# The Scottish Legal System

**Robin M White LLB, LLM, Cert Soc Anth, AIL, JP**
Senior Lecturer in Law, University of Dundee

**Ian D Willock MA, LLB, PhD**
Emeritus Professor, University of Dundee

Third edition

LexisNexis™ UK

**Members of the LexisNexis Group worldwide**

| | |
|---|---|
| United Kingdom | LexisNexis UK, a Division of Reed Elsevier (UK) Ltd, 4 Hill Street, EDINBURGH EH2 3JZ and Halsbury House, 35 Chancery Lane, LONDON WC2A 1EL |
| Argentina | LexisNexis Argentina, BUENOS AIRES |
| Australia | LexisNexis Butterworths, CHATSWOOD, New South Wales |
| Austria | LexisNexis Verlag ARD Orac GmbH & Co KG, VIENNA |
| Canada | LexisNexis Butterworths, MARKHAM, Ontario |
| Chile | LexisNexis Chile Ltda, SANTIAGO DE CHILE |
| Czech Republic | Nakladatelství Orac sro, PRAGUE |
| France | Editions du Juris-Classeur SA, PARIS |
| Germany | LexisNexis Deutschland GmbH, FRANKFURT, MUNSTER |
| Hong Kong | LexisNexis Butterworths, HONG KONG |
| Hungary | HVG-Orac, BUDAPEST |
| India | LexisNexis Butterworths, NEW DELHI |
| Ireland | Butterworths (Ireland) Ltd, DUBLIN |
| Italy | Giuffrè Editore, MILAN |
| Malaysia | Malayan Law Journal Sdn Bhd, KUALA LUMPUR |
| New Zealand | LexisNexis Butterworths, WELLINGTON |
| Poland | Wydawnictwo Prawnicze LexisNexis, WARSAW |
| Singapore | LexisNexis Butterworths, SINGAPORE |
| South Africa | LexisNexis Butterworths, DURBAN |
| Switzerland | Stämpfli Verlag AG, BERNE |
| USA | LexisNexis, DAYTON, Ohio |

© Reed Elsevier (UK) Ltd 2003

A CIP Catalogue record for this book is available from the British Library.

**First published in 1993**
**Second Edition 1999**

ISBN 0 406 95962 5

Typeset by Phoenix Photosetting, Chatham, Kent
Printed and bound in Scotland by Thomson Litho, East Kilbride

**Visit LexisNexis UK at www.lexisnexis.co.uk**

# Preface

We have written this book in the hope that it will be of use in courses on the Scottish Legal System, under whatever title, in Scottish universities and colleges. But we hope also it will be of interest to general readers who wish to learn about its subject.

We have attempted to present the legal system and law of Scotland as a unique and constantly evolving human enterprise, intertwined with the changing political and social conditions of Scotland. So as well as looking back into the history of Scotland, we have attempted to look forward and give more prominence than in other works on this subject to the over-arching law and institutions of the European Community, to the role of bodies other than the legal profession in the provision of legal services, and to the modern concern with the appraisal and improvement of the law, which is most manifest in the work of the Scottish Law Commission. We draw attention to works which study the law in operation in its social setting, although limits of space have precluded full summaries. Where appropriate too we have tried to quantify legal activity and thus present its importance in numerical as well as hierarchical terms.

The third edition of this work has allowed us to incorporate the effects of the first four years of the Scottish Parliament and Scottish Executive, and of the operation of the Human Rights Act 1998 together with other general updating.

However, while it was in press, two events occurred which require some discussion. These were: firstly, the unexpected announcements of certain constitutional changes, and proposals for change, within the United Kingdom, and secondly, the rather more expected proposals for constitutional changes within the European Union. Some of the proposals from both sources are less than fully worked out, and all are liable to be amended. The United Kingdom proposals will require legislation and the European Union proposals will require amendment to the treaties. Therefore, neither set of proposals is by any means in its final state. We have nevertheless tried to describe the relevant changes and proposals in outline in an Appendix to this Preface, and references have been added to the text in relevant places to cross-refer back to this Appendix.

Our thanks are due to our colleagues Ann Duncan, David Hart, Silvère Lefèvre, Colin Reid and Yannos Tolias for helpful comments on sections of the text. They are not responsible for what we have made of those comments.

We have attempted to state the law as at 1 June 2003, but where practicable, have made revisions up to 18 July 2003 (including those contained in the Appendix to this Preface).

Robin M White
Ian D Willock
*July 2003*

# Appendix to preface

## PART I – UK CHANGES AND PROPOSALS

The changes and proposals for changes within the United Kingdom initially emerged on 12 and 13 June 2003 out of a Cabinet reshuffle[1]. Some of the changes took, to all intents and purposes, immediate effect. Some of the proposals which relate directly to Scotland, however, were further discussed in a Consultation Paper published on 14 July 2003[2], and some which do not relate directly to Scotland in two other Consultation Papers published on the same date[3].

It is fair to say that much (though by no means all) of the controversy surrounding these changes and proposals for change was generated by the fact that, although of considerable constitutional significance, they were initially announced without prior consultation, and without a number of aspects being clear. Even after publication of the Consultation Papers, many questions remain. Thus, it appears likely that there will be much more discussion both before and during the passage of the necessary legislation.

The changes which occurred, effectively from 12 and 13 June 2003, were broadly as follows.

(1) **Scotland Office and Secretary of State for Scotland:** the Scotland Office continued to have a separate existence, and the office of Secretary of State for Scotland was not abolished, but the previous holder (Helen Liddell, MP) resigned and the post was given to the existing Secretary of State for Transport (Alistair Darling, MP, who represented a Scottish constituency). He thus held both posts, and spoke in the House of Commons on Scottish affairs as well as on transport. (The Wales Office underwent a similar change). This seemed an

---

1 See Prime Minister's Official Spokesman's Press Briefings of 12 and 13 June and contemporary press comment thereon.
2 Constitutional Reform: a Supreme Court for the United Kingdom (CP 11/03).
3 Constitutional Reform: a new way of appointing judges (CP 10/03); and Constitutional Reform: the future of Queen's Counsel (CP 08/03).

vii

unstable situation, and was thought possibly to presage absorption of the Scotland Office into another Department, perhaps the new Department of Constitutional Affairs (for which, see below).

(2) **Advocate-General for Scotland:** the office of Advocate-General for Scotland remained (as did its incumbent, Dr Lynda Clark, QC, MP), but rather than being regarded as part of the Scotland Office, became attached to the new Department of Constitutional Affairs.

(3) **Lord Chancellor and the 'Secretary of State for Constitutional Affairs':** the office of Lord Chancellor remained transitionally, but the previous holder (Lord Irvine of Lairg) resigned and the post was given to the promoted junior minister in charge of criminal justice in the Home Office (Lord Falconer of Thorogood). However, this was seen as a temporary measure, pending abolition of the office of Lord Chancellor on the grounds that its simultaneous holding of executive, legislative and judicial responsibilities was anomalous (and more obviously so since the Human Rights Act 1998) so they should be split from each other. The new incumbent of the office was, however, also appointed at the same time to a new office of 'Secretary of State for Constitutional Affairs' (the 'Department of Constitutional Affairs'[1] – 'DeCAf', for short – being in essence a rebranding of the Lord Chancellor's Department), and continued to sit as a Minister in Cabinet (in one or other capacity), and to act as Speaker of the House of Lords (pending new arrangements), but not to sit as judge in the Appellate Committee of the House of Lords (the Lord Chancellor's traditional judicial role).

The further proposals for change which were made at the same time were broadly as follows.

(i) **Appellate Committee of the House of Lords and Judicial Committee of the Privy Council – a 'Supreme Court':** the Appellate Committee of the House of Lords was to be replaced by a 'Supreme Court' for the United Kingdom. This proposal was discussed in the Consultation Paper Constitutional Reform: a Supreme Court (CP 11/03), but it is a possible criticism of that Consultation Paper that, while it was usefully descriptive, it did not consider some significant matters, and was not fully reasoned.

1 www.dca.gov.uk: this should not be confused with the Dundee Contemporary Arts website www.dca.org.uk.

Two initial difficulties were with the title. Firstly, it was assumed by some that any 'Supreme Court' would be in the mould of the United States Supreme Court, with the power to override legislation, and a possible political element in the appointment of its judges. The Consultation Paper expressly denies any intention as to the former (Executive Summary and paras 23–25, 45), and the simultaneous publication of one of the other Consultation Papers[1] makes it plain that there was no intention of the latter. Secondly, the term 'Supreme Court of Judicature' was in fact already in use as the technical, if little-used, title for the principal courts of England and Wales. The Consultation Paper does not mention this. Other more substantial issues arising included the following.

(a) *The relationship of the proposed Court to Parliament*: the Consultation Paper noted the apparent oddity of judicial appeals being heard by what was technically a Committee of one House of Parliament, and the fact that its judges, as peers, might speak in that House, though also noting certain possible advantages (paras 1, 3, 5, 7, 34–37). (The anomalous position of the Lord Chancellor noted above was perhaps simply the most obvious version of this oddity: paras 3, 6). The Consultation Paper proposals worked from the premise that this was indefensible and must change (para 36).

(b) *The jurisdiction of the proposed Court in relation to civil appeals from Scotland*: the Consultation Paper did not seek to change the possibility of such civil appeals to the proposed Court, but raised the possibility of restricting the right to appeal to the narrower grounds applying to English and Welsh appeals (paras 27, 55–56).

(c) *The jurisdiction of the proposed Court in relation to criminal appeals from Scotland* (which have never been heard by the House of Lords): the Consultation Paper did not to seek to change the position (paras 11, 26).

(d) *The relationship of the proposed Court to the Judicial Committee of the Privy Council*: since the judges of the Appellate Committee of the House of Lords are effectively identical with those of the Judicial Committee of the Privy Council, there is an argument for the economy and simplicity of a merger (para 20). Questions arose in relation to appeals from other Commonwealth countries which the JCPC

1 Constitutional Reform: a new way of appointing judges (CP 10/03).

heard (and might do so with Commonwealth judges as members), and the Consultation Paper envisaged retaining the JCPC for this purpose (para 28). They also arose in that the JCPC heard 'devolution issues' ie, broadly, issues as to whether the Scottish Parliament and Scottish Executive were acting outwith their powers (paras 19–20). The Consultation Paper rather briefly concluded that '[o]n balance, the Government believes that it would be right to transfer the jurisdiction on devolution cases from the Judicial Committee to the new Supreme Court with arrangements which enable additional Scottish . . . judges to sit on cases raising devolution issues where that is appropriate' (para 21, see also paras 31 and 60–61). This did seem an inadequate discussion of the issue, for instance failing to take on board the different, constitutional, nature of 'devolution issues', or to see the proposed Court as a truly United Kingdom Court, rather than an essentially English and Welsh court, occasionally hearing appeals from elsewhere. (It should be noted that the Lord Chancellor has been Lord Chancellor of Great Britain, but that the Lord Chancellor's Department was an essentially England and Wales Department, being responsible for running the court system there, and the new Department of Constitutional Affairs appeared to have inherited these responsibilities).

(e) *The membership of the proposed Court:* the Consultation Paper was inclined to continue the existing arrangement of a dozen full time judges, supplemented by others, ad hoc, although the question of whether it should continue to sit in panels of (typically) five, or as a full bench was raised (paras 51–52). If supplemented by others, it was not clear who might be used by way of supplement (paras 29–32, also 36–37), although the possibility of legal academics being appointed was hesitantly suggested (para 46). It was clearly concluded that existing tenure was appropriate.

(f) *The means of appointment to the proposed Court:* the Consultation Paper leaned heavily upon the simultaneously published Consultation Paper on judicial appointments in England and Wales[1] and favoured a Commission making recommendations to the Prime Minister, who would consult the First Minister for Scotland (and First and Deputy First Ministers of Northern Ireland) (paras 40–43). While acknowledging that the process of appointment would be

1 Constitutional Reform: a new way of appointing judges (CP 10/03).

different from that of English and Welsh judges, it did envisage the proposed English and Welsh appointments commission doing the job (para 43). Also, while an open and transparent application process was considered, in line with thinking on judicial appointments generally, traditional arguments against seemed favoured (para 44).

Finally, it was clear both that some senior judges were not enthusiastic about the proposals[1], and that there was no consultation with the Scottish Executive before the proposal was announced[2].

(ii) **Judicial Appointments:** there was to be a Judicial Appointments Commission for England and Wales[3]. This clearly did not directly impinge on Scotland (though the Judicial Appointments Board was mentioned as a model in Annex B of the Consultation Paper).

(iii) **Queen's Counsel:** the role, and indeed existence, of Queen's Counsel was to be reconsidered[4]. Although the title of the Consultation Paper did not make the point clear, this did not directly affect Scotland. However, were there to be radical change in England and Wales, it is likely Scotland would follow suit.

## PART II – EU PROPOSALS

The report of the 'Convention on the Future of Europe', the body charged with considering the constitutional changes to the European Union in consequence of the impending accession of 10 new Member States, was published on 13 June 2003 as a 'Draft Treaty establishing a Constitution for the European Union' (CONV 850/03, available at http://europcan-convention.eu.int/bienvenue.asp?lang=EN. This was

---

1 See eg Lord Hope of Craighead, the senior Scottish judge in the House of Lords, who publicly expressed concern for the integrity of Scots law under such a system (wondering whether the proposals were consistent with the Acts of Union) and concern for the devolution settlement (wondering if such a new court was equipped to be a constitutional court): see eg Scotsman 27 June 2003; and Lord Woolf, the Lord Chief Justice of England & Wales, who also publicly expressed concern in respect of the independence of judges and related matters: see speech at Annual Dinner for HM judges 9 July 2003 at www.lcd.gov.uk/judicial/speeches/lcj090703.htm, reported in press on 10 July, and speech at Lord Mayor's Annual Dinner for Judges 18 July 2003 www.lcd.gov.uk/judicial/speeches/lcj180701.htm).
2 See eg First Minister's Official Spokeswoman's Media Briefing 14 July 2003.
3 Constitutional Reform: a new way of appointing judges (CP 10/03).
4 Constitutional Reform: the future of Queen's Counsel (CP 08/03).

a lengthy document, at over 250 pages, and difficult to summarise. In any case, its proposals would have to be discussed by the existing Member States (in consultation with the applicants), and some were controversial, so it was not clear what the final form would be.

However, it opens with a Preamble quoting Thucydides on democracy and continuing 'Conscious that Europe is a continent that has brought forth civilisation . . .' and similar assertions, and the principal recommendations of interest were:

(1) in relation to the Council of the Union (alias Council of Ministers), an elected President to replace the rotating six-monthly presidency and in relation to qualified majority voting, a new weighting system and extension to many more areas (though not including tax and social security);

(2) in relation to the European Commission, each Member State to continue to have a Commissioner, but only 15 Commissioners to be fully voting;

(3) in relation to the European Parliament, a new allotment of members as between Member States;

(4) in relation to Member States' national parliaments, attempts to involve them in the EC legislative process;

(5) in relation to 'human rights', adoption of the Charter of Fundamental Rights;

(6) in relation to the European Union as a whole, a merger of the three 'pillars', and a single legal personality for the whole.

Numerous other recommendations were made, including merger of the EU Commissioner for Foreign Affairs with the Council's 'High Representative for the Common Foreign and Security Policy' (an office held by the Secretary General of the Council), into an 'EU Foreign Affairs Minister' within the European Commission.

# Contents

# Abbreviations

| | |
|---|---|
| AC | Law Reports, Appeal Cases (House of Lords and Privy Council) 1890– |
| All ER | All England Law Reports 1936– |
| App Cas | Law Reports, Appeal Cases (House of Lords) 1875–90 |
| APS | Acts of the Parliament of Scotland (Record Edition, 12 vols) |
| Bell App | S S Bell's Scotch Appeals (House of Lords) 1842–50 |
| CMLR | Common Market Law Reports 1962– |
| Ch | Law Reports, Chancery Division 1890– |
| Co Rep | Coke's Reports 1572–1616 |
| Cox CC | Cox's Criminal Cases 1843–1941 |
| ECR | European Court of Justice Reports 1954– |
| EHRR | European Human Rights Reports 1979– |
| F | Fraser's Session Cases 1898–1906 |
| F(J) | Justiciary cases in Fraser's Session Cases 1898–1906 |
| ICR | Industrial Cases Reports 1972– |
| IRLR | Industrial Relations Law Reports 1972– |
| Irv | Irvine's Justiciary Reports 1851–68 |
| JC | Justiciary Cases 1917– |
| JLSS | Journal of the Law Society of Scotland |
| JR | Juridicial Review |
| KB | Law Reports, King's Bench Division 1900–52 |
| LJR | Law Journal Reports 1947–49 |
| M | Macpherson's Session Cases 1862–73 |
| Macq | Macqueens House of Lords Reports 1851–65 |
| Mor | Morison's Dictionary of Decisions (Court of Session) 1540–1808 |
| PD | Law Reports, Probate, Divorce and Admiralty Division 1875–90 |
| Pat | Paton's House of Lords Appeal Cases 1726–1821 |
| QB | Law Reports, Queen's Bench Division 1891–1901, 1951– |

| | |
|---|---|
| QBD | Law Reports, Queens Bench Division 1874–90 |
| R | Rettie's Session Cases 1873–98 |
| R(J) | Justiciary cases in Rettie's Session Cases 1873–98 |
| Rob | Robertson's Scotch Appeals (House of Lords) 1707–27 |
| SC | Session Cases 1907– |
| SCCR | Scottish Criminal Case Reports 1981– |
| SCLR | Scottish Civil Law Reports 1987– |
| Shaw's Appeals | P Shaw's Scotch Appeals (House of Lords) 1821–26 |
| SJ | Scottish Jurist 1829–73 |
| SLT | Scots Law Times 1893– |
| SLT (Lands Tr) | Lands Tribunal for Scotland Reports in Scots Law Times 1971– |
| Swin | Swinton's Justiciary Reports 1835–41 |
| TLR | Times Law Reports 1884–1952 |
| WLR | Weekly Law Reports 1953– |

# Table of statutes

# Table of cases

xxiii

# 1. Introduction

## WHY HAVE LAW?

Law is everywhere. It is, like the air we breathe, part of our environment. But unlike the air it is man-made. Why is it made? There is no one universally agreed answer, but a plausible one that would fit most societies is this. People live together in communities. They have competing wants and limited resources to satisfy them. Therefore they make arrangements to share things out and minimise or repress conflict. These arrangements can take various forms, such as morality, etiquette, conventions and law. Law consists of rules. These are not necessarily fair or accepted by all. They may be written by a small elite who wield some form of power and impose them on a reluctant majority. But some such arrangements are indispensable. The bigger and more complex the community, the more the scope for conflict; and so the more likely there are to be rules of law. As one writer puts it, society is not a suicide club.

## SOME KINDS OF LAW WE ALL KNOW

If law is everywhere about us, we must be enveloped in it from our earliest days. In a family the parents have power over young children by virtue of their greater size and strength and knowledge. Ideally the relationship is imbued with love. But it still involves the children doing what they are told on such matters as bed-time, dress, going to school, and play-mates. If the parents are consistent in what they require the children to do, then unwritten rules emerge. They can still be rules, even though exceptions may be made for special occasions or they are relaxed as the children grow older. In school too the pupils find themselves in a regime of rules, concerning time-tables, holidays, absentee notes and so on. In many schools there will be no list of school rules as such. But the children are taught by the teachers what a rule is when the consequences of unacceptable behaviour are explained to them and they are told what conduct to avoid for the future. If they still do not conform, then some punishment, such as loss of privileges, will be imposed and as a last resort exclusion from the school.

As children grow older and become more self-reliant they become aware of a system of control that affects nearly everything that people do outside their homes. Probably it first impinges on them when as pedestrians they become aware of the rules that make drivers of vehicles behave more or less consistently in certain situations; stopping at a red light or giving way to someone on a pedestrian crossing or obeying the lollipop man's signal. Sooner or later they will also watch the result of not complying, when police stop and question the errant driver.

## SO WHAT EXACTLY IS LAW?

Already from these simple situations we can see some of the elements of law. It seems to be the words of someone in authority who has the power to intervene in other people's affairs. It imposes patterns of conduct on other people; and if they do not comply something unpleasant is liable to befall them. A single example of these effective words is called a rule or a law. Some people would want to add that the law must be fair to be a true law. Others would say that if the law comes from a person whose authority is generally recognised, then that is good enough. Some laws actually compel conduct, whether you like it or not. For example, a speeding motorist may be stopped by traffic police and warned to obey the speed limit. A persistent offender will be fined by a judge and may be disqualified from driving. But a lot of law simply provides opportunities to do things effectively. If you want to buy a house, there are rules you must observe to obtain the desired result. You don't need to go near a court. You can ignore such laws if you choose, but you are likely to find that somebody takes your house from you or you cannot get anyone to buy it from you. So some laws are primarily compelling ones and some are primarily enabling ones. But if you ignore either kind, some harm or loss or detriment is likely to befall you. Some laws are very precise; they tell you exactly what you can and cannot do. Others shade off into discretion. Thus, on divorce the matrimonial property is to 'be shared fairly' between the couple (Family Law (Scotland) Act 1985, s 9(1)(a)). The couple will be the best people to decide what will be a fair sharing of their belongings. But if they cannot, then a judge will do it for them.

We have only just touched on some of the most profound questions in the subject called jurisprudence or legal philosophy, which university students of law will have to study later. There are many aspects of this topic which will then be examined, such as: must the law-maker obey his own laws?; is there any duty to obey the laws of a tyrant?; what law is to be obeyed during and after a revolution? But for our purposes in this book that picture of the standard form that law takes will suffice.

However, there is a variant of law that we must mention at this stage. It is law without a law-giver. It simply rests on the general observance of some pattern of behaviour. The person who steps out of line will be criticised and may suffer some harm, such as being ostracised. In a narrow street where all the cars are parked on one side to let the traffic flow, a driver who parks on the other side will soon be made to feel unpopular. This is custom or convention. It is unwritten law and is associated with an early stage of legal development, when means of making law and imposing punishments had not yet been developed. So we can call it embryonic or inchoate law. Yet, paradoxically, some of the most basic parts of the United Kingdom's constitution exist only in the form of conventions, such as the duty of a Prime Minister whose government is defeated on a matter of confidence in the House of Commons to offer his resignation to the Sovereign.

## THE LAW OF A STATE

So far we have been describing a very simple model of law. But of course in a modern state it is much more complex. Indeed, to issue and uphold its own laws is one of the marks of a state. The laws of a state are arranged in a hierarchy of authority and importance. In the United Kingdom the highest tier of law has for centuries been the statutes or Acts issued by Parliament. But since the United Kingdom accepted the Treaty of Rome and entered the European Community, and the consequences of this decision were spelled out by Parliament in the European Communities Act 1972, there is a higher tier of law, that of European Community law, which takes precedence over United Kingdom law. In theory, Parliament could repeal the European Communities Act and free itself of that level of law. But the problems of disengaging itself from the European Union make that possibility highly unlikely. Likewise,

the United Kingdom Parliament has tied its hands by incorporating substantial parts of the European Convention on Human
Rights in the Human Rights Act of 1998. Parliament could repeal
that Act but is most unlikely to do so.

Much modern statute law is of an outline kind. The details are
provided in regulations drawn up by government departments
under the authority of a parent Act. They can thus be varied easily,
for example to take account of inflation. Most social security law is
of this kind. As we shall see, there are many other subordinate
forms of enacted law, such as laws made by courts for their own
procedure, by local authorities and by transport undertakings.

Alongside the law created on purpose, there is a kind of law
which is extracted as a by-product from something else. To justify
their decisions in disputed cases judges issue judgments applying
the existing law to the new situation which has come before them.
In so doing they make law in a limited sense in that they clarify or
extend the existing law, including the law emerging from the decisions of previous judges. Lawyers reading such published judgments try to formulate a brief rule of law which epitomises the
reason underlying the decision. Judges in their judgments have to
respect what Parliament appears to have enacted, if anything, on
the subject; and their statements of the law and even (though
rarely) their decisions could be overridden by Parliament. They
also have to adhere to expositions of the law in courts higher than
their own. So this judge-made law is also arranged in tiers of
authority.

As well as this structure of enacted and judge-made law – what
we might call official law – which is of general application, there are
sets of law applying to people in particular circumstances; for
example, members of the armed forces, of the universities, of the
established Churches of Scotland and of England and of certain
professions such as medicine, law and teaching. The laws of these
bodies require some degree of state approval and the decisions of
their courts and tribunals are usually subject to final appeal to the
courts of the land.

There are also many other bodies which have a legal structure
which in a limited way imitates that of the state; for example,
trade unions and professional associations, the non-established
churches, and sports associations. But only if they act in an
oppressive way or fail to observe the basic rules of natural
justice, as laid down by the law courts, do they become subject
to the law of the land.

The laws of such private organisations do not have to be obeyed.
If, as a member, you do disobey them the worst that can happen is

that you will be made to leave the organisation. But all the other kinds of law mentioned above have a pedigree which could be traced back to the ultimate source of legal authority which in the United Kingdom we refer to by the symbol of the Crown and personify in the person of the monarch. If you come within the scope of such an official law, you have to comply or take the prescribed consequences.

## IS LAW A GOOD OR A BAD THING?

A modern law system extends to every corner of a nation, and in limited ways beyond its boundaries. It touches the lives of every inhabitant and to some degree even those of temporary residents such as tourists. Most laws probably strike the law-abiding citizen as restrictive. They stop them from doing what they want to do. Yet provided laws as a whole are generally respected they create a climate of security in which people can go about their everyday affairs, confident that they are not going to be harmed in their persons or property. If they are, something will be done about it. For example, we can be reasonably sure in this country, though not perhaps in Madrid or Rome, that if we drive through a road crossing on the green light we are not going to collide with someone driving across on a red light.

The other kind of laws, those which enable us to do things and get results, are more obviously beneficial. They could be compared to the telephone network which enables us to make contact with people all over the country and even beyond. This sort of law enables us to perform transactions with people everywhere, whom we may never have seen and know little about, with some assurance that they will be honoured; and if not, we shall be able to get some redress. From Scotland we might send to a nursery firm in Cornwall for some plants, in the confidence that they would send the plants ordered to us, properly packed. If they did turn up dead on arrival, we would have a good chance of getting our money back. If we were paying by credit card or cheque we would be counting on the bank to make payment on our behalf. Again, we might get married in Scotland and, armed with a marriage certificate, we could be assured of being treated as married here and elsewhere in the world. It is this comprehensive system of law that enables people to enter transactions like these with assurance.

## LAW IS ALWAYS SUBJECT TO CHANGE

One of the problems about law is discovering what exactly it is at any given point of time. If one is trying to do exactly what the law requires or to discover the law that should settle a dispute, then it is vitally important to ascertain all the rules applicable at the relevant date. Why so? Surely it might be thought the law is as clear and certain as the law-maker can make it? The trouble is that law is always subject to change so that it can be kept up to date. This is true of individual rules of law. That means that although a new statute may get plenty of publicity in the media, what may not be so clear is how it amends previous statutes, or when it comes into force (for different parts of it may be operative from different dates), or whether it has any retrospective effect. So lawyers have to rely on publications such as the monthly periodical *Current Law* to keep them abreast of legal changes. The Internet is proving a valauble aid in this regard.

But although law is always evolving, it is mainly at the margins. There are broad core areas of the law, such as the law of contract and of property, and the main crimes such as murder and theft, where change is minimal. These heartlands of the law enable it to have a conserving and a stabilising role in societies. The very existence of the modern nation-state depends on reliable rules of law and the means to find them and enforce them. Thus, the law of companies enables property to be set apart for certain economic purposes and for the ownership of that property to be fragmented among many people and other companies, without putting at risk the rest of their assets. Without that device the capitalist or free enterprise system could not flourish.

In this book we are more concerned with structures and with broad movements and trends in the law, although some rules will be mentioned; and we shall have to strive to state them as accurately as possible at a named date. There are different kinds of legal change. There is the step-by-step kind of change, which we may call incremental. Most judge-made law is of that kind. There is innovative change, when a new area of legal regulation is opened up, for instance, by the Sex Discrimination Act of 1976; or an existing one is drastically changed, such as making divorce rest on the breakdown of the marriage, instead of the commission of a matrimonial fault. And there is evolutionary change, which takes the form of broad trends such as the increasing role of civil servants in detailed law-making. Of course, if all the laws were in a constant state of flux it would defeat the purposes of law to create certainty and security. But a certain amount of change can be lived with in the interests of keeping the law in line with people's expectations.

Another way in which a small element of uncertainty creeps into the law arises out of laws which remain on paper but are not actually enforced. Thus, in 1972 the Lord Advocate let it be known that he would not initiate prosecutions of male adults for engaging in private homosexual activities by agreement in Scotland, in circumstances such that they would not be criminal in England. The police, like prosecutors, in the nature of their duties have much discretion, but in 1982 they publicly declined to operate the powers conferred on them in the Transport Act 1982, s 27, to issue fixed penalty notices for a variety of minor traffic offences, including speeding. In 1993 (now under the Road Traffic Offenders Act 1988, s 54) they announced that they would now do so. Bodies affected by a new law may protest that they need time to prepare for it. Thus the Freedom of Information (Scotland) Act 2002 affecting all governmental and many quasi-governmental bodies will not come into force until 1st January 2005. This shows that legal institutions have the power to vary the operation of legal rules.

## LAW AND POWER

Law is indissolubly linked with power; that is, the ability of a person or group to determine the behaviour of others. From what we have already said about laws, they are obviously ideal instruments by means of which to control others. Power may take many and varied forms. Sometimes it is visible and very forceful, as when massed policemen, their arms linked, try to contain demonstrators to bar street and stop them marching, then handcuff those they arrest. Sometimes it is more subtle. Those who are in charge of the mass media have the power to influence what people think, and thus do, by their ability to select which facts to publicise and which opinions to advance. Power may be exercised by an individual or by a group or class. The trade union movement used to attribute its power against employers to the ability of its members to take strike action. But now strikes must be preceded by a strike ballot, otherwise the union funds are put at risk, and employees are free to join or not join a trade union. An individual employer still has the power to dismiss an employee but if he does so unfairly he may have to pay the employee compensation. These forms of power are legitimate in that they are either authorised by law or at least not forbidden by it. But the power a bank robber exercises when he holds up the staff of a bank would be regarded as illegitimate.

## LAWS AS WAYS OF GETTING THINGS DONE

In a modern democratic society there is a constant ferment of debate on things that are wrong and how to correct them. For example, road accidents have long been blamed on driving with excessive alcohol in the system. Now there is concern about the effect of drugs, whether medicinal or forbidden, on driving. People who sleep on the streets regardless of the weather are seen as an embarrassment and a scandal. Pressure groups, television documentaries and articles in the newspapers draw attention to such social evils. Political parties may put them into their election manifestos. The method of correction usually uses law. It may be simply some new use of existing legal powers which have been conferred on officials such as the police or head teachers or environmental protection officers. Or it may require new parliamentary legislation. Relying on law assumes that, for the most part, people respect law and approve of the objectives that are embodied in particular laws. If they ignore a law then some sanction can come into operation to compel or persuade them to comply. It need not be as overt as imprisonment. It might be the payment of compensation to someone hurt by the failure to obey the law. In the case of professionals it might be loss of promotion or humiliating publicity. So the legitimate power of law is drawn upon to achieve reforms in all walks of life. But the job is never done. There are always calls for new laws and the amendment of existing ones. Whole new areas may be made subject to law, such as racial relations and sexual discrimination.

# 2. Scotland – nation and state

In this chapter we shall be looking in a broad-brush manner at the history of Scotland and seeing the ways in which law has been entwined with it. In so doing we may hope to find the answer to the question: how did that peculiar, indeed unique, association enjoyed by the legal system of Scotland within the United Kingdom arise?

## NATION AND STATE

A nation is a cultural concept, rooted among people and their belief that they have a shared identity that distinguishes them from other peoples. It is manifested in what they produce as a people – their art, music and literature, their language, their pastimes and games, in their beliefs about themselves and their place in the world. A nation may or may not have the organs of government which signify a state; a central administration holding sway over a defined area; armed forces to defend its boundaries; police and courts to maintain order within them. That apparatus is the sign of a state and if it is functioning effectively gives it a claim to recognition by other states. It marks a society which claims independence from all others, although in the modern world of instant communications, mutual economic dependence and treaties and alliances that independence is more apparent than real.

When we examine the law in Scotland certain unique problems confront us. Most Scots would claim that Scotland is a nation. Certainly in most sports (though not at the Olympic Games) it counts as a nation. But it is not in itself a state. In the Scottish Executive it has only some of the apparatus of a state; part of that of the United Kingdom of Great Britain and Northern Ireland. Its representatives as MPs participate in special ways in the Parliament of the United Kingdom. Since May 1999 it has had its own Parliament sitting in Edinburgh and dealing with matters devolved to it by the United Kingdom Parliament. It does have its own courts, but it shares with the rest of the United Kingdom common highest courts in civil and devolution cases. Most of its tribunals are part of a United Kingdom organisation. It has its own legal profession. Some of its laws are peculiar to Scotland, some are common to the whole of Britain (ie England, Scotland and Wales), some are shared with the rest of the United Kingdom (ie with Northern Ireland as well). Some are separate in form, but almost identical in substance. It will be one of our main tasks to tease out these similarities and differences.

## THE EMERGENCE OF SCOTLAND

The emergence of a Scottish nation and later a Scottish state was a slow and painful process lasting several centuries. It began in the 11th century when four rival peoples had by warfare coalesced into one kingdom under King Malcolm II (1005–34). They were the Picts of the east of Scotland, the Angles of the south-east, the Scots of Dalriada in the west and the Britons of the south-west.

### Custom

The law before David I (1124–53) was probably entirely custom and in the Celtic, Gaelic-speaking areas of the west was spoken to by hereditary oracles called Brehons. In the nature of things customary law, being unwritten, is hard to identify later. But numerous references to *leges et consuetudines* (laws and customs) in the statutes of the 12th and 13th centuries testify to the existence and recognition of some law other than the enacted written law[1]. Custom is also often referred to in charters. Some of it, especially in charters, is local[2]. Some of it is general; what in England was called the common law, a term which in Scotland is used both for the law common to the whole of Scotland and less frequently the

---

1 Thus, the *Laws of the Four Burghs* (of Edinburgh, Roxburgh, Berwick and Stirling) are more properly the *Leges et Consuetudines Quatuor Burgorum* and were adopted by many other Scots burghs. See APS I, 333. The *Laws of the Marches* were the outcome of a process of recognition in 1249 by magnates from England and Scotland of the laws and customs of the marches (or frontiers). See APS I, 413–416, conveniently and fully translated in DM Walker *A Legal History of Scotland* (1988) vol I pp 63–66.
2 For example, Malcolm IV in a charter to the Abbey of Scone of 1164 allowed it to have three tradesmen with the same liberties and customs as those of his Burgh of Perth (Barrow, *Regesta of Malcolm IV*), No 243).

Roman or civil law common to Europe[1]. Stair, the authoritative institutional writer on Scots law, uses the term 'common law' to mean primarily, as in England, 'our ancient and immemorial customs'[2]. As examples he includes the law governing most rights of succession as being 'anterior to any statute'[3]. To these might be added the early ways of trying criminal accusations, the ordeal, trial by combat and even the early jury. Custom flourished for centuries in the law observed by mariners and traders among nations, where there was no sovereign authority to enact it, and to a minor extent this is still so. But most maritime law is now embodied in judicial precedent (the authoritative statement of the law by a court), statute and international convention. Customs of trade may sometimes be used to interpret a contract[4]. In employment law the custom and practice of a workplace may be paid regard to by employment tribunals and courts. Thus, custom had a formative role in the law of Scotland and despite the spread of written law still has a minor part to play.

## EARLY MEDIEVAL SCOTLAND

Custom with its local roots could be a divisive force. But through a documentary form of law uniformly introduced and enforced from the centre the country was to become much more united. This came about through the arrival of the Normans who pacified England within a few years of their victory over King Harold at Hastings in 1066 and then began a peaceful penetration of Scotland. The marriage of Margaret, an English Saxon princess[5], to Malcolm III of Scotland and the marriages of their sons, Alexander I and David I, to English noblewomen led to the coming to Scotland of many families hailing from Normandy, such as the Bruces, the Stewarts (formerly Fitzallans) and the Grahams. Margaret's piety drew many religious orders to Scotland during her reign and after. The Scottish kings then followed Norman practice in conferring lands upon these incomers, in return for their

---

1 For numerous medieval examples, see DM Walker *A Legal History of Scotland* vol II (1990) pp 252–254. Later Stair was also to use 'common law' as the law 'common to many nations' (*Institutions of the Law of Scotland* (ed 1981) I, 1, 11).
2 Stair *Institutions* I, 1, 16.
3 Stair *Institutions* I, 1, 16.
4 See, eg, *Wilkie v Scottish Aviation* 1956 SC 198 (custom as to remuneration of chartered surveyor followed if reasonable, certain and notorious).
5 Though born in Hungary.

homage and the promise of armed knights in time of war. These tenants-in-chief could create their own sub-tenants. At the lowest level were the peasants, the husbandmen and cottars who tilled the land and whose return was in produce and days of labour on their overlord's land. These land rights carried with them the right to hold a court. In this way disputes as to tenure and succession could be settled. The kings also conferred on religious houses extensive lands. For them the return was usually in prayers and masses.

### Feudal tenure

This system was known as feudal tenure. Worked out initially in relation to land, it was soon to be extended to towns. Burghs were royal creations, part of a deliberate policy to maintain peace and raise standards of life. This plan had three elements: royal castles manifesting the king's authority and power; sheriffs there resident to represent the king in administration, tax-gathering and law enforcement; and townships whose inhabitants were encouraged to engage in trade and manufacture. They too were given plots of land, for which they paid a return in rent and in other obligations such as attendance at the burgh court.

In this way a legal device, rooted in the staple resource of land, carried the monarch's authority throughout the country. It was a centralised form of government in that all rights derived from the Crown and the forms of land tenure were uniform everywhere. The Royal Chancery issued the charters conferring the lands or confirming them; and when any kind of dispute arose it ordered in the form of legal writs called brieves an inquiry in the local court. After hearing evidence from local people it reported back as to the true state of affairs. But it was also decentralised in so far as the monarch gave his tenants-in-chief powers similar to his own within their territories. By the 14th and 15th centuries these so-called regalities were to be a source of division and conflict in the country.

Thus, feudalism reinforced class stratification, at least in the rural areas. Burghs were more loosely bound into the system. The burghers had a strong sense of community, focused on their town church and burgh court, and often maintained a doughty independence from adjacent large land-owners, even those who had the powers of sheriffs.

Feudalism in time tended to disperse power, for the successors of those who were entrusted with lands by the sovereign did not always remain faithful to him or his successors. But it did give Scotland many of the signs of statehood, even although they and that concept were not fully developed until the 16th century. It emphasised the loyalty owed by everyone in the country to the person of the king, who was both leader and the symbolic embodiment of the nation. It facilitated the raising of an army when needed. It sustained courts in every community. Yet paradoxically, at the centre, the *curia regis* or royal court was just an informal gathering of a varying number of those clerics and titled laymen who gave counsel to the king. Out of it grew eventually the Scots Parliament, law courts and the Privy Council[1].

The pervasiveness of the linked institutions we call feudalism has been equalled by its durability. Its concept of concurrent interests in land is still the basis of Scottish land law, for example, between landlord and tenant or owner-occupier and security holder. In 1991 the Scottish Law Commission (charged with the reform of Scots law) published a discussion paper entitled *Property Law: Abolition of the Feudal System*. This led to the Abolition of Feudal Tenure etc (Scotland) Act 2000 which is being brought into force in stages. From this era too we derive the cleavage in Scots property and succession law between, on the one hand, the law of land, all buildings attached to land, trees and growing crops, mines and quarries and, on the other, all other items of value; that is between heritable and moveable property, respectively.

## Documents of title

The distinctive form of law derived from this period is the charter, the all-important document of title which evidenced the rights over land of the wealthy, both individuals and institutions such as religious houses. The stout charter-chest can still be seen in many castles. In the 19th century, groups of (usually) titled people formed clubs, such as the Maitland and the Bannatyne, to publish the surviving charters and other documents of title, often of their own families, and these form invaluable historical records, as well as a chain of ownership. Today many owner-occupiers still have his title deeds, though often deposited as security with a building society which holds a standard security (a form of mortgage) over the home. From a legal proposition of the most general kind, that the Crown is the ultimate owner of all the land of Scotland, fragments of that ownership descend to the level of the home-owner and give him legal rights. Tenants of lands, homes, factories etc

1 See pp 17, 20, 26.

likewise have the enjoyment of that property, though limited in duration and other ways.

## Feudalism and independence

Feudalism also led to a growing sense of Scots independence from England, though it was from England that the feudal institutions had been imported. At one level it was a disagreement over feudal law that precipitated the Wars of Independence. On the death in Orkney en route to Scotland of the Maid of Norway, who was to succeed to the Scottish throne following the accidental death of Alexander III in 1286, Robert Bruce, the Lord of Annandale, and John Balliol, the Lord of Galloway, were in dispute as to who had the right to succeed to the throne of Scotland. Edward I of England claimed to be overlord of Scotland and in support of his claim could argue that the contenders and other Scots nobles, like the Comyns, owned lands in England for which they paid him homage. Eventually Bruce and Balliol and certain lesser claimants conceded that Edward was lord superior of Scotland and promised to abide by his decision. After many sessions of legal argument Edward gave judgment in favour of John Balliol who then paid him homage at Newcastle.

The humiliation implied in the outcome of this so-called Great Cause was emphasised by Edward who went on to hear appeals on questions of Scottish feudal rights, insisting that King John Balliol be present. When war broke out between England and France Scots envoys signed an alliance with the French. Edward invaded Scotland in 1296, stripped John of the symbols of his kingship and removed the Scots records and Stone of Destiny to Westminster. There then followed the Wars of Independence, with Scotland's defeat under William Wallace at Falkirk in 1298 and victory under Robert Bruce against Edward II at Bannockburn in 1314. This formative period in Scotland's development ended in 1328 with a peace treaty signed at Edinburgh and Northampton, prior to which Edward III accepted that Scotland was to be 'separate in all things from the kingdom of England, assured forever of its territorial integrity, to remain forever free and quit of any subjection, servitude, claim or demand'.

## Beliefs sustaining legal independence

The victory at Bannockburn gave a great boost to Scotland's sense of nationhood. This is manifested in the sonorous prose of the

Declaration of Arbroath of 1320. In it the nobility, the barons, free-holders and whole community of the kingdom of Scotland beseeched Pope John XXII to persuade Edward III of England to allow the Scots to live in peace and liberty. They are portrayed as a nation (*nacio*) of ancient lineage, governed by a succession of 113 kings of native stock, and under the patronage of St Andrew, brother of St Peter[1]. Mythology much of it may be, but it gave the Scots a certain pride of ancestry and confidence as a people for the future. Its rhetoric is echoed in a populist form as Scots supporters sing 'Flower of Scotland' at international rugby and football matches. Confidence that Scotland is still a nation underlies the Scotland Act 1998 which affirms that Scotland should retain a separate legal system from that of England.

The Declaration was composed by Bernard de Linton, Abbot of Arbroath and Chancellor of Scotland. Leading churchmen had given their support and recognition to King Robert Bruce, speaking on behalf of the people and commons of the Kingdom of Scotland, in a declaration of 1310. A century earlier the Church had successfully fought off the claims of the Archbishop of York to jurisdiction over the dioceses of Scotland by securing from Pope Honorius III in 1218 a bull declaring the bishops of the Scottish Church to be directly subject to Rome. So the Church had an interest parallel to that of the state in proclaiming the indepen-dence of the Scottish nation.

Bernard de Linton wrote a poem in celebration of the victory of Bannockburn and later in the century another churchman, John Barbour, Archdeacon of Aberdeen, further boosted the national sentiment in his epic poem *The Bruce*. In it he gives an account of the Wars of Independence, portraying Bruce as the hero and the English kings as holding the Scottish people, rich and poor, in a state of 'thryllage' or serfdom, until led to freedom by Bruce[2].

Rather than stressing the stratification of society, imposed by feudalism, Barbour portrays one 'kynrik' or country and one folk, certain of whose members are chosen to act for the common weal (or good). This theme is to be found too in the Declaration of Arbroath. According to it, it was 'the consent and assent of all the people', as well as divine providence and (very questionably) right of succession, that made Robert Bruce King of the Scots. The class divisions of feudalism were no doubt real enough, but an attempt

1 The Declaration of Arbroath, in Latin with an English translation, is printed in Lord Cooper *Selected Papers 1922–1954* (1957) p 334.
2 See Archibald AH Duncan *The Bruce, An Epic Poem*.

was being made to subsume them into a united national conscious-
ness.

## THE LATER MIDDLE AGES

The years following the Treaty of Edinburgh and Northampton
were turbulent ones politically, though not without cultural
achievements, in poetry, architecture and learning. Edward III
went back on his word and the 1330s were a decade in which
English troops captured Scottish castles and were ousted from
them one by one. The Scots made an alliance with the French and
thus became embroiled in the Hundred Years War. There were
many dynastic feuds. Several kings such as David II and James I
came to the throne in childhood. Both of these kings spent periods
in captivity in England. Yet throughout these vicissitudes there was
no doubt that Scotland remained a nation and had much of the
apparatus of a state, though it functioned imperfectly. The chroni-
clers of the 14th and 15th centuries, John of Fordoun, Walter
Bower, and Andrew Wyntoun, all churchmen, recount Scotland's
history in strongly nationalist terms.

### Emerging statehood

One way in which statehood was evidenced was in boundaries. The
Tweed and the Solway became accepted natural divisions between
Scotland and England, though Berwick on the north bank of the
Tweed remained English. In between there were disputed
marches, east, middle and west. These were policed by wardens,
the Scottish ones being appointed by Parliament or the Council
from the families of the Humes, the Kerrs and the Maxwells. They
kept rough and ready order, at times engaging in warfare, at times
upholding truces. Although raids were frequent and there was
strife as to the exact boundaries, there was no doubt that here was
an international frontier.

Treaties too evidence Scotland's international standing. Thus,
before James IV married Margaret Tudor, daughter of Henry VII,
in 1503, a Treaty of Peace was signed between the two monarchs,
promising 'a true, sincere, whole and unbroken peace, friendship,
league and alliance'. But no union was contemplated. If the King
of England waged war against another country, the King of
Scotland promised to refrain from invading England, but might
still give succour to England's enemy.

## Courts, central and local

By the 16th century Scotland had developed many of the judicial institutions of a legal system. Some were akin to those of England; others adapted from continental models. The development is one from local and diverse institutions to centralised and uniform ones. Many of them emanated from the feudal system. Participation in the doing of justice was one of the returns made for the right to hold lands, large and small. At the top it meant attendance by the king's tenants-in-chief, lay and ecclesiastical, at the king's court, the *curia regis*. It advised the monarch on all matters of government. Out of it, by the 15th century, there emerged various combinations of Lords – of Council and of Session[1]. In 1532 they were placed on a permanent footing, financed out of church revenues, as the Court of Session, which remains Scotland's premier civil court.

From the reign of the first effective feudal king, David I (1124–53), an attempt was made to maintain order throughout Scotland by travelling civil and criminal courts presided over by judges called Justiciars. These courts operated very irregularly, perhaps because the Justiciars were also magnates with more pressing interests and ambitions of their own. Repeated attempts were made over the centuries to make them travel on circuit or ayre, 'on the grass and on the corn' (in spring and autumn). The civil side of the Justiciars' work had decayed by the 15th century. The revival of their criminal jurisdiction was one of the achievements of James VI. Eventually central criminal justice was put on a permanent footing with the founding of the High Court of Justiciary in 1672, composed for the most part of Court of Session judges in the role of Lords Commissioners of Justiciary.

The inadequacies of the central courts were remedied to some extent locally. Trusted nobles and churchmen were granted from the 14th century powers of regality enabling them in their own territory to exercise justice on the gravest crimes, the pleas of the crown which normally had to await the coming of the Justiciar's court. Regality courts could repledge or recall their own subjects from other courts[2]. Some, such as those of St Andrews and the

---

1 On the antecedents and creation of the Court of Session, see RK Hannay *The College of Justice*, republished by the Stair Society in 1990. For a vivid account of the part played by a leading churchman in judicial decisions, see LJ Macfarlane *William Elphinstone and The Kingdom of Scotland, 1431–1514*.

2 ID Willock *The Origins and Development of the Jury in Scotland* (Stair Society, vol 23, 1966) p 84.

Abbeys of Dunfermline and Arbroath, even had their own chancery. The surviving regalities were finally abolished in the Heritable Jurisdictions (Scotland) Act 1746. Although they could be divisive in the hands of unruly noblemen, the records of the best regalities run by religious foundations suggest that they provided a high quality of justice[1].

At the level of the shire or county, sheriffs existed as local judges, civil and criminal, from the reign of David I and remain as the mainstay of Scottish justice to this day. But like the lords of regality, the office of sheriff became a hereditary one, which could be turned against the king and his policies[2].

Sheriffs were in competition with the burghs which were created by the early medieval kings as centres of royal influence and economic development through trade and manufacturing. They enjoyed their own courts over which provosts and baillies presided. At the principal or head courts of both burgh and sheriff courts, usually held four times a year, all the adult males with a title to land had to attend. This was known as suit of court. From them jurors would be selected[3].

Until the 15th century the burgh courts were supervised by the Chamberlain, a high officer of the king's household, who also heard appeals from the burgh courts. In the later Middle Ages wealthy magnates set up their own burghs, free of the king's influence and strengthening their own power. Burgh courts are the predecessors of today's district courts. Lesser landowners, called barons or lairds, also had the right and the duty to do justice in barony courts, and usually appointed a baron-baillie to act as judge in their name. In both civil and minor criminal matters he would be assisted in establishing the facts by the suitors of court, those tenants who were bound to attend[4].

As well as these courts of the land, there operated in Scotland a parallel set of courts set up by the Church. Every bishop had his own court, with a judge called the official and in larger dioceses

---

1 See JM Webster and AAM Duncan *Regality of Dunfermline Court Book, 1531–1538; Court Book of the Regality of Broughton 1569–1573.*

2 For a comprehensive account of the functions of the sheriff and the records of a well-run sheriff court, see WC Dickinson *The Sheriff Court Book of Fife, 1515–1522* (Scottish History Society).

3 For a similar account of burgh courts, prefacing the earliest surviving records of a burgh court, see WC Dickinson *Early Records of the Burgh of Aberdeen, 1317, 1398–1407* (Scottish History Society). On burgh juries, see ID Willock *The Origins and Development of the Jury in Scotland* p 52.

4 See, eg, WC Dickinson *The Barony Court Book of Carnwath, 1523–1542* (Scottish History Society).

archdeacons also. As well as dealing with internal church disputes, it had jurisdiction over marriage, legitimacy, wills and moveable property, and contracts made under oath. Appeal lay to the supreme courts of the Catholic Church in Rome. Because of the unreliability of the courts of the land, people often voluntarily submitted their disputes to the arbitrament of the ecclesiastical courts[1] and registered agreements in their records.

## The substantive law

Unless courts are just going to decide cases on a whim or according to what seems just and reasonable, they need law to apply, general formulae which will enable cases to be determined with consistency. Feudal law, except in the individualised form of deeds, is rather scanty; but it has a voluminous procedural law, stating the manner in which decisions are to be reached. Thus, it had an order of succession to land on the death of the holder. The procedure of determining who was the entitled successor to particular lands was commenced by a claimant obtaining a brieve, a short document issued by the chancery of the king or of a regality. It ordered the sheriff or other judge to make inquiry of faithful men, the inquest or jury, whether the deceased died 'vest and seized' of certain lands, and by what tenure, and what was the relationship of the claimant to the deceased. Most of the law was of this procedural character. When much later in 1605 the first book giving a narrative account of Scots law was written it was the *Jus Feudale* or *Feudal Law* of Sir Thomas Craig. Criminal law was simpler. Killing, stealing, robbing and raping were crimes. The rules of law were concerned more with detailed procedures than deciding whether certain acts constituted a crime.

## Law from the courts

If law was to emerge from the decisions of courts, there had to be judges sitting regularly and giving reasoned decisions on what the law meant which were in some way recorded and stored. There had also to be people knowledgeable about the law and able to argue from it; in other words, a legal profession. Its history is described in Chapter 7. It was not until the early 19th century that such a fully

---

1 See further Simon Ollivant *The Court of the Official in Pre-Reformation Scotland* (Stair Society).

fledged system of judicial precedent emerged. But in the 16th and early 17th centuries, judges began to keep notebooks, initially for their own convenience, of decisions which demonstrated the practice of the courts, like a form of custom. These were called *Practicks*. The fullest are those of Sir James Balfour and Sir Thomas Hope, who wrote *Major* and *Minor Practicks*, and Robert Spotiswoode. All of these were eventually printed. But printing was slow to be applied to the law and for a long time they circulated in handwritten copies. Some *Practicks* are mere collections of decisions of the highest courts. Others, called by historians *Digest-Practicks*, contain extracts from statutes, Roman law and Canon law as well[1].

## Law from Parliament

Long before these personal collections of rules of law appeared, a book of Scots law of venerable antiquity existed. This was *Regiam Majestatem*, a rather disorderly collection of laws from various sources. Some of it is native Scots law taken from Scots statutes of the 12th and 13th centuries. But the major source is the *Tractatus* or *Treatise on the Laws and Customs of England*, attributed to Glanvill, the Justiciar of Henry II, some of the borrowings being unchanged and others amended to fit Scottish circumstances. Other sources include writers on medieval Roman and Canon law. It is uncertain how this collection began; it may well have been merely collections made by a clerk of court for his own use. But by the 15th century it was regarded as one of 'the bukis of law of this realme' and a commission was appointed to 'mend the lawis that nedis mendment'[2]. The return of James I from captivity in England produced a spurt of legislation from Parliament in 1424 and subsequent years, much of it designed to improve the quality of justice and some of it apparently inspired by English examples[3]. The substantive law was still very incomplete and a statute of 1473 deplored the 'divers obscure matters that are now in our law'[4]. The first printing press was introduced into Scotland in 1507, but it was not until 1541 with the printing of the Black Acts that it was

---

1 The largest and most authoritative *Practicks* are those of Balfour of probably 1579, but not printed until 1754. See PGB McNeill *The Practicks of Sir James Balfour* (Stair Society, vols 21, 22).
2 APS II, 10; one of several such Acts.
3 On the content of that statute law, see JJ Robertson 'The Development of the Law' in Jenny Brown *Scottish Society in the Fifteenth Century*.
4 APS II, 105.

applied to legislation. Thus, the problem of identifying the authentic text of an Act was eventually solved.

## The study of law

Despite the political and dynastic upheavals, the vitality of the cultural life of Scotland in the 15th century was attested to by the founding of three universities, all under papal bulls; in St Andrews in 1413, Glasgow in 1451, and Aberdeen in 1494. All were founded on the initiative of local bishops; James Kennedy, the second founder of St Andrews, William Turnbull of Glasgow and William Elphinstone of Aberdeen were all graduates in Canon law, that is, the law of the Church. All the universities taught some law from the beginning, mainly to clerical students, who thus no longer had to travel to continental universities such as Paris and Orleans. But their existence justified a statute of 1496 requiring barons and freeholders to spend three years in the 'sculis of art and jure' (i e law) 'that thai may have knawlege and understanding of the lawis'[1]. With some interruptions the teaching of law in universities has continued to the present day.

Scots law is often said to have been influenced by Roman law – sometimes referred to as civil law. In so far as this is true, the influences have come through academic study in the universities. The first channel was through the Canon law of the Catholic Church which provided a complete and self-sufficient legal apparatus from the 12th to the mid-16th centuries and made up for many of the deficiencies of the native law. It employed the terminology and procedures of the later Roman law which reached its peak of development under the Emperor Justinian in 6th-century Byzantium. A second channel was through the *Regiam Majestatem*, the compiler of which supplemented his mainly English materials with extracts from continental writers on Roman law (see above). The third channel was through legal study by Scots in continental universities, where as a matter of course the law worthy of study was taken to be updated Roman law and not the local customary law. In the early Middle Ages, Bologna and Pisa were favoured, in the 14th and 15th centuries, Paris and Orleans, and after the Reformation, Utrecht and Leiden in the Protestant Netherlands. Many Scots, such as William Elphinstone, also taught in these overseas universities. Their influence is to be found in the often

---

1 APS II, 238. On the place of law in the first Scottish universities, see DM Walker *A Legal History of Scotland* vol II, pp 277–285.

cumbersome Romanistic pleadings used in the Scots courts and in the style and phraseology of writers such as Sir Thomas Craig and Viscount Stair (though the latter denied that Roman law formed part of the law of Scotland)[1]. But influence of Roman law on Scots law has been very limited and spasmodic in comparison with that of English law[2].

## THE REFORMATION

The Reformation brought about several changes in political and thus legal doctrine. The latent concept of the state emerged in England, France and Spain and a long struggle began to align nations and states. In those countries which accepted the doctrines of Martin Luther, religion became in effect a department of state and all subjects were required to follow the religion of their prince. In this respect, England followed Lutheranism. The Sovereign became the head of the Church of England, to which all subjects had to belong. Allegiance to the Pope was made a matter of treason. Scotland, on the other hand, followed the doctrines of John Calvin, as applied in Geneva. He distinguished two kingdoms, a civil one and a spiritual one, the latter with Christ as its only head. These two jurisdictions were complementary.

The magistrates of the civil power should submit to the ministers of the ecclesiastical power in matters of conscience and religion, just as the ministers submitted to the magistrates in matters of civil and criminal law. As expounded in the Second Book of Discipline, drawn up by Andrew Melville in 1578, this doctrine threw a challenge to the king, which was taken up by James VI who was something of a theologian. It lay behind many of the divisive religious conflicts of the 17th century and tended to dilute the concepts of nation and patriotism. In place of bishops, Presbyterianism chose government by committees – in ascending order the Kirk Session, the Presbytery, the Synod and the General Assembly. They provided many Scots men with experience of argument from theological principles and a belief in the principles of equality and community. Arguably the Scots resistance to laws in the making of which they have had only a minor part or which

1 Stair Inst I, 1, 12: 'though it be not acknowledged as a law binding for its authority, yet being, as a rule, followed for its equity'.
2 For a slightly more favourable account, see P Stein 'The influence of Roman law on the law of Scotland' 1963 JR 205. He concludes 'many parts (of Scots law) still bear an unmistakeably Roman stamp'.

seem to embody excessive individualism derives in part from this group experience. It certainly made natural and acceptable the theological slant to the work of Viscount Stair, the late 17th century consolidator of Scots law[1].

In the ten years before and after the Reformation Act of 1560 there was popular hostility to the French counsellors and soldiers who accompanied Mary of Lorraine, the Queen Regent, and later her daughter Queen Mary. This was more than equalled by hatred of the English, following the invasions of Scotland by the Earl of Hertford in 1544 and 1545 and by the Earl of Somerset in 1547, during which many churches and towns were destroyed. When the Reformation came it took a distinctively Scottish course which owed nothing to the example of England and arguably strengthened the Scots sense of nationhood, albeit as a branch of a reformed universal church.

## UNION OF THE CROWNS

The first of the three major steps which brought about the present constitutional position of Scotland was the Union of the Crowns in 1603. Queen Mary of Scotland had one child, James. When she fled to England and was imprisoned there by her cousin, Queen Elizabeth, her son was educated by tutors, including George Buchanan, an intellectual of European renown. At the age of 12 James took up the powers of kingship and was an able and vigorous monarch in trying to pacify the more disorderly parts of his realm and play off the various political and religious factions. On the execution of Mary in 1587, James became heir to the English throne, a prospect he had long relished. When Elizabeth died in 1603, James immediately made a ceremonial procession to London, feted in every town. He rarely returned to Scotland. During his reign James VI and I took as close an interest in the government of Scotland as that of England. The introduction of Justices of the Peace into Scotland in 1609 and the creation in 1617 of the still extant Register of Sasines, providing a register of all deeds concerning title to land (outside the burghs till 1681), were two of his lasting innovations. Above all, looking at his reign over Scotland as a whole, he gave stable central government, which it had not known during many centuries of factional strife.

1 See p 29.

Throughout his reign over the two kingdoms James cherished a scheme for their union. He derived it from his belief in the Divine Right of Kings. Since God had appointed him to rule the two realms, they should be treated as one. In his first address to the English Parliament in 1603 he fancifully compared himself to a husband wedded to the whole island of Britain as his wife. In 1604, the two Parliaments at his request appointed Commissioners from Scotland and England to discuss the project of unification. One of the Scots, Sir Thomas Craig, author of the *Jus Feudale*, wrote a treatise in 1605 arguing for union on mainly practical grounds[1]. In it he asserted 'that at the present day there are no nations whose laws and institutions more closely correspond than England and Scotland' (at p 304). Although the Commissioners reported in favour of a fuller union, the proposals were opposed by both Parliaments and nothing came of them.

One of the issues driving the king to raise the question of unification in some form was the legal status of Scots in England. Nationality was by now such a strong force that Scots and English were treated as foreigners in each other's country, a handicap felt much more by Scots than English. Despairing of finding a solution through the English Parliament, James arranged a collusive case before the highest English judges called *Calvin's Case*[2]. Land in London was bought for an infant born in Edinburgh in 1606. Its seizure by others was challenged. The judges held that *post-nati*, i e persons born in Scotland since the accession of James to the throne of England, were entitled to hold land in England, since they owed allegiance to him as King of England and he owed them protection. This limited form of naturalisation removed one of the grievances of Scots in England.

## THE 17TH CENTURY; RELIGIOUS FEUDS

Throughout most of the 17th century disputes about religion took precedence over nationhood. James following out his doctrine of the Divine Right of Kings (to rule) contemplated a single church in England and Scotland led by bishops appointed by him. This provoked resistance in Scotland in his reign and even more so in that of his successor, Charles I. Charles was about to introduce

---

1 *De Unione Regnorum Britanniae Tractatus*, with translation by CS Terry (Scottish History Society). See also BP Levack 'The Proposed Union of English and Scots in the 17th Century' 1975 JR 97.
2 (1608) 7 Co Rep 1a.

Episcopacy in Scotland. The Scots of all classes reacted in 1638 by signing a National Covenant, which echoed some of the arguments of the Declaration of Arbroath in portraying the Scots as a chosen people, like the Jews, covenanted to God. This elevated form of nationalism was not long persisted in as a matter of policy, but it led to the raising of a Scottish army, which gave a boost to the concept of Scottish identity. The Scots troops invaded the North of England and occupied Newcastle. In the face of this threat Charles gave way and in 1641 ratified laws of the Scots Parliament against Episcopacy. Emboldened by this success, the Scots Covenanters then sought to impose their Presbyterian form of church government on England. Commissioners of the English Parliament, by now in conflict with the king, sought the support of the Scots. In a Solemn League and Covenant signed in 1643 the Scots and English agreed that the Church of England should be reformed on the model of the reformed faith practised in Scotland, so that there would be one form of church government throughout Britain. The Scots took this as acceptance of Presbyterianism.

This incursion into English affairs was to lead to years of skirmishes and minor battles among the armed sectarians, as an off-shoot of the English Civil War. Most Scots, though rejecting the ecclesiastical claims of Charles and his son, were shocked at the English Parliament's execution of the king in 1649 and refused to accept the ensuing Republic under Oliver Cromwell. They also were concerned that Cromwell declined to endorse Presbyterianism and instead showed a tenderness to the consciences of most believers (except of course Catholics). The period of the Commonwealth from 1649 to 1659 was thus for Scotland one of military occupation and a forced union with England.

Some Scots welcomed that unity. But when the monarchy was restored in 1660 in the person of Charles II, it was a restoration of the status quo and the two Parliaments resumed their separate existence. The religious feuds continued, but no longer reinforced nationalism, for Scots were much divided as to whether Scotland was still covenanted to impose Presbyterianism on England. Constitutional issues then came to the surface. Charles ruled in Scotland through the Scottish Privy Council, which had more power than it had enjoyed since the Middle Ages. It exercised both legislative and judicial functions, thus challenging the Parliament and the Court of Session respectively, and purported to do so under the royal prerogative, the residual powers of the king as the fountain of justice.

Resentment against this autocratic style of government eventually led to the dethroning of Charles' successor, his brother James

VII (in Scotland) and II (in England). His successor (and son-in-law), William of Orange, was invited to Britain by some English nobles, prompting James's precipitate flight. The question was thus posed: who was now the King of Scotland? The Estates of Scotland (or Parliament) answered by offering the Crown to William and his spouse Mary. In a long preamble they denounced the abuses by James, who was in any case disqualified as a 'papist'. He had thus 'invaded the fundamental constitution of the Kingdom, and altered it from a legal limited Monarchy, to an arbitrary despotic Power' leading to 'the violation of the laws and liberties of the Kingdom, inverting all the ends of Government'. The Estates then declared William and Mary to be King and Queen of Scotland, confident they would preserve the rights they had asserted. Thus, the Estates were appealing to a fundamental law, by which sovereignty resided in the people (represented by the Estates of Parliament), who conferred the Crown on one who would respect that fundamental law. Indeed, the whole document is styled the Claim of Right and is the Scottish equivalent of the English Bill of Rights[1].

For much of the 17th century men's energies were thus taken up with argument and warfare on essentially religious issues. Amid the clash of arms the laws were often silent. What did emerge from this epoch of legal significance was a constitutional settlement in which the autocratic powers claimed by the Stewart monarchs were rejected and parliamentary government put in place. From it by gradual extensions of the franchise the form of parliamentary democracy now in existence in the United Kingdom emerged.

## THE 18TH CENTURY

### Union of the Parliaments

The inconveniences of governing two kingdoms under one king became more obvious in the reign of William, who was often absent on the continent. Scots resented their exclusion from England's foreign trade and engaged in a disastrous attempt to establish a colony at Darien in Central America. When William was succeeded by Anne, who outlived all her many children, matters came to a head, for the English Parliament, without consulting the Scots, passed the Act of Succession in 1701, declaring that the Electress Sophia of Hanover and her offspring should succeed

1 See APS IX, 38.

to the English throne. So Scots who wished the Union of the Crowns to continue would have to accept the English choice. Those who did not would have to find an alternative. James VII and II and his descendants could provide one.

Faced with this deterioration in relations, Queen Anne took the initiative and instructed that commissioners should be chosen from each country to negotiate a complete union. The Scots commissioners chosen were wholeheartedly in favour, their price being that Scots should have complete equality in trade with England. The English were luke-warm. Negotiations collapsed when the Scots demanded an 'equivalent' or compensation for taking on a share of the English national debt. The Scots Parliament reacted by passing in 1703 an Act of Security declaring that on Anne's death it would nominate a successor from the royal house of Scotland provided he or she was a Protestant. The English retaliated by passing the Aliens Act 1705, making Scots aliens in England and restricting trade between the two countries.

It seemed as if the two countries were on a track leading to complete separation. But in 1706 Anne restarted negotiations, this time nominating the commissioners herself, with on each side a majority in favour of an incorporating union under one Parliament. Working on the drafts of the earlier meetings, a draft treaty was produced within a few months[1].

The resultant articles of union then had to be approved one by one by the Estates of Scotland in Parliament. They were unpopular with several groups, as well as with the ordinary people of the towns. The Presbyterians of various persuasions resented the lack of protection for that form of church government. They were placated by the passing of an Act for Securing the Protestant Religion and Presbyterian Church Government, which was declared to be 'a fundamental and essential condition of any Treaty or Union ... in all time coming'[2]. In the same Act the then four universities of Scotland were to 'continue within this Kingdom for ever'. The legal profession had already had its doubts met by articles preserving the private law of Scotland and forbidding Scottish cases to be heard in any court 'in Westminster Hall'. Noblemen who saw their offices of state about to disappear were won over with sinecures, pensions, arrears of salaries (paid out of the agreed equivalent) and the retention of their hereditary rights of

1 The Articles of Union are printed in G Donaldson *Scottish Historical Documents* (1970) p 268.
2 *Scots Statutes Revised*, 201.

dispensing justice on their own lands. But the greatest lure of the union was the promise of freedom of trade with England and its colonies, which could be presented as the means to raise living standards in Scotland to equal those enjoyed in England.

The articles of union were debated by the one-chamber Scots Parliament over several months and each was voted on separately by the nobles, barons and burgesses[1]. They were all approved, with minor amendments, on 16 January 1707, together with the Act on Presbyterian Church Government. The English Parliament, urged by Queen Anne, then with less deliberation ratified the Treaty and passed an Act of Union in terms corresponding to and incorporating the Scots Act[2]. The Scots Privy Council by a proclamation dissolved the Scots Parliament on 28 April 1707 and on 1 May the United Kingdom of Great Britain, as defined in Article II, came into being. There was no corresponding dissolution of the English Parliament, but the existing members of the English Parliament, unlike members of the Scots, automatically became members of the Parliament of Great Britain and it followed the procedure of the English Parliament.

The main features of the Treaty of Union are these. The two kingdoms were united under the name of Great Britain, the succession to the monarchy being conferred on the Electress Sophia of Hanover and her descendants, as the English Parliament had decreed. There was to be one Parliament of Great Britain, in the Commons of which there should be 45 Scots representatives, and in the Lords 16 peers elected by their fellows. All subjects of Great Britain were to have full freedom of trade and navigation in Britain and the Dominions. The same customs and duties were to apply throughout the kingdom and the same coinage and weights and measures. The Court of Session and Court of Justiciary were to remain in all time coming in Scotland. 'No causes in Scotland [were to] be cognisable by the Courts of Chancery, Queen's Bench, Common Pleas or any other Court in Westminster Hall', a sentence the meaning of which was to be later the subject of debate[3]. The Scots Privy Council was to continue until altered by Parliament (which promptly abolished it). Heritable jurisdictions and offices were reserved to their owners. Laws concerning 'Public Right, Policy and Civil Government may be made the same throughout the whole United Kingdom', but 'no alteration be made in Laws which concern private Right, except for the evident

1 Minutes of the debates are printed in APS XI, 322.
2 APS XI, 446.
3 APS XI, 411.

utility of the Subjects within Scotland' (Article XVIII). The rights
and privileges of the royal burghs of Scotland were preserved. Laws
and statutes of either kingdom so far as inconsistent with the
Articles were void[1].

## Rational exposition of the law

Apart from Craig's defence in Latin of feudal law, writing about
the law as distinct from collections of laws in the 17th century had
scarcely gone beyond the stage of *Digest-Practicks* (see p 20). Sir
George Mackenzie, Lord Advocate under Charles II and founder
of the Advocates' Library (the precursor of the present National
Library of Scotland), was a man of learning who wrote much on
morality, religion and heraldry. But in writing his *Laws and Customs
in Matters Criminal* he gathered together pieces of law from many
varied sources under subject-headings with only minor analysis.
James Dalrymple, Viscount Stair, then with one massive and
masterly work transformed the civil (ie non-criminal) law of
Scotland from unco-ordinated fragments of law from various
sources of uncertain weight and priority into a coherent and
rational system of law, expounded in magisterial style. This work
was *The Institutions of the Law of Scotland* of 1681 (extensively
revised and republished in 1693)[2].

Stair's achievement is summed up in the sub-title 'Deduced
from its originals, and collated with the Civil [ie Roman] Canon
and Feudal Laws, and with the Customs of Neighbouring
Nations'. Stair had been a Regent (or Professor) of Philosophy at
Glasgow University from 1641 before embarking on a legal career
which carried him to the top post of Lord President of the Court
of Session in 1671. In 1681 he refused to take an oath under the
Test Act 1681, had to resign and retired in 1682 to Leiden in the
Netherlands, where he remained until the deposition of James VII
and II in 1688. He then returned to Britain in the company of the
future King William of Orange who re-appointed him Lord
President[3].

Stair's concept of a work expounding as a system the whole of a
nation's civil law had no counter-part in England until William
Blackstone's *Commentaries* of 1765, but he may have been inspired
by the similar treatment of the civil law of the Netherlands by

1 For text with subsequent amendments, see *Scots Statutes Revised* 203.
2 The 1693 text was used in a new edition, edited by DM Walker in 1981.
3 For a fuller account of his life, see *Stair Tercentenary Studies*, edited by DM Walker
   (Stair Society, 1981).

Hugo Grotius, who is celebrated as the founder of international law. Stair's achievement thus put Scots law in line with the major systems of law which took Roman law as their inspiration. In Scotland his example was followed by the *Institute* of Andrew McDouall, Lord Bankton, of 1751, the *Institute of the Law of Scotland* of John Erskine, Professor of Scots Law at Edinburgh, of 1773, and the *Commentaries on the Law of Scotland and the Principles of Mercantile Jurisprudence* of 1804 and the *Principles of the Law of Scotland* of 1829 of George Joseph Bell. The weakness of legal literature on the criminal side was remedied by David Hume (nephew of the philosopher of the same name) in his *Commentaries on the Law of Scotland Respecting Crimes* of 1797, which performed the same organising role for criminal law as Stair had done for civil law a century earlier. Erskine, Bell and Hume were all holders of the Chair of Scots Law at Edinburgh University and evidence the contribution that the Universities of Edinburgh and, to a lesser extent, Glasgow (in William Forbes and others) were making to the development of Scots law, following the establishment of Chairs of Law there in the early 18th century.

As such they were part of the movement in scholarship called the Enlightenment in which Scotland played a leading role through the writings of men such as David Hume, the philosopher, Adam Smith, the economist and jurist, John Millar and Adam Ferguson, the forerunners of modern sociology. Stair, though founding his work on theological assumptions that were undermined by the philosopher Hume, had in common with the Enlightenment movement of the next century his claim that the constitution rested on rational foundations and his imposing order on the hitherto disorderly and incomplete civil law of Scotland. Within the 18th century the most prominent contributor from the legal profession to the Enlightenment movement was Henry Home, Lord Kames (1696–1782). Kames was an enthusiastic polymath, whose interests extended to agricultural improvement, transport, town planning, history, philosophy and literature, as well as law and its science, jurisprudence. His main work on the law is his *Principles of Equity* of 1760, in which in typical Enlightenment fashion he precedes his account of equitable procedures in Scots law and English law with a discussion of the principle of utility under which courts have a role to play in advancing the well-being of people[1].

---

1 For biographies of Kames, see Ian S Ross *Lord Kames and the Scotland of his Day* (1972) and William C Lehmann *Henry Home, Lord Kames, and the Scottish Enlightenment* (1971).

# THE 19TH CENTURY

The transformation of the social life of Scotland through the Industrial and Agricultural Revolutions could not fail to have an impact on its legal system and in several ways it adapted itself to meet the challenge. The upsurge of trade and manufacturing made new demands on the legal concepts of contract and property. Innumerable daily deals for the supply and transformation and transport of commodities required an environment in which they could be entered into with confidence that they would be carried out. Insurance and bankruptcy laws had to be available to cope when they were not. But land law, still rooted in the feudal law handed down from the Middle Ages, was ill-adapted to industrial needs and in the hands of rapacious landlords could become an instrument of oppression in rural areas, most notoriously in the Highland Clearances. Police forces were rudimentary, until the Police (Scotland) Act 1857 required all counties and the larger burghs to maintain a local force. Thus, conditions of law and order in which industrial and commercial activity could flourish were secured.

At the start of the century the law could enable people to come together in business only by means of partnership and unincorporated joint stock companies. Their resources could be pooled in the enterprise, but each individual's own entire assets remained fully liable if it failed. From the creditor's point of view there was the handicap that each contributor to the enterprise had to be sued separately. By means of several statutes this brake on commercial enterprise was removed by 1862 through the creation of incorporated companies, which have an existence in law distinct from that of the individuals who as shareholders are their members. Their personal liability for the company's debts is limited to the value of their shares, including any unpaid ones. Banks, however, were excluded from incorporation until after the disastrous collapse of the City of Glasgow Bank in 1878 which brought ruin to many in the West of Scotland.

## Restructuring of the courts

Early in the century the Court of Session was restructured and thus became better able to deal with the later upsurge of commercial litigation. It had sat since its inception in 1532 as a single court of fifteen judges, one of whom in turn sat in the 'Outer House' to take evidence, while the rest sat in the 'Inner House'. In 1808 the

Inner House was made an appellate court, sitting in two divisions, each of four judges[1]. The remainder dealt with cases at first instance, that is, on first hearing. Procedure was also facilitated by cutting down the length of written pleadings. Later in the century, shorthand writers were admitted to record evidence. Appeals from the Court of Session to the House of Lords, which had begun immediately after the Union of 1707 and flourished in the 18th century, were curtailed by the Court of Session Act of 1808. Many of the sheriff courts had been poorly served since the abolition of heritable jurisdictions in 1747, for the sheriffs were Edinburgh advocates, who seldom attended, but acted through unqualified resident sheriff-substitutes. From 1825 this abuse was remedied in that sheriff-substitutes had to be advocates or solicitors of at least three years' standing.

## Growth of case law

The smaller appellate courts led to the judges feeling an onus upon each of them to justify his decision; and as the century wore on these tended to become fuller and supported by the authority of past cases and, in their absence, of the class of authorities who became recognised as institutional writers. From 1821 the judgments, mainly of the Inner House, were collected and published in annual volumes which form part of the series now known as Session Cases. In this manner the essential requirement for the emergence of a practice of judicial precedent, namely accurate reports of litigation and reasoned judgments upon it, gathered by advocates in a standardised form, was met. Previously it had been left to the initiative of individuals, of whom two of the best qualified were Stair and Kames, to publish such decisions as they selected. Now the material was available and the structure was in place to operate a system of judicial precedent. In the 19th century the typical form of law was thus the published judgment. As more and more issues arose for decision from the industrial and commercial community, Scots advocates cited and Scots judges used more and more English decisions to justify their judgments and thereby gave the business users of the law a legal environment which was nearly uniform throughout Great Britain. Statutes such as the Mercantile Law Amendment Act of 1856 and the Sale of

---

1 On the reform of the Court of Session, see Nicholas Phillipson *The Scottish Whigs and the Reform of the Court of Session* (Stair Society, vol 37) ch V.

Goods Act of 1893, applying throughout Great Britain, accentuated this trend.

## THE 20TH AND 21ST CENTURIES

While the decisions of judges still play a creative role, now in most of the law there is less scope for innovation and development than before. In part this is because more law is already settled. But chiefly it is because of the dominance of enacted law, both in changing existing areas of law such as family law, and in opening up new areas of legal regulation; for example, road traffic law, planning law, social security law, race and sex discrimination, employment protection, misuse of drugs and new forms of taxation. In these areas the role of the courts is a secondary one, clearing up ambiguities in the law that comes from Parliament. The courts too play a less dominant role than before, because most of the work of decision-making is entrusted to specialised tribunals, such as social security appeal tribunals, employment tribunals, and Commissioners of Income Tax. Road traffic law remains with the courts, but the volume of cases has been lessened by procedures allowing many minor criminal, including road traffic, offences to be dealt with by the acceptance of a penalty offer, recourse to the courts being at the option of the alleged offender.

Nearly all these new areas of statutory law are common to Great Britain or the United Kingdom and represent the notional will of the whole electorate as mediated through the United Kingdom Parliament. Thus, they diminish the proportion of the law prevailing in Scotland which is distinctively Scots. Most of the tribunal systems operate on a British basis and so offer little or no scope for a distinctive Scottish contribution. Occasionally in road traffic and drug law the Scots courts will differ from their English counterparts, but such disagreements do not usually last long.

Parliaments are ill-equipped to deal with these demands for new and complex legal regulation. Much of such law calls for a response to changing circumstances; for instance, new drugs, new vehicles, new forms of disability. For this reason and the sheer volume of regulations required, most enacted law takes the form of regulations classed as statutory instruments and produced by government departments, under powers delegated by Parliaments, but with little or no parliamentary scrutiny. Often, as in the Social Security Act 1986, the Act itself is a mere framework, authorising the creation of benefits through easily amended statutory instruments such as in that example income support and housing benefit.

During the years of Conservative rule from 1979 to 1997 a ground-swell of discontent arose at the imposition of policies on Scotland which were opposed by the majority of MPs elected in Scottish constituencies. This first took the form of a pressure-group called the Campaign for a Scottish Assembly. This demand was taken up in a formal way by the formation of a Scottish Constitutional Convention composed of representatives of certain political parties, local authorities, trade unions and churches. It published a Claim of Right deliberately echoing that of the late 17th century and asserting the right of the Scottish people to determine the form of government that best suited their needs. The Labour government that returned to power on 1 May 1997 was, with the Liberal Democrats, pledged 'to create a Scottish Parliament. This commitment was fleshed out in a White Paper, *Scotland's Parliament*. Its terms were put to a referendum of voters registered in Scotland and supported by a large majority. The first Scottish Parliament was elected in May 1999 and exercises authority over all matters which are not specifically reserved to the United Kingdom Parliament . During its first fixed term of four years the Parliament passed over 62 Acts.

The continuing parts of the law of Scotland have the means of being kept up to date through the research and reports of the Scottish Law Commission, regardless of whether they engender appeals to the courts[1]. It has been supported by a resurgence of the academic study of law in the university law schools, substantial evidence of which is to be seen in the volumes of the Scottish Universities Law Institute (SULI) and *The Laws of Scotland: Stair Memorial Encyclopaedia*. But, as we shall see, there have been some difficulties in securing the enactment of the Commission's draft Bills, which should be remedied by the Scottish Parliament. Other changes to Scots law have sometimes been made as part of mainly English measures, such as the Unfair Contract Terms Act 1977 and the Criminal Justice Act 1988. Even today, Acts which apply throughout Britain and have special applications to Scotland, such as the Proceeds of Crime Act 2003, may be passed in the Westminster Parliament.

The United Kingdom's membership of the European Community creates a layer of legal regulation above that emanating from Parliament and thus diminishes to some degree the identity of the Scots law[2]. The characteristics of the law produced by the

---

1 See ch 8 below.
2 See p 47 below.

European Commission have much in common with the statutory instruments produced by United Kingdom ministries. They are difficult to discover and to understand because of their technical expression and lack of a context. They are prone to frequent unannounced change. Any disadvantage emerging to the detriment of the issuing authority can quickly be corrected by amendment, sometimes with retrospective effect. The legal profession tends to be reluctant to become involved with regulations. Thus, this law is weighted in favour of its creators, who are also its enforcers, and any rights it appears to confer on individuals are purely theoretical. We may call this law bureaucratic law, and with its adjunct in tribunals it is the typical legal product of the 20th century.

However, just as the volume of law of all kinds seems to be in danger of collapsing under its own weight, computer technology is starting to come to the rescue in the form of data retrieval bases. These have been in operation for some ten years in the form of LexisNexis, WESTLAW and others which give access to decisions (some unreported) and statutory materials in the United Kingdom, Commonwealth countries, USA, France and to a minor extent the European Community. *Statutes in Force* and the Land Register of Scotland can also be accessed by computer. A database of sentences passed on offenders in various circumstances has been provided for High Court judges to promote consistency in sentencing. Judgments of the Court of Session and High Court are now available on the Internet on the day of publication.

## CONCLUSION

It is a far cry from the trading customs of Scottish burghs in the 12th century to a print-out of the latest statutory instrument in the early 21st. All they have in common is the capacity to change people's behaviour, at the behest of those who control them, from what it would otherwise be. But that is the tenuous essence of law. Scotland in its chequered but well-documented history has generated the full range of forms that law can take.

# 3. Institutions

## INTRODUCTION: CONSTITUTIONS AND CONSTITUTIONAL REFORM

In the first edition of this book, it was remarked that the United Kingdom constitution had been described as a 'medieval theme park', implying that it was antiquated and in need of reform. There have been very considerable changes since then. For instance, human rights have been entrenched, the Westminster Parliament has radically altered in composition and, behind all that, the European Community has generated the European Union. These may have pulled it, at least to some extent, into the 21st century.

The change with most immediate effect in Scotland has, however, been devolution[1], the history of which was somewhat protracted. During the 18 years of Conservative government from 1979 to 1997 there was an increasing perception that the policies of the government did not reflect the wishes of the Scottish electorate as demonstrated through the ballot-box, and that representative institutions situated in London provided a very inaccessible and inefficient means of registering Scottish opinion on political questions. This has been summed up in the phrase 'the democratic deficit'. The distinctively Scottish institutions and traditions in law, education, religion and sport became viewed as embodying Scotland's identity as a nation.

There had been an opportunity for a devolution of power to Scotland in the Scotland Act 1978. But it provided that if in a referendum less than 40% of those entitled to vote voted 'Yes' to the question 'Do you want the Scotland Act 1978 to be put into

---

1 Only devolution to Scotland is dealt with here, but it should be remembered that there was simultaneous, though much more limited, devolution introduced in Wales. At much the same time, though in very different circumstances, a form of devolution (originally introduced in 1922) was re-introduced into Northern Ireland. England is devolution-free at the time of publication, though there is a possibility of devolution to English regions.

effect?', or a majority voted 'No', then it should be repealed by Order in Council[1]. Only 33% voted 'Yes' in the Referendum on 1 March 1979 and so the opportunity was lost. The sense of disappointment led to the formation a year later at a public meeting in Edinburgh of a Campaign for a Scottish Assembly to keep alive the case for Scottish self-government. After the 1987 election it set up a committee of prominent Scots, led by the late Sir Robert Grieve[2], which produced *A Claim of Right for Scotland*, asserting the sovereignty of the Scottish people and invited debate on how it should be given expression. This led to the formation of a Scottish Constitutional Convention which adopted the Claim of Right at its inaugural meeting in the Church of Scotland's Assembly Hall in Edinburgh on 30 March 1989.

The Convention was composed of representatives of the Labour, Liberal Democrat and some smaller political parties, of almost all the local authorities, of the Scottish Trade Union Congress, of the Churches, and of a variety of organisations, including the Law Society of Scotland. In 1995, after several years of debate, the Convention presented to the people of Scotland a fairly detailed proposal for the creation of a Parliament for Scotland with specified functions, to be set up by Act of the United Kingdom Parliament.

The inspiration of the Convention was acknowledged in the Labour Party's Manifesto for the 1997 general election. It supplied the outlines of the Scotland Bill, which was one of the first pieces of legislation introduced by the Labour government of May 1997. It was explained in a White Paper entitled *Scotland's Parliament* and published as early as July 1997 and formed the subject of a Referendum on 11 September in which the Scottish electorate voted overwhelmingly in favour of creating a Scottish Parliament and giving it limited tax-varying powers[3]. Although the Scotland Act 1998 which resulted is of a constitutional nature, the division of powers is not carved in stone. Any modifications that seem necessary or expedient can be made by Order in Council with the agreement of both Parliaments.

The election for the Scottish Parliament in May and the opening of the Parliament in July made 1999 a year of transition in the constitutional arrangements of the United Kingdom. A few years

---

1 Scotland Act 1978, s 85, Sch 17.
2 Who was Professor of Town and Country Planning at Glasgow University.
3 On a 60.4% turnout, 74.3% were in favour of a Scottish Parliament and 63.5% were in favour of tax-raising powers.

on, these changes have become embedded, and judgments are emerging as to how well they have operated[1].

## THE UNITED KINGDOM

The state is properly called 'the United Kingdom of Great Britain and Northern Ireland'. This title was assumed after Southern Ireland seceded in 1922. It does not include the Channel Islands and the Isle of Man, which are technically dependencies of it. The preceding title, 'the United Kingdom of Great Britain and Ireland', was created when Great Britain and Ireland were formally amalgamated by the Union of 1801.

'Great Britain' comprises Scotland, England and Wales. The title was adopted when the two previous states (Scotland, and England and Wales, respectively) were combined in 1707, after sharing monarchs since 1603. (Wales had been conquered by England in the 13th century, and was legally and administratively combined with it in the 16th century.)

The laws and legal institutions of Scotland and of England and Wales were not merged by the Union of 1707. Thus, they remain separate 'law areas', with separate court systems (as does Northern Ireland), and it is necessary to distinguish Scots law and English law (and Northern Irish law). However, a single legislature was created by the 1707 Union (and continued by the 1801 Union). This legislature is common to all the law areas and much legislation is passed which applies to the whole of Great Britain or of the United Kingdom. It makes sense, therefore, to speak of 'Great Britain law' and 'United Kingdom law' in fields such as tax and social security law, as well as of 'Scots law' and 'English law'[2].

With effect from 1 January 1973 the United Kingdom acceded to the European Community, which was incorporated into the European Union[3] in 1992. The full effects of this are still being worked out. Certainly, however, it has had considerable legal and governmental effects in what is now more than three decades of

---

1 The typescript for this edition was completed almost simultaneously with the second election to the Scottish Parliament, on 1 May 2003.

2 'British' is a very ambiguous word in constitutional terms, and has no specific legal meaning, save in specific contexts, such as 'British citizenship', as created by the British Nationality Act 1981. On the Treaty and Acts of Union, see ch 2.

3 The European Union comprises the 'three pillars' of: the European Community; the 'Common Foreign and Security Policy'; and 'Police and Judicial Co-operation in Criminal Matters' (previously 'Justice and Home Affairs'): see below.

United Kingdom membership. Principally, in the context of the legal system, there are institutions generating and judging the law created by the European Community ('Community law'), and this law can apply in the United Kingdom and, indeed, displace Scots or English law.

## United Kingdom government and Parliament

### The Crown and government

'The Crown' is a term used to mean, in effect, the state. It is a symbol of the power of the state, which was formerly vested in the monarch. Thus, for example, prosecution of crime is said to be on behalf of 'the Crown'. For very few purposes does 'the Crown' refer to the monarch personally. When reference is made to the Queen's formal powers and duties, the term 'Sovereign' is often used.

Government is carried on in the name of 'the Crown', so the Crown often comes to mean the government of the UK. This comprises the Prime Minister and some 25 senior ministers (those in charge of departments usually being called 'Secretary of State'[1]) who form the Cabinet, and up to 100 or so junior ministers (usually called 'Minister of State' or 'Parliamentary Under-Secretary of State') and unpaid 'Parliamentary Private Secretaries'. By a 'convention of the constitution' (that is, an unwritten rule of the constitution), members of the government must be members of one or other House of Parliament. The Prime Minister is appointed by the Sovereign. However, her discretion is extremely constrained, for there is another strong convention of the constitution that she appoint the person who can command a majority in a vote in the House of Commons. In practice this means the leader of the party which won the last general election. Other ministers are also appointed by the Sovereign, but in practice on the nomination of the Prime Minister. It is the UK government which proposes most legislation in the UK Parliament, including some which relates to Scotland. The UK government is sometimes referred to as 'Whitehall', after the name of the street in which most central government offices are.

---

1 Thus, e g, Secretary of State for the Home Department ('Home Secretary'), Secretary of State for Foreign and Commonwealth Affairs ('Foreign Secretary') etc.

**Secretary of State for Scotland.** Before devolution, the Scottish Office, headed by a Secretary of State for Scotland, was the UK government department responsible for Scotland. Responsibility for most Scottish matters, including the legal system, is now, however, devolved to the Scottish Executive (and Scottish Parliament). However, a Scotland Office remains in the UK government, under a Secretary of State for Scotland, despite the reduction in his functions, and he is able to participate in decisions on matters reserved to the UK government as they affect Scotland[1]. He is authorised by s 58 of the Scotland Act 1998 to forbid any action proposed by a member of the Scottish Executive which he believes would be incompatible with any international obligations, including Community law and rights under the European Convention of Human Rights, and likewise to order action to be taken to give effect to such obligations. He can also revoke Scottish subordinate legislation which he believes to be incompatible with international obligations or the interests of defence and national security or which purports to modify reserved matters. So he can be said to have a supervisory function to ensure that the Scottish authorities do not exceed their powers. However, while the Secretary of State may be said to have a number of roles (including representing Scotland in Westminster and Whitehall, and vice versa; resolving issues between the two; determining whether proposed Scottish legislation is within devolved powers and challenging legislation which is not; and being the channel of funds from the United Kingdom government to the Scottish Executive and negotiating in relation to them), it has been doubted whether there is, since devolution, a real role for the office, and the suggestion has been made that the offices of the Secretaries of State for Scotland, Wales and Northern Ireland be merged[2].

1 The Secretary of State for Scotland in early 2003 was Helen Liddell MP, and the Scotland Office (also containing a Parliamentary Under-Secretary, the Advocate-General for Scotland – for whom, see below – and an 'official spokesman in the House of Lords' and a Parliamentary Private Secretary) was situated in Dover House, Whitehall, London. However, The Secretary of State became a part time job, held by another Minister (Alistair Darling MP) in June 2003, and the future of the Scotland Office put in doubt: see Appendix Part I to Preface. Its website is at www.scottishsecretary.gov.uk/.
2 See eg House of Lords Committee on the Constitution, Second Report 2002–03, HL Paper (2002–03) no 28, paras 57, 68 and ch 2 generally. It recommended more formal 'intergovernmental relations' within the UK. In early 2003, there was a Cabinet Ministerial Committee on Nations and Religion chaired by the Deputy Prime Minister, but it was not clear that it had an important function. See also previous note.

**Advocate-General for Scotland.** The Scotland Act 1998 has also made provision for an Advocate-General for Scotland who can advise the Westminster government on matters of Scots law[1]. There is no requirement that he be a member of Parliament, nor even qualified in Scots law. He is one of those who can initiate court proceedings to determine any dispute or doubt that has arisen over the operation of the Scotland Act[2]. By virtue of s 33 he (and also the Attorney-General for England and Wales) can raise proceedings before the Judicial Committee of the Privy Council which, despite its name, is a court, and is the ultimate authority on the meaning of the Scotland Act, including the question of whether a Bill of the Scottish Parliament is one which it has power to pass.

*The United Kingdom Parliament*[3]

The Parliament of the United Kingdom comprises the Sovereign, the House of Lords, and the House of Commons. In this it reflects the traditions of the English Parliament rather than the Scots. It is sometimes referred to as 'Westminster', as the building it meets in is technically the Palace of Westminster.

The Sovereign is a ceremonial element of Parliament only. The House of Lords used to comprise all hereditary peers (who latterly numbered some 750, though few sat regularly) and all life peers (who numbered some 500)[4]. The House of Lords Act 1999

---

1 The Advocate-General for Scotland should not be confused with the European Court of Justice Advocates General (see below). The Advocate-General for Scotland in early 2003 (who had been since devolution commenced) was Lynda Clarke QC, MP: see 2002 SLT (News) 139. The office, formerly attached to the Scotland Office, became attached to the new Department of Constitutional affairs in June 2003: see Appendix Part I to Preface. The Lord Advocate (see below) formerly exercised this function, but is now a member of the Scottish Executive by virtue of the Scotland Act 1998, s 44(1).

2 See Sch 6, Pt II of the Act. This is known as a 'devolution issue' and is discussed further below.

3 The United Kingdom Parliament website is at www.parliament.uk/, and live webcasts of parliamentary proceedings can be viewed at www.parliamentlive.tv.

4 From the Union until the Peerage Act 1963, while all holders of post-1707 peerages, and all holders of (pre-1707) English peerages, might sit in the House of Lords, only 16 elected 'representative' holders of (pre-1707) Scottish peerages could sit. The 1963 Act permitted all Scottish peers to sit, and also allowed life peers to be created.

allowed all the life peers to continue to sit[1], but only 92 hereditary peers, chosen by election from among themselves, radically altering the composition of the House[2]. It also continues to contain certain Church of England bishops and the Lords of Appeal in Ordinary (for whom, see below). However, the 1999 Act was seen as only the first stage of House of Lords reform, though it is unclear what form it will take, as there is dispute between those who seek a House wholly or largely appointed by the government, and those who seek one wholly or largely elected by the electorate. The House of Lords, as such, is to be distinguished from the Appellate Committee of the House of Lords, which is a court staffed by judges who are made life peers (mostly 'Lords of Appeal in Ordinary') in order to sit in it (see below).

The House of Commons comprises 659 MPs, elected in single-member constituencies of roughly equal population. There are 72 Scottish constituencies, a larger number than warranted by Scotland's proportion of the United Kingdom population. It is probable that the number of Scottish constituencies will be reduced to remove that overprovision, now that there is a Scottish Parliament[3].

The UK Parliament is (subject to Community legislation) the legislature, in which most law for the UK is made. It is also the forum in which government policy is discussed, and provides the means by which governments are created. The party which can command the largest number of votes in the House of Commons is, by convention, entitled to form the government. The system of simple majority voting in general elections has had the effect that the party which receives most votes in total usually has a disproportionate number of members returned[4]. Coalition governments are therefore almost unknown, except in war-time.

The United Kingdom constitution has usually been said to

---

1  Life peers are, in effect, nominated by the Prime Minister, typically as party political appointments from the major political parties, though not all. In 2000, the government set up a House of Lords Appointments Commission to recommend non-political appointments ('people's peers'). It nominated 15 in 2001, one of whom was Sir Stewart Sutherland, Principal of Edinburgh University. For details, see www.houseoflordsappointmentscommission.gov.uk.

2  The method of election was complicated, designed to prefer those holding office in the House, and to reflect party balance. *Lord Gray's Motion* 2000 SC(HL) 46 unsuccessfully challenged the change as a breach of the Treaty of Union. The other hereditary peers may now, incidentally, stand for election to the House of Commons.

3  This reduction would be reflected in the size of the Scottish Parliament unless Sch 1, para 1(c) to the Scotland Act 1998 is amended.

4  As discussed below, in order to avoid this outcome, election to the Scottish Parliament is not by simple majority voting. It may be that this method will be abandoned for the UK Parliament in the future.

display 'parliamentary supremacy' (alias 'parliamentary sovereignty'); that is, there are no legal boundaries to Parliament's legislative power: it may pass any law to any effect[1]. As governments almost invariably have a majority in the House of Commons (indeed, that is why they are the government), and a convention of the constitution requires that the House of Lords not veto legislation which the Commons insist upon, there has long been in practice 'executive dominance of the legislature', or more bluntly 'governmental supremacy'[2].

Parliamentary supremacy as a constitutional principle is extremely unusual, for nearly all other states have a written constitution which, among other things, limits the powers of the legislature. In any case, accession to the European Community has required that Acts of Parliament be subordinate to Community legislation, apparently fatally compromising this 'supremacy'.

There is in the House of Commons a Scottish Grand Committee, comprising all Scottish MPs, which can debate government policy[3], and the second reading stages of Scottish Bills. There can also be Scottish Standing committees which take the Committee stages of Scottish Bills, their membership reflecting party strengths (so ensuring a government majority). There is also a Select Committee on Scottish Affairs. It consists of back-benchers, again reflecting party strengths, who scrutinise the policy and decisions of the Scotland Office. For as long as the office of Secretary of State remains after devolution (albeit with fewer duties and a smaller staff), there seems no reason why the Select Committee should not continue. The survival of the other two kinds of committee is likely to be dependent on the degree to which, despite devolution, legislative and executive power remain at Westminster.

## The Scottish Parliament and Executive

The Scotland Act 1998 introduced a large measure of devolution into the running of Scotland. It creates a Scottish Parliament

---

1 It has been argued that this is an English principle, which the Scots constitution never recognised (see e g, *MacCormick v Lord Advocate* 1953 SC 396; SLT 255); also that it is a 19th-century invention. Be that as it may, it has been the constitutional orthodoxy for over a century. Thus, the Scottish Parliament's power to make law derives from the Scotland Act which could be amended or repealed by the UK Parliament.

2 Lord Hailsham, a former Conservative Lord Chancellor, described it even more bluntly as 'elective dictatorship'.

3 In December 2002, it debated the Scottish economy and, in February 2003, the Scottish fishing industry.

(sometimes referred to as 'Holyrood', as its intended home is next to the Palace of Holyrood) and a Scottish Administration (in effect a Scottish government, though that word is not used in the Act), led by a Scottish Executive (in effect, a Scottish Cabinet, though that word is not used in the Act either). The Act grants powers and responsibilities which used to be exercised by the United Kingdom Parliament and United Kingdom government to these new devolved institutions.

A lot of issues arise concerning the nature and progress of devolution which cannot be addressed here. However, it can be noted that there are many successes, such as the reform of landownership, and there are interesting initiatives, such as the plan to set up a Human Rights Commission. It can also be suggested that, while no reversal of devolution is seriously discussed, the first four years of devolution were not wholly successful. Two particular issues have tended to overshadow all others. The first is the rapid turnover of First Ministers (see below). The second is the new Scottish Parliament building which will be very late in completion, and very much over budget[1].

The Parliament's own Procedures Committee reported at the end of the first Parliament on the four 'founding principles' of the Scottish Parliament, that is, access and participation, equal opportunities, accountability, and power-sharing[2]. It concluded that there was a good deal of evidence of success in these areas, and support for the Parliament, although a need to improve in certain areas.

### Devolved matters and reserved matters

The basic principle of Scottish devolution is that everything is devolved unless specifically reserved. The powers and responsibilities devolved are essentially domestic ones, but the division is not simple and unavoidably leaves a large number of debatable lands. Schedule 5 to the Scotland Act 1998 contains the detailed list of 'reserved matters'[3]. They are divided into 'General Reservations' and 'Specific Reservations'.

---

1 In early 2003, it was predicted to be two years late in completion and ten times the estimate of cost originally given.
2 Procedures Committee, Third Report 2003, SP Paper 818 (2003). For the source of these principles, see the All-Party Steering Group Report *Shaping Scotland's Parliament*.
3 Note that the list can, and has, been modified: Scotland Act 1998, s 30(2) and Scotland Act 1998 (Modifications of Schedules 4 & 5) Order 1999, SI 1999/1749.

The **General Reservations** are the Constitution, Political Parties, Foreign Affairs, the Civil Service, Defence, and Treason. These are clearly United Kingdom responsibilities. Some of these have exceptions, however. An important one is that, while relations with the European Community are reserved, 'observing and implementing international obligations, obligations under the Human Rights Convention, and obligations under Community law' are not, and are therefore devolved so far as Scotland is concerned.

The **Specific Reservations** are set out under 11 subject-heads, often with reference to particular statutes and again with exceptions. These are cases where there is tension between the wide sweep of devolution on the one hand and the desire to reserve certain specific matters on the other. They are therefore much more complicated, and are as follows:

A – Financial and Economic Matters

But not including council tax and non-domestic rates. Money-laundering is reserved.

B – Home Affairs

A miscellaneous assortment, reflecting the interests of the Home Office. The Misuse of Drugs Act 1971 and legislation on drug-trafficking and international control of substances used for manufacture of controlled drugs are reserved. Confiscation orders are not. The prosecution of drug offences and police, social work and health involvement with controlled drugs are not reserved.

Also reserved are the Data Protection Act 1998, elections, firearms, classification of films and video-recordings, immigration and nationality, the Animals (Scientific Procedures) Act 1986, most of the Official Secrets Acts, betting gaming and lotteries, emergency powers and extradition.

C – Trade and Industry

A lengthy list with many detailed exceptions. Among the reservations are business associations, covering limited liability companies, but not charities; insolvency, including preferred or preferential debts under the Bankruptcy (Scotland) Act 1985, but not other aspects of Scots bankruptcy law; anti-competitive practices law, but not as it affects the legal profession; intellectual property; import and export control; sea fishing; consumer protection; product standards, safety and liability, but not as concerns food safety or items used in agricultural and fisheries; weights and measures; telecommunications and wireless telegraphy, including the Internet; postal services; research councils; industrial development.

D – Energy

Electricity, oil and gas; coal; nuclear energy; energy conservation.

E – Transport

Road transport, including the Road Traffic Act 1988 and Road Traffic Offenders Acts 1988, but not road safety; rail transport; marine transport, except ports and harbours; air transport.

F – Social Security

Social security schemes; child support; occupational and personal pensions; war pensions.

G – Regulation of Professions

Specifically architects, health professionals, as defined, and auditors; but not the legal Profession.

H – Employment

Employment and industrial relations, except the Agricultural Wages (Scotland) Act 1949; health and safety at work; job search and support.

J – Health and Medicine

Abortion; xenotransplantation (i e from a non-human species to a human); embryology, surrogacy and genetics; medicines; poisons; welfare foods.

K – Media and Culture

Broadcasting; public lending rights; (but not the Scottish Arts Council, National Galleries, Library and Museums).

L – Miscellaneous

Remuneration of judges; equal opportunities, including Equal Pay Act 1970, Sex Discrimination Act 1976, Race Relations Act 1976 and Disability Discrimination Act 1975; control of weapons of mass destruction; the Ordnance Survey; and finally, perhaps unsurprisingly, Outer Space.

Thus, most obviously important for present purposes, responsibility for the legal system is devolved, save for the remuneration of judges (and also, in fact, responsibility for the appointment of the most senior judges: see below), and regulation of the legal profession. Other noteworthy matters which are devloved are education and training at all levels, the National Health Service (though regulation of the health professions is not), housing, the environment, agriculture, forestry and fisheries, and the arts. Transport is reserved, but with numerous exceptions.

The practical significance of the list of 'reserved matters' is this. Firstly, the list is the basis of the Scottish Parliament's 'legislative competence', that is, its ability to make law (Scotland Act 1998, ss 29, 30). Secondly, this legislative competence is, in turn, the basis of the Scottish Executive's 'devolved competence', that is, its ability to exercise any function (including making delegated legislation: for which, see Chapter 5). However, the list of reserved matters does not actually define the legislative and devolved competencies, which are considered separately below.

It should also be remembered that 'power devolved is power retained' and the United Kingdom Parliament retains its powers to make laws for Scotland, as the Scotland Act, s 28(7) expressly declares.

The constitution and role of the Scottish Parliament and Executive (including their 'competences'), and the concept of 'devolution issues', are considered below in this Chapter, and Acts of the Scottish Parliament and 'Scottish Statutory Instruments' in Chapter 5.

## The Scottish Parliament[1]

**Election of the Scottish Parliament.** There are 129 Members of the Scottish Parliament ('MSPs'). However, the total number may be reduced in future if the number of constituencies for the Westminster Parliament is reduced, as has been discussed[2]. Unlike MPs in the United Kingdom Parliament, MSPs are elected by two simultaneous ballots. The first ballot is for 73 'constituency members', one for each of the existing Westminster seats (except

---

1 The Scottish Parliament website is at www.scottish.parliament.uk/, and live webcasts of Scottish parliamentary proceedings can be viewed at www.scottishparliamentlive.com/.
2 No firm plan existed in early 2003.

that Orkney and Shetland have one seat each, instead of forming one constituency). On this ballot the 'first-past-the-post system', familiar from Westminster, is used.

Because 'first-past-the-post' tends to produce an unrepresentative result, a further 56 'additional members' are elected by the somewhat complicated second ballot. For this ballot, the eight 'regional' constituencies formerly used for European parliamentary elections are used[1]. Each political party draws up a list for each of these constituencies. The voters in each of these constituencies vote for one of those lists (or for an independent candidate). Reflecting the voters' preferences between those lists (or independent candidates), the top-scoring names in each (selected on a mathematical formula designed to give each party about the same proportion of MSPs as their proportion of the total vote once the constituency member results are declared), provide seven 'additional' (or 'regional') members for that constituency[2].

A person may be a member of both the House of Commons and the Scottish Parliament and a member of the House of Lords may be elected to the Scottish Parliament. Electoral arrangements may alter if the total number of MSPs is reduced.

The Parliament is elected for a fixed period of four years, the election being held on the first Thursday in May. But exceptionally it may be dissolved if two-thirds of the membership vote for a resolution to that effect, or if it fails to nominate a First Minister.

**The law-making powers of the Scottish Parliament – 'legislative competence'.** Section 28 of the Scotland Act 1998 declares that 'the Parliament may make laws, to be known as Acts of the Scottish Parliament'. However, s 29 limits this to Acts within its 'legislative competence', and any provision which is 'outside the legislative competence of the Parliament' is declared to be 'not

---

1 These are: Central Scotland, Glasgow, Highlands and Islands, Lothians, Mid-Scotland and Fife, North East Scotland, South of Scotland and West of Scotland: European Parliamentary Constituencies (Scotland) Order 1996, SI 1996/1926. Their boundaries are defined by those of the Westminster parliamentary constituencies within them. Thus, North East Scotland comprises Aberdeen Central, Aberdeen North, Aberdeen South, Angus, Banff and Buchan, Dundee East, Dundee West, Gordon and West Aberdeenshire and Kincardine.

2 The formula can be found in the Scotland Act 1998, ss 6–8. It is expressed more simply in Annex C of the White Paper, *Scotland's Parliament*. See also the hypothetical worked example in Page, Reid and Ross *A Guide to the Scotland Act* 1998 (1999) App 1. Designedly, this method is one very likely to produce coalition governments, since the largest party may not have an overall majority: see below.

law'. Section 29 seems to contain a simple list, but it is far from
straightforward, and requires some explanation. A provision is
declared to be outside the legislative competence if it:

(i)    purports to apply outwith Scotland – This is an obvious limi-
       tation, but raises interesting questions where legislation
       concerns personal status which may have effect abroad, such
       as in relation to marriage or recognition of professional
       qualifications.

(ii)   relates to 'reserved matters' – These are described above.
       Section 29(3) requires that the question as to whether a
       provision of an Act of the Scottish Parliament relates to a
       reserved matter or not is to be determined from the purpose
       of that provision (having regard among other things, to its
       effects). This makes the boundaries of legislative competence
       a little elastic. Legislative competence is also potentially
       extended into reserved matters by s 29(4). This provides that
       if the Scottish Parliament makes an incidental foray into a
       reserved matter in the course of making an Act modifying
       Scots private law[1] or Scots criminal law[2], the offending provi-
       sion is not to be treated as dealing with a reserved matter if it
       makes 'the law in question apply consistently to reserved
       matters and otherwise'. This somewhat obscure piece of
       drafting seems to mean that if the Scottish Parliament is
       legislating on, say, the law of contract (which is devolved),
       and its legislation carries implications for consumer law
       (which is not), then the legislation is nevertheless to be
       treated as not affecting reserved matters[3].

1  This is defined in s 126(4) as the general principles of private law (including
   private international law), the law of persons (including natural persons and
   unincorporated bodies), the law of obligations (including those arising from
   contract, unilateral promise, delict, unjustified enrichment and *negotiorum gestio*),
   the law of property (including heritable and moveable property, trusts and
   succession), the law of actions (including jurisdiction, remedies, evidence, procedure, diligence, recognition and enforcement of court orders, limitation of
   actions and arbitration) and judicial review.
2  This is defined in s 126(5) as: criminal offences, jurisdiction, evidence, procedure
   and penalties and treatment of offenders.
3  Thus, suppose that, in its wisdom, the Scottish Parliament sought to introduce
   the 'doctrine of consideration' into Scots contract. It could do so in relation to
   contract, as such, under its ordinary devolved powers without reference to this
   provision, but not to consumer contracts, or any other contracts within reserved
   matters. This provision would allow it to do so even though it would affect
   consumer contracts and any other contracts within reserved matters.

(iii)   is in breach of certain further specific restrictions – In addition to the limit on reserved matters, there are further consequential restrictions, listed in Sch 4. These, in effect, protect the actual devolution settlement from amendment by the Scottish Parliament. The most important of these restrictions is that (subject to exceptions) an Act of the Scottish Parliament cannot modify (a) the Scotland Act itself, (b) certain other basic provisions of existing law (including the parts of the (English) Acts of Union with Scotland 1706 and (Scottish) Act of Union with England 1707 which relate to freedom of trade; the essential parts of the European Communities Act 1972; and any part of the Human Rights Act 1998); and (c) 'the law on reserved matters'. This last, in drafting of quite outstanding complexity and some uncertainty, is a belt-and-braces provision preventing the Scottish Parliament from amending Acts of the United Kingdom on reserved matters, or altering the common law on reserved matters (subject to exceptions).

(iv)   is incompatible with Convention rights or Community law – Another obvious limit to the legislative competence of the Scottish Parliament is the inability to pass Acts incompatible with Convention rights (that is, rights derived from the European Convention on Human Rights: see below) or Community law (that is, the law of the European Community: see below).

(v)   would remove the Lord Advocate from his position as head of the systems of criminal prosecution and investigation of deaths – Finally, this curiously specific limit is designed to protect the Lord Advocate (see above) from improper pressure by the Scottish Executive in exercising his prosecutorial and related functions.

However, note that, within that legislative competence, the Scottish Parliament may amend or repeal Acts of the United Kingdom Parliament, typically those not concerned with devolved matters[1].

The policing of the boundaries of legislative competence is considered below in relation to 'Devolution disputes and "devolution issues"', and in Chapter 5 in relation to Acts of the Scottish Parliament.

---

1  Acts of the United Kingdom may, of course, amend or repeal Acts of the Scottish Parliament, as its legislative omnicompetence is unaffected: Scotland Act 1998, s 27(8).

**Activities of the Scottish Parliament.** In its first four-year session, the Scottish Parliament passed 62 Acts on a variety of topics. Some of these were very controversial, and ranged from the abolition of feudal land-holding and fox-hunting to reform of the means of appointing judges and of the Scottish Qualifications Agency. However, a surprising amount of legislation for Scotland is still passed in Westminster (see below and Chapter 5).

But the Scottish Parliament is not only a legislature, it is also a forum for discussion of important matters, and it has oral and written questions to Scottish Ministers on a wide range of devolved topics, and debates on a yet wider range (including reserved matters, such as defence, for topics for discussion are not limited to the Parliament's legislative competence).

The Parliament operates to a considerable extent through a committee structure[1]. This includes Committees on the devolved areas (such as the Education, Culture and Sport, and Health Committee, the Community Care Committee, and two Justice Committees), and on other matters (including a Standards Committee, a European Committee and a Public Petitions Committee)[2]. It has made considerable efforts to involve the public in its activities, including special procedures to permit petitions on almost any matter of public interest, holding sittings of committees (and even the Parliament itself, on occasion) outwith Edinburgh, and actively employing IT (including developing a useful website).

A House of Lords Committee Report in 2003 discussed 'inter-parliamentary relations' between the Westminster Parliament, the Scottish Parliament, and the devolved Assemblies in Wales and Northern Ireland[3]. It concluded that such relations were excessively informal and insufficiently scrutinised, in part because the Scottish Parliament had no committee on the subject, while in Westminster, the Select Committee on Scottish Affairs and

---

1 This was a theme running through the Scottish Constitutional Convention Report *Scotland's Parliament, Scotland's Right*, the White Paper *Scotland's Parliament* and the All-Party Steering Group Report *Shaping Scotland's Parliament*.

2 Its 'business committee' , chaired by the Presiding Officer and attended by the party business managers, to discuss forthcoming business was noted in the House of Lords Committee of the Constitution Second Report 2002–03, HL Paper (2002–03) no 28, (*House of Lords Constitution Report*) paras 146, 147 as a better means of operating than the Westminster equivalent. These committees produce an Annual Report on the Scottish Parliament Committees (available of the Scottish Parliament website: see above).

3 See previous note.

Scottish Grand Committee had not prioritised consideration of such relations. It also noted (as mentioned above) that there had been much more Westminster legislation applying to Scotland than expected. This appeared to be for several reasons, including electoral expectations, administration of policies by United Kingdom bodies, the need to apply European Community law and international obligations uniformly, and 'simply seeing no good reason why the law should differ'. However, it seemed that this position also suited the Scottish Executive, as United Kingdom legislation allowed reliance on Whitehall to initiate reforms, prevented disruption of the Executive's legislative programme, and avoided risk of uncertainty about the validity of Scottish legislation[1]. The Committee recommended joint enquiries into matters spanning reserved and devolved matters and noted the value felt by the Presiding Officers of all three devolved legislatures of their membership of the House of Lords, a relationship it felt should be institutionalised[2].

*The Scottish Administration and Executive*[3]

**Appointment of the Scottish Executive.** There is a Scottish Administration headed by a Scottish Executive (comprising 'the Scottish Ministers'), which is in effect the Scottish Cabinet[4].

The Scotland Act 1998, ss 45(1) and 46 state that the First Minister, that is, the head of the Scottish Executive, is to be nominated by the Scottish Parliament, and 'appointed by Her Majesty', from among MSPs[5]. Section 47(1),(2) state that he appoints other Ministers to the Executive from among the remaining MSPs 'with the approval of Her Majesty' and the agreement of the Scottish

---

1 *House of Lords Constitution Report* paras 127, 128.
2 *House of Lords Constitution Report* paras 129, 144, 145. Smooth running so far had resulted from the fact that the Labour Party provided the United Kingdom government and was a predominant partner in the coalition making up the Scottish Executive.
3 The Scottish Executive website is at www.scotland.gov.uk.
4 The first Scottish Executive was a coalition of Labour and Liberal Democrats, the first Scottish parliamentary election having given no party a majority: see above. So was the second.
5 During the life of the first Scottish Executive, the First Minister changed twice. The initial appointment, Donald Dewar, architect of devolution, died in office: the second, Henry McLeish, resigned: the third, Jack McConnell was in office at the time of the second Scottish Parliamentary election in May 2003 and remained in office thereafter, as that election produced another Labour/Liberal Democrat coalition. All three were leaders of the Labour Party in Scotland.

Parliament[1]. However, the Lord Advocate and the Solicitor-General for Scotland (see below) who are also members of the Scottish Executive, and are also recommended by the First Minister to Her Majesty for appointment, need not be MSPs, though they may speak in the Parliament. The ministers can be given titles showing their functions. Among these in the Executive formed from the first Scottish Parliament was a Justice Minister, with general responsibility for the Scottish legal system[2].

Junior ministers can also be appointed by the First Minister from among MSPs, but they are not part of the Scottish Executive[3].

The Scottish Ministers are supported by the staff of the Scottish Administration, who are civil servants of all levels. They are in the main drawn from the staff of the Scottish Office prior to devolution. There is also a small number of non-career civil servant 'special advisers' who work to individual ministers or the Executive as a whole, and are appointed by them and leave with them. The Civil Service is a reserved subject. Under s 51 of the Scotland Act, civil servants remain members of the Home Civil Service and subject to the same terms of service. Although the Prime Minister is in overall charge of the United Kingdom Civil Service, in accordance with recent policy their appointment and management is a matter for the Scottish Ministers and, in respect of lower-rank appointments, their senior civil servants. The fact that the Civil Service remains organised on a United Kingdom basis at the higher levels may have operated as a limit upon devolution, as the machinery of government remains firmly Whitehall-oriented.

**Functions of the Scottish Executive – 'devolved competence'.** The purpose of the Scottish Executive is to run Scotland for broadly the same range of functions as the United Kingdom government's pre-devolution Scottish Office did. This apparently straightforward proposition needs clarification, however.

Firstly, where governmental functions were conferred before devolution upon the Secretary of State for Scotland, and other

---

1 There were some 10 Scottish Ministers at any one time during the first Scottish Executive, including a Deputy First Minister, also holding the Justice portfolio (Jim Wallace, leader of the Scottish Liberal Democrats), plus the Lord Advocate and the Solicitor-General for Scotland (see below). The second Scottish Executive Commenced with 11 Scottish Ministers (Jim Wallace being Enterprise Minister).

2 For the Justice Minister in the first Scottish Executive, see previous note. In the second it was Cathy Jamieson.

3 There were some further ten Junior Ministers at any one time during the first Scottish Executive, but the second commenced with 8.

members of the UK government, so far as they are to be exercised within the 'devolved competence', they are now conferred upon the Scottish Ministers[1]. Thus, where a pre-devolution Act of the United Kingdom Parliament refers to 'the Secretary of State', in relation to devolved matters it is implicitly amended to read 'the Scottish Ministers' instead. This 'devolved competence' thus covers the same range of topics as permitted by the Scottish Parliament's 'legislative competence'.

Secondly, these functions now conferred upon the Scottish Executive are exercised by them exclusively. However, there are two important exceptions to this. In the first place, there is a variety of disparate matters from road safety information and training to the funding of scientific research, via arrangements for employment and training, which are 'shared powers', and are therefore carried out on a shared basis by the Scottish Executive and the UK government[2]. In the second place, although it is important to realise that carrying out Community law obligations is devolved, and they are therefore commonly carried out in Scotland by the Scottish Ministers' functions, the United Kingdom government can also still act to carry them out in Scotland[3]. These two provisions further obscure the already complicated difference between reserved and devolved matters.

However, thirdly, although certain matters are clearly reserved to the UK government, there are powers enabling it to transfer reserved matters to the Scottish Executive[4]. This process, which clearly enables the UK government without further legislation to extend the functions of the Scottish Ministers beyond the devolved

---

1 Scotland Act 1998, ss 52–54. For certain purposes the First Minister and the Lord Advocate (in the latter case, in order to preserve his independence as head of the criminal prosecution service) are in a special position. Also, in a belt-and-braces provision, by s 57(2), the Scottish Executive is explicitly denied the power to do any act (including making delegated legislation) incompatible with Convention rights or Community law, although they are in any case outwith their delegated competence because they are outwith the Scottish Parliament's legislative competence.

2 Scotland Act 1998, s 56.

3 Scotland Act 1998, s 57.

4 Scotland Act 1998, s 63. A lengthy list of such transfers, including functions under legislation from the Small Landholders (Scotland) Act 1911 to the National Health Service (Scotland) (Injury Benefits) Regulations 1998, were transferred by the Scotland Act 1998 (Transfer of Functions to the Scottish Ministers, etc) Order 1999, SI 1999/1750, art 2 and Sch 1. There are also powers to transfer functions from the Scottish Ministers to the United Kingdom government in s 108, not exercised by early 2003.

competence (further blurring the reserved/devolved boundary), is sometimes referred to as 'executive devolution'.

Fourthly, the UK government can, in any case, make an 'agency arrangement' for the Scottish Ministers (and vice versa)[1]. This means that the Scottish Ministers carry out specified functions on behalf of the UK government; or concurrently with the UK government; or are carried out by the UK government but only in agreement with, or after consultation with, the Scottish Ministers (and vice versa). This renders the reserved and devolved distinction yet more opaque.

Fifthly, in any case further Acts of United Kingdom and Scottish Parliaments may add further functions.

Finally, as an interesting long-stop measure, the Secretary of State (in effect, the United Kingdom government) may direct that a proposed action not be taken, if he has reasonable grounds to believe it would be incompatible with international obligations (which would include the European Convention on Human Rights, and obligations under the various treaties constituting the European Union), or to order that a particular action be taken in order to give effect to such obligations[2].

Thus, there is much scope for working out at ministerial and Civil Service level the exact interface between Whitehall and the Scottish Administration, and the pattern of devolved executive powers is extremely complex[3]. Electricity provides a good example[4]. The generation and supply of electricity is a reserved matter, so is outwith the devolved competence of the Scottish Ministers. However, the power to grant consents for generating stations and overhead lines in Scotland has been transferred to the Scottish Ministers, though not as part of the general conferring of powers under ss 52–54, but rather by an order transferring responsibility made under s 63. But the same order provides that powers

1 Scotland Act 1998, s 93. There are lengthy lists of such functions in the Scotland Act 1998 (Transfer of Functions, etc) Order 1999, SI 1999/1750, arts 3–5 and Schs 2–4, including examples from functions under the Police (Scotland) Act 1967 to the Broadcasting Act 1996.
2 Scotland Act 1998, s 58.
3 In addition to the functions of the Scottish Executive, as such, the Scotland Act 1998, ss 88–90 creates a regime for 'cross border public authorities', that is, bodies which operate on a UK or GB basis and are concerned with reserved and devolved matters, such as the Council on Tribunals.
4 The authors are grateful to their colleague Colin Reid who supplied this example, fully explained in his 'Devolution and the Environment' in Ross (ed) *Environment and Regulation (Hume Papers on Public Policy vol 8, no 2)* (David Hume Institute, 2000) at 104.

to require certain statistical information are to be exercised concurrently by Scottish Ministers and the Secretary of State, though it also provides that the power to license suppliers of electricity remains a power of the Secretary of State, but only after consultation with the Scottish Ministers.

Interestingly, the House of Lords Committee Report of 2003 concluded that 'inter-governmental relations' within the United Kingdom had no statutory basis, in practice resting on a Memorandum of Understanding, various 'concordats' and a Joint Ministerial Committee, and while these relations were intensive, they were in general highly informal, which could cause problems when different parties formed the United Kingdom government and the Scottish Executive[1].

**Lord Advocate and Solicitor-General for Scotland.** These two offices require special mention. They are, as noted above, members of the Scottish Executive, and may speak in the Scottish Parliament, but need not be MSPs. They are members of the Scottish Executive as 'Law Officers'[2]. This means that they are responsible for providing legal advice to the Executive, and can sue and be sued on its behalf. They must therefore, on the one hand, be politically acceptable to the Executive (and before devolution, to the UK government). However, on the other hand, they are also the head and deputy head of the prosecution service and responsible for fatal accident enquiries so hold a quasi-judicial office and must, in dealing with these responsibilities, be independent of the Executive. Their position is therefore constitutionally odd[3].

1 The current Memorandum of Understanding was published as Cm 5240 (2001), and it and the concordats can be found on the Scottish Executive website at www.scotland.gov.uk/concordats.
2 In early 2002, the Lord Advocate was Colin Boyd QC, and the Solicitor-General for Scotland was Elish Angiolini QC. While the former was an advocate, as has invariably been the case, the latter performed a hat-trick in being the first solicitor, the first procurator fiscal, and the first woman to hold the office. The Law Officers for the Westminster government are the Attorney-General, the Solicitor-General and (for advice in relation to Scotland) the Advocate-General for Scotland: and for Northern Ireland, the Attorney-General for Northern Ireland.
3 The anomaly is less than it was, as the Lord Advocate's powers are more restricted than was once the case. In the 18th century, they were essentially Governors of Scotland on behalf of the Westminster government. In more recent times, they had considerable powers in appointing judges (and not infrequently appointed themselves). On the appointment of judges now, see below.

**Financial arrangements.** Checks as to income and expenditure by the Scottish Administration follow the well-tried United Kingdom model. A Scottish Consolidated Fund is created by s 64(1) of the Scotland Act 1998. Into it all Scottish Administration income is paid. Out of it all Scottish Administration expenditure is paid. This must be authorised by some enactment and under Treasury rules. There is an Auditor General for Scotland to check that all expenditure is properly authorised. The main source of income is the Block grant from the Treasury, to be spent as determined by the Executive and authorised by the Parliament. It can be supplemented or reduced if the Parliament votes in favour of a tax-varying resolution moved by a member of the Scottish Executive varying the basic rate of income tax payable by Scottish tax-payers by no more than 3 pence in the pound, up or down for one assessment year (Scotland Act, ss 73, 74 and 75).

*Devolution disputes and 'devolution issues'*

Plainly, there is scope for a lot of questions to arise concerning the devolved institutions and the United Kingdom government and Parliament. These will have to be worked out through experience over the years. However, to avoid such problems so far as possible, an extra-statutory 'Memorandum of Understanding' and 'concordats' have been devised[1]. These are working arrangements on such matters as relations with the European Union and application of Community law. Also, if problems arise in relation to making delegated legislation, they can be aired through the normal processes of approval of such legislation (see Chapter 5). Where both the United Kingdom government and the Scottish Executive are of the same political hue, or largely so, all such problems can be worked out relatively simply and amicably. However, if they are not, then the risk of friction will be intensified, as noted above.

In any case, since any Act of the Scottish Parliament beyond its legislative competence is ultra vires (that is, 'beyond the powers'), it is void. Indeed, s 29 of the Scotland Act expressly says that any such purported Act 'is not law'. Any action of the Scottish Executive beyond its devolved competence is in like case (though there is no equivalent of s 29). Thus such matters may arise in the course of ordinary civil litigation (for example, answers in a claim for damages) or criminal prosecution (for example, a defence to a prosecution). They may also arise through a person directly

1 See above.

challenging such Act or action through judicial review (for which, see below)[1]. Such cases may include challenges in terms of human rights (for which, see below[2]) or otherwise.

However, there are specific devices in the Scotland Act 1998 for dealing with devolution disputes. Firstly, there are various scrutiny devices in the process of enactment of Acts of the Scottish Parliament to try and ensure they are within its legislative competence. These are dealt with in Chapter 5, when such Acts are discussed.

Secondly, there are special procedures to deal with what the Scotland Act 1998 calls 'devolution issues'. These are defined rather elaborately in Sch 6 to the Scotland Act 1998 and can take any one of six forms, that is, questions as to:

- whether or not an Act of the Scottish Parliament (or part of one) is in fact within its legislative competence (thus recognising the scrutiny in the enactment process might not have worked);
- whether or not a governmental function is one which is conferred on Scottish Ministers, the First Minister or the Lord Advocate (in other words, whether it is one which has been devolved);
- whether or not the actual exercise of a governmental function by a member of the Scottish Executive is within its 'devolved competence' (for which, see above);
- whether or not such an actual exercise would be incompatible with Convention rights or Community law;
- whether or not a failure to act is incompatible with Convention rights or Community law; and
- any other question about whether a function is within the devolved competence or relates to Scotland or which concerns reserved matters (for which, see above).

Where a 'devolution issue' thus defined arises in any court or tribunal of whatever level[3], then (provided it is not dismissed there as 'frivolous or vexatious'), it can be separated from the rest of the

---

1 Attempts to subject Acts of the Scottish Parliament to judicial review had been, by early 2003, unsuccessful: see below in relation to human rights.
2 The power to do this under the Scotland Act 1998 is expressly preserved by s 100.
3 Devolution issues have arisen in District Courts, for example: see e g *Kelly v Clark* 2003 SLT 308.

proceedings, and intimation made to the Lord Advocate and Advocate-General for Scotland in case they wish to participate. These separated proceedings are as elaborate as the definition of 'devolved issues'.

A court or tribunal faced with a devolution issue may decide the matter itself, or may refer it to the Inner House (in civil proceedings) or High Court acting as an appeal court (in criminal proceedings)[1]. At least in the early years of devolution, any such case is likely to be referred unless very straightforward[2]. The court to which reference is made must decide the matter itself, but its decision can be appealed in all cases to the Judicial Committee of the Privy Council (which is a court: see below). If the Inner House or High Court acting as a court of appeal are faced with a devolution issue directly, they may also either decide it themselves or refer it to the Judicial Committee of the Privy Council. If they decide it themselves, the matter can be appealed to the Judicial Committee of the Privy Council (unless appeal would normally be to the House of Lords). In the early years of devolution, there were in fact hundreds of devolution issues raised, mostly concerning human rights, as discussed below.

In any case, the Lord Advocate[3] or the Advocate-General for Scotland may institute proceedings on a devolution issue on their own initiative (and the Lord Advocate may defend proceedings instituted by the Advocate-General[4]); they (and the law officers of England and Wales, and of Northern Ireland) may require any court or tribunal to refer such a case direct to the Judicial Committee; and they (and those other law officers) may forestall a dispute by referring to the Judicial Committee action proposed by a member of the Scottish Executive before it happens.

Thus, incidentally (and as noted below in relation to that court), the Judicial Committee has imposed upon it a role akin to a Constitutional Court.

---

1 For these courts, see below.
2 A problem occurs where the devolution issue arises in the middle of a trial, for halting proceedings for some months for such a reference is impractical.
3 Given the Lord Advocate's membership of the Scottish Executive and the opportunities to challenge a private member's Bill before the royal assent (for which, see ch 5), such occasions are likely to be rare.
4 Indicating, in effect, a disagreement between the UK government and the Scottish Executive which has not been resolved by other means.

*Interlinking of the Human Rights Act 1998 with the concept of 'devolution issues'*

'Human rights' and the Human Rights Act 1998 are dealt with below. However, it is useful to recall here, as noted above, that the powers of the Scottish Parliament and Scottish Executive are limited by the devolution legislation to, among other things, actions compatible with Convention rights under the Human Rights Act 1998[1]. Inevitably, some legislation passed by the Scottish Parliament will turn out to be incompatible, despite the scrutiny during the enactment process designed to weed it out (described in Chapter 5). Equally, some actions of the Scottish Executive will too (including making delegated legislation and performing administrative acts whether by Ministers themselves or by their civil servants). These are thus ultra vires, i e beyond the powers the Parliament and Executive have, and may be dealt with as described above as 'devolution issues'.

And it is thus worth noting, that, while the Human Rights Act 1998 came into full force throughout the United Kingdom in 2000, it was brought partly into force in Scotland in 1998, through the Scotland Act 1998, as part of the devolution arrangements.

One result of this is that all the early human rights cases in United Kingdom law are Scottish ones, under the 'devolution issue' provisions of the Scotland Act rather than under the Human Rights Act directly. As noted above, some hundreds were initiated, though few made their way as far as the Judicial Committee[2]. The vast majority were challenges to actions of the Scottish Executive, not the Scottish Parliament. In particular, they were challenges to decisions by the Lord Advocate to prosecute, and related decisions, so arose in criminal cases, relied on the right to a fair trial under art 6 of the European Convention on Human Rights (see below), and were referred from, or via

---

1 Scotland Act 1998, ss 29(2)(c),(d), 30, Schs 4, 5 (which define the 'legislative competence' of the Scottish Parliament) and ss 54 and 57(2) (which – read with s 53 – define the 'devolved competence' and rule-making power of the Scottish Executive) respectively. (S 29(1) roundly declares the legislation outside the legislative competence 'is not law'.) There is no saving provision for those adversely affected by such a finding. Remedial action does not arise. Fresh legislation would have to be made.
2 By early 2003, only a dozen.

the High Court[1]. This is discussed further in relation to the Human Rights Act, below.

## Scottish local government

The organisation of Scottish local government has changed considerably over the last 50 years. 'Counties of cities', burghs, large and small, and counties were abolished in 1975. They were replaced by a two-tier system of local government consisting of regions and districts, together with three all-purpose single-tier authorities for the Western Isles, Orkney and Shetland[2].

This was changed again by the Local Government etc (Scotland) Act 1994, which replaced the two-tier system with 32 unitary authorities[3]. The Fife, Dumfries and Galloway, Borders and Highlands authorities were based on the old regions. Strathclyde Region was broken up into 13 authorities. The three islands authorities remained as before. The new arrangements were to give a clearer understanding of who was responsible for what. The one-tier system was expected to be cheaper, since fewer senior executives would be needed. However, in relation to the protective services of the police and fire service it was thought necessary to have larger groupings. The eight police forces remain as before, and they and the fire service are administered by joint boards, consisting of representatives of all the local authorities in their area. Strategic planning, formerly a regional and islands function, is now, on the mainland, a function of the unitary authorities. But because these areas might be inappropriately small or large, there is provision for joint arrangements and for more than one planning district within the one authority's area.

An exception to the trend towards small, locally responsible authorities was the creation of, originally, three Boards, but now one ('Scottish Water'), to cover the provision of water and sewage disposal throughout Scotland[4]. It was thought the costly

1 Early examples included *Starrs v Ruxton* 2000 JC 208, 2000 SLT 42, 1999 SCCR 1052 (temporary sheriffs), *HM Advocate v McNab* 2000 JC 80, 2000 SLT 99, 1999 SCCR 930, *HM Advocate v McLean* 2000 JC 140, 2000 SLT 299, 2000 SCCR 112 (both delays in prosecution), *HM Advocate v Montgomery and Coulter* 2000 JC 111, 2000 SCCR 959 (pre-trial publicity), and *Brown v Stott* 2000 SLT 379, 2000 SCCR 314 (self-incrimination).
2 Local Government (Scotland) Act 1973.
3 Sch 1, Pt 1 to the 1994 Act. Election remains 'first-past-the-post', but proportional representation by single transferable vote was promised in a Local Governance [sic] (Scotland) Bill in 2003.
4 Section 62 of the 1994 Act, as amended by the Water Industry (Scotland) Act 2002

improvement of these services to comply with European Community requirements called for provisions on a much larger scale than any authority's area.

Local authorities can set up community councils to express to them and other public authorities the views of the residents of their neighbourhood on matters for which the authorities have responsibility. Made possible under the Local Government (Scotland) Act 1973, s 51, they have not proved very popular and do not exist in all areas, but were retained under the Local Government etc (Scotland) Act 1994.

With the arrival of the Scottish Parliament, local councils are no longer the only elected tier of government operating in Scotland.

## 'EUROPE'[1]

### The Council of Europe[2] and the European Convention on Human Rights

*The Council of Europe and 'human rights'*[3]

The Council of Europe (not to be confused with the European Community and European Union: see below) is a treaty organisation set up by Western European states in 1948 to promote democracy and human rights. The United Kingdom was a founder member. It has now expanded its membership to over 40 Western,

---

1 See Appendix 3.
2 The Council of Europe portal is at www.coe.int/portalT.asp. See also Appendix 3.
3 'Human rights' has become a popular phrase to describe certain obligations considered by their exponents to be more fundamental than ordinary law, indeed perhaps more fundamental than law itself. There are important questions to be asked as to what makes a claim a 'human right', and who decides. Numerous treaties assert a range of human rights, fundamental freedoms and the like, including the United Nations Universal Declaration of Human Rights (1948), and related documents like the International Covenant on Civil and Political Rights and International Covenant on Economic, Social and Cultural Rights (both 1966), not to mention a host of others on specific rights such as those concerned with the treatment of prisoners, the death penalty, torture, genocide, prisoners of war, children and so on. Further, the European Union is expanding into the field, by introducing legislation on race and gender discrimination; requiring Member States to adhere to respect for human rights, democracy and the rule of law; 'proclaiming' its own Charter of Fundamental Rights (though without any means of enforceability at present); and it might one day accede to the European Convention on Human Rights and Fundamental Freedoms.

Eastern and Central European states. There is a Committee of Ministers (comprising the Foreign Ministers of the signatory states) and a Parliamentary Assembly[1], as well as a European Court of Human Rights[2]. (These should not be confused with the European Commission, Council of the Union, European Parliament and European Court of Justice, all of which are institutions of the European Union: see below.) The European Court of Human Rights, which deals with cases under the European Convention on Human Rights (discussed below), comprises over 40 judges, one for each of the member states. However, they are not representatives of their states, though they will be familiar with its legal system. They are appointed by the Parliamentary Assembly of the Council of Europe for a period of six years and sit full-time[3]. The full Court elects its President and two Vice-Presidents for a period of three years[4]. The Court is divided into four Sections, each led by a Section President. Within each Section, Committees of three judges are set up for 12-month periods. The official languages of the Court are French and English only. It is the responsibility of the Committee of Ministers of the Council of Europe to ensure that the judgments of the Court are complied with and corrective measures introduced where necessary.

The Council of Europe has promoted the creation of treaties between its members. There are nearly 200 to date, and they cover a wide variety of subjects, ranging from terrorism to nationality and social security to cybercrime. However, the first and most important Council of Europe treaty is the European Convention for the Protection of Human Rights and Fundamental Freedoms (commonly called the 'European Convention on Human Rights', and abbreviated to 'ECHR'). The United Kingdom was joint first signatory in 1950, the Convention came into force in 1953, and it has been signed by all Council of Europe members. The ECHR is an attempt to implement the United Nations Universal Declaration of Human Rights of 1948, and requires its signatories to 'secure' (that is, not to allow breach of) certain specified human rights, such as a right to life, freedom from torture or inhuman or degrading treatment, a right to liberty and security of person, and

1 The Parliamentary Assembly website is at http://assembly.coe.int.
2 The European Court of Human Rights website is at www.coe.int.
3 In early 2003, the United Kingdom judge was Sir Nicolas Bratza, a barrister and QC and formerly a Recorder. The Registrar, Paul Mahoney, is also from the UK.
4 In early 2003, the President was Swiss and the Vice-Presidents Greek and French.

a right to family life. There are amending Protocols which add further rights, but the United Kingdom has not signed up for all of these.

## The European Convention on Human Rights ('ECHR')

The ECHR is designed to limit 'official' action by declaring certain obligations which the signatories accept as binding. The United Kingdom has accepted (subject to certain derogations) the following obligations[1]:

CONVENTION
Article 1 All signatory states agree to secure to everyone within their jurisdiction the rights and freedoms listed.
Article 2 Everyone's life shall be protected by law, except where the death penalty is provided by law or where death results from defence from unlawful violence, to effect arrest, to prevent escape from detention, or in quelling a riot or insurrection.
Article 3 'No one shall be subjected to torture or to inhuman or degrading treatment or punishment'.
Article 4 'No one shall be held in slavery or servitude. No one shall be required to perform forced or compulsory labour'.
Article 5 'Everyone has the right to liberty and security of person' except under lawful arrest or detention. In such cases he must be given reasons and must be brought promptly before a judge.
Article 6 Everyone is entitled to a fair and public hearing in civil and criminal law. Everyone charged with a criminal offence is presumed innocent until proved guilty.
Article 7 No one shall be guilty of an offence which was not one under national or international law when it was committed, except for an act

---

1 Those listed below in quotation marks are quoted verbatim. The full text, and details of derogations, etc, can be found through the Council of Europe website (see above). In particular, note that the United Kingdom has not ratified the Fourth Protocol (art 1: 'No one shall be deprived of his liberty merely on the ground of inability to fulfill a contractual obligation', art 2: Freedom of movement within the state, and freedom to leave it, art 3: No expulsion of nationals or deprivation of their right to enter the country) or the Seventh Protocol (art 1: Expulsion of aliens only after a reasoned decision with appeal and representation, art 2: Right to have criminal convictions reviewed by a higher tribunal governed by law, art 3: Compensation for those wrongly convicted of a crime, art 4: No one subjected to double jeopardy in criminal proceedings, art 5: Equality of rights and responsibilities of spouses).

which was criminal according to general principles of law recognised by civilised nations.

Article 8 'Everyone has the right to respect for his private and family life, his home and correspondence' (with certain exceptions).

Article 9 'Everyone has the right to freedom of thought, conscience and religion' (with certain exceptions).

Article 10 'Everyone has the right to freedom of expression' and opinions (with certain exceptions).

Article 11 'Everyone has the right to freedom of peaceful assembly and to freedom of association with others' (with certain exceptions).

Article 12 'Men and women of marriageable age have the right to marry and to found a family'.

Article 13 Everyone whose rights or freedoms have been violated to have an effective remedy before a national authority.

Article 14 'The enjoyment of the rights and freedoms set forth in this Convention shall be secured without discrimination on any ground such as sex, race, colour, language, religion, political or other opinion, national or social origin'.

Article 15 In time of war or other public emergency threatening the life of the nation, measures limiting the application of the rights may be taken, except from article 2 (other than in respect of deaths from lawful acts of war), Art 3, Art 4 (in respect of slavery or servitude), and article 7.

Article 16 Restrictions may be imposed on the political activity of aliens.

Article 17 Nothing must be done that is aimed at the destruction or limitation of the rights.

Article 18 Permitted restrictions to the rights and freedoms must not be used except for the purposes for which they are prescribed.

## FIRST PROTOCOL

Article 1 The peaceful enjoyment of possessions is protected. No one can be deprived of possessions, except in the public interest.

Article 2 'No person shall be denied the right to education'. The right of parents shall be respected.

Article 3 Free elections shall be held at reasonable intervals by secret ballot.

## SIXTH PROTOCOL

Article 1 'The death penalty shall be abolished. No one shall be condemned to such penalty or executed'.

Article 2 A state may make provision for the death penalty in time of war or imminent threat of war.

Article 3 'Collective expulsion of aliens is prohibited'.

Certain of the Articles and Protocols are subject to qualifications. Thus, the right to peaceful enjoyment of possessions is subject to the right of the state to control the use of property and to secure the payment of taxes. They are also subject to possible derogations and reservations (that is, ad hoc exceptions and exclusions[1]).

However, the underlying message is clear, that is, the United Kingdom, its government and Parliament, the Scottish Executive and Scottish Parliament, and all other 'official' institutions, are bound by its terms.

*Enforceability of the ECHR*

But what does the agreement to 'secure' these rights mean?

**Enforceability of the ECHR by states and by individual petition.** By art 1 all signatory states, including the United Kingdom, agreed to secure to everyone within its jurisdiction the rights and freedoms declared in subsequent articles. That agreement, being a matter of international law, did not make the Convention part of the law of the United Kingdom. It merely allowed states, and (so far as the United Kingdom is concerned) from 1966 individuals who had exhausted possible remedies for their grievances in the courts of the United Kingdom, to petition for redress at the Court of Human Rights in Strasbourg, claiming that they had been treated in a manner which contravened one or more articles of the Convention.

Procedure is as follows[2]. The Court first deals with matters of the competence of applications, such as whether the applicant had

---

1   The United Kingdom entered a derogation from art 5(3) concerning arrest and detention in Northern Ireland after an adverse European Court of Human Rights decision (*Brogan v UK* (A 145-B) [1988] 11 EHRR 117). It also entered a derogation from art 5(1)(f) concerning detention in any part of the United Kingdom through the Human Rights (Designated Derogation) Order 2001, SI 2001/3644 to allow ss 21–23 of the Anti-Terrorism, Crime and Security Act 2001 which permit those subject to deportation as suspected international terrorists to be detained indefinitely if they cannot be deported because it would subject them to the risk of torture (thus breaching art 3) or it is impossible because no state will take them, or like reason.

2   Until 1998, the petition was considered first by the European Commission on Human Rights (not to be confused with the European Community's European Commission) which, having decided whether or not the petition was admissible, would seek a friendly settlement. If it failed to achieve a settlement, it considered whether or not to pass the matter to the Court, or to the Committee of Ministers (not to be confused with the European Community's Council of Ministers). If it did so, the Court might proceed to a judgment, or the Committee to a decision, respectively. In all of this complicated procedure, enforceability depended upon the state in question agreeing to comply with the conclusion of Commission, Court or Committee.

exhausted remedies in his own state and whether a violation of one or more articles had been validly raised. Attempts to promote a friendly settlement are then made by the Registrar and his staff. If they fail, and the application against a state is admitted to the Court, it goes before a seven-judge Chamber of a Section (for the internal structure of the Court, see above), which considers written submissions and may hear evidence. Decisions are by majority, and dissenting judgments, contrary to the practice in most countries of Continental Europe, can be issued. In cases of major importance, it is possible for the case at various stages to be referred to a Grand Chamber of 17 judges. Nevertheless, enforcement remains a matter of the state agreeing to comply.

There have been a considerable number of petitions from Scotland, concerning trials, prisoners' rights, and other matters, and there are a number of examples of such indirect enforceability by individual petition following a judgement of the Court. *Campbell and Cosans* (1982) 4 EHRR 293 concerned corporal punishment in schools. The parents of Campbell, who went to school in Bishopbriggs, objected to the use of corporal punishment and sought assurance from Strathclyde Regional Council (then the relevant local authority) that it would not be inflicted upon their son. This was refused. Cosans, who went to school in Cowdenbeath, refused to submit to corporal punishment, a form of punishment which Fife Regional Council (then the relevant local authority) permitted. He was suspended. The petitioners claimed corporal punishment breached art 3 of the ECHR (inhuman or degrading punishment) and art 2 of the First Protocol (requirement for respect for parents' right to ensure education is in conformity with their religious and philosophical beliefs). The matter eventually went to the Court of Human Rights, which held that art 3 had not been breached, but (by a majority only) that article 2 of the Protocol had been.

The case was adjourned on the question of compensation, with a view to the parties agreeing a sum. More importantly, after this case, the law on corporal punishment in state schools was abolished by the Education (No 2) Act 1986, s 48. However, the process from petition to judgment took seven years, and from petition to the change of law, a decade.

It is important to remember that the implementation of the content of the ECHR by the Human Rights Act does not remove a victim's right of individual petition. It merely requires the victim, when exhausting possible remedies for their grievances in the courts of the United Kingdom before petitioning, to invoke any remedies under that Act.

**Enforceability of the ECHR through Community law.**
Although the ECHR and its institutions are separate from the
European Union and its institutions (considered below) and
although the European Union is experimenting with its own
'fundamental rights', the ECHR may be enforceable through
Community law

This is discussed in Chapter 5 in relation to Community law,
however, it should be noted that, therefore, Community law is
applied by the European Court of Justice subject to the ECHR.

**Enforceability of the ECHR through United Kingdom law –
'entrenchment'.** Before the Human Rights Act 1998, the
Scottish courts had, over time, changed from the view that
the ECHR was a non-legislative document, so to be ignored, to the
view that it should be used, at least to require statutes to be interpreted in conformity with it. However, the position has been
further changed radically by the Human Rights Act 1998. That Act
does not incorporate the ECHR into United Kingdom law (as is
sometimes said), for its terms do not have 'direct effect' as
Community law has (see Chapter 5). Rather, it 'entrenches' it.
Section 1 of the Act takes most of the contents of the ECHR, and
its First and Sixth Protocols[1], and puts them in its Sch 1, calling
them 'Convention rights'. These Convention rights have thereby
become part of United Kingdom law and, broadly speaking,
United Kingdom law is intended (though not necessarily required)
to be 'compatible' with them.

This compatibility is sought in various ways. The Act imposes
requirements in relation to parliamentary scrutiny during the
process of legislation of all subsequent Acts, in relation to statutory
interpretation, and in relation to the Scotland Act 1998. These are
dealt with in the relevant sections in Chapter 5.

The Act also creates rights for victims of breaches of Convention
rights, which are dealt with here. Section 6 of the Human Rights
Act makes it 'unlawful for a public authority to act in a way which
is incompatible with a Convention right' (subject to exceptions)
and s 7(1) allows a 'victim' to 'bring proceedings against the
authority . . . in the appropriate court or tribunal' or to 'rely on the
convention right . . . concerned in any proceedings' (within certain

1 The Act thus omits arts 1, 13 and 15 of the Convention. Arts 1 and 15 are
omitted because they do not add anything to the obligations listed in the
Schedule. Omission of art 13 is more controversial. It can be seen, like arts 1 and
15, as adding nothing. However, another view is that it was omitted because
judges might use it to extend the range of remedies available. It also omits
Protocols 4 and 7 entirely, because the United Kingdom has not ratified them.

time limits). Thus, he can both sue and defend himself on the basis of Convention rights. 'Public authority' is defined so as to include any court or tribunal (including the House of Lords in its judicial capacity), and 'any person certain of whose functions are of a public nature' (other than the Westminster Parliament or a person exercising functions on its behalf[1]). This is clearly very wide and includes the Scottish Parliament, all government departments (including the Scottish Executive), local authorities, quangos, universities etc (including the Law Society of Scotland and the Faculty of Advocates). 'Victim' is also defined widely in terms of art 34 of the ECHR itself as 'any person, non-governmental organisation or group of individuals'[2]. Such challenges have been attempted[3].

Where a court or tribunal finds an act of a public authority unlawful, by s 8, it can 'grant such relief or remedy, or make such order' as it considers 'just and appropriate', subject to certain limitations.

**Human Rights Act cases in Scotland.** The immediate effect of the Human Rights Act 1998 was considerable. A large amount of litigation arose, mostly by way of devolution issues (because the cases were initiated in the period between the coming into force of the Scotland Act 1998 and the complete coming into force of the Human Rights Act, as noted above) and mostly concerning the criminal law. A number affirmed the law as fulfilling the requirements of the Convention rights, such as *Brown v Stott* 2001 SC(PC) 43, 2001 SLT 59, 2001 SCCR 62, [2001] 2 WLR 817 and *Clark v Kelly* (2001 UKPC D1, unreported). In the former case, despite doubts in courts below, the Judicial Committee of the Privy Council (see below) concluded that requiring a driver to take a breath test did not breach the requirement against self-incrimination and therefore prejudice a fair trial in terms of art 6. In the latter, it decided that the position of the clerk of court and legal adviser (a local authority employee with limited security of tenure) in the District Court did not compromise that court as being the independent and impartial tribunal required by art 6.

1 Human Rights Act 1998, s 6(3)
2 Human Rights Act 1998, s 7(7) (and see above).
3 By early 2003, only unsuccessfully: see *A v Scottish Ministers* 2002 PC 63 (judicial review of Mental Health (Public Safety and Appeals) (Scotland) Act 1999 sought for incompatibility with Convention right art 5), *Adams v Scottish Ministers* 2002 SCLR 881 (judicial review of Protection of Wild Mammals (Scotland) Act 2002 sought for incompatibility with Convention right arts 8 and 14 and Protocol 1, art 1).

However, some had far-reaching effects. The best-known example was *Starrs v Ruxton* 2000 JC 208, 2000 SLT 42, and it illustrates the considerable power of the Act. The case concerned temporary sheriffs, that is, advocates or solicitors appointed to serve part-time, and who undertook some 25% of the criminal work of the court. As they were appointed by the Lord Advocate, a member of the Scottish Executive and (of more immediate relevance) the head of the prosecution service, their appointments were clearly acts of a public authority. On an appeal from a decision by a temporary sheriff, the High Court of Justiciary decided that, because their appointments were short term and they could be sidelined by being given no work, or dismissed at will, temporary sheriffs lacked security of tenure. This breached the requirement for 'an independent and impartial tribunal' in art 6 of the ECHR (which was clearly one of the Convention rights listed in Sch 1 to the Human Rights Act 1998), it was clearly incompatible with a Convention right. As a result, temporary sheriffs ceased to be appointed or used, and the Bail, Judicial Appointments, Etc (Scotland) Act 2000 abolished the office (replacing it, however, with that of 'part-time sheriff' with greater security of tenure).

## The European Community and European Union[1]

The European Community and European Union are not the same thing as the Council of Europe. Three original 'communities', the European Coal and Steel Community (ECSC), the European Atomic Energy Community (Euratom), the European Economic Community (EEC) were set up in the 1950s under separate treaties. The main one was the last mentioned, set up by the 'Treaty of Rome'. Each community had its own with separate institutions to carry out its purposes. The communities were set up by six European states[2] to promote economic and political integration, to a degree still disputed among the member states. After a Preamble reciting that the member states are 'Determined to lay the foundations of an ever closer union among the peoples of Europe' and similar sentiments, and art 1, actually establishing the Community, the EC Treaty[3], continues:

1 See Appendix 3 and Appendix Part II to Preface. The European Union website is at http://europa.eu.int/.
2 I e Belgium, France, Germany, Italy, Luxembourg and the Netherlands.
3 Consolidated Version of the Treaty Establishing the European Community: *Official Journal* C325 of 24 December 2002.

Article 2 'The Community shall have as its task, by establishing a common market and an economic and monetary union and by implementing common policies or activities referred to in Articles 3 and 4, to promote throughout the Community a harmonious, balanced and sustainable development of economic activities, a high level of employment and of social protection, equality between men and women, sustainable and non-inflationary growth, a high degree of competitiveness and convergence of economic performance, a high level of protection and improvement of the quality of the environment, the raising of the standard of living and quality of life, and economic and social cohesion and solidarity among Member States.

Article 3 refers to prohibition of customs duties, a common commercial policy, an internal market with free movement of goods, persons, services and capital, etc, and Article 4 to adoption of a common economic policy and a single currency.

The significance of this to the Scottish legal system is that the institutions set up by the treaties can enact legislation (usually referred to as 'Community law') which takes direct effect in member states.

A number of other treaties have amended the original ones, some radically, over the succeeding half-century. The Merger Treaty of 1965 merged the institutions, while leaving the three communities technically separate under the new collective title of 'the European Communities'. The Single European Act 1986 altered significantly some internal procedures (for instance, introducing qualified majority voting of member states, instead of unanimity in some matters) and sought to extend co-operation over a new area of 'justice and home affairs' under the title 'European political co-operation'.

By means of accession treaties, the six original members have been joined by nine more, including the United Kingdom in 1972[1]. The European Communities also created the 'European Economic Area' (EEA) with the remaining members of a rival organisation, the European Free Trade Area (EFTA). This allowed EFTA members to participate in the free movement of workers, goods and services within the Communities, but without participating in the Community institutions. (Later, Switzerland, though not a member of EFTA, also joined the EEA.)

Considerable further changes were effected by the Treaty on European Union[2] (the Maastricht Treaty) which does not replace,

---

1 I e Denmark, Ireland and the United Kingdom (1972), Greece (1981), Spain and Portugal (1986) and Austria, Finland and Sweden (1995).
2 Consolidated version of the treaty on European Union: *Official Journal* C325 of 24 December 2002.

but builds on, the EC Treaty. After a Preamble reciting that the Member States 'Resolved to mark a new stage in the process of European integration undertaken with the establishment of the European Communities', and similar sentiments, art 1 establishes the European Union and continues:

Article 1 'This Treaty marks a new stage on the process of creating an ever closer union among the peoples of Europe, in which decisions are taken as openly as possible and as closely as possible to the citizen.

The Union shall be founded on the European Communities, supplemented by the policies and forms of co-operation established by this Treaty. Its task shall be to organize, in a manner demonstrating consistency and solidarity, relations between the Member States and their peoples'.

Article 2 sets the objectives of economic and social progress, high employment and balanced and sustainable development through the creation of an area without internal frontiers; to assert an identity on the international scene through a common foreign and security policy; to maintain and develop an area of freedom, security and justice etc.

Thus, firstly, the Treaty on European Union sought to re-emphasise the aim of closer union of member states by renaming the three communities simply 'the European Community' (EC) and by institutional changes within the Community. Secondly, it sought to entrench co-operation between member states outwith the Community in justice and home affairs (now renamed 'police and judicial co-operation in criminal matters') and extend co-operation over another such area, that is, foreign and security policy. Joint action in these areas is by 'intergovernmental co-operation', that is by agreement among governments as such, involving the Community institutions to only a limited degree, and thus without the degree of integration achieved in the Community. These two areas were described as second and third 'pillars', respectively, being added to the first pillar of the European Community itself. The resulting edifice, comprising all three pillars, is called 'the European Union' (EU). In addition to these changes the Treaty sought to include the principle of subsidiarity, whereby, in areas in which either member states or the Community might act, member states should do so.

Further changes are being wrought as a result of the Treaty of Amsterdam 1997. This amends the aims of the EC and EU in a number of ways. It also renumbers articles of the EC Treaty (as amended), which makes reference to them hazardous. However, a principal result is to blur the distinction between the pillars, for instance, by incorporating the part of the justice and home affairs (third) pillar concerned with visas, asylum and immigration, into the EC (first) pillar. It also encourages different member states to integrate at different speeds and assists non-member states which are associated with the EC/EU and likely to become members.

The Treaty of Nice in 2000 concluded yet further institutional changes, including the extension of majority voting in the European Community, strengthening the role of the Court of First Instance (see below) and further encouraging integration of different members at different speeds. However, from the point of view of the legal system, it was principally concerned with two matters. Firstly, as an alternative to acceding to the European Convention on Human Rights ('ECHR': see above), the European Union adopted a 'Charter of Fundamental Rights'. This contains provisions similar to those in the ECHR, but goes beyond it to include 'social rights' in relation to education, employment, asylum, data protection and the freedom to conduct business. Nevertheless, it does not have legal force at present, although it may already influence decision-making (including judicial decision-making by the Court of First Instance and the European Court of Justice: see below) and is intended to have some such force in the future. Secondly, the Treaty of Nice prepared the way for enlargement of the EU, by the accession of ten states with effect from 2004[1]. However, not all questions concerning consequential changes (such as the composition of the European Commission and the European Parliament) have been resolved and in early 2003 the conclusions of a 'Convention on the Future of Europe' representing the governments and parliaments of member states and acceding member states, and the European Commission and European Parliament[2] was published as a Draft Treaty establishing a Constitution for Europe.

Thus for some years, the European Union has appeared to be in a state of continuous revolution, and the whole enterprise is becoming more complex and difficult to understand. Its most important effect as far as Scotland is concerned is that some Community law has direct effect and thus without further adoption becomes part of the law of Scotland (see Chapter 5).

1 I e Cyprus, Czech Republic, Estonia, Hungary, Latvia, Lithuania, Malta, Poland, Slovakia and Slovenia.
2 CONV 820/1/03. The 'Convention' website is at http://European_convention. eu.int/bienvenue.asp?lang=EN for outline content, see Appendix Part II to Preface.

*The European Commission*[1]

The Commission, which sits in Brussels, exists to further the interests of the Community. It initiates and implements Community policy, and can legislate under its own powers and under powers delegated by the Council of Ministers. Its deliberations, however, are confidential.

There are, at the time of publication, 20 Commissioners, two from each larger member state, one from each smaller, nominated by the Council of the Union (see below) but involving the European Parliament)[2]. Nevertheless, Commissioners are required to owe their political allegiance to the Community, not the nominating government. One Commissioner is President, and the others each have responsibility for an area of Community policy[3]. They can be removed by a no confidence vote of the European Parliament. They are supported by a Civil Service with some 25 directorates-general and other agencies such as the Legal Service and the Translating Service.

The European Commission should not be confused with the European Commission on Human Rights (see above).

*The Council of the Union (sometimes referred to as 'the Council of the European Union' and formerly called 'the Council of Ministers')*[4]

The Council of the Union, which also sits in Brussels, exists to represent the member states, and co-ordinate their views. It must approve most Community legislation, and therefore has a central role in the legislative process of the Community. Voting involves 'qualified majority voting' ('QMV'), a complicated weighted system (which will be amended in the light of the enlargement of the Union) to allow larger states a greater say without squeezing out the smaller, but its deliberations are also secret.

1 The European Commission website is at http://europa.eu.int/comm./. See also Appendix 3 and Appendix Part II to Preface.
2 These arrangements will change upon the accession of the ten new member states in 2004, but in early 2003, the new arrangements had not been decided upon. However, see Appendix Part II to Preface.
3 United Kingdom governments have nominated one Commissioner from each major United Kingdom party. In early 2003, they were Neil Kinnock (a former Labour Leader of the Opposition), who is a Vice President and is in charge of transport policy, and Chris Patten (a former Conservative Cabinet Minister and Governor of Hong Kong) who is responsible for external relations.
4 The Council of the Union website is at http://ue.eu.int. See also Appendix 3 and Appendix Part II to Preface.

It comprises one minister from each member state's government. Membership is not constant. For discussions on agriculture, it will be Agriculture Ministers, and so on. The Presidency rotates every six months. The Council of the Union has a general secretariat, with several directorates-general and a legal service.

The Council of the Union is easily confused with the European Council, which is a formalised quarterly meeting of Member State heads of government, designed to further political co-operation. It is also easily confused with the Council of Europe (see below).

## COREPER (the Comité des Réprésantants Permanents or Committee of Permanent Representatives)[1]

COREPER is the French acronym usually used for the Committee of Permanent Representatives. Because meetings of the Council of the Union are infrequent, involve different ministers on different occasions, and because ministers have other responsibilities, work is carried on by Permanent Representatives from each member state, who are national civil servants, and their staff[2].

The significance of COREPER is great. It deals with all business going to the Council of the Union and, if it is unanimous, the Council will rubber-stamp its decision.

## The European Parliament[3]

The European Parliament, despite its name, is not the legislature of the Community, but a supervisory, consultative and deliberative body which participates in the legislative process. It exists to represent the population at large of the member states, and is directly elected. It must be consulted on some proposals. The Treaty on European Union gave it a veto in certain legislation and co-decision with the Council of Ministers in other legislation and the Treaty of Amsterdam strengthened it further.

The Commission must be approved by the European Parliament, must report to it and answer questions, and could be

---

1 COREPER does not have a website, as such.
2 In early 2003, the United Kingdom Permanent Representative was Sir Nigel Sheinwald, a career diplomat and civil servant.
3 The European Parliament website is at http://www.europarl.eu.int. See also Appendix 3 and Appendix Part II to Preface.

dismissed by a vote of censure[1]. The Council of the Union must also make certain reports to it, and it has powers in relation to the Community budget.

There are at the time of publication 626 members of the European Parliament, allotted in various proportions to member states. The United Kingdom currently has (like France and Italy) 87 MEPs of whom 8 are elected in Scotland, which for this purpose now forms one constituency. However, the Treaty of Nice raised the total to 732 in anticipation of seats being given to the new Member States, and the number allotted to existing Member States will change. MEPs sit in political groupings, but there are no 'government party' and 'opposition parties'.

The Parliament sits for only a short part of the year, and most of its work is done by committees. It has a secretariat, with five directorates-general. As a result of a compromise, the European Parliament itself sits in Strasbourg, committees in Brussels, and the secretariat in Luxembourg.

### The European Court of Justice (the Court of Justice of the European Communities), Court of First Instance and 'judicial panels'[2]

The European Court of Justice (ECJ) exists to ensure that Community law is correctly interpreted, and is observed. Since 1989 there has been attached to it a Court of First Instance (CFI), which was created because of the large workload, and consequent enormous delays, in the Court of Justice. For certain cases, there is a right of appeal from it to the Court on a point of law.

Between them they decide several classes of case. Firstly, there are several types of 'direct action', in which the court hears the whole proceedings. These include actions against Community institutions (for instance, where an institution is accused of acting ultra vires or otherwise improperly; appeals against penalties imposed by Community institutions; actions for damages against Community institutions for wrongful acts; 'staff cases' by those employed by Community institutions, against their employer; and 'enforcement actions' brought by Community institutions against member states alleged to have failed to carry out their Treaty

---

1 In 1999, the European Parliament threatened to dismiss the Commission, but all the Commissioners resigned. Most were re-appointed.
2 The European Court of Justice website is at http://curia.eu.int/en/index.htm. See also Appendix 3.

obligations[1]. The CFI has usually heard staff cases, competition law cases, and anti-dumping cases, other cases going to the ECJ itself. (Thus, generally, the ECJ hears cases brought by states and institutions, the CFI hears cases brought by individuals.)

Secondly, and of much more importance in the context of the Scottish legal system, the ECJ (and probably in the future the CFI) hear preliminary references under art 234 (numbered 177 before the Treaty of Amsterdam). Here the proceedings neither start nor finish in the Court, but in ordinary national courts and tribunals. Community law may have 'direct effect'. This is discussed in more detail in Chapter 4, but means, among other things, that it is to be applied by the usual national courts. As these courts stretch from Shetland to the Peloponnese, the possibility of conflicting decisions is great. Article 234 (ex article 177) therefore permits any national court hearing a case involving the validity or interpretation of Community law to send that question (but not the rest of the dispute) to the European Court of Justice for an authoritative ruling, which binds that national court. The national court nevertheless decides all questions of fact, and any questions of national law, and gives the final judgment. Final courts of appeal are required to make preliminary references, subject however, to the *acte clair* doctrine, which dispenses with it where the law is clear (whether because it is inherently clear or because there is already a clear ruling).

There are currently 15 judges of the European Court of Justice, one from each member state[2], one of whom is elected President. This is likely to change after the enlargement of the European Union in 2004. There are also nine Advocates General, an office for which there is no United Kingdom equivalent[3]. They present to the judges a fully reasoned preliminary judgment. The Court is by no means bound to follow the Advocate General's view, but is

---

1 For example, art 141 (numbered 119 before the Treaty of Amsterdam) requires sexual equality in employment, and the Equal Pay Directive (75/117), furthering that policy, was made in 1976. The Commission considered that the relevant United Kingdom legislation, the Equal Pay Act 1970, did not fulfil the requirements of Community law and successfully brought enforcement proceedings (Case 51/81 *Commission v United Kingdom* [1982] ICR 578).

2 At the time of publication, the United Kingdom judge in the European Court of Justice was David Edward QC, an advocate and former professor at Edinburgh University.

3 The Advocates General of the European Court of Justice are not to be confused with the Advocate General for Scotland (see above). In early 2003, one of the Advocates General was Francis Jacobs QC, an English barrister and former professor at London University.

likely to[1]. The Court may sit in full session, or in chambers of smaller numbers, depending upon the type or importance of the case. There are 15 further judges, but no separate Advocates General in the Court of First Instance[2] (though a judge may act as Advocate General).

In addition, since the Treaty of Nice, there may be 'judicial panels' attached to the Court of First Instance to deal with certain classes of case, subject to appeal to the CFI. The judges will have similar qualifications to those in the CFI. It remains to be seen how this innovation will work.

Procedure in both courts follows civil law rather than common law patterns (for example, relying heavily upon written submissions, with very limited oral argument), and the language of the case is usually that of the applicant, although it uses French as its working language.

The European Court of Justice, which sits in Luxembourg, is not to be confused with the European Court of Human Rights, which sits in Strasbourg.

### Other Community institutions

There are other Community institutions, such as the Economic and Social Committee (ECOSOC), a committee composed of 224 members (24 from the UK) representing functional interests, that is, 'the various economic and social components of civil society, and in particular producers, farmers, carriers, workers, dealers, craftsmen, professional occupations, consumers and the general interest'. It gives its opinion on draft legislation and under the Treaty of Amsterdam can be consulted by the European Parliament. Under the Treaty on European Union, there is a consultative Committee of the Regions with similar size of membership (including 5 from Scotland), representing regional and national bodies. It operates through 'Commissions' on a variety of topics such as 'territorial adhesion' and 'economic and social policy'.

---

1  The difference between the two styles of judgment has importance for judicial reasoning and the operation of precedent. This is discussed in ch 6 below.
2  In early 2003, the United Kingdom judge was Nicholas Forwood QC, an English barrister.

# UNITED KINGDOM COURTS, TRIBUNALS AND RELATED INSTITUTIONS

## Courts and tribunals

There are two hierarchies of courts in Scotland: the civil and the criminal. England and Wales and Northern Ireland have their own hierarchies, similar to the Scottish ones, but separate. Nevertheless, all three national hierarchies are connected. The Scottish civil hierarchy (but not the criminal) ends with a final appeal to the House of Lords. The civil and the criminal hierarchies in England and Northern Ireland also end there. Further, from all courts in the United Kingdom there is the possibility of a 'preliminary reference' to the European Court of Justice in relation to European Community law (see above).

In addition to the courts, there are a number of tribunals, generally organised on a United Kingdom basis (although there is a Scottish Committee of the Council on Tribunals). These deal with certain types of legal dispute, but are not regarded as courts. Well-known examples are the Employment and the Social Security Tribunals. Tribunals vary considerably in structure and personnel, but in general are less formal than courts, and litigants are often unrepresented by lawyers. There may be appeal from them to the courts and, as with the courts, the possibility of a preliminary reference to the European Court of Justice.

Dissatisfaction with the efficiency of the administration of criminal justice led to several reports on the subject[1], and these may produce significant changes in the running of the criminal courts.

Dissatisfaction with the method of appointing sheriffs and judges produced the Judicial Appointments Board in 2002, briefly preceded by an ad hoc Selection Board (see below).

## The Scottish courts

### The district court[2]

District courts are local courts dealing with minor crime, staffed by lay justices of the peace. In Glasgow, there are also salaried

---

1 E g *Improving Justice: 2002 review of the practices and procedures of the High Court of Justiciary* (2002) (the 'Bonomy Report').
2 Most of the relevant law is in the District Courts (Scotland) Act 1975, as amended by the Bail, Judicial Appointments Etc (Scotland) Act 2000. There is no district courts website, but the District Courts Association (see below) website is at www.district-courts.org.uk.

stipendiary magistrates. The district courts deal with approaching about a third of all criminal proceedings in Scotland[1], although these proceedings all concern minor crime.

**The court.** District courts, created by the District Courts (Scotland) Act 1975, are an amalgamation of the previous burgh police courts (in the burghs) and justice of the peace courts (in some landward areas).

They are run, somewhat anomalously, by local authorities rather than the Scottish Courts Service. The structure of local authority areas has altered since district courts were set up, so their territorial jurisdiction no longer closely coincides with local authority boundaries, and some local authorities have several district courts[2]. In cities and towns the justices sit alone (as in the old burgh police courts), and in the landward areas in twos or more (as in the former justice of the peace courts). An assessor (usually the clerk of court) is always present to offer legal advice, but not to take part otherwise[3]. Frequency of sitting is decided locally. In rural areas only a few court days a month may be required, while in the cities the court sits every day, and sometimes two or more courts may sit simultaneously.

Every court must have a justices' committee. This decides the duty rota of justices, makes training arrangements, and takes other steps to secure the effective administration of justice. The clerk of the court (and if necessary, deputes) is appointed by the council. The clerk of the court must be a solicitor or advocate, and usually acts as assessor[4]. The council must also appoint a clerk of the peace (who may be the clerk of court), to advise the justices generally on the performance of their duties, and to carry out administrative duties for the justices' committee. The council is also responsible

1 In 2001, of the 139,345 persons summoned to criminal courts 41,075 (29%) were dealt with by lay justices of the peace, and 5,644 (4%) by stipendiary magistrates: *Scottish Executive Statistical Bulletin: Criminal Justice Series* CRJ/2002/9 (December 2002). This is, in both cases, less than half the number of a decade before. The decrease is attributable to the increased use of alternatives to prosecution of minor crime, such as police conditional offers.

2 For example, Fife has district courts in Cupar, Dunfermline and Kirkcaldy. For the locations of district courts, see the District Courts Association website (see above), or the annual *Directory of the Law Society of Scotland* ('the Blue Book') (Law Society of Scotland/LexisNexis UK) or the annual *Scottish Law Directory* ('the White Book') (LexisNexis UK).

3 For discussion of the role of clerk to the district court, and indeed, general discussion on its origins, see *Kelly v Clark* (DRA No 2 of 2002, PC unreported)

4 District court clerks of court and their (principal) deputes are listed in the entry for the relevant court in the White and Blue Books (see n 1 above).

for providing suitable premises for the court, and servicing it.

The First Minister has oversight of the work of justices of the peace generally, advised by the Central Committee on Justices of the Peace, which is chaired by the Lord Justice-Clerk. The First Minister has specific obligations in respect of training justices, although most arrangements are made locally. Prosecutions in the district court are undertaken by the Procurator Fiscal Service, which thus can decide whether the district court or the sheriff court is appropriate for minor crimes. There is a voluntary association, the District Courts Association, representing the views of those concerned in their operation.

**Justices.** The First Minister appoints most justices, in the name of the Sovereign and upon the recommendation of local advisory committees on justices of the peace. There are few formal requirements for appointment, save an obligation to live in or near the district (but there has been a tendency in some areas to seek 'political balance'). The local advisory committee's role is to ensure that appointees are honest, sensible local people. They number about 4,000. The justices' committee selects justices for the duty rota from among those suitably trained. Justices are formally divided into 'full' justices, who actually sit on the bench, and 'signing' justices, who may only sign warrants and other documents. 'Full' justices may be removed only on specified grounds, and after investigation by a tribunal appointed by the Lord President of the Court of Session and chaired by a sheriff principal[1]. 'Signing' justices are on a 'supplemental list', and at the age of 70, all justices are in any case put on that list. A justice may also be placed on that list by reason of infirmity or negligent attention to duties. In practice only a small proportion of justices sit on the bench.

Councils may also nominate up to a quarter of their members to serve as justices. These constituted, in early 2003, only some 10% of all justices, and they may be only 'signing' justices. Stipendiary magistrates are all appointed by the local authority, and must be solicitors or advocates of at least five years' standing.

---

1 This division and security of tenure were introduced after the High Court of Justiciary decided in *Starrs v Ruxton* 2000 JC 208, 2000 SLT 42 that temporary sheriffs did not constitute 'an independent and impartial tribunal', contrary to art 6 of the European Convention on Human Rights. A particular problem was presented by those justices who were appointed by virtue of being councillors.

**The work of the district court.** The district court hears cases concerning offences which a statute has declared competent to it, and which occur within its area. This includes a number of common law offences (such as, subject to limitations, minor assault, breach of the peace, and theft), and statutory ones (such as minor road traffic offences).

All cases are prosecuted by summary procedure. As all such cases are competent in the sheriff court as well, it is the procurator fiscal who decides which cases go to which court in the light, among other things, of the limits to the district court's sentencing powers[1]. A justice may impose up to 60 days' imprisonment and/or a fine at level four of the standard scale[2]. A stipendiary magistrate, however, has the same powers as a sheriff in summary criminal proceedings.

Appeal is possible against conviction and/or sentence, to the High Court of Justiciary, sitting as an appeal court. It is available to both the person convicted, and (on a point of law only) to the prosecutor.

*The sheriff court[3]*

Sheriff courts are local courts with very wide jurisdiction, both civil and criminal, and legally qualified judges. There is a sheriff court in every city and most towns. Thus, for many purposes it is the most important court in the land. In its civil jurisdiction (largely overlapping that of the Court of Session) it deals mostly with debt and divorce[4]. However, many of these are simple, and much of a

---

1 Thus, speeding under 100mph in a 70mph limit might go to the district court; above that figure to the sheriff court.

2 At the time of publication level four of the standard scale under the Criminal Procedure (Scotland) Act 1995, s 225, as amended, was £2,500.

3 Much of the relevant law is to be found in the Sheriff Courts (Scotland) Acts 1907 and 1971, as amended. Information on sheriff courts is available on the Scottish Courts website at www.scotcourts.gov.uk.

4 In 2000, 45,402 small claims (i e for less than £750) were initiated and disposed of, nearly all for debt. In the same year, 38,551 summary causes (i e for less than £1,500) were disposed of, 22,921 by decree for the pursuer. Of these, some 13,000 were for land and some 9,000 for debt. These actions are competent in the sheriff court only. In that same year, there were also 30,965 ordinary causes disposed of. Of these, some 15,000 were for debt, and some 5,000 concerned mortgage lenders, while over 6,000 were for divorce. These actions might all have been brought in the Outer House of the Court of Session. (See *Civil Judicial Statistics Scotland 2000* Scottish Executive (2001).)

sheriff's time may be taken up with the small proportion of difficult and important cases which may be debt or divorce or some
other matter. In its criminal jurisdiction (largely overlapping that
of the High Court of Justiciary on the one hand, and that of the
district court on the other), it deals with about two-thirds of all
criminal proceedings[1].

**The court.** Sheriff courts are organised into six sheriffdoms,
based on the former local government regions[2]. Each sheriffdom
(except Glasgow and Strathkelvin) is divided into sheriff court
districts, giving 49 sheriff courts in all[3]. The First Minister decides
how many sheriffs there shall be in each sheriffdom, and sheriff
courts often have more than one (Glasgow and Strathkelvin has
22). Sheriffs are appointed to a sheriffdom, and usually sit in only
one sheriff court district. There are also, however, 'floating
sheriffs', part-time sheriffs and honorary sheriffs.

The First Minister has overall responsibility for the efficient
organisation and administration of the courts, which he discharges
through the Scottish Courts Administration. It is responsible to
him for the performance of the Scottish Court Service and central
administration pertaining to the judiciary in the supreme and
sheriff courts and to the Lord Advocate for certain aspects of court
procedures. The Scottish Court Service is an Executive Agency
within the Scottish Courts Administration. It is responsible for
provision of staff, court-houses etc. It employs over 800 people.
However, each of the six sheriffdoms has a sheriff principal who is
responsible for the speedy and efficient disposal of business, and
each sheriffdom has a regional sheriff clerk and a sheriff clerk (and
deputes if necessary) for each court, who run it day-to-day[4].

---

1 In 2001, of the 139,345 persons summoned to criminal courts, 4,073 (3%) were
   dealt with by sheriff and jury and 87,438 (63%) by sheriff summary proceedings:
   *Scottish Executive Statistical Bulletin: Criminal Justice Series*: CRJ/2002/9
   (December 2002). This is a broadly similar number to that a decade ago.
2 The Sheriffdoms of Glasgow and Strathkelvin; Grampian, Highland and Islands;
   Lothian and Borders; North Strathclyde; South Strathclyde, Dumfries and
   Galloway; and Tayside, Central and Fife.
3 For instance, the Sheriffdom of Tayside, Central and Fife is divided into the
   sheriff court districts of Alloa, Arbroath, Cupar, Dundee, Dunfermline,
   Falkirk, Forfar, Kirkcaldy, Perth and Stirling. For a complete list, see, for
   example, the Scottish Courts website (see above) which gives addresses and
   maps, the annual *Scottish Law Directory* ('the White Book') (LexisNexis UK)
   or *Directory of the Law Society of Scotland* ('the Blue Book') (Law Society of
   Scotland/LexisNexis UK).
4 The identities and addresses of sheriff clerks are given on the Scottish Courts
   website, and in the White and Blue Books.

**Sheriffs.** The office of sheriff is ancient, and sheriffs were long a principal part of local law and administration. The office became largely hereditary in the Middle Ages, but sheriffs appointed deputes to do the work, and they in turn appointed substitutes. Heritability was finally abolished after the 1745 rebellion by the Heritable Jurisdictions (Scotland) Act 1746. No-one was thereafter appointed to the office of sheriff, but the office of sheriff depute was continued, and its holders were called by that title until the 19th century, when they became known as sheriffs (or sheriffs principal). The appointment was part-time, and held by advocates. In 1971 they became formally entitled sheriffs principal, and the post became full-time.

The sheriff deputes continued to appoint substitutes after the heritable jurisdictions were abolished. These substitutes became the full-time sheriffs, with the title Sheriff Substitute, salaried and legally qualified from the early 19th century, but appointed by the Crown only later. In 1971 the substitutes finally fell heir to the title Sheriff. The actual means of appointment, clear in formal terms, was somewhat obscure in practical ones, involving consultations with the Dean of the Faculty of Advocates and Sheriffs Principal, until the Judicial Appointments Board was set up in 2002 (see below).

Today sheriffs, including sheriffs principal (but excluding part-time and honorary sheriffs), are appointed by 'Her Majesty' on the nomination of the First Minister[1], and after consultation with the Lord President and recommendation by the Judicial Appointments Board (see below)[2]. Those who have been advocates or solicitors for at least ten years are eligible to be appointed sheriff, but few are appointed with less than a couple of decades of experience, or more in the case of sheriffs principal (who are usually appointed from among QCs and those who are sheriffs already). Vacancies are advertised informally to sheriffs and sheriffs principal, the Faculty of Advocates and Law Society of Scotland, and those eligible who have expressed interest, and also more recently by public advertisement. Sheriffs may hold office until the age of 70. They are salaried[3].

1  Scotland Act 1998, s 94(5). In early 2003, there were some 130 full-time sheriffs, some 20 of them women. A list of their identities, sheriffdoms and sheriff court districts is found in the White and Blue Books.
2  Sheriff Ian Macphail, appointed Sheriff Principal of Lothian and Borders in 2002, was the first to be so appointed.
3  In early 2003, the Senior Salaries Review Board (Cm 5718) recommended that sheriffs receive a salary of £110, 362 and sheriff principals £119,160, both with non-contributory pensions.

Full-time salaried 'floating sheriffs'[1], appointed to a particular sheriffdom or as 'all-Scotland floating sheriffs', may be directed to sit anywhere to relieve pressure of business. There are also up to 60 part-time sheriffs, appointed by the Scottish Ministers from those qualified to be sheriffs. They are appointed for five-year terms, are normally to be re-appointed, may sit in any sheriff court district, normally sitting between 20 and 100 days a year. Like the floating sheriffs, they add some flexibility to the system, enabling it to respond to the ups and downs of business and the availability of full-time sheriffs[2]. If solicitors, they would not normally be used in the sheriff court district in which they practise. A part-time appointment provides judicial experience for possible appointees to a full-time post.

Honorary sheriffs are appointed by the sheriff principal[3]. They require no legal qualification (although many are senior solicitors). The office is honorary but may involve some judicial duties. In that role honorary sheriffs have the same powers as other sheriffs.

Sheriffs can be removed from office. The Lord President and the Lord Justice-Clerk on their own initiative, or on that of the First Minister, may investigate the fitness for office of any sheriff or sheriff principal. They report that he is fit for office, or that he is not 'by reason of inability, neglect of duty, or misbehaviour', in which case the First Minister may make a statutory instrument (subject to annulment by the Scottish Parliament) removing him. This has only been done twice. In 1977, a sheriff was removed for having organised local political plebiscites, and in 1992 another was removed for inability[4]. A part-time sheriff may be removed if, at the request of the Scottish Ministers, the Lord President of the

1 In early 2003, there were some 20 floating sheriffs.
2 Part-time sheriffs replaced the former 'temporary sheriffs' after it was decided in *Starrs v Ruxton* 2000 JC 208, 2000 SLT 42 that the latter did not provide 'an independent and impartial tribunal', as required by art 6 of the European Convention on Human Rights., because of their lack of tenure. The method of appointing, terms of office and means of removal of part-time sheriffs is laid down in the Bail, Judicial Appointments, Etc (Scotland) Act 2000. At the time of publication there was no published list of the actual number, or their identities.
3 The identities of honorary sheriffs are given in the entry for the relevant sheriffdom in the White and Blue Books.
4 See the Sheriff (Removal from Office) Order 1992, SI 1992/1677 and *Stewart v Secretary of State* 1995 SLT 895, 1996 SLT 1203, 1998 SLT 385.

Court of Session appoints a tribunal (consisting of a Court of Session judge, a person of at least ten years' legal experience, and another person) which finds him unfit on the same grounds as for removal of a sheriff. Honorary sheriffs are appointed by the sheriff principal, so may be removed by him.

The Judicial Studies Board (see below) now provides training and professional development

**The work of the sheriff court.** In civil proceedings, the basic principle is that a pursuer must bring his case in the sheriffdom of the defender's domicile. This is much broadened, however, to include other connections with the sheriffdom, such that the relevant contract was performed there, or the relevant delict occurred there[1].

Within these limits, a sheriff court may take almost any kind of civil case, including contract, delict, property and divorce (though that has its own grounds of jurisdiction). It also hears appeals from, or review of, a large number of local authority and other administrative decisions, such as licensing appeals. There are some types of case it cannot hear[2]. On the other hand, it has privative (i e exclusive) jurisdiction in relation to actions for sums of £1,500 or less, and to many statutory applications and appeals. As a civil court, it employs small claims, summary cause and ordinary cause procedures and also summary application procedure for the great variety of emergency and administrative applications under common law and legislation.

Appeal in civil cases depends upon the procedure used. In small claims, appeal is to the sheriff principal on a point of law only, and no further. In summary causes, it is to the sheriff principal on a point of law only and thence (by leave only) to the Inner House of the Court of Session and thereafter to the House of Lords. In ordinary causes, it is to the sheriff principal and then (generally as of right) to the Inner House, or direct to the Inner House, and thereafter in either case, on a point of law only, to the House of Lords.

---

1 Sheriff Courts (Scotland) Act 1971, s 7: Civil Jurisdiction and Judgments Act 1982, Pt II; Sch 8.
2 By virtue of the Companies Act 1985, s 515, for example, the sheriff court cannot hear petitions to wind up a company with fully paid-up share capital of greater than £120,000.

The number of appeals is small compared with the number of cases dealt with[1].

In criminal proceedings, generally speaking, the sheriff court has jurisdiction only over offences occurring within the sheriffdom. Also, there are certain offences, the main ones being murder and rape, which cannot be tried in a sheriff court. There are limits too on a sheriff's sentencing powers. In summary proceedings, a sheriff can impose up to three months' imprisonment and/or a fine at level five of the standard scale[2], and in solemn proceedings (used in serious cases with a jury), three years' imprisonment (or in some cases more[3]) and/or an unlimited fine. Within these limits, however, a sheriff can try any criminal case, and by summary or solemn procedure, as appropriate. Prosecution is by the Procurator Fiscal Service, and the fiscal chooses between summary or solemn procedure where a choice is available.

Appeals in criminal cases may be against conviction and/or sentence, and are to the High Court of Justiciary. In summary proceedings, the person convicted can appeal against conviction and sentence or other disposal. The prosecutor may appeal, but only on a point of law, against conviction or sentence. In solemn procedure, only the person convicted may appeal. Appeals are a small proportion of cases heard[4].

1  In 2000 there were 431 small claims appeals, 48 summary causes appeals, and 34 ordinary cause appeals initiated to the sheriff principal (most of which were unsuccessful). There were 20 further appeals to the Inner House, and 662 went direct to the Inner House (most of which were also unsuccessful). (No sheriff court decision was appealed to the House of Lords.) Yet 115,013 actions were disposed of by sheriff courts in that year: *Civil Judicial Statistics Scotland 2000* (Scottish Executive) (2001).

2  But six months for a second or subsequent offence of dishonest appropriation or personal violence (Criminal Procedure (Scotland) Act 1995, s 5(3)). At the time of publication level five on the standard scale under the Criminal Procedure (Scotland) Act 1995, s 225 was £5,000.

3  CP(S)A 1995, s 3(3). Section 13 of the Crime and Punishment (Scotland) Act 1997, raising the custodial sentencing powers of sheriffs in solemn procedure to five years, has not yet been brought into force. However, by s 219(8) of the Criminal Procedure (Scotland) Act 1995 a sheriff can in such cases remit the accused to the High Court for sentence, if he considers that his powers are inadequate. Particular statutes may confer specific greater sentencing powers.

4  In 2001 there were 3,495 criminal appeals from all courts (approximately 3% of all convictions), two-thirds of them from the sheriff summary courts. Nearly 90% overall concerned sentence rather than conviction, and most of those concerned a custodial sentence. Only 12% of appeals overall were successful. But in that year 139,345 persons were proceeded against in all courts

*The High Court of Justiciary*

The High Court of Justiciary is the trial court for major crime, and the appeal court for all crime in Scotland. As a trial court, it goes on circuit to a number of towns and cities, with a single judge. It deals with a very small proportion of all crime, although all that it does deal with is serious[1]. As an appeal court (sometimes called the Court of Criminal Appeal in appeals under solemn procedure), it sits only in Edinburgh, in the old sheriff court-house in the Lawnmarket, opposite Parliament House, usually with a bench of three judges, although a larger bench can be convened to review precedents which are doubted. The judges are the same as those who staff the Court of Session. It is the supreme criminal court for Scotland.

**The court.** In 1672, the High Court of Justiciary was set up to replace the previous system of lay 'justices-general' (earlier called 'justiciars') appointed to tour the country dealing with crime (and other matters) of particular concern to the sovereign. The sovereign might directly interfere in the business, and the system was ineffective even by the standards of the day. The High Court originally comprised the Lord Justice-General (a layman who often did not sit[2]), the Lord Justice-Clerk (originally the clerk of court to the lay justiciars), and five Lords Commissioners of Justiciary from among the Court of Session judges.

In 1837, the office of Lord Justice-General was passed to the Lord President of the Court of Session, and in 1887 all Court of Session judges became Lords Commissioners of Justiciary and the court took its present form.

The court may sit anywhere in Scotland. It used to go on four fixed circuits, but now sits where the Lord Justice-General determines after consultation with the Lord Advocate. Half a dozen Lords Commissioners will be on circuit much of the time (with a permanent sitting in Glasgow), and three more sitting in Edinburgh hearing appeals.

The Lord Justice-General is responsible for the administration of the court, acting through the Principal Clerk of Session and Justiciary and his staff, who may act as clerks of court on circuit.

---

1 In 2001, of the 139,345 persons summoned to criminal courts, 1,078 (1%) were dealt with by the High Court: *Scottish Executive Statistical Bulletin: Criminal Justice* Series CRJ/2002/9 (December 2002). This is a slightly lower number than that of a decade ago.

2 The office became hereditary in the Dukes of Argyll.

**High Court of Justiciary judges (Lords Commissioners of Justiciary).** The Lord President of the Court of Session is the Lord Justice-General, and all Court of Session judges (Senators of the College of Justice) are High Court judges (Lords Commissioners of Justiciary) *ex officio*[1]. Temporary judges of the Court of Session are also temporary judges of the High Court.

**The work of the High Court.** As a trial court, the High Court of Justiciary has jurisdiction over all offences in Scotland (unless excluded by statute). Thus, its jurisdiction overlaps that of other criminal courts, and it is the prosecutor's decision in most cases whether a case goes to the High Court or elsewhere. However, no other court may try certain offences, principally murder and rape, and the High Court also wields the *nobile officium* (see Chapter 6), and a 'declaratory power' to create new offences (although the use of the latter is very constrained). On the other hand, it does not deal with offences triable by summary proceedings, so trials are always by solemn procedure, before a single judge and a jury of 15. Prosecution is by one of some 20 Advocates Depute in the name of the Lord Advocate, but occasionally by the Lord Advocate or the Solicitor-General.

Appeal from the High Court sitting as a trial court is to the High Court sitting as a court of appeal, in which usually three judges sit. It also sits as the appeal court from all summary proceedings in the district court and the summary and solemn proceedings in the sheriff court. In practice, one or other of the Divisions of the Inner House of the Court of Session, under their presiding judges, almost always provides the criminal appeal court. (There is no further appeal save in a devolution case: see above.)

*The Court of Session*

The Court of Session has jurisdiction over most civil matters in Scotland, but sits only in Parliament House in Edinburgh. It comprises the Outer House and the Inner House. Judges of the former (known as Lords Ordinary) sit singly, and deal with cases at first instance. Judges of the latter are assigned to one of two divisions of five (until recently four), of whom three customarily sit at one time, and chiefly hear appeals (although they also hear petitions in which one party seeks some special permission usually

---

1 For a list of their identities, see the Scottish Courts website (see above), the White and Blue Books (see above) or the bound volumes of the Scots Law Times.

without opposition). It is the supreme civil court in Scotland, although appeal from it to the House of Lords is possible.

**The court.** The date traditionally taken to be the year of the court's foundation is 1532. Since the late 15th century the King's Council had been sitting intermittently to dispense civil justice. Its funding and the limited availability of the nobility around the time of Kings James IV and V impeded its efficiency. An Act of 1532 (later called the College of Justice Act) made arrangements for a central royal court under the name of the College of Justice to be set up[1]. It comprised fifteen men (eight, including the Lord President, being clerics) appointed as Lords of Council and Session to be professional judges, supported financially by church endowments and exhorted to sit daily. But it was not until an Act of Parliament of 1541, confirming that of 1532 and a Bull of Pope Paul III of 1535, that the court began to function regularly with some semblance of sufficient funding.

At first it dealt only with cases at first instance, with possible appeal to the Privy Council, and it had no jurisdiction over marriage and some other matters, which were then dealt with by ecclesiastical courts. It rapidly expanded its jurisdiction, however, and became an appeal court as well. The leading writer on Scots law, Viscount Stair, referred to the court in his *Institutions* of 1681 (IV,1,22) as 'the Session' or 'the College of Justice'. By the time of the Union of 1707, it was called the Court of Session.

Until the Union rendered Parliament House vacant, 'the Haill Fifteen' usually sat in an inner room in the Edinburgh Tolbooth[2], save for one or two judges dealing with witnesses and preliminary matters outside before reporting back to them. This practice

---

1 On this complex subject, see RK Hannay, *The College of Justice* (Stair Society, 1990).

2 Or rather, it sat in the Tolbooth itself till 1560, and from 1564 to 1640 in an upstairs room in an annexe to St Giles church, referred to as the 'Over' or 'Upper Tolbooth' (the High Court of Justiciary sitting in a lower room). McQueen 'Two Visitors in the Session, 1629 and 1639' in McQueen (ed) *Miscellany IV* (Stair Society, 2002) reproduces two 17th-century accounts by English visitors, including a sketch map of the lay-out of the 'Upper Tolbooth'. One of the visitors (Sir C Lowther) recorded (p163) that in the Outer House 'is allway grete noyse and confusion, but the Inner House very orderly . . . it onely medleth with things not determined or where his [*scil* the Outer House judge's] judgment is disliked'. The other visitor (Sir W Brereton) also recorded (at p166) that 'I observed the gretest rudeness, disorder and confusion that ever I saw in any court of justice, no, not the like disorder in any of our sessions, for here two or three plead and speak together, and that with such a forced, strained voice as the strongest only caries it . . .'.

persisted when the court moved into the adjacent Parliament Hall. They would send one of their number in turn to hear evidence on the other side of a partition and report back to them. Thus the titles 'Inner' and 'Outer House' arose. In 1808 and again in 1825 a number of reforms resulted in the court taking its present form. It is still 'collegiate' in that decisions are given in the name of the whole court, judges from one House may sit in the other, and all are said to be of equal status (although Inner House judges are paid slightly more, and the Lord President most of all).

There is provision for 32 Court of Session judges. Additional temporary judges may be appointed, usually from the ranks of senior sheriffs and practising advocates. One judge is always seconded to the Scottish Law Commission as whole- or part-time chairman. The more junior ones (that is, those who are not members of the Inner House) sit as Lords Ordinary in the Outer House. But they will not do so every working day. Some may be sitting as Lords Commissioners of Justiciary in the High Court of Justiciary, usually away from Edinburgh on circuit. Others may be sitting in other judicial capacities, such as Chairman of the Employment Appeal Tribunal, and yet others may be undertaking other functions, such as judicial inquiries[1].

The Inner House comprises the First and Second Divisions, which are, however, of equal status. The First is composed of the Lord President of the Court of Session and four senior judges, and the Second, the Lord Justice-Clerk and four other senior judges. Both have a quorum, and normal complement, of three (for the others may be performing other tasks, such as sitting in the Outer House). An Extra Division may also be convened. Also, occasionally, a Court of Seven (or more) Judges is convened for a point of special difficulty, or where overruling a precedent of a Division is in contemplation.

The Lord President is responsible for administration of the court, acting through the Principal Clerk of Session and Justiciary and his staff.

## Court of Session judges (Senators of the College of Justice).

The judges of the Court of Session, the senior permanent Scottish judges, are technically Senators of the College of Justice[2]. The

---

1 Lord Cullen, now Lord President, conducted the Public Inquiry into the Piper Alpha disaster between 1988 and 1990, the Public Inquiry into the Dunblane Primary School shootings in 1996, and the Ladbroke Grove Rail Inquiry in 1999, for instance.
2 A list can be found on the Scottish Courts website, in the White and Blue Books (see above) and in the bound volumes of the Scots Law Times.

power of appointment lies with Her Majesty, on the recommendation of the First Minister and after consulting the Lord President
(Scotland Act 1998, s 95(4)) and receiving recommendations from
the Judicial Appointments Board (see below). Those eligible are
sheriffs and sheriffs principal of five years' standing, and advocates
and solicitors with five years' right of audience in the Court of
Session[1]. Vacancies are now advertised, and candidates are considered by the Judicial Appointments Board (see below), which makes
recommendations to the First Minister[2]. On appointment judges
take the courtesy title 'Lord' or 'Lady'[3]. They are not thereby
members of the House of Lords (although a few such as Lord
McCluskey and Lord Cameron of Lochbroom had been made life
peers for other reasons). Some follow an old tradition and take a
territorial title, which may some times be justified as avoiding the
surname of another judge[4]. In addition, temporary judges may
now be appointed by the First Minister from among retired judges
for a year at a time up to the age of 75 and also from those eligible

1 Until the Law Reform (Miscellaneous Provisions) (Scotland) Act 1990, s 35, it
  was not even clear who was eligible. There was no legislation on this matter, but
  art 19 of the Treaty of Union permitted (on various conditions) advocates,
  Writers to the Signet and Principal Clerks of Session to be appointed. Only
  senior advocates who were not sheriffs had been appointed for many years, so the
  1990 Act broadened eligibility considerably. However, advocates as such are not
  mentioned in the 1990 Act, so while they are undoubtedly still considered
  eligible, it is presumably on the basis of the Treaty of Union, art 19.
2 The first two judges appointed under the new system were Phillip Brodie QC,
  who took the courtesy title of Lord Brodie, and Alistair Campbell QC, who took
  the courtesy title of Lord Bracadale. However, see below on the appointment of
  Lady Smith.
3 At the time of publication there were three women judges: Lady Cosgrove
  (appointed 1996, an advocate, having been a sheriff and Temporary Judge, and
  who became in 2003 the first woman to serve in the Inner House); Lady Paton
  (appointed 2000, direct from the Bar, having been an advocate-depute); and
  Lady Smith (appointed 2001, from the Bar, having been a temporary sheriff and
  an advocate-depute: she was appointed by a temporary formal selection process
  which briefly preceded the Judicial Appointments Board).
4 Among judges sitting at the time of publication, Lord Marnoch was Michael
  Bruce QC, Lord Abernethy was John Cameron QC, Lord Eassie was Ronald
  Mackay QC, and Lord Carloway was Colin Sutherland QC. This practice is far
  from invariable, and incidentally raises the subject of Scottish judicial dynasties.
  Lord Clyde (appointed 1985, Lord of Appeal in Ordinary 1996–2001) is son of
  the late Lord Clyde (Lord President 1954–72) and grandson of the late Lord
  Clyde (Lord President 1928–35). Lord Kingarth (appointed 1997) and Lord
  Emslie (appointed 2001) are both sons of the late Lord Emslie (appointed 1970,
  Lord President 1972–89). Lord Wheatley (appointed 2000) is the son of the late
  Lord Wheatley (appointed 1954, Lord Justice Clerk 1972–85).

to be appointed as full-time judges[1]. The latter do not have the title of 'Lord' or 'Lady'.

However, under the Scotland Act 1998, s 95, the Lord President of the Court of Session and the Lord Justice-Clerk 'continue to be' appointed by Her Majesty on the recommendation of the Prime Minister, after consulting the Lord President and the Lord Justice-Clerk, unless the office is vacant. Occasionally they are appointed straight from the Bar, but otherwise from among existing judges[2].

Senators are paid[3]. They are required to retire at 70 and when they do so they retain their title. Provision is now made for the removal of a judge of the Court of Session. Formerly it was thought that only an Act of Parliament could prematurely remove a judge[4]. The Scotland Act, by s 95(6) to (11), provides that if the removal of a judge is contemplated the First Minister must convene a tribunal of at least three persons, chaired by a member of the Judicial Committee of the Privy Council, who are to report whether the judge is unfit for office 'by reason of inability, neglect of duty or misbehaviour'. If such a report is made, the First Minister may recommend to the Scottish Parliament that the judge be removed and if it so resolves he shall make a recommendation to Her Majesty to that effect. The procedure is similar to that for the removal of a sheriff.

The Judicial Studies Committee (see below) now provides some training and career development of judges.

**The work of the Court of Session.** The Outer House of the Court of Session is a court of first instance, and can hear most types of civil case. Therefore many cases can be brought either there or in the sheriff court, and pursuers choose on the basis of

1 Judicial Pensions and Retirement Act 1993, s 26(4)–(7); Law Reform (Miscellaneous Provisions) (Scotland) Act 1990, s 35(3)
2 The Lord President in early 2003 (Lord Cullen) was previously Lord Justice-Clerk. His immediate predecessor (Lord Rodger, now a House of Lords judge) was appointed from the Outer House, but his predecessor, (Lord Hope, now also a House of Lords judge), was appointed from the Bar where he was Dean of the Faculty of Advocates. The current Lord Justice-Clerk (Lord Gill) was an Outer House judge, and Chairman of the Scottish Law Commission. His immediate predecessor was Lord Cullen (see above), whose predecessor (Lord Ross) was appointed from the Inner House.
3 In early 2003, the Senior Salaries Review Board (Cm 5718) recommended that the Lord President be paid £181,176, the Lord Justice Clerk £175,055, Inner House judges £166,394, and Outer House judges £147,198, all with non-contributory pensions.
4 The position in England was covered by the Supreme Court Act 1981, which does not apply in Scotland.

cost, importance, convenience etc. Some cases, however, such as judicial review over certain administrative bodies and exercise of the *nobile officium*, are reserved to the court. Some others though, such as actions for £1,500 or less and a number of appeals from administrative decisions, are reserved for sheriffs. There is a limited degree of specialisation among the Court of Session judges, for instance, in judicial review cases and in intellectual property, commercial and patent cases there are special provisions to enable them to be dealt with quickly[1]. Most cases, however, are debt and personal injury cases[2].

The Inner House of the Court of Session is primarily a court of appeal from the Outer House, sheriffs principal and sheriffs, certain specialised courts (such as the Scottish Land Court), and a variety of tribunals (such as the Employment Appeal Tribunal and the Social Security Commissioners). As a court of first instance, it hears 'special cases', that is, certain ones in which the facts are agreed, and only the law is disputed (for example, on the interpretation of a will), and certain petitions, generally purely formal (such as to appoint solicitors as notaries public), but also including those seeking variation of trusts.

Appeal from the Outer House to the Inner House is as of right and is called a reclaiming motion, as one part of the collegiate court is reviewing the decision of another part. Thereafter it is to the House of Lords, provided it is from a final judgment, or the judges were not unanimous, or the Inner House gives leave. Where the appeal originated in the sheriff court, there are restrictions on appeal to the Inner House. It may go thereafter go to the House of Lords on a point of law. The number of appeals (as from other courts) is not large[3].

The Court of Session has the power of judicial review over the decisions of lower courts and tribunals and of government, on grounds of procedural impropriety, such as ultra vires (acting beyond one's powers), or lack of 'natural justice' (for instance, not

1 In early 2003, Lords Macfadyen, Eassie and Clarke had been nominated as commercial judges.
2 In 2000, there were 2,993 actions disposed of in the Outer House, and 98 in the Inner House. By far the biggest category was personal injury actions. There were also 837 petitions disposed of by the Inner House (other than petitions for judicial review, of which there were 141). The biggest single category was sequestration petitions: see *Civil Judicial Statistics Scotland 2000* (Scottish Executive, 2001).
3 In 2000, there were (in addition to the appeals from the sheriff courts, for which, see above), 34 appeals from the Outer House to the Inner House, and 14 from the Inner House to the House of Lords: see *Civil Judicial Statistics Scotland* 2000 (Scottish Executive, 2001).

hearing both sides of the case). This is considered further below in relation to civil procedure.

It can also exercise the *nobile officium* (see Chapter 6).

## Appellate Committee of the House of Lords[1]

Subject always to the decisions of the European Court of Justice on Community law matters, the final court of appeal from civil courts (but not from criminal courts, except in England and Wales and Northern Ireland) is that referred to as 'the House of Lords'. However, it is the Appellate Committee of the House of Lords, comprising a number of judges, which is the actual court. It sits in the Palace of Westminster, that is, the United Kingdom Parliament building in London.

**The court.**  There was no Scottish House of Lords, as Scottish peers did not meet as a separate body. The present House of Lords is descended from the House of Lords of Great Britain, set up in 1707, but which follows the traditions of the English House, which heard appeals from the courts. There was dispute as to whether the new House could hear appeals from Scottish courts, but it quickly assumed jurisdiction[2], and there were many Scottish appeals until the present century. The House of Lords only grew into a professional court in the 19th century, when a convention grew up that lay peers should not sit on appeals, judges were ennobled in order to hear such appeals, and finally the Appellate Committee was set up in 1876.

The Appellate Committee usually sits as a bench of five, in a committee room in the House of Lords, but judgment is given in the Chamber itself.

## Judges of the Appellate Committee of the House of Lords[3]

The Appellate Committee comprises the Lord Chancellor[4],

---

1 It is likely that the Appellate Committee of the House of Lords will be partly amalgamated with the Judicial Committee of the Privy Council and rebranded as a 'Supreme Court': see Appendix Pt II to Preface.
2 The first reported case, *Greenshields v Magistrates of Edinburgh* (1710–11) Rob 12, was in 1710. An Episcopalian minister was imprisoned by the magistrates, at the behest of the Presbytery, for using the Anglican form of service. The Court of Session upheld their decision, but the House of Lords set its stamp on the matter by overturning it.
3 The relevant law is largely found in the Appellate Jurisdiction Act 1876, as amended but see now Appendix I to Preface.
4 In June 2003, Lord Irvine of Lairg resigned and was replaced by Lord Falconer of Thoroton, but with a view to abolition of the post in the near future: see Appendix Part I to Preface.

Lords of Appeal in Ordinary (see below), and any other peers who have held high judicial office. Collectively, but informally, they are referred to as the Law Lords.

Lord Chancellors are members of the government[1]. They are therefore, in some sense, political appointments, and they have been either active members of the ruling party who are legally qualified (such as Lord Hailsham), or persons of distinction in the law who are at least sympathetic to that party's objectives (such as the Conservative Lord Mackay of Clashfern and the Labour Lord Irvine of Lairg). Their tenure therefore depends upon the continued trust of the Prime Minister and the outcome of general elections, so more than one past Lord Chancellor may be available for judicial duties.

Up to 12 Lords of Appeal in Ordinary are appointed as peers for life from among those who have held high judicial office for at least two years, or have been practising advocates (or barristers in England and Wales or Northern Ireland) for 15 years[2]. By convention, at least two are Scottish[3]. Thus, as the House of Lords normally sits as a bench of five, Scottish appeals have usually been heard by a majority of non-Scottish judges. Lords of Appeal in Ordinary are appointed by the Crown on the recommendation of the Prime Minister, but there is, however, no formal selection procedure or scrutiny of appointments[4]. They hold office until the

---

1 The office of Lord Chancellor is a constitutional anomaly, spanning the legislative, executive and judicial branches of government. See Appendix Part I to Preface.

2 A list of their identities is also to be found in the White and Blue Books.

3 In early 2003, they were Lord Hope and Lord Rodger. A retired Lord of Appeal in Ordinary, Lord Clyde, was still eligible to sit. Also, three retired Scottish peers who had held high judicial office were still eligible to sit, that is, Lord Mackay of Clashfern, Lord McCluskey and Lord Cameron of Lochbroom (see text). Those appointed as Lords of Appeal in Ordinary are almost invariably already judges, but Lord Reid of Drem (appointed 1948, retired 1975), who had been both Solicitor-General for Scotland and Lord Advocate (while an MP, thus acquiring no peerage) and Dean of the Faculty of Advocates, was appointed direct from the Bar.

4 The Lord Chancellor's Department paper *Judicial Appointments* (2002) declared that they are 'appointed by the Queen on the recommendation of the Prime Minister, who receives advice from the Lord Chancellor. Before giving advice the Lord Chancellor customarily [sic] consults serving Lords of Appeal in Ordinary and other senior members of the judiciary'. The Judicial Appointments Board has no formal role, nor has the Judicial Appointments Commission in England and Wales (see below). However, see now Appendix Part I to Preface.

age of 70, but remain eligible on a temporary basis up to the age of 75. They remain peers for life, and are salaried[1].

Peers who have high judicial office includes past Lord Chancellors, retired Lords of Appeal in Ordinary, if not disqualified by age, and judges of the Court of Session (and their equivalents in England and Wales and Northern Ireland) who happen to hold peerages[2]. Typically, these are judges who have received peerages through holding some other office attracting a peerage before appointment to the bench, such as Lord McCluskey, a former Solicitor-General for Scotland, and Lord Cameron of Lochbroom, a former Lord Advocate. The availability of such judicial peers is unpredictable[3].

**The work of the Appellate Committee of the House of Lords.** The Appellate Committee is the final court of appeal from the Scottish civil courts (and their equivalents, and the criminal courts, in England and Wales and Northern Ireland). Appeals to it are few[4]. The House of Lords also has a rarely exercised jurisdiction at first instance in cases of impeachment and claims to peerages.

**The Judicial Committee of the Privy Council**[5]

The Privy Council is the surviving remnant of the former English Privy Council, the Privy Council of Scotland having been

1 Judicial Pensions and Retirement Act 1993, s 26. In February 2003, the Senior Salaries Review Board (Cm 5718) recommended that the senior Lord of Appeal in Ordinary (Lord Bingham of Cornhill in early 2003), who has administrative responsibilities, be paid £181,176, and the others £175,055, all with a non-contributory pension. The Lord Chancellor's salary is determined by other means, and has been fixed by legislation at £2,500 more than the Lord Chief Justice of England and Wales (recommended to be £200,236). The effect of the SSRB's recommendation was therefore to give the Lord Chancellor an increase some £22,000 year on year (i e 12.6%). As this was controversial, the Lord Chancellor agreed his salary should be reviewed individually, and the outcome of this review was awaited in early 2003.

2 A list of their identities is to be found in the White and Blue Books. In early 2003, there were seven retired Lords of Appeal in Ordinary who were still eligible to hear appeals and five other retired peers who had held high judicial office and who were still eligible to hear appeals. (Others were ineligible by reason of age.)

3 In early 2003, there were a dozen technically available, including former Lord Chancellors.

4 In 2000, there were 14 appeals initiated from the Inner House to the House of Lords, and 8 disposed of: see *Civil Judicial Statistics Scotland 2000* Scottish Executive (2001). See also Appendix I to Preface

5 The JCPC website is at www.privy-council.org.uk. It is likely that the Judicial Committee of the Privy Council will be amalgamated with the Appellate Committee of the House of Lords, and rebranded as a 'Supreme Court': see Appendix Part I to Preface.

abolished. It was an advisory body to the sovereign at a time when sovereigns wielded real political power. The Privy Council, as such, still has a shadowy existence as a dignified, but not useful, part of the United Kingdom constitution. Membership is a form of honour for certain ministers of the Crown and senior opposition politicians and others. Prerogative Orders in Council (for which, see Chapter 5) which are used for some constitutional legislation are technically Orders of the Sovereign in Privy Council.

However, it has various committees which do have serious functions. For instance, it exercises certain regulatory powers over Scottish Universities through a committee. Another of these committees is the Judicial Committee, set up in 1833, which is in effect a court.

At one time the colonies of the British Empire and later the Commonwealth countries (other than the United Kingdom) had a final right of appeal to the Judicial Committee of the Privy Council, which was thus a sort of central imperial court. Only a few countries and territories retain this right of appeal. They include Trinidad and Tobago, the Bahamas, and Antigua, as well as the Channel Islands and the Isle of Man (which technically are not part of the United Kingdom). Until 1997 (when it was returned to China) there was a small but steady flow of appeals from Hong Kong, but the number of countries using it as their final court of appeal has diminished and this work therefore declined. In addition, the Judicial Committee acts as a final court of appeal from certain professional disciplinary bodies, such as the General Medical Council and the General Dental Council[1].

However, the significance of the Judicial Committee has recently increased considerably under the Scotland Act 1998 in relation to devolution. Firstly, there is a specific power for the Advocate-General for Scotland or the Lord Advocate, during the passage of a Bill through Parliament, to refer to the Judicial Committee the question of whether that Bill is in fact within the Parliament's competence. Secondly, in any case (as discussed above), in relation to 'devolution issues' generally (that is, questions as to whether the Scottish Parliament or Scottish Executive have exceeded their powers) there are various procedures. The issue may be raised by the Advocate-General or the Lord Advocate, as such. They may also be raised by any person adversely affected in any existing proceedings. In either case, the court may decide the issue itself or refer it to the Inner House or the High Court, from which it may

---

1 This source has produced 50–70 cases a year recently.

be appealed to the Judicial Committee[1]. Thus the Judicial Committee has taken on a role as a sort of Constitutional Court in relation to devolution[2].

As it is, strictly speaking, a committee of an advisory body rather than a court, the judgments of the Judicial Committee used to conclude with words tendering advice to the Sovereign in Council. Traditionally, there is a single 'judgment', but occasionally the right to give a dissenting judgment is exercised[3]. In devolution cases, however, the format has followed that of the House of Lords.

The membership of the Judicial Committee is laid down in the Judicial Committee Act of 1833. It comprises all the Lords of Appeal in Ordinary (the House of Lords judges), the Lord Chancellor, Lord Justices of Appeal and any members of the Privy Council who hold or have held high judicial office in the United Kingdom or (save in devolution cases[4]) been judges in the highest courts of those Commonwealth territories from which appeals still go to the Judicial Committee. Appeals are in practice nearly always heard by three or five of the Law Lords and so it is effectively the same court as the Appellate Committee of the House of Lords and can therefore include those trained in Scots law, and presumably always would in relation to a Scottish devolution matter.

*Other courts*

There are several specialised courts of limited jurisdiction.

The Scottish Land Court deals with agricultural tenancies and crofting lands[5]. It has a legally qualified chairman, and four lay members with agricultural experience, including at least one Gaelic speaker. There is appeal on a point of law to the Inner House.

The Restrictive Practices Court is a United Kingdom court, concerned with certain monopolistic practices. One of its judges is a Court of Session judge, who sits with two lay members.

1 Similar powers exist in relation to England and Wales, and parallel ones for Northern Irish devolution. See now, however, Appendix I to Preface.
2 As noted above, by early 2003, some hundreds of devolution issues had been raised, but only a dozen heard by the Judicial Committee, almost all criminal cases referred from or via the High Court. This jurisdiction raised some controversy in relation to the likely amalgamation with the Appellate Committee of the House of Lords as a 'Supreme Court': see Appendix Pt I to Preface.
3 Permitted by the Judicial Committee (Dissenting Opinions) Order 1966, SI 1966/1100.
4 There is, however, no requirement for the Judicial Committee to reflect any balance between the constituent parts of the United Kingdom is a devolution case.
5 In 2000, it disposed of 204 cases: see *Civil Judicial Statistics Scotland 2000* (Scottish Executive, 2001).

There are also the Lands Valuation Appeal Court (concerned with disputes arising out of local rates), the Court of the Lord Lyon (concerned with heraldry), the Court of Teinds (concerned with teinds, or tithes), the Registration of Voters Appeal Court, and the Election Petition Court. The Lands Tribunal (concerned with compensation for compulsory purchase of lands, and the 'right to buy' council houses), is presided over by a judge, so is a court in all but name.

## Judicial Appointments Board for Scotland[1]

After a consultation exercise in 2000, and brief use of an ad hoc formal Selection Board, the Judicial Appointments Board for Scotland was set up in 2001[2]. Its creation marked a very big change in the method of appointment[3]. It receives guidance from ministers, but decides its own procedure. Its function is to provide the First Minister with a list of candidates recommended for appointment as judge of the Court of Session, sheriff principal, sheriff or part-time sheriff (but not justices of the peace) and to do so on merit while considering ways of making representative recommendations. The Board comprises a lay Chair, four lay members, a Court of Session judge, a sheriff principal, a sheriff, an advocate and a solicitor[4].

---

1 The Judicial Appointments Board for Scotland's website is at www.judicial appointmentsscotland.gov.uk. It includes downloadable application forms.
2 In England and Wales, the Judicial Group of the Lord Chancellor's Department (LCD) is responsible for judicial appointments: see *Judicial Appointments* (which is very detailed) and *Judicial Appointments – Annual Reports* (which give enormous amounts of information) at the LCD website at www.lcd.gov.uk/. There is also now a Commission for Judicial Appointments which acts as a sort of ombudsman for the system.
3 Formerly, appointment procedure for judges and sheriffs was very opaque, and the Lord Advocate played a highly influential role: see Stott *Lord Advocate's Diary* (1991), pp 173, 195.
4 In early 2003, the Chair was Sir Neil McIntosh (a retired senior local government official); the lay members were Barbara Duffner (a personnel specialist), Sir Robert Smith (a businessman), a legal academic (Prof Alan Paterson), and an academic administrator (Prof Joan Stringer); the judge, Lord MacLean; the sheriff principal, Sheriff Principal Bruce Kerr; the sheriff, Sheriff Douglas Allan; the advocate, Colin Campbell QC; and the solicitor, Michael Scanlan.

**Judicial Studies Committee[1]**

Until recently, there was no training and professional development for sheriffs and judges. Since 1997, however, there has been a Judicial Studies Committee to provide this. The Committee comprises two judges, a sheriff principal and three sheriffs (one of whom is Director of Judicial Studies), an advocate, a solicitor and a civil servant from the Justice Department of the Scottish Executive[2]. It organises induction courses for sheriffs and judges, refresher courses and seminars on specific topics, and publishes an annual report.

## COURT PROCEDURE[3]

With few exceptions, all court proceedings are public. The Lord President and sheriffs principal have given permission for television cameras to be used in court in limited circumstances. These are, broadly, that the programme is educational or documentary, that the proceedings do not show witnesses or juries, that proceedings are not disrupted, that the presiding judge approves (and he may set further conditions), and that the parties approve[4].

### Civil procedure

Most civil disputes are settled out of court, because litigation is slow, expensive and uncertain (though a private settlement may be adopted by the court at the request of the parties). Decisions of courts affect such settlements, as they show how the dispute might be determined if it were litigated, and litigation may be started as a threat to induce settlement

---

1 The Judicial Studies Committee website is at www.judicialstudies_ scotland.org.uk. For the Judicial Studies Board for England and Wales, see www.jsboard.co.uk, and see also the European Judicial Training Network site at www.etjn.net.
2 In early 2003, they were Lords Wheatley and Philip, Sheriff Principal Nicholson, and Sheriffs Brian Kearney, AL Stewart and NMP Morrison (Director of Judicial Studies), John Sturrock QC, Graeme Warner WS, and J Gallagher.
3 Most of the relevant law is in the Sheriff Courts (Scotland) Act 1907, Act of Sederunt (Small Claim Rules) 2002, SI 2002/133, Act of Sederunt (Summary Cause Rules) 2002, SI 2002/132, Ordinary Cause Rules 1993, SI 1993/1956, Court of Session Act 1988 and Rules of the Court of Session 1965, SI 1965/321.
4 See 1992 SLT (News) 249 and 332.

Civil procedure is (like criminal) usually adversarial. That means, broadly, that the judge does not actively seek to discover what happened and what the law is on the subject, but leaves it to the parties to put their best case before him. Thus, in this context, the person who initiates the case (the pursuer), bears the burden of proof (which is on the balance of probabilities) and puts before the court the evidence and arguments he considers appropriate to support his case, and to entitle him to a remedy. The person called upon to answer the claim (the defender), may put his evidence and arguments to show why a remedy should not be granted. The judge is referee, intervenes little, and decides if the pursuer has proved his case.

The precise procedure depends upon the remedy sought and the court used. In most forms, the pursuer initiates matters by issue of a summons or initial writ, specifying the parties and the remedy sought. The defender must reply to this or risk judgment against him in default. Most proceedings are not defended, so the pursuer may not have to prove his case.

Where proceedings are defended, there may be written pleadings, that is, answers by the defender to the pursuer's claims, to specify more closely the facts and law in dispute. When these are complete, the proceedings continue in court in order to determine the result. These proceedings may be a proof in the case of disputed facts (or possibly, in the Court of Session, a jury trial with a jury of 12), and a debate in the case of disputed law.

Proof depends upon witnesses and other evidence. Witnesses are examined in chief by the side which calls them, and cross-examined by the other side. Examination in chief is designed to bring out the witness's story in his own words. Cross-examination is designed to cast doubt upon it, and may do so by asking leading questions; that is, questions suggesting an answer. In legal debate, the parties' lawyers argue as to what the applicable law is, which requires them to refer to relevant sources of law such as Acts of Parliament and precedents.

There may be proof before answer, whereby facts are determined before legal debate, and pleas to the relevancy, in which the defender argues that even if the facts are true, they do not entitle the pursuer to the remedy sought[1]. Commonly, a judge will not

---

1 Thus, in the celebrated *Donoghue v Stevenson* 1932 SC(HL) 31, 1932 SLT 317, the presence of the snail in the bottle was never admitted or proved. Stevenson's argument was that, even if there were a snail, it did not entitle Mrs Donoghue to any remedy from him.

give an *ex tempore* judgment, but 'take it to *avizandum*', that is take time for consideration.

Decisions by the judge on matters which arise as the case proceeds are called interlocutors. At the end of the proceedings the judge states his findings of fact and law, and justifies his decision. This leads to the final interlocutor in which, if he upholds the pursuer's claim, he grants decree against the defender and authorises enforcement.

The principal forms of adversarial civil procedure are small claims, summary cause, and ordinary procedure in the sheriff court, and Court of Session procedure[1].

Small claims procedure, a recent attempt at a truly simple and cheap procedure, is for sums less than £750 (excluding aliment claims)[2]. A *pro forma* summons initiates procedure, but thereafter it is largely at the sheriff's discretion, and intended to be informal. It may not be in practice, as complicated questions of law may arise and be dealt with by sheriffs in strict legal fashion.

Summary cause procedure, an earlier attempt at simplicity, is for sums between £750 and £1,500[3]. It is more formal (and the actual rules are lengthy and complicated). Nevertheless, many summary causes are straightforward, and the sheriff has a large discretion over procedure.

Ordinary cause procedure and Court of Session procedure are similar. They are much more formal, and there are full written pleadings. The summons must state what are called 'craves' in sheriff court procedure and 'conclusions' in Court of Session procedure (the remedy sought), the 'condescendence' (facts averred) and the 'pleas-in-law' (rules and principles which, applied to those facts, entitle the pursuer to a remedy). The defender enters formal defences, and these claims and counterclaims form the 'open record', which is adjusted (amended) by the parties to identify the points of agreement and, as closely as possible, the issue between them, resulting in the 'closed record', upon which any proofs or debate proceed. This process may take months.

The delays and lack of expertise associated with the court were identified in the Coulsfield Report of 1993, as leading members of the commercial community begin to resort to arbitration or the

---

1 These are found in updated form in the annual *Parliament House Book*.
2 For the number of small claims, see above in relation to the sheriff court. The great majority are raised by large businesses, such as mail order companies and public utilities, against individuals (*Small Claims in the Sheriff Court in Scotland* (Scottish Office Central Research Unit Papers, 1991)).
3 For the number of summary causes, see above in relation to the sheriff court.

English courts to settle their disputes. In 1994, by the simple device of amending the Rules of Court, a simplified commercial procedure was provided, though still within the Court of Session. Three judges are allotted to this work[1]. They take a proactive role in helping the parties to set out what they agree on and narrow the area of dispute. The procedure is informal, often around a table, without wigs and gowns.

In addition to these proceedings of an adversarial nature, which are usually contentious, there are also the usually non-contentious petition procedures. There is a large number of types of petition. Very many are of a formal nature, such as those seeking appointment of a trustee where a trust lacks one, and like cases). Others concern the dissolution of companies and sequestration of bankrupts. Others yet, involving contentious issues, include seeking interdict, an order forbidding a person or persons from acting in an unlawful way.

One form of petition (noted above in relation to the Court of Session) that deserves particular mention is 'judicial review'. In a nutshell, judicial review is a procedure whereby the Court of Session exercises its 'supervisory jurisdiction' over government departments and local authorities and other 'official' decision-takers. It is not an appeal, but a procedure whereby the court is asked to quash the decision because it was taken in a wrong fashion. Typical examples are decisions taken ultra vires (acting beyond one's powers), or with a lack of 'natural justice' (for instance, not hearing both sides of the case). It has become a powerful remedy against improper government action.

*Remedies*

The most common remedies are an order to pay a sum owed (such as the price under a contract); specific implement (an order requiring a person to carry out a legal obligation other than payment of money); damages (an order to pay compensation, such as for injury done); declarator (a declaration that an individual or corporate body has a specific right or duty, such as that a local authority is obliged to house a homeless person); interdict (an order forbidding the commission of a wrong, such as publishing a defamatory statement); reduction (an order nullifying a document,

---

1 In early 2003, Lord Macfadyen full-time and Lords Eassie and Clarke part-time.

such as an invalid will); aliment (an order to give financial support to dependants); divorce; and adoption.

There is also a large number of specific remedies under statute for specific circumstances. The Court of Session may provide a remedy in exceptional and unforeseen circumstances (the *nobile officium*).

## *Appeal*

It is possible to appeal against almost every decision taken at first instance, and often thereafter further appeal is possible. Appeals are nevertheless a small proportion of cases heard[1].

Appeals may be on both law and fact, but are often limited to points of law, in part because of the difficulty of reopening the facts, for appeal is never by way of a complete rehearing (although appeal from a jury trial may be by way of a new trial).

An appeal court can usually affirm the decision below, substitute its own judgment, or remit the case to the lower court for further procedure (such as proof) or final decision in the light of the appeal court's judgment.

## *Diligence and expenses*

A court's order is usually obeyed. If it is not, the pursuer can do diligence, that is enforce it. There are many forms of diligence. Most common are charges (formally requiring payment) and arrestment (arresting a debtor's funds held by a third party such as a bank). The former method of 'warrant sale', technically 'poinding' (pronounced 'pinding') and sale (whereby sheriff-officers, or, if decree is from the Court of Session, messengers-at-arms, removed and might sell the debtor's moveable property) has been repealed and replaced by 'debt arrangement and attachment'. Diligence is also possible against heritable property by inhibition (forbidding sale of it), followed by adjudication, that is, its transfer to the creditor. Exceptionally there can even be diligence against the person, that is, imprisonment for debt, although this is available only for aliment, and is very rare.

Courts generally have discretion to award expenses, and usually the losing party is required to pay the judicial expenses of the winning party (that is, those in connection with the action).

1 See relevant references in relation to individual courts.

**Criminal procedure**[1]

Criminal proceedings are held in public, but the judge, by s 92(3) of the Criminal Procedure (Scotland) Act 1995, is entitled to exclude all those not immediately involved in cases of rape and the like.

*The public prosecution system*[2]

Criminal proceedings are almost always brought by the Crown through the public prosecution system. Private prosecutions are possible with the consent of the Lord Advocate, failing which, if brought by someone with a direct interest, with the consent of the court, but are extremely rare.

The Lord Advocate, assisted by the Solicitor-General for Scotland[3], is in charge of public prosecutions, through the Crown Office[4] , which is effectively the headquarters of the Procurator Fiscal Service.

In district and sheriff courts, prosecutions are brought by the Procurator Fiscal Service[5]. Previously organised on the basis of the six sheriffdoms, the Procurator Fiscal Service is now organised on the basis of the eight police forces, save that Strathclyde is divided into four, giving a total of eleven areas. Each of these has an area procurator fiscal who administers the service within that area and is the procurator fiscal for the sheriff court district in which he is. Prosecution is carried out by depute procurators fiscal[6].

In the High Court of Justiciary, prosecutions are brought by Advocates-Depute (alias 'Crown counsel') or, on occasion, the Lord Advocate or the Solicitor-General for Scotland in person.

---

1 The relevant law is largely found in the Criminal Procedure (Scotland) Act 1995.
2 The Crown Office and Procurator Fiscal website is at www.crownoffice. gov.uk.
3 These offices are discussed above.
4 The Crown Office is situated in Chambers Street, Edinburgh. It produces annual reports, a guide to its work, and its prosecution code. At the beginning of the 21st century, it was undergoing considerable change. An inspectorate is also planned.
5 For a description of the Procurator Fiscal Service, see the Crown Office and Procurator Fiscal Service website and annual reports.
6 The identity of area procurators fiscal, and all deputes, can be found on the Crown Office website and under the relevant sheriff court districts in the White and Blue Books.

Advocates-Depute are advocates employed (temporarily and part-time) to prosecute on the Crown's behalf[1].

## Public defenders

In 1998, in response to the rising cost of criminal legal aid, a Public Defence Solicitor's Office was set up as a five-year pilot scheme in Edinburgh, covering district court and sheriff court cases (see Chapter 7)[2].

## Procedure[3]

Criminal proceedings are (like civil) generally adversarial. Thus, it is not the judge who seeks to discover if there has been a crime or not[4]. It is for the prosecution to decide what crime it considers may have been committed, and it bears the burden of proof (which is beyond reasonable doubt). It therefore seeks and presents to the court the evidence it considers sufficient to prove it. The defence generally need prove nothing, but is entitled to have the case against it proved, to cast doubt on prosecution evidence, and to bring evidence if it chooses. Indeed, it may move that 'there is no case to answer' at the end of the prosecution evidence, seeking to have the case dismissed for want of proper evidence. The judge is referee and intervenes little. He charges the jury if there is one, that is, reminds them of the main evidence presented and instructs them on the applicable law. It is, however, entirely for the jury to decide what conclusions they draw from the facts, and thus whether the prosecution has proved its case.

The two forms of criminal procedure are summary and solemn. Most common law offences are triable by either procedure. Statutory offences are declared by statute to be triable by one or both. The district court uses only summary procedure, the sheriff court both, and the High Court only solemn.

In both forms the prosecution must serve on the accused a precise accusation, to which he pleads guilty or not guilty. If he

1 There were in early 2003 over 20 Advocates-Depute. Their identities are given in the White and Blue Books. There are now to be three categories: Senior Advocates – Depute, Advocates – Depute, and Ad Hoc Advocates – Depute.
2 The Public Defence Solicitor's Office website is at www.pdso.demon.co.uk.
3 In 2003, a Court Reform Bill was promised and a White Paper published, intending to alter aspects of solemn procedure (see below), including the 110 day rule. This followed the Bonomy report (see above).
4 Continental systems tend to use inquisitorial procedure, whereby a judge actively pursues the investigation.

pleads not guilty, a later date is fixed for trial. The trial may require facts to be proved, and law to be determined. These are done in essentially the same way as in civil proceedings, although the burden of proof, which is on the prosecutor, is higher ('beyond reasonable doubt'), and the accused must generally be present. Facts are proved by evidence, from witnesses and otherwise, and the law is determined by argument. After evidence has been given, the prosecution and defence address the court. At the end of the trial, the accused may be found guilty, not guilty, or the charge is not proven. A verdict of not proven is equivalent to an acquittal, and an acquitted person may not be retried. If found guilty, before sentence is passed, a list of previous convictions (if any) is produced by the prosecutor, and any plea in mitigation (that is, information tending to suggest a lenient sentence should be passed) is made by the defence.

In summary proceedings, the procurator fiscal details the charge in a complaint. The accused may appear in court to plead to this, but in many cases will plead by letter or be represented by a solic-itor instead of appearing. If he pleads not guilty, a later date is fixed for trial, which is conducted before a sheriff, justice of the peace or stipendiary magistrate, without a jury. If found guilty, the court sentences him.

In solemn procedure, the procurator fiscal drafts a petition alleging a named person committed a specified crime, and requesting authority to arrest him. The accused appears before the sheriff in private for a brief first examination. Usually no plea or declaration is made and the accused is released on bail or committed in custody for trial (in which case, the trial must begin within 110 days). There may be further judicial examination before the sheriff in which the prosecutor may put a limited range of ques-tions to the accused, to discover if he is going to use certain defences, or concerning any alleged confession. The accused is not on oath, and can decline to reply. The prosecutor then drafts the indictment detailing the charges upon which the accused will be tried (which is served upon the accused) and decides if the case is to go to a sheriff or the High Court. In either case there will be a jury. There may then be a preliminary diet, if the accused objects to the competency or relevancy of the indictment; for example, arguing that the facts alleged in the indictment disclose no crime known to the law, as happened in *Khaliq v HM Advocate* 1984 JC 23 where the accused were charged with supplying glue-sniffing kits to children.

The trial diet follows on similar principles to that in summary proceedings, but after the evidence and the addresses by the prosecution and defence, the judge charges the jury (as described above) before they retire to consider their verdict.

*Guilty pleas*

However, the great majority of those charged, whether under summary or solemn procedure, are not tried, because they plead guilty, usually at an early stage. (Indeed, if this were not so, the courts could not cope.) This plea may result from plea negotiation, an informal procedure whereby the accused, through his agent, agrees with the Crown to plead guilty (so there is a conviction), but only to some charges, amended charges, or lesser charges (so he may expect a lesser sentence). The court takes no part in this negotiation.

*Diversion schemes*

The pressure upon the criminal courts has led to diversion from prosecution schemes[1]. The police may make a conditional offer of a fixed penalty to the accused in certain minor road traffic offences[2], and a procurator fiscal may do so in certain other offences triable in the district court[3]. Accepting it avoids going to court and risking a higher penalty on conviction. However, it may be declined, and the accused may be summoned to court and there seeks acquittal. These are popularly referred to as 'fiscal fines'. They are separate from other diversion schemes, such as the fixed penalty notice for parking and similar offences, whereby a traffic warden affixes a notice to an illegally parked car, rendering the owner liable to a fine.

In any case, it has long been accepted that fiscals are able to issue directly, or through the police, a formal warning, which is not

1 Thus, the vehicle defect rectification scheme deals with 30,000 road traffic offences a year; police fixed penalty conditional offers with another 175,000; and there is an unknown number of police warnings, references to other agencies and cases dealt with by detecting agencies (such as the Television Licensing Authority) all without their being reported to the procurator fiscal. Of the 284,141 crimes and offences reported to procurators fiscal in 2001, there were procurator fiscal warnings in 20,333 cases, 'fiscal fines' in 18,855 cases; procurator fiscal fixed penalty conditional offers for motor vehicles offences in 7,548 cases; other forms of diversion in 1,057 cases; and simple 'no pros' (that is, a decision not to prosecute or do anything else) in 42,898 cases: *Scottish Executive Statistical Bulletin: Criminal Justice Series* CRJ/2002/9 (December 2002).

2 At the time of publication the offer was £60 for an endorsable offence and £30 for any other: Fixed Penalty Order 2000, SI 2000/2792.

3 At the time of publication, the offer was £25, £50, £75 or £100: Criminal Procedure (Scotland) Act 1995, ss 302, 303.

recorded as a conviction. Fiscals may also divert cases to social work or psychiatric services. Further, a fiscal is always entitled to decide not to prosecute although there appears to be sufficient evidence, if the offence is trivial, or it is otherwise not in the public interest to prosecute.

*Penalties*

The principal penalties are: a fine (unlimited, or to a maximum permitted by statute); admonition (a warning); imprisonment or detention in a young offenders' institution; a community service order; probation; and a compensation order in favour of the victim, which may be combined with another penalty[1]. Imprisonment or a supervised attendance order (requiring attendance at a certain place for some form of training) can be imposed to replace an unpaid fine.

Sentence is often deferred. This may be a brief deferral of, normally, some three weeks for social background, psychiatric, or other reports, or a lengthy one (such as six months) for good behaviour or restitution to a victim. In the latter case, it is in effect a sentence in itself, as the penalty is likely to be reduced if there has been good behaviour or restitution of property stolen or damaged.

*Appeals and the Scottish Criminal Cases Review Commission*[2]

A person convicted after summary procedure may appeal as of right to the High Court of Justiciary sitting as an appeal court by stated case[3] on the ground of miscarriage of justice. If convicted after trial, he may appeal against conviction and/or sentence; if after a guilty plea, against sentence only. He may seek to introduce

1 In 2001, there were 75,643 fines (63% of all disposals); 12,225 imprisonments (10%); 11,975 admonitions (10%); 8,171 probation orders (7%); 4,869 community service orders (4%); 4,228 committals to young offenders institutions (4%); and 1,138 compensation orders (1%). The proportion varies enormously with the offence, of course. The total number of court disposals has dropped considerably in recent years with the growth of alternatives to prosecution, such as 'fiscal fines'. The proportion of fines and admonitions has therefore dropped, and the proportion of imprisonment therefore risen. See *Scottish Executive Statistical Bulletin: Criminal Justice Series* CRJ/2002/9 (December 2002).
2 The Scottish Criminal Cases Review Commission website is at www.sccrc.co.uk.
3 In a stated case, the charges are listed and procedure outlined, and the judge lists the facts he found, or were admitted, indicates the reasons for his decision, and asks a question such as 'On the facts admitted or proved, was I entitled to convict the accused?'.

new evidence unavailable at trial, but this is rare. He may also appeal by way of a bill of suspension on the ground of procedural irregularity.

The prosecutor may also appeal, on a point of law only, against conviction or sentence by stated case or, on the ground of procedural irregularity, by bill of advocation.

A person convicted after solemn procedure (again whether by guilty plea or trial) may appeal in like terms, save that the appeal is usually by note of appeal. The prosecutor may not appeal at all against conviction, but after conviction on indictment, the Lord Advocate may appeal against sentence on the grounds of undue leniency.

The High Court is entitled to dismiss an appeal and affirm the verdict and sentence, quash a conviction, substitute conviction of a lesser offence, or impose a lesser or (unless appeal was against conviction only) a heavier sentence. It may authorise a retrial but is unlikely to do so if there was any fault on the part of the prosecution or the evidence was weak. It is for the Crown within two months to decide whether to prosecute again.

Two other procedures exist which are related to appeals. Both have been used, but rarely. Firstly, the Lord Advocate may refer any question of law which has arisen in a trial by solemn procedure resulting in an acquittal to the High Court for an opinion. This is not an appeal, so cannot overturn the acquittal, but the person acquitted may appear, and the High Court can give an authoritative view on the point of law.

Secondly, the Secretary of State may refer a case to the High Court, whether or not there has been appeal, to be heard as if it were an appeal. This is appropriate where new evidence emerges after an appeal.

In addition, the Scottish Criminal Cases Review Commission[1] has powers to refer a case to the High Court for re-consideration after the appeal process has been exhausted (or, exceptionally, where it was not invoked). A person concerned may refer a conviction or sentence to the Commission, and it decides whether or not to accept such application. If it does accept it, the Commission receives any representations, and may make its own inquiries through its staff (and this may involve interviewing witnesses and taking evidence on oath, and using the services of expert advisers) as well as examining the trial and appeal papers. It only refers the

---

1 Set up in 1999 under powers in the Criminal Procedure (Scotland) Act 1995, and sitting in Glasgow with seven members.

matter to the High Court if it believes a miscarriage of justice has occurred and that it is in the interests of justice to make the reference. This might be because of new evidence which has emerged since the appeal[1]. If the Commission does not refer the case, it gives its reasons to the applicant. If it does refer the case, it gives its reasons to the High Court, copied to the applicant and Crown Office. However, the Commission does not represent the applicant in the High Court re-consideration, which is conducted much as an ordinary appeal. Thus the applicant requires to obtain representation (for which legal aid will be available) or conduct it himself[2]. The Commission publishes an annual report.

*Expenses*

Generally speaking, criminal courts cannot award expenses. The expenses of prosecution are paid by the prosecution. Those of the defence are usually paid from criminal legal aid.

**Tribunals**[3]

In modern times the state has entered into, or extended, numerous legal relationships with its citizens. Personal taxation and social security are two obvious examples. These give rise to legal rights and duties, on which disputes may arise. These disputes might have been entrusted to the courts, like any other justiciable issues. But courts would have been swamped by the number of such disputes and arguably forced to change in character to cope. They might have been left to the government departments concerned to decide internally at a higher level. But that would have contravened the principle of 'natural justice', that no-one should be judge in his

---

1 There are 'case-studies' available on the Commission's website, giving an indication of how the Commission works and what sorts of cases might be successful.

2 In the first three full years of operation, the Commission received 304 cases, and concluded consideration of 164 of them. It referred 17 of these to the High Court, which had determined 4 of them: *Boncza-Tomaszewski (aka Fraser) v HM Advocate* 2000 SCCR 657 (in which the High Court concluded there had been a miscarriage of justice), *Crombie v Clarke* 2001 SCCR 231 (in which it did not), *Dalton v HM Advocate* (3 May 2001, unreported) and *Gibson v Heywood* (12 June 2001, unreported).

3 The Council on Tribunals' (see below) website is at www.council-on-tribunals.gov.uk.

own cause. So in fact a new type of decision-making body has been devised. They are independent and impartial like the courts, but less formal and more accessible. These are the tribunals.

Tribunals are now enormously varied in subject-matter, extent and degree of formality. Among those that cover major areas, Social Security Appeal Tribunals deal with disputes over all kinds of benefits, except ones for the disabled, for which specialised Disability Appeal Tribunals were set up in 1992. The General Commissioners and the Special Commissioners of Income Tax deal with disputes on matters of personal taxation. National Health Service Tribunals and Service Committees handle complaints by patients against medical and related practitioners. These could affect any citizen. Others affect only people in special occupations and capacities, such as the Police Appeals Tribunal for Scotland which handles appeals by constables against dismissal and other penalties, and the Immigration Tribunal system which hears appeals from individuals refused entry into the United Kingdom and related decisions.

Although most tribunals stem from central government functions, a few relate to local authority activities. Housing Benefit Review Boards deal with questions about entitlement to or the amount of housing benefit, and Education Appeal Committees were set up to hear complaints arising out of parents' requests that their children be placed in a certain school.

The tribunal format has been extended to situations where private citizens are in dispute with each other or with a company or other corporate body. Industrial Tribunals were set up under the Industrial Training Act 1964 to handle questions arising from the imposition of levies on employers to help finance schemes of training in particular industries such as haulage contracting. In this and other roles they were so successful that in 1971 they were extended to claims for compensation for unfair dismissal brought by ex-employees against employers. This remains their largest type of business but, under various Acts of Parliament, and now called Employment Tribunals, they have about 15 kinds of jurisdiction, including complaints of discrimination on grounds of gender or marital status, of failure to give equal pay, to supply written particulars of a contract of employment, to make a redundancy payment and to give time off work to safety representatives. Another private relationship in which tribunals are involved, though now less so than in the past, is that between landlord and tenant. Rent Assessment Committees establish fair rents when the parties cannot agree on them.

*Characteristics*

Since tribunals have such diverse functions it is not easy to generalise about their characteristics. Moreover, the strengths of some of
them have been somewhat weakened with the passage of time.
However, there would be general agreement that the following
features are among the advantages of most kinds of tribunal and
are in fact exhibited in most of them.

**Informality.** In comparison with courts all tribunals are
informal. At some, such as Children's Hearings and Social
Security Appeal Tribunals, all the participants sit round a table and
a relaxed discussion is encouraged, though not always achieved.
Employment (formerly Industrial) Tribunals, have become
increasingly formal. The chairman and members sit on a raised
dais, and evidence by the parties and witnesses they have
summoned is usually given on oath and always subject to cross-
examination. The Lands Tribunal for Scotland is also formal in its
layout and presided over by a judge of Court of Session rank.

**Representation.** Informality tends to be eroded by the participation of lawyers accustomed to the procedure of courts. Employers
in Employment Tribunal cases usually find it worthwhile to employ
a lawyer; and appeals to the Employment Appeal Tribunal, which
is chaired by a Court of Session judge, and from there to the
courts, are not infrequent. This means that judgments by
Employment Tribunal chairmen have to be fully supported in law
and in facts established in evidence. It also means that case law
from the courts and Employment Appeal Tribunal feeds back into
the tribunals and will be invoked by lawyers there.

On the other hand, lawyers scarcely ever appear before
Children's Hearings or Social Security Appeal Tribunals, which
have remained relatively informal. But people appearing before
them are allowed and encouraged to bring a friend or relative to
help them bring out the points they wish to make. More formal
representation is given by appropriate non-lawyers before some
tribunals, such as a trade union official at an Employment
Tribunal. A guidance teacher might accompany a child at a
Children's Hearing. Some Citizens Advice Bureaux also offer help
at the less formal tribunals.

**Cheapness.** Unlike civil courts, where a fee usually has to be paid
to initiate proceedings, tribunals are almost entirely free. Unlike
courts again, the loser does not have to pay the winner's expenses.

A minor exception is in Employment Tribunal procedure. If a party has acted frivolously, vexatiously or otherwise unreasonably (on which there may have been a finding at a pre-hearing assessment of the case) then he may be ordered to pay the other side's expenses, which might include the fees of the employer's lawyer.

**Speed.** Tribunals are intended to provide a rapid settlement of disputes. Unfortunately, for a variety of reasons, they do not always fulfill that expectation. As in courts, one side may use delaying tactics in the hope that the opponent will give up or evidence may be lost. In tribunals dealing with social security benefits, upsurges in claims and cuts in staffing can produce long delays. Thus, claims for the disability living allowance introduced in 1992 far exceeded expectations and led to the operation of disability appeal tribunals being held up and thus decisions being subject to long delay.

**Specialisation.** All tribunals are specialised to some extent, some highly so. Thus, there is at one extreme the National Appeal Panel for Entry to the Pharmaceutical Lists (which received 18 cases in 2001–02). Others cover a range of related questions, such as the Employment Tribunals which handle nearly all disputes arising in the workplace and involving individuals (and received 10,240 cases in Scotland in 2001–02). Thus, people with relevant background knowledge can be appointed to sit on tribunals and, given a sufficient flow of cases, can apply and extend that knowledge in contentious situations. So the part-time lay members of Employment Tribunals are appointed from panels nominated by organisations representative of employers and of employees, in Scotland, the CBI and the STUC. Disability Appeal Tribunals have a medically qualified member and one with knowledge or experience of the needs of disabled people.

*Legal authority*

Despite the appearance of informality of many of them, tribunals are vested with legal powers, just as much as are courts. The rules of law which they apply can be very complex, especially in the social security area. Their decisions are just as enforceable as court decrees and sentences. Appeal to the courts on a point of law is usually possible, as is judicial review by the Court of Session, that is, an inquiry on the adequacy of the procedure, but both are uncommon. In their conduct of cases, tribunals are bound to observe the same broad standards of fairness to all parties as courts. They must clearly state their decisions in writing, usually amplified by their findings on the facts and the reasons for the decision (in the case of Children's Hearings, only if requested to do so).

For all these reasons nearly all tribunals are now presided over by a legally qualified chairman. (One conspicuous exception is Children's Hearings.) For example, Employment Tribunal chairmen must be solicitors or advocates of at least seven years' standing.

There is a danger that lawyer-chairmen may come to dominate the proceedings, unless the lay members have the confidence to make their own distinctive contribution.

*Supervision*

In their early days each tribunal was set up on an ad hoc basis, usually on the initiative of a government department. It could thus come under the influence of the department and conform to its expectations. The department's ascendancy could be exacerbated when it appointed the chairman and members, as was the case with the now extinct National Insurance Appeal Tribunals and Supplementary Benefit Appeal Tribunals. In 1957, the Franks Committee[1] urged that common standards of openness, fairness and impartiality should be observed by all tribunals. It scrutinised the mode of appointment and procedure of all the then tribunals and made recommendations for improvement. To provide a permanent form of supervision the Committee proposed a Council on Tribunals.

Such a Council, with a Scottish Committee, was set up and now operates under the Tribunals and Inquiries Act 1992[2]. It is consulted by departments and other bodies setting up or changing tribunals and sees the draft statutory instruments authorising them[3]. It also pays visits to tribunals and inquiries. However, since

1 *Report of the Committee on Administrative Tribunals and Enquiries* (1957) (Cmnd 218).
2 Its Statement of Purposes includes ensuring that tribunals and inquiries are: open, fair and impartial; accessible to users; have the needs of users as their primary focus; offer cost effective procedures; are properly resourced and organ-ised; and are responsive to the needs of all sectors of society: see *Council on Tribunals Annual Report 2001–02*. (The Scottish Committee seems more generous: see *Council on Tribunals Scottish Committee Annual Report 2001–02*.)
3 It has issued Model Rules of Procedure for Tribunals (Cm 1434) which in early 2003 it was updating.

it has some 70 tribunals and comparable bodies such as the Civil Aviation Authority (which grants licences) under its supervision (of which some are under the direct supervision of its Scottish Committee), plus office-holders such as the Data Protection Registrar and the Director General of Fair Trading[1], visits to any single tribunal are few and far between. It does not have power to correct individual complaints, but these may indicate a failure to follow procedures which can be taken up with the organisation concerned.

Many tribunals are organised on a Great Britain or United Kingdom basis. But a few, such as Children's Hearings, the Crofters Commission and the Lands Tribunal for Scotland, are peculiarly Scottish. Others such as Employment Tribunals, Pensions Appeal Tribunals and Criminal Injuries Compensation Adjudicators, have a Scottish organisation, similar to that operating in England and Wales. The Scottish Committee of the Council of Tribunals supervises these bodies in the same manner as the parent Council. The Committee has fifteen members, all prominent people with a variety of backgrounds and other public appointments (three of whom, together with four other persons, constitute its Scottish Committee) with a staff of a dozen[2]. It operates through four subject-based committees (Education, Social Security, Health and Property & Land) and three general ones (Legal, Standards and Performance, and Training). During 2001–02 they considered some 30 statutory instruments, and paid numerous visits to tribunals and inquiries (including many in Scotland, several to Children's Panel Hearings). Notice is given of the attendance of a member, who writes a report to the Committee. The Scottish Committee also published a special report on Children's Hearings.

*Tribunal performance*

Tribunals are big business. In 2001–02, tribunals and inquires received 1,213,321 cases, and decided 664,267 (many of the difference being withdrawn)[3]. Employment Tribunals decided 29,124 cases; the General Commissioners of Income Tax, 10,743; Immigration Adjudicators, 57,531 (including 1,022 in Scotland);

---

1 Tribunals and Inquiries Act 1992, Sch 1, Pts I and II and *Annual Reports*.
2 For a list of members, see the current annual report of the Council.
3 See *Council on Tribunals Annual Report 2001–02*.

and the Social Security and Pensions Appeals Service, 328,796 (including 42,158 in Scotland)[1].

However, relatively little research has been carried out on their performance. One large-scale piece of work[2] gives the results of a study commissioned by the Lord Chancellor's Department focusing on Social Security Appeal Tribunals, Immigration Adjudicators, Industrial (now Employment) Tribunals and Mental Health Review Tribunals (not found in Scotland). The researchers found that appellants did not regard the tribunals as informal, which they equated with being able to talk freely about the fairness of the decision in question. Instead they found themselves up against incomprehensible law in Social Security Appeal Tribunals and Immigration Adjudications and a formal procedure, with a confident opposing lawyer familiar with it in Industrial Tribunals. In all four tribunals the presence of a representative significantly increased the probability that appellants and applicants would succeed in their cases; but in Industrial (now 'Employment') Tribunals this was dependent on the respondent being unrepresented. In Industrial (now 'Employment') Tribunals, barristers and solicitors had the greatest impact on success, and in Social Security Appeal Tribunals lay agencies specialising in welfare law.

Another report[3], commissioned by the Independent Tribunal Service, reported the same feeling of disappointment at the formality of the proceedings among appellants, who had the additional disadvantage of being disabled and for various reasons found it a stressful experience. They had medical as well as legal jargon to contend with. The average clearance time for all cases in 1990 was 27 weeks, leading to hardship and anxiety for appellants. Representatives found little scope for advocacy skills, but had a useful role in marshalling evidence for the appellant.

It would seem that some formality is inseparable from any system which expresses entitlements in legal form and thus makes them open to disputed interpretation.

1 *Scottish Committee of the Council on Tribunals Annual Report 2001–02; Council on Tribunals Annual Report 2001–02.*
2 Genn and Genn *The Effectiveness of Representation at Tribunals* (1989).
3 Sainsbury *Survey and Report into the Working of Medical Appeal Tribunals* (1992).

*The future*

In 2001, a major review of tribunals operating in England and Wales was undertaken by the government[1]. It made numerous recommendations, summed up as offering a more independent system, a more coherent system, and a more user-friendly system. In particular, appointments to tribunals should be undertaken by the Lord Chancellor, to ensure greater separation between them and the government authority whose policies and decisions are being tested. Further, there should be a single over-arching structure for tribunals in a Tribunals Service. Also, tribunal procedure should be altered to assist users to present their own cases. There were also numerous recommendations in relation to specific tribunals. In early 2003, the government had promised legislation to implement the Report, introducing the largest reform of the tribunal in fifty years. However, it was far from clear how this plan would impact upon Scotland, as the Report was unable to take account of devolution in the time available[2].

## Other related institutions

*Arbitration and alternative dispute resolution*

A popular alternative to litigation in some areas of industry and the professions is arbitration. Indeed, a number of trade and professional bodies have arbitration schemes for their members, including the building and engineering industries, the Scottish Motor Traders' Association, and the Association of British Travel Agents. The Law Society of Scotland also offers an arbitration scheme. Arbitration may also be international, between companies in different countries.

Essentially, arbitration is the submission of a dispute to a private judge (called an arbiter), whose decision is final. The courts are thus largely excluded. Arbitration may have advantages for those in dispute. The matter is disposed of privately and probably more rapidly than in the courts. The award may be a compromise acceptable to all parties, rather than (as commonly occurs in litigation) finding a winner, and thus a loser. No precedent is set for later disputes. The dispute may be on technical matters, so the

---

1 *Tribunals for Users: One System, One Service: report of the review of tribunals by Sir Andrew Leggat* (2001) (the '*Leggat Report*').
2 See *Leggat Report* ch 11 and responses in the *Council on Tribunals Annual Report 2001–02* and *Council on Tribunals Scottish Committee Annual Report 2001–02*.

arbiter can be someone technically qualified. Arbitration may also be cheaper than litigation, although this depends upon the procedure used, which may be quite formal, with the parties legally represented, and a lawyer as arbiter.

Commonly, arbitration is contractual, that is, the parties to a contract have agreed that any dispute arising out of the contract shall be dealt with thus. Probably the contract will be a standard form contract used in such cases, incorporating an arbitration scheme. The arbiter is likely to be identified by office (for example, the president for the time being of a professional association), but may be nominated by the parties. The parties may be able to nominate an arbiter each, in which case there may also be appointed an 'oversman' to determine the matter if the arbiters cannot agree. What disputes can be arbitrated, what procedure followed, and what awards made, are matters for the parties.

Although the aim is to exclude the courts, there is a good deal of law on the subject, and the courts do have a role. For example, an arbiter may be required to 'state a case', that is, to obtain a legal opinion from the Court of Session. Also, although there is no appeal to the courts from the arbitration, the award may be open to challenge on the grounds of procedural irregularity, such as want of honesty or impartiality on the part of the arbiter. Further, an arbiter's award may be enforceable by the courts. International arbitrations are decided under the Model Rules laid down by international agreement by the UN Committee on International Trade Law. There are also statutory arbitration schemes, for example under the Agricultural Holdings (Scotland) Act 1991.

While arbitration is as old as litigation, recently 'alternative dispute resolution' has come to prominence. 'ADR' is said to be widely used in many countries for many types of issue, from commercial to family disputes. Because of this wide usage, however, it is difficult to give exact meaning to the term. It refers to a variety of means of settlement alternative to litigation. These means include a well-known repertoire of processes such as arbitration, conciliation, mediation and negotiation, all of which have accepted semi-technical definitions. The means may also include variations upon, and combinations of, that repertoire (and indeed of litigation as well). Thus, for example, one ADR method is described as 'med-arb' or 'concilio-arb', in which mediation is used, failing which, arbitration[1]. In Scotland the Law Society keeps

1 For a review of ADR, see the memoranda prepared for the English Law Society called 'Alternative Dispute Resolution' (1991) and 'Alternative Dispute Resolution: Second Report' (1992).

a Register of Accredited Mediators called ACCORD. There is also a Group called CALM (Comprehensive Accredited Lawyer Mediators). Family Mediation Scotland supports branches in some parts of Scotland where trained lay volunteers try to bring about agreement mainly on the relationships of divorcing or separated parents with their children.

Because ADR is argued for in such a variety of disputes, it is a matter for discussion which means or combinations of means are appropriate for each dispute. This in turn depends upon the perceived disadvantages of litigation, but these are not the same in all disputes. For example, in a commercial dispute between trading partners of roughly equal power, confidentiality may be all-important to both, and be a reason to avoid litigation, while cost is irrelevant. In one between a consumer and a supplier, however, firstly, the perspectives of the two disputants may be very different from each other, and secondly, from the consumer's point of view, it is cost that may be all-important and a reason to avoid litigation, and confidentiality may be irrelevant. Considerations are yet further different in, say, family disputes. In all cases the possibility of greater speed, however, is usually an advantage.

The significance of ADR probably does not lie in the novelty of the means of dispute resolution that it offers. Arbitration, conciliation and mediation have long been widely used in the United Kingdom in industrial disputes, for example, and were a strongly preferred alternative to litigation until legislation in the 1980s. The Advisory, Conciliation and Arbitration Service (ACAS) is well known and active in the field, and is the descendant of government services set up for this purpose as long ago as the late 19th century.

The significance lies rather in the existence of a conscious search for alternatives to litigation, premised upon a dissatisfaction with litigation, perhaps parallel to that which caused the enormous growth in tribunals a generation ago. This is important to the study of a legal system for it may indicate a declining relevance and use of courts, and the growth of alternative quasi-legal institutions. This particularly affects a legal system reliant upon precedent. It may also have importance in relation to civil liberties, in questions as to how far individuals may seek to use private means of dispute settlement, and whether stronger disputants may be enabled to force weaker ones into unsatisfactory arrangements.

*Ombudsmen*[1]

A method of redressing grievances imported from Scandinavia (via New Zealand) in the last few decades is the ombudsman, that is, an official who is not a judge, but who can examine critically the conduct of officials in a more effective way than could a court or tribunal (though usually only after the complainant has exhausted all other remedies). The first ombudsman, technically called the Parliamentary Commissioner for Administration (PCA), was appointed in 1967 under the Parliamentary Commissioner Act of that year[2].

The PCA is appointed by the Crown, and may be removed only by an address of both Houses of Parliament, so has protection of tenure similar to that of a judge, though most appointees have been civil servants. The PCA is entitled to investigate complaints of injustice resulting from 'maladministration' (a term given a technical meaning) by government departments in the exercise of their administrative functions. Various areas are specifically excluded from oversight, including foreign relations, the investigation of crime, and appointment and discipline within the Civil Service. Nor may the PCA investigate where the complainant has a legal remedy which could reasonably be pursued (such as an appeal against refusal of a benefit). On the other hand, the PCA has powers equivalent to those of the Court of Session to require production of papers and the attendance of witnesses (save in relation to Cabinet proceedings).

A complainant cannot approach the PCA directly, however, but only via an MP, who is not required to pass the complaint on. The PCA's conclusions after investigation are passed back to the MP, though he may also make a special report to Parliament. This indirect approach was the result of MPs' jealousy of Parliament's role as the place where grievances against government are dealt with. Thus, also, the PCA cannot order any remedy where maladministration is found, and it is up to the department concerned what it does. There is a Select Committee which reports to the House of Commons, and

---

1 A directory of Ombudsmen can be found on the British and Irish Ombudsman Association website at www.bioa.org.uk.
2 The PCA website is at www.ombudsman.org.uk. The PCA in early 2003 was Ann Abraham (previously Legal Services Ombudsman for England and Wales, and before that Chief Executive of the National Association of Citizen's Advice Bureaux), who was simultaneously Health Service Ombudsman for England and Wales.

which in practice assists in obtaining a remedy. The PCA issues an annual report and reports on specific issues.

In 2001–02, the PCA received the highest ever number of complaints, at 2,319 (an increase of nearly a quarter over the previous year), and settled 1,988 complaints. A proportion of complaints received each year is clearly outside the PCA's jurisdiction (109 in 2001–02), and in a further substantial number of cases, after consideration of the papers the matter is taken no further, for example because there is no evidence of a continuing injustice to the complainant (812 in 2001–02). Where, after consideration, there does seem to be maladministration producing such injustice, the PCA makes inquiries. Many complaints are settled by this means, whether in favour of the complainant (344 in 2001–02) or otherwise (437 in 2001–02). Others require a statutory investigation, which may result in settlement or in a conclusion that no worthwhile remedy can be given (91 in 2001–02) or in a report which is sent to the MP who initiated the matter and the offending body (195 in 2001–02). Many complaints are received concerning the Department of Work and Pensions (53% in 2001–02), frequently concerning disability- or incapacity-related benefits and non-payment of Child Support Agency payments. Other complaints are spread over a wide range of government departments.

There is also a Scottish Public Services Ombudsman[1], an office set up by the Scottish Public Services Ombudsman Act 2002 to replace the Scottish Parliamentary Ombudsman, the Health Service Ombudsman for Scotland, the Local Government Ombudsman for Scotland, and the Housing Association Ombudsman for Scotland. Consequently, the office covers a very wide range of organisations, including the Scottish Administration, health service bodies, local authorities, and a variety of other governmental bodies from the Audit Commission for Scotland to the Water Industry Commission for Scotland (via the Crofters' Commission, the Parole Board for Scotland and the Scottish Arts Council). It also includes a large number of 'cross-border public authorities', that is, Great Britain or United Kingdom ones, some of whose activities relate to devolved matters, such as the Criminal Injuries Compensation Authority, the National Consumer Council and the Unrelated Live Transplant Regulatory Authority. Also,

---

1 The website of the Scottish Public Services Ombudsman is at www.scottish ombudsman.org.uk. The SPSO is Alice Brown, a political scientist from Edinburgh University, and there are three deputes.

there is a Scottish Legal Services Ombudsman (discussed in Chapter 7)[1].

In addition, there is a UK-wide Financial Ombudsman Service (replacing the former Banking, Building Society, Insurance and Investment Ombudsmen) and Pensions Ombudsman, and several other ombudsmen whose jurisdiction relates to England and Wales only. Some of these schemes are closer to arbitration than to the usual role of an ombudsman.

## Principal English and Welsh courts[2]

### Civil courts

Magistrates' courts are organised on a county basis, with lay justices of the peace assisted by a legally qualified clerk, but also in many urban areas with full-time district judges. They deal with certain family law matters including adoption proceedings (when they are termed 'family proceedings courts'), recovery of charges from public utilities, and act as a licensing court for alcohol licensing.

County courts are found in all major towns. They take a wide variety of civil cases within their areas, subject to certain limitations. District judges may hear cases up to a limited figure, circuit judges hear above that limit, and there are small claims procedures.

The High Court of Justice (not to be confused with the Scottish High Court of Justiciary) sits mainly in London, and comprises three Divisions. These are called, respectively, Queen's Bench (which includes the Commercial Court and the Admiralty Court), with some 80 judges, headed by the Lord Chief Justice (abbreviated to 'LCJ' after his surname: thus 'Lord Woolf LCJ'); Chancery, with some 20 judges headed technically by the Lord Chancellor (LC: thus 'Lord Irvine LC[3]'), but in practice by the Vice-Chancellor (VC: thus 'Sir Robert Morritt VC'); and Family (once known as the Probate, Divorce and Admiralty Division), also with about 20 judges, headed by the President (P: thus 'Dame Elizabeth Butler-Sloss P'). The judges

---

1 The Scottish Legal Services Ombudsman website is at www.slso.org.uk. The SLSO in early 2003 (reappointed till 2006) was Linda Costelloe Baker, a management consultant, formerly member of the Parole Board and the Criminal Injuries Compensation Authority.

2 The Courts Bill 2003 will affect significant changes in the operation of English and Welsh courts.

3 But see now Appendix I to Preface.

without titles are styled 'Mr Justice' ('J', after the surname; 'JJ' in the plural: thus, for instance, 'Bell J'[1]). The High Court takes important civil litigation at first instance, and each Division has a small appeal jurisdiction. This is exercised by two or more judges and is known as the Divisional Court.

The Court of Appeal (Civil Division) chiefly takes appeals from the county courts and from the High Court. It has some 40 judges, called Lords Justices of Appeal (abbreviated to 'LJ' after the surname; 'LJJ' in the plural, and not to be confused with the Lords of Appeal in Ordinary of the House of Lords: thus, for instance, 'Auld LJ'[2]), headed by the Master of the Rolls (MR: thus 'Lord Phillips MR'). They sit in threes, usually.

The House of Lords hears appeals from the Court of Appeal, but also occasionally, with the consent of the parties, on questions of statutory interpretation of general public importance, direct from the High Court.

### Criminal courts

Magistrates' courts, essentially the same courts as for civil purposes, try minor offences, which constitute the overwhelming majority of all criminal cases, with restricted sentencing powers (rather like district courts and sheriff summary courts in Scotland). As the Youth Court, they try those aged between 14 and 17 years (as there is no equivalent to the Children's Hearings). They also act as a court of committal, for which there is no Scottish equivalent. Any serious crime is tried 'on indictment' (roughly similar to solemn procedure) before the Crown Court, but traditionally, the person had first to appear before examining magistrates whose function was to decide if there were a prima facie case against the accused. If they decided there was, the case was committed to the Crown Court for trial. If not, the accused was discharged. However, the unwieldiness of the proceedings means that they are now considerably watered down.

Crown courts (descended from the old 'Assizes' and 'Quarter Sessions') hear more serious criminal cases, including all trials on indictment, and are organised on a circuit basis with several levels of judge (High Court judges, circuit judges and recorders). The courts are organised into three tiers, reflected in the seriousness of the cases they may try. The Old Bailey is the London Crown

---

1 Though English High Court judges are made knights or dames, as appropriate, on appointment, so 'Bell J' is in fact Sir Rodger Bell.
2 Who is in fact Sir Robin Auld.

Court, technically known as the Central Criminal Court. Crown courts also hear appeals from magistrates' courts.

The Court of Appeal (Criminal Division), headed by the Lord Chief Justice, hears appeals against conviction and sentence, and other matters, from the Crown Court, and the House of Lords is the final court of criminal appeal.

# 4. Sources of law

## THE MEANINGS OF 'SOURCES OF LAW'

'Sources of law' is a widely used phrase. It has several meanings, all of which have their importance, and which must be distinguished.

### Historical sources

Legal rules and principles do not spring into existence, fully formed. They have their origins in political, moral and social ideas. Specific pieces of legislation (for example, the Race Relations Act 1976), and fundamental organising legal principles (such as contract), encapsulate such ideas. Thus, any legal provision has historical sources. Chapters 1, 2 and 8 look further at the process by which such ideas become law.

### Formal sources

The most common use of the phrase 'sources of law' relates to the form in which the law appears. The formal sources of any legal system will be specific to it. Thus, the formal sources of Scots law are not identical to those of English law, and a good deal more different from those of, say, French law. The formal sources of Scots law are conventionally divided into major and minor, reflecting their relative importance.

The major formal sources can be said to be:

(a) legislation, including:
- Acts of the United Kingdom Parliament, two of which, the Human Rights Act 1998 and the European Communities Act 1972, have special status;
- laws made by Ministers of the Crown and others under powers delegated by the United Kingdom Parliament;

- Acts of the Scottish Parliament also made under powers delegated by the United Kingdom Parliament;
- laws made by Scottish Ministers, again under powers delegated by the United Kingdom Parliament; and
- European Community legislation of various types;

(b) precedent (rules produced by courts without reference to Parliament or any other legislature).

The minor formal sources can be said to be:

(a) prerogative legislation (remnants of the former power of the Crown, now exercised by the government, some of them being legislative in form);
(b) institutional works (that is, certain writings on the law by individual authors who have won respect in the courts and elsewhere, their writings therefore being treated as authoritative); and
(c) custom (practices observed by certain groups of people, or by people generally).

This typology of formal sources is the basis upon which the rest of this chapter, and Chapters 5 (Legislation) and 6 (Precedent) proceed. Its importance is reflected in the most significant feature of a law library, visible at a glance. Half the books are textbooks, monographs, commentaries and other books about the law. The other half are the law itself, that is, they are collections of legislation, and reports of cases etc. It is the most characteristic part of a law student's work that he must 'look up the law', that is, find not just summaries of the law and comments on it but the actual legal provisions themselves.

### Other uses of sources of law

The term 'sources of law' can be used in other senses. For example, it is sometimes used to indicate that a rule is to be found in a specific piece of legislation or a particular precedent (that is, a particular decided case), as when the legal rules on how a valid marriage is contracted are said to have as their source the Marriage (Scotland) Act 1977, and the legal rules on what constitutes a contract to have as their source a large number of identifiable cases in which they were laid down. This usage might be termed the 'locational source'.

## Quasi-sources

Some rules, although not actually rules of law, are similar in some important ways. These require examination, and can be described as 'quasi-sources'.

## RANKING OF SOURCES

If there is more than one source of law, they might contradict each other. This would be intolerable, for it would be impossible to discover what the law was on any topic. So the sources must be ranked in an order of precedence.

Unfortunately, the details of how this ranking works are very complicated. Nevertheless, nine principles broadly express this ranking:

### 1 Legislation – 'Convention rights'

These are listed in the Human Rights Act 1998 and embody most of the rights laid out in the European Convention on Human Rights (for which, see Chapter 3 and Appendix 3). All other existing and future law is to be interpreted consistently with them, save that legislation of the United Kingdom Parliament may override them if it does so clearly.

### 2 Legislation – 'Community law'

This is the law created by the European Community (for which, see Chapter 3 and Appendix 3). All other existing and future law is valid only in so far as it is consistent with Community law, as is required by the European Communities Act 1972 (and Community law is to be interpreted consistently with the European Convention on Human Rights).

### 3 Legislation – United Kingdom Parliamentary legislation

This is the law passed by the United Kingdom Parliament in Acts of Parliament. Subject to the above, the United Kingdom Parliament may pass any Act, to any effect, that it wishes, and this legislation is therefore more powerful than the law created by the following means.

#### 4 Legislation – Scottish parliamentary legislation

This is law passed by the Scottish Parliament in Acts of the Scottish Parliament. As it has law-making power only by virtue of the United Kingdom Parliament having delegated such powers in the Scotland Act 1998, such legislation is valid only in so far as permitted by the delegation in that Act.

#### 5 Legislation – other delegated legislation

This is law made by members of the United Kingdom government, or the Scottish Executive, or other governmental bodies such as local authorities, in the form of statutory instruments (and Scottish statutory instruments), by-laws etc. It also is possible only by virtue of the United Kingdom Parliament (or, in the case of the Scottish Executive and Scottish local authorities, the Scottish Parliament) delegating appropriate powers. Such legislation is thus valid only in so far as it is permitted by the delegation in the relevant legislation.

#### 6 Legislation – Earlier and later legislation

Within any of the above classes of legislation, later legislation repeals or amends earlier inconsistent legislation implicitly, even if it does not do so explicitly.

#### 7 Judicial precedent

This is the law made by judges in deciding cases in courts, in the absence of legislation. Such law is valid only in so far as it is compatible with any of the above legislation. Higher courts can overturn the law created by judicial precedent in lower courts. (Something like judicial precedent operates in cases interpreting legislation, that is, working out a meaning where the legislation is unclear, for such interpretations become embedded as precedents.)

#### 8 Judicial precedent – earlier and later judicial precedent

Those operating the system of judicial precedent, from whatever time, assume that no precedent contradicts any other, so are reconcilable until proved otherwise, and strive to maintain it as a coherent and consistent whole.

## 9  Minor sources

This is law made by a variety of disparate bodies (see above). Law made by the minor sources may be drawn on in default of any of the above.

## THE MAJOR FORMAL SOURCES OF LAW

### Legislation and precedent: civil law, common law and mixed systems

It may be useful to start with the distinction between the civil and common law families of legal systems, for this throws light upon the relationship between legislation and precedent.

Civil law systems claim to be the intellectual heirs of Roman law, and many of their legal rules are descended from it. Civil law is a translation of the Latin *ius civile*, the name given by Roman lawyers to the bulk of their law. In general, civil law systems are codified systems, in the sense that much law is set out in logical, reasoned and encyclopaedic form in legislative codes. In such a system, in principle, not only do all legal rules derive from legislation (principally the codes), but also the underlying principles of the system are set forth there. In such systems, precedent is not recognised as a source of law at all, or at least only as a minor, supplementary one. The legal systems of most of Continental Europe, such as France, Belgium, Spain, Italy and Germany and to a large extent those parts of the rest of the world which were colonised by these European powers, such as South America, are civil law.

Common law systems are usually seen as the heirs of English law. English law itself never adopted Roman law as other European countries did. The native law it developed depended heavily upon precedent. Indeed, only in the 19th century did legislation become a significant source of law. The name given to the kind of law created by precedent, common law, is the very name identifying this type of legal system. Thus the rules, and the principles underlying them, are found in precedent. For example, the organising concepts of law such as contract, and the basic rules on the creation of contracts, the effect upon them of error by a party, and on performance or non-performance of contracts, are found in precedent. Legislation merely alters the application of those principles, to a greater or lesser extent, in respect of specific contracts (such as consumer credit contracts). Even great new areas of law such as company law, which were created by legislation, depend upon underlying common law rules and principles. English law was exported to colonies, and thus became the type of law found in much of the rest of the world, including most of North America and the Commonwealth.

Scots law forms one of a small group of mixed or hybrid systems, which partake of both. It is said to be a civil law system, in so far as Roman law, and the law of civil law countries, influenced it in the past, not least through the institutional writers. However, it is not codified and since the early 19th century it has accepted precedent as a source of law on the common law model.

## Legislation

'Legislation' is surprisingly hard to define. It is easiest to say that, so far as Scotland is concerned, legislation is the law created by certain European Community institutions, by the UK and Scottish Parliaments and by delegates of them. This, however, begs the question of what these bodies have in common.

It is better therefore to say that legislation is deliberately and formally created law. Acts of the UK Parliament have commonly been regarded as the standard example, in as much as they prevailed over all other forms of law until the coming of European Community law. Legislation is commonly, but not necessarily, produced by a deliberative body (sometimes referred to as a legislature, and sometimes elected). It nearly always deals in general rules rather than specific cases. While in civil law countries the whole law can be presumed to be the result of legislation (often in the form of encyclopaedic codes), in common law countries, which admit precedent as a formal source of law, this is not so, for the purpose of legislation is to change (or possibly restate) the law. Legislation in common law countries is thus essentially ad hoc.

The various types of legislation applying in the UK are discussed in Chapter 5.

## Precedent

Precedent is law created incidentally, by an adjudicative body (usually a court) in the course of judging disputes in an area where there is no legislation. It is found, therefore, in cases dealing with specific facts, and the actual rules of law applied must therefore be inferred, as further described in Chapter 6 and Appendix 1. Acceptance of precedent as a means of creating law effectively defines common law legal systems. These inferred rules purport to express timeless principles inherent in the system, rather than specific contemporary policy. While it is possible for the law to be changed through precedent, the process is usually slow, limited and uncertain, so legislation is usually sought for this purpose. Thus, the underlying principles of the legal system are to be found in the common law, that is the law created by precedent, rather than in legislation, which merely modifies or adds to it. Indeed, common law can be put into abeyance by legislation, but not wholly destroyed, for it takes force again if the legislation replacing it is repealed.

## THE MINOR FORMAL SOURCES OF LAW

The minor sources are prerogative legislation, institutional works, and custom.

### Prerogative legislation

Generally speaking, the Crown (that is, in practice, the government of the day) has no power to create law, for that is the job of Parliament. However, it does have some limited residual powers, dating from the powers of the monarchs before the 'Glorious Revolution' of 1688–89 to legislate without reference to Parliament. These powers are part of the royal prerogative, which is the name given to the ill-defined bundle of legal powers which the Crown has[1].

These powers are chiefly executive rather than legislative, and include the Sovereign's power to appoint ministers to form a government, and the powers of the government (in the name of the Crown) to conduct foreign affairs including, for example, the power to sign treaties and declare war.

Among these prerogative powers certain residual legislative ones exist, however. Although they are essentially legislative, they are minor, so are dealt with here, rather than in Chapter 5. They are residual in that they are the remains of the broad legislative powers claimed by the Crown before the 'Glorious Revolution', that is, the constitutional settlement of the 17th century in both England and Scotland (who had shared a king from 1603). In this settlement,

---

1 In *Laker Airways v Department of Trade* [1977] 1 QB 643, Lord Denning described the royal prerogative as 'a discretionary power to be exercised for the public good' and so was examinable by the courts.

Parliament took most of these powers away from the Crown, and what remains could also be removed by Parliament. The prerogative powers therefore continue to exist on sufferance[1], and there remains no general right on the part of the Crown to legislate[2], only a limited right to do so in relation to certain topics. These included colonies, internal governmental matters, and possibly certain emergencies and otherwise.

Examples of its use are therefore few and disparate. One, concerned with colonial legislation, was the constitution of Hong Kong (until it was handed back to China in 1997). This constittuion was contained in certain acts of prerogative legislation (called Letters Patent)[3]. All legislation made in Hong Kong by the Governor in the Legislative Council (Hong Kong's Parliament) was therefore valid by virtue of the fact that the Letters Patent created the post of Governor, set up the Legislative Council and provided for its composition, and gave legislative powers to the Governor in Legislative Council.

A second example, concerned with internal governmental matters, is the principal regulations for the internal operation of the Civil Service[4], and a third, concerned with emergencies, is certain legislation made on the outbreak of war in 1914, when no standing emergency legislation existed[5], and more recently at the time of the Falklands emergency[6].

A fourth example was the former Criminal Injuries Compensation Scheme. When the government decided in 1964 that persons suffering injuries as a result of criminal acts should receive some compensation from the state (being unlikely to obtain it from the criminal) it used the prerogative to set up a scheme of awards, based on the level of damages that the courts in Scotland or in England would grant. The justifications for circumventing Parliament were that the scheme was experimental and the costs to the state uncertain. In fact, dissatisfaction with this arrangement led eventually to the Criminal Injuries Compensation Act 1995

---

1 See, for example, the English case of *Attorney-General v de Keyser's Royal Hotel* [1920] AC 508.
2 Claim of Right 1689; *Grieve v Edinburgh and District Water Trustees* 1918 SC 700, 1918 2 SLT 72; also the English *Case of Proclamations* (1611) Co Rep 74.
3 Letters Patent of 14 February 1917 (as amended); also Royal Instructions of 14 February 1917 (as amended) etc; see Wesley-Smith *Constitutional and Administrative Law in Hong Kong* (1987) vol 1, ch 4.
4 For example, the Civil Service Order of 22 December 1982 (as amended).
5 For example, the Trading with the Enemy Proclamation 1914.
6 Requisitioning of Ships Order of 4 April 1982.

which requires Parliament to give its approval to a draft scheme. The Scheme is, however, one which enables the government to keep some control over expenditure by fixing a tariff or price for each kind of injury.

While acts of prerogative legislation answer to a variety of names[1], such as Letters Patent, Royal Instructions, Proclamations and Royal Warrants, they are usually issued in the form of (prerogative) Orders in Council, that is, Orders purportedly made by the Sovereign on the advice of the Privy Council[2]. The title 'Order in Council' is misleading. Firstly, the same name is used for another much more common type of legislation, that is (delegated) Orders in Council, a form of delegated legislation (see Chapter 5). Secondly, the involvement of the Sovereign and the advice of the Privy Council are fictional as the content is dictated by the government of the day.

## The institutional works

In the 17th century, Scots law was an untidy amalgam derived from various sources. It included old unwritten custom, custom and other rules recorded in medieval writings, such as that called *Regiam Majestatem*[3], which were considered authoritative, ad hoc Acts of Parliament of various vintages, and decisions of the Court of Session, at least in so far as available in the *Practicks*.

Scots law was not the only system with such characteristics, and the advantages of a systematic treatment were clear to lawyers and others across Europe. A widely known model for systematising native law was the *Corpus Iuris Civilis*. This was a codification of late Roman law, produced in the 6th century AD in Constantinople (which was by then the capital of the Eastern part of the Roman Empire) under the auspices of the Emperor Justinian. It comprised four parts, two of which were of greater importance than the rest. The 'Pandects' (or 'Digest') was a reconciliation of the commentaries of the major Roman legal writers of

1 Acts of prerogative legislation are cited by name and date, as the examples above show. Some are bound in the annual volumes of *Statutory Instruments*, so can be cited by that reference.
2 The Privy Council, originally a sort of forerunner of the Cabinet, is almost fictional in that it never meets as a whole, and the title 'Privy Councillor' is a sort of honour bestowed upon leading politicians, judges and bishops.
3 See ch 2. It appears that *Regiam Majestatem* was heavily based upon an earlier English work, called *Glanvil* after the name of its presumed author. '*Regiam majestatem* . . .', meaning 'Royal Majesty . . .', are its opening words.

previous centuries. The 'Institutiones' was a general introductory book on Roman law, dedicated to law students.

In Scotland such attempts to produce a systematic treatment took place from the mid-17th to the early 19th centuries. The writers of these works have become known as 'institutional writers', as several of their works adopted the title 'Institutes' or 'Institutions' in imitation of the title of Justinian's *Institutiones*, even though they might imitate the 'Digest' in content. Their work remade Scots law.

It can be debated whether a particular writer or work is institutional. However, undoubtedly Stair's *Institutions of the Law of Scotland* is regarded as the greatest, and certain works are in all lists.

They are[1]: Sir Thomas Craig's *Jus Feudale* (1655); Sir George Mackenzie's *Laws and Customs of Scotland in Matters Criminal* (1678); James Dalrymple, Viscount Stair's *The Institutions of the Law of Scotland* (1681); Andrew McDouall, Lord Bankton's *An Institute of the Laws of Scotland* (1751–53); Professor John Erskine's *An Institute of the Law of Scotland* (1772); Baron David Hume's *Commentaries on the Law of Scotland Respecting the Description and Punishment of Crimes* (1797); Professor George Joseph Bell's *Commentaries on the Law of Scotland and Principles of Mercantile Jurisprudence* (1804) and *Principles of the Law of Scotland* (1829); and Archibald Alison's *Principles of the Criminal Law of Scotland* (1833) and *Practice of the Criminal Law of Scotland* (1833)[2]. Sometimes included are Mackenzie's *The Institutions of the Law of Scotland* (1684); Erskine's *Principles of the Law of Scotland* (1759); and Henry Home, Lord Kames' *Principles of Equity* (1760).

The current significance of these works is that, at least since the middle of the 19th century, they have been accorded a special status. That is, they are regarded not as commentaries upon, illustrations of, opinions about, or textbooks concerning, the law, but

1 All dates given are of the first edition. Later editions may be more authoritative. The first edition of Stair's *Institutions* was defective, for example, and the second, published in 1693, is more reliable. In any case, later editions of all the works are usually preferred.
2 References to Stair are usually cited by name, book, title and section, for example, Stair I, 1, 22 (or, more traditionally I, i, 22), but sometimes in the form Stair *Institutions* I, 1, 22. Bankton (commonly abbreviated to Bankt) and Erskine's *Institute* are cited in essentially the same way, for example, Bankt I, 5, 28 and Erskine III, 1, 2 (and Erskine's *Principles* similarly, but with *Prin* inserted). Bell's *Commentaries* are cited as, for example, Bell *Comm* I, 343, but his *Principles* (which has continuous paragraphing throughout), as Bell *Prin* 267. Hume is cited as, for example, *Hume* 1, 52.

as in themselves actually constituting the law[1]. Thus, in effect, the institutional writers have been regarded as akin to legislators.

While it is undeniable that the institutional writers are sources of law, explicit recognition of the position is actually limited to a small number of 19th-century cases, decided at a time when attitudes to the nature of law were different from today's, buttressed by a few authoritative, but less than comprehensive, 20th-century cases[2]. No works have been added to the canon since the middle of the 19th century and none deleted, although, so far as institutional authority depends upon judicial recognition, in principle either event could occur.

When an institutional work is cited, the question of its weight in comparison with other sources arises. There is little guidance on the answer. Lord Normand, a distinguished Scottish judge, observed in an often quoted[3] published lecture of 1941 that they were as respected in court as decisions of the House of Lords. However, because there are few cases explicitly dealing with the authority of the institutional writers, judges have rarely discussed the matter explicitly. Clearly, the institutional works carry less weight than any legislation and, given their status, it is unlikely that any judicial decision will flatly contradict them, but in many areas, such as family law and employment law, social and moral changes have been so substantial as to reduce their persuasiveness considerably, or justify use of the maxim *cessante ratione legis, cessat ipsa lex*[4], and the deference suggested by Lord Normand now seems exaggerated[5]. Thus, they may be regarded as potentially decisive, but only where no legislation or clear precedent exists, and in areas

---

1 It is unusual for legal systems to regard such writers as sources of law. South African law is the only other system which appears to do so. There, rules may be regarded as legal rules simply by virtue of having been written by one of the 'old authorities', chiefly internationally renowned Dutch writers on law, such as Grotius (Hugo de Groot 1583–1645): see *The Laws of Scotland: Stair Memorial Encyclopedia* vol 22, para 435, and Cairns 'Institutional Writings' in Kiralfy and MacQueen *New Perspectives in Scottish Legal History*.

2 For example, *Sugden v HM Advocate* 1934 JC 103, 1934 SLT 465; *Fortington v Lord Kinnaird* 1942 SC 239, 1943 SLT 24.

3 For example, in *The Laws of Scotland: Stair Memorial Encyclopedia* vol 22, para 437.

4 I e, approximately, 'if the reason for the law ceases, so does the law'.

5 See *HM Advocate v Stallard* 1989 SCCR 248, 1989 SLT 469. The learned commentator on the SCCR report of that case observed that 'it is not necessary to convene a Full Bench [i e an enlarged bench of judges, capable of giving more authoritative decisions] to depart from a proposition of Hume, which was repeated by later authorities and has been unchallenged by any authority for almost two centuries'.

of law in which the principles have not altered significantly since the institutional writers were at work.

In any case, although institutional works were of enormous importance in the past, it would be very unusual for any court today to justify its decision solely by reference to one. Indeed, although the High Court refers to Hume's works from time to time in relation to major common law offences[1], it is unusual for institutional writers even to be cited in court, in part because the tide of precedent and statute has washed over so much law in the last hundred years. Their role is thus, perhaps, to supply a moral and intellectual sheet anchor for the law while not excluding legal change.

Other, non-institutional, works may be referred to in argument or decision in court, and increasingly are. Indeed, some highly respected but non-institutional works, such as Gloag's *Law of Contract* (2nd edn, 1929) and McBryde *The Law of Contract in Scotland* (2nd edn, 2001), are cited more frequently than institutional works. In such cases, if the judge adopts the rule described, he is not accepting it as the actual law, but making it law by his decision. Thus, in *Black v Carmichael; Carmichael v Black* 1992 SLT 897 at 902 and 903 the judges accepted a statement in Gordon's *Criminal Law* at para 14–63 that in theft it is the owner's loss, not the thief's gain, that is important. In *Morgan Guaranty Trust Co v Lothian Regional Council* 1995 SLT 299, Lord President Hope acknowledged 'the work of academic lawyers whose detailed research and vigorous criticism has already had a marked influence on debate among the judiciary'.

## Custom

The common law (in the sense of law not created by Parliament) emerged from unwritten custom. Institutional writers digested it in their works, and judges adopted it in their judgments, which clearly made it law which was common to the whole country. Local custom might also be recognised. For example, Stair and other institutional writers recognised 'udal tenure', a form of land-holding found only in Orkney and Shetland, as custom enforceable through the courts[2].

---

1 As in *Khaliq v HM Advocate* 1984 JC 23, where Hume was relied upon, and *HM Advocate v Stallard* (see note above), where he was mentioned only to reject him.
2 Stair IV, 22, 2.

It remains possible for custom to be a source of law. Nevertheless, because most rules once referred to as customs, such as legitim (rights held by a deceased person's children to his moveable property), have now been enshrined in precedent, and thus incorporated into the common law, even that possibility exists only in limited circumstances. It is thus very rare today to assert the existence of a custom, and the leading case, *Bruce v Smith* (1890) 17 R 1000 (which concerns the rejection of a claim by the owner of land abutting the shore in Shetland, by virtue of owning the land, to one third of the value of pilot whales driven onto that shore and slaughtered), is over a century old.

In so far as a custom might still be declared enforceable in the courts, it must pass certain tests. The custom must not contradict the general law[1], it must be certain[2], it must be generally accepted or acquiesced in as being obligatory[3], it must be reasonable (although what this means is not clear and might be difficult to decide), and it must have continued for a long time, although no particular period is required and interruption is not fatal. But a custom may be regarded as falling into desuetude, or by losing authority by contrary usage[4]. Any enforceable custom is likely to be restricted to a locality or trade, because any more general custom will either have been absorbed into the common law by judicial precedent, or be regarded as contrary to the general law.

Although the test of an enforceable custom has been laid down by precedent, it is of the essence of the idea of custom that it can be binding without judicial recognition. Explicit recognition of a custom is very rare. But one modern example is *Stirling Park & Co v Digby Brown and Co* 1996 SLT (Sh Ct) 17. A firm of solicitors as agents for a client instructed sheriff officers to serve a charge and carry out a poinding in order to recover a debt. The solicitors did not pay the sheriff officers' fees and expenses and were sued. On appeal a sheriff principal held there was a custom 'so certain, uniform, notorious and reasonable' as to be binding on the solicitors, as if it were part of a contract. Legislation may implicitly or explicitly delegate to custom, as when a statute uses words such as 'reasonable', which give judges a wide interpretive discretion. For

1 *Anderson v McCall* (1866) 4 M 765.
2 Erskine I, 1, 44.
3 *Bruce v Smith* (1890) 17 R 1000.
4 *Bruce v Smith* (1890) 17 R 1000; *McAra v Edinburgh Magistrates* 1913 SC 1059, 1913 2 SLT 110; *Royal Four Towns Fishing Association v Dumfriesshire Assessor* 1956 SC 379, 1956 SLT 217.

example, by virtue of s 8(4)(a) of the Employment Rights Act 1996, part of the test of whether an employee was unfairly dismissed is that the employer 'in the circumstances . . . acted reasonably . . .'. In applying this test, judges have regard to what is commonly called 'custom and practice', that is, what is commonly regarded as acceptable in that employment.

In addition, custom-like rights may be recognised in other ways. Rights of way, for example, may arise from prescription, that is, continuous use over a period, now fixed by statute at 20 years[1]. Also, trade practices may be incorporated into a contract.

Most important of all, however, custom may affect the law in a major fashion without being explicitly recognised as such, as a 'historical source'. Judges' views of what people, generally or within a particular milieu, consider acceptable will influence the way they take their decisions, both in applying and developing precedent, and in statutory interpretation. An example may be Lord Atkin's implicit, but clear, adoption of Christian morality in his 'neighbour test'[2] in *Donoghue v Stevenson* 1932 SC(HL) 31.

## QUASI-SOURCES

As well as the major and minor sources of law, there are also 'quasi-sources'. This term refers to a great and amorphous variety of rules and principles which are not unequivocally law, which therefore do not fit into the generally accepted categories of formal sources of law, but which are nevertheless connected to law, look like law, or are treated much as if they were law.

### Constitutional conventions

One of the most important types of quasi-source is constitutional conventions. The United Kingdom has no single document called 'the constitution'. Constitutional laws, therefore, are found in the same sources as other laws, chiefly legislation (such as the Scotland Act 1998) and precedent. There are no fundamental laws such as

---

1 Prescription and Limitation (Scotland) Act 1973, s 3.
2 See Matthew xix, 19 and the Catechism in the (English) Book of Common Prayer.

exist in Germany and the United States[1]. Unwritten rules affect the way in which the constitution operates in practice in all states, no doubt. Because of the unwritten nature of the United Kingdom constitution, these unwritten rules, usually termed 'conventions of the constitution', have assumed special significance.

For example, there is no law requiring there to be a Prime Minister, let alone stipulating how he or she is to be appointed. In law there is simply a power on the part of the Sovereign to appoint ministers. Nevertheless, there is an unwritten rule, a constitutional convention, that the Sovereign will appoint the person who can command a majority of the votes on an issue of confidence in the House of Commons[2]. Indeed, it is only by convention that members of the government must have a seat in one or other House of Parliament[3] and that the Speaker of the House of Commons is an impartial chairman once elected to that office by the House, although he will invariably be an MP who is a member of a political party. Another important convention is that the Sovereign should not refuse assent to a Bill which has passed both Houses of Parliament. Indeed, the role of the Sovereign as one who 'reigns but does not rule', that is one who acts in accordance with the basic constitutional conventions, has grown up by convention only.

Conventions are created by behaviour which becomes strictly observed because thought to be right, but by the same token can be tacitly altered by simple non-observation. For example, until the beginning of the 20th century, the convention was that a Prime Minister might be a member of either House, as long as his party had a majority in the House of Commons. Thus, the Marquess of Salisbury was Prime Minister from 1895 to 1902 because the Conservative Party had a majority in the Commons. However, at some time in the 20th century, it became accepted that the Prime

1 It has been argued that various documents, such as the Acts of Union of the two Parliaments which created Great Britain in 1707, in fact form at least part of a constitution, and are fundamental law. Also, accession to the European Community has considerably altered the constitutional map, and the EC and EU Treaties bear to be the constitution of the United Kingdom as well as any other document. Further, the entrenched position of the Human Rights Act (see chap 5) was intended to make it, in some sense, fundamental.

2 To command a majority in the House of Commons requires in practice that one be an MP, and leader of the party which won the last general election. As party leaders are elected by party members according to various rules, it is an interesting question as to whether such party rules are part of the constitution of the United Kingdom, and quasi-sources.

3 This convention has occasionally not been observed for brief periods, and the ease of creating life peers provides a means of avoiding embarrassment.

Minister must be a member of the elected House, and the convention altered, so no peer has been thought eligible for at least half a century. Indeed, the Earl of Home renounced his peerage in 1963 and successfully sought election for Kinross and West Perthshire in order to be eligible to become Prime Minister (an aim he achieved shortly thereafter).

The Scottish Parliament and Administration may be expected to develop practices which will be observed with a sense of duty and so become constitutional conventions. The relationship between them and the UK Parliament and government will, if it is to be harmonious, require to be regulated by fresh conventions.

Constitutional conventions are certainly not enforceable by courts, but can be argued to be law in so far as they are respected and acted upon and thus, like laws, have a certain obligatory character. Like a jigsaw, they interlock with one another and so give a certain coherence to the public life of a society. They are part of the political morality of the state. Indeed, 'unconstitutional' in the United Kingdom more readily fits a breach of convention than one of ordinary law.

### Administrative quasi-legislation[1]

Governments produce among other things, guidance, guidelines, advice, plans, information upon their intentions, and so on. Various regulatory agencies set up by government do likewise. Within this mass of communications there are rules and principles, not contained in legislation, but intended to be acted upon, and often directed to officials. Indeed, the process is sometimes referred to as administrative rule-making or (somewhat misleadingly) 'soft law'[2]. To some extent, its growth parallels that of delegated legislation, for it has increased through an increase in the activities of government and regulatory agencies, but it may also have grown through a desire to influence activities through self-regulation rather than directly.

On the other hand, some of this guidance etc reflects a need for comprehensibility, which the United Kingdom style of legislative drafting does not promote, and is aimed at the general public, or those engaging in particular occupations or activities.

---

1 'Quasi': '. . . (a) kind of; resembling or simulating, but not really the same as . . .' (*Shorter Oxford English Dictionary*, 3rd edn, revised with addenda, 1970).
2 The learned editor of the entry on Legislation in *The Laws of Scotland: Stair Memorial Encyclopaedia of the Laws of Scotland* vol 22, paras 233ff used the phrase 'ersatz legislation'.

There are concerns over the growth of administrative quasi-legislation. While legislation comes under parliamentary and other scrutiny (albeit sometimes of a limited kind), quasi-legislation may come under less or none. Indeed, it may actually be secret, and in any case may be seen as reflecting too cosy a relationship between government and some interest-groups. Although any government must be entitled to produce internal rules for its civil servants, some quasi-legislation may appear to be legislation by government, outside the royal prerogative and without recourse to Parliament.

This quasi-legislation includes many types of communication, including codes of practice, professional codes of conduct, government circulars, and perhaps the Citizen's Charter.

*Codes of practice*

The Highway Code is a well-known example, though not necessarily typical, of a code of practice, one form of administrative quasi-legislation which is increasingly common. Such codes are in general relatively brief, but systematic and reasonably comprehensive sets of precepts, produced by government or a regulatory agency, and addressed to the public. They are produced in order to allow a particular activity to be carried out more safely, or better in some other way, so are written in standard English for the layman rather than in watertight drafting for the lawyer and judge.

Usually they are required or permitted by an Act of Parliament, and may require parliamentary approval. They are not, however, legislation, but paraphrases or interpretations of it, or embellishments upon it. They have varying legal force. Some offer only guidance, and are wholly unenforceable, as, for example, the Secretary of State's 'guidance' to be issued under the Transport Act 1985, s 125 in relation to the transport needs of disabled persons. Others are indirectly enforceable, for example, the Highway Code. The Road Traffic Act 1988, s 38 stipulates that a breach of the Highway Code renders no-one liable to criminal proceedings, but may be relied upon in civil or criminal proceedings to assist in establishing liability. In short, failure to signal a right turn, for example, is not an offence, but if an accident occurs in the course of such a manoeuvre, it can be used to help prove the offence of careless driving or negligence creating liability to compensate somebody injured. Other examples of codes, breach of which may result in some form of liability, are the code of practice on employment under the Race Relations Act 1976, and the Code of Practice on Picketing, now under the Trade Union and Labour Relations

(Consolidation) Act 1992, s 199, which by s 201(3) courts and tribunals are bound to 'take into account'[1].

### Professional codes of conduct

Suppliers of services organised as a profession often have a registration procedure as a precondition of practice, and a code of conduct, breach of which may be punished, and may even result in deregistration. It is part of the orthodox notion of a profession that the code of conduct is produced and enforced by the profession itself. This is modified in some cases by legislation requiring and otherwise controlling such a code.

For example, under ss 34, 35 and 53 of the Solicitors (Scotland) Act 1980 (as amended), the Law Society of Scotland is required to make such rules, usually called practice rules and accounts rules. Breach, judged by the independent Scottish Solicitors' Discipline Tribunal, may constitute professional misconduct, attracting one of a range of penalties, including 'striking off the roll', that is deregistration. (This procedure is more fully dealt with in Chapter 7.)

### Government circulars

Government circulars form a miscellaneous category of quasi-legislation, comprising a variety of advice and guidance, diversely titled, issued as a formal letter to officials in central or local government, or in the National Health Service, or to police, or otherwise[2]. Some are very important, for example, Crown Office Circulars to procurators fiscal are presumed (for they are secret) to detail procedures to be followed and how discretion is to be exercised in prosecuting offences. At the other extreme, Scottish Home and Health Department Circular 6/1992 (ref: CPF/2/7) dated 30 April 1992 to chief executives of islands and district councils informs them of rates of travelling and subsistence allowances to be paid to justices of the peace.

Circulars are not legislation, so cannot vary the enacted law. Thus, in *Inglis v British Airports Authority* 1978 SLT (Lands Tr) 30, a woman claimed compensation for depreciation in the value of

---

1 Applied as to number of picketers in *Thomas v National Union of Mineworkers* [1986] Ch 20 at 70.
2 In 2002, for instance, the Home Office published nearly 50 circulars (most relating to police in England and Wales): see www.homeoffice.gov.uk/circulars/index.htm.

her house by reason of the construction of a new runway at Edinburgh Airport. The Airports Authority resisted her claim, relying on advice as to its obligations contained in the Scottish Development Department Memorandum No 85/1973. The Lands Tribunal described the memorandum as 'an administrative circular', and decided it was mere guidance to public authorities as to the scope of the relevant legislation on compensation, and could not be used as an aid to construe the wording of a statute. So compensation was awarded.

There are few other cases directly in point, but some decisions from the House of Lords in English cases broadly support the conclusion. In *Gillick v West Norfolk and Wisbech Area Health Authority* [1986] AC 112, [1985] 3 All ER 402, the health authority, following advice from the Department of Health and Social Security in Circular HSC(IS)32 (memorandum of guidance on family planning), gave contraceptive advice to young people, including those under 16. Mrs Gillick (who had five children under 16) sought a declaration that this was unlawful. Although this point was not the main issue in the case, the House of Lords concluded that it could issue a declaration correcting erroneous advice on the law issued by government departments in a public, non-statutory document such as a circular. This clearly involved concluding that such legal advice could be wrong, and that a circular could not alter the law.

However, it is certainly the case that some circulars can be enforced indirectly. For example, if local planning authorities ignore planning circulars, their decisions can be overturned on appeal.

Also, circulars addressed by central government to civil servants are from the Crown to Crown servants, and from employers to employees, and may be enforced through disciplinary proceedings[1]. Thus, in *Palmer v Inverness Hospitals Board* 1963 SC 311 a circular of the Department of Health concerning hospital disciplinary proceedings was held to create a right to a hearing, which could be read as part of the contract of employment of a dismissed house surgeon. In *Tehrani v Argyll and Clyde Health Board (No 1)* 1989 SLT 851 the suspension of a hospital consultant on full pay in accordance with a Scottish Home and Health Department circular was not disputed. But the absence of reasons and the duration of the suspension were held to be not unreasonable.

1 See *R v Ponting* [1985] Crim LR 318.

*Chartermarks and benchmarks*

One interesting example of quasi-legislation emerged through the 'Citizens' Charters', designed as a means to set and raise standards in the provision of public sector services by mechanisms such as performance targets, publication of information, and encouragement of means of complaint and redress. There are now some 200 'national charters', from the Benefits Agency's 'Caring for the Carer' to Customs and Excise's 'Traveller's Charter', and the Cabinet Office's Centre for Management and Policy Studies encourages both national and local 'charters'[1].

Such charters, while indicating good practice, and how to complain about service, do not create legal rights or new means of redress in themselves. Nor do they have any parliamentary approval.

---

1 See www.servicefirst.gov.uk/. Curiously, its list of 'national charters' includes several relating to England and Wales only, or Northern Ireland only, but none relating to Scotland only.

# 5. Legislation

The meaning of 'legislation' is discussed in Chapter 4. This chapter discusses the various types of legislation, that is, European Community legislation (Part 2), parliamentary legislation (Part 3), Acts of the Scottish Parliament (Part 4), and other delegated legislation (Part 5), and the application of legislation (Part 6), though commencing with an example of parliamentary legislation with special features, that is, human rights legislation (Part 1). Prerogative legislation, as a minor source of law, is discussed in Chapter 4.

## PART 1: HUMAN RIGHTS LEGISLATION

### The meaning of 'human rights', the ECHR and the Human Rights Act 1998

For present purposes, 'human rights' can be taken to refer to the content of a particular treaty, the European Convention on Human Rights and Fundamental Freedoms (or 'ECHR'), made under the auspices of the Council of Europe (already considered, along with the European Court of Human Rights, in Chapter 3). As noted there, the United Kingdom, as a member of the Council of Europe, was one of the original signatories of the ECHR in 1950, and ratified it in 1951. (There are also amending Protocols which add further rights, but not all of these have been ratified by the United Kingdom.) Thus it adheres to the ECHR.

However, what is of present interest is human rights legislation which, in the United Kingdom, effectively means the Human Rights Act 1998. This is, in some senses, simply another Act of Parliament, and to be mentioned below, if at all, in relation to Acts of Parliament in general. However, it has a special status which makes it necessary to give it special mention at the beginning of this chapter.

## Human Rights Act 1998 and the 'entrenchment' of human rights

The ECHR is enforceable in various ways, including through the European Court of Human Rights by states or by individual petition (discussed in chapter 3) and through Community law (noted in Chapter 3 and discussed below in Part 2 of this chapter). However, of much more importance, it is now enforceable through the Human Rights Act 1998, which has had radical effects. As noted in Chapter 3, the Human Rights Act does not, as is sometimes said, actually incorporate the ECHR into United Kingdom law. Its terms do not have the 'direct effect' which Community law does (see Part 2 of this chapter, below).

Nevertheless, it can be said to 'entrench' human rights. What it does in s 1 is to take most of the contents of the ECHR[1], and its First and Sixth Protocols[2], and put them in its Sch 1, under the name of 'Convention rights'. These Convention rights are thus part of United Kingdom law. Further, in broad terms, United Kingdom law is intended to be 'compatible' with them (though not necessarily required to be).

There are various means of seeking this compatibility. Firstly, the Act imposes requirements in relation to parliamentary scrutiny during the process of legislation of all subsequent Acts. This is discussed in relation to Acts of the United Kingdom and Scottish Parliaments below in Parts 3 and 4 of this chapter. Secondly, the Act imposes requirements in relation to statutory interpretation. This is discussed in relation to the application of legislation below in Part 6 of this chapter. Thirdly, it imposes requirements in relation to devolution. This is discussed above in chapter 3, and below in relation to Acts of the Scottish Parliament.

Finally, the Act also creates rights for victims of breaches of Convention rights, which was dealt with in Chapter 3

---

1 It omits arts 1, 13 and 15. As noted in ch 3, the omission of art 13, requiring 'an effective remedy before a national authority', is controversial. The government considered that it added nothing as the very Act itself provided the effective remedies. Another view is that it wished to avoid judges creating new ones based on the Act.
2 That is, those Protocols creating further rights which the United Kingdom has signed.

# PART 2: EUROPEAN COMMUNITY LEGISLATION

European Community and European Union institutions are discussed in Chapter 3.

## The meaning of 'Community law'

European Community law is usually called simply 'Community law'. The Community was set up by the various treaties in order to promote certain aims. The most important are explicitly stated in the opening articles of the original European Economic Community Treaty of 1957, which, as amended and now called the European Community Treaty (or Treaty on the European Community: 'TEC'), remains in force. The Preamble speaks of the intention 'to lay the foundations of an ever closer union among the peoples of Europe', and the Treaty articles specify numerous policies to that end, including free movement between member states of goods, persons, capital and services, and non-discrimination against their nationals on the ground of nationality or sex.

In order to fulfil these aims, the treaties do something of enormous significance, that is, they give the Community the power to make its own law. Community law is thus a separate legal order from those of the member states. However, Community law exists only for the purpose of achieving the aims specified, so any piece of Community legislation might be ultra vires, that is, beyond the powers granted to the Community's institutions by the various treaties, and thereby invalid[1]. It is important to realise that anything done within the Community must be justified by reference to a treaty provision. Nevertheless, the Community's aims are

---

1 Articles 230 and 231 (173 and 174 before the Treaty of Amsterdam) allow the European Court of Justice to review the legality of acts of the Commission and Council of Ministers on specified grounds including ultra vires, and to declare them void. For example, the UK sought to have the 'Working Time Directive' (EC) 93/104 (which imposes regulation of working hours, rest breaks, night work and annual leave) set aside as ultra vires because it was based on art 118a of the treaty (now art 138: which concerned health and safety at work and required only a qualified majority vote, from which the United Kingdom in fact abstained), when it should have been based on art 100 or art 235 (now arts 94 and 308: which allow legislation to fulfil the purposes of the treaty in areas not specifically covered, and requires unanimity, and thus could be vetoed by the United Kingdom). In Case C–84/95 *UK v EU Council (working time)* [1996] 3 CMLR 671, the European Court of Justice rejected the argument, however. Health and safety were the essential objectives of the directive.

so broad, and so broadly interpreted by the European Court of Justice, that this is not a major limitation

The subsequent creation of the European Union out of the European Community and other elements, and later developments (discussed in Chapter 3) have complicated the matter considerably. For present purposes, what requires noting principally is that the second and third 'pillars' of the European Union operated 'inter-governmentally' rather than 'supranationally' as the European Community (the first 'pillar') does. Thus, they did not create Community law, so were not subject to the jurisdiction of the European Court of Justice.

However, thereafter the Treaty of Amsterdam allowed the United Kingdom to opt out of parts of an amended first 'pillar' (so as not to be bound by those parts)[1], and also allowed member states to conclude agreements between only some of them and not others (creating further areas in which some member states are bound, but not others)[2]. It also integrated the third 'pillar' more closely to the first, giving the ECJ a restricted role in relation to it. Thus, the term 'European Union law' is used by some commentators. However, for most purposes, it is only the law of the Community with which we are concerned, so the title 'Community law' is retained here.

Community legislation (as opposed to Community law) is not a term much used, no doubt because all the founding member states were civil law states, in which precedent is, broadly speaking, not a source of law, so for whom 'legislation' and 'law' can be equated[3].

### Community law and the European Convention on Human Rights

The European Convention on Human Rights is fully considered in Chapter 5, and above in Part 1 of this chapter.

However, here it should be noted that, although the ECHR and its institutions are separate from the European Union and its

---

1 Indeed, complexity was even greater, for the Treaty of Amsterdam transferred a large part of the third 'pillar' to the first 'pillar', which was the part the United Kingdom (and Ireland and Denmark) were allowed to opt out of (though they might also opt in to bits of it later if they wished).
2 While the Treaties refer to this as 'flexibility', 'enhanced co-operation' and 'closer co-operation', it is popularly termed 'variable speed Europe' and the United Kingdom is clearly one of the slower participants.
3 The creative role of the European Court of Justice means that while it would be very unorthodox to refer to 'Community precedent', there is effectively Community law which is not legislation. This is discussed in ch 6.

institutions (and the European Union is experimenting with its own 'fundamental rights'), the former may be enforceable through the latter.

In Case 11/70 *Internationale Handelsgesellschaft* [1970] ECR 1125, the European Court of Justice (not the European Court of Human Rights) held, in a creative decision, that respect for the fundamental freedoms enshrined in the ECHR was an integral part of the general principles of law which it had to uphold. In Case 4/73 *Nold* [1974] ECR 419, the court went further and declared that international treaties for the protection of human rights to which member states were signatory could supply guidelines to be followed within the framework of Community law. A United Kingdom case, Case 63/83 *R v Kirk* [1984] ECR 2689, [1984] 3 CMLR 522, concerned penalties for illegal fishing. Regulation 170/83 appeared to permit a retrospective penalty, but the court interpreted the Regulation to exclude this, expressly by reference to art 7 (non-retroactivity of criminal law) of the ECHR.

Therefore, Community law will be applied by the European Court of Justice subject to the ECHR. As such decisions are binding on the courts of member states, Scots courts must loyally apply the same principle when deciding Community law cases.

## Types of Community legislation and their forms

Four types of Community legislation can be said to exist: treaties; regulations; directives; and decisions. (In addition, other Community documents of no clear legal force are issued.) The decisions referred to are those of Commission or Council, not of the European Court of Justice. The powers of this Court, which also develops Community law, are dealt with in Chapter 6. (Under the second 'pillar' created by the Treaty on European Union, the European Union may adopt 'common strategies', 'joint actions', 'common positions' and 'systematic co-operation', and under the third 'pillar', may adopt 'common decisions'; 'framework decisions' and 'decisions' and 'conventions', which may variously resemble Regulations, Directives and Decisions, but are not part of Community law, so are not considered here.)

*Treaties*

The treaties, sometimes referred to as the Community's 'primary legislation', form its constitution (although some parts concern very detailed provisions of other sorts, for instance on customs duties). They have lengthy names, but are often referred to by abbreviations, such as 'the TEC'. The principal ones[1] are:

- the European Economic Community Treaty of 1957 (the EEC Treaty, once often referred to as the Treaty of Rome, but now, after many amendments, referred to as the EC Treaty or 'TEC');
- the Merger Treaty of 1965;
- the First Accession Treaty of 1972 (and subsequent accession treaties);
- the Single European Act ('SEA') of 1986;
- the Treaty on European Union ('TEU') of 1992;
- the Treaty of Amsterdam ('ToA') of 1997; and
- the Treaty of Nice ('ToN') of 2000.

The original EEC Treaty was drawn up in the four languages of the original six member states. More recent treaties are drawn up in the official language of each member state. Each version has to be equally authentic, which has caused problems where there are discrepancies.

The form of all the principal treaties is broadly similar[2]. They start with a series of statements of purposes[3]. They may be divided into parts, subdivided into titles and chapters[4], but the basic unit is the article. Articles are usually numbered sequentially throughout, ignoring the parts, titles etc[5]. The Treaty of Amsterdam also

1   For the purpose and significance of these treaties, see ch 3. Other treaties entered into by the Community (such as the Lomé Convention, with West African states), and possibly some entered into between member states (such as the Convention on Jurisdiction and Enforcement of Judgments) are also relevant. Other agreements, such as the 'Luxembourg Accord', by which member states promised informally not to exercise majority voting where one of them claims its vital national interests are involved, are not treaties.
2   The structure of the TEU is more confusing than most, but this has been overtaken by the amendments in the ToA.
3   The TEC Preamble commences 'Determined to lay the foundations of an ever closer union among the peoples of Europe . . . ', and the opening articles specify the establishment of a common market, and a variety of specific policies to that and other ends, such as the elimination of customs duties, and the approximation of the laws of member states
4   The TEC is divided into six numbered and named 'Parts', 'I – Principles', 'II – Citizenship of the Union' etc. Parts III and V are divided into 'Titles' (Part V into XXI Titles), several of which are divided into 'Chapters' (Part V, Title VII is divided into five Chapters), and some of those even further into 'Sections' (Part V, Title I, Chapter 1 is divided into five Sections).
5   The numbering of the TEU, however, had its articles identified by letters ('Article A', 'Article B' etc, including 'K.1','K.2', etc, and even 'K.3(2)(c)'). This system is obsolete, having been replaced by numbers by the ToA (see below), but contemporary literature necessarily contains reference to the letter form.

renumbered the articles of the principal treaties, which means that commonly articles are referred to by both pre- and post-Amsterdam numbers, as, for example, 'article 18 (ex 8a)' or 'article 234 (ex article 177) (or 'article 8a (now 18)' or 'article 177 (now article 234)')'[1]. To avoid confusion between treaties, articles may be referred to as, for example, 'article 205 EC' or 'article 205 (TEC)' to identify the treaty in question.

The articles may be brief or lengthy[2], and may be divided into paragraphs and sub-paragraphs. These in turn may be identified by number and letter in the United Kingdom fashion (for example, article 39(3)(b) (ex article 48(3)(b)) or otherwise (for example, article 43 (ex article 52) which has two paragraphs identified by neither number nor letter, while article 40 (ex article 49) has no numbered paragraphs, but four lettered ones expanding upon the first). This can make citation of specific passages difficult[3]. Commonly the treaties also have numbered annexes and unnumbered Protocols. These are essentially schedules, containing material too detailed or too specific for the body of a treaty, though they may reflect the fact that unanimity was not achieved on a matter, but the majority are going ahead anyway as between themselves[4].

As is common with treaties generally, some articles are simple exhortation. Others are specific enough to be applied by courts, and may therefore have 'direct effect' (for which, see below).

Article 249 (ex article 189) specifically permits the Commission and the Council of Ministers, under various powers elsewhere in the treaty, to make regulations, directives and decisions, which are collectively referred to as 'acts', but sometimes colloquially as 'secondary legislation'. The difference between each type is significant for the legal effect they have in member states, which is dealt with below.

---

1 Or in relation to TEU articles, for example, 'article 33 (ex K.5)'. Indeed, some articles have changed number more than once. The SEA introduced an Article 8a, renumbered by the TEU as art 7a, renumbered again by the ToA as art 14. The possibilities of confusion are thus great. Good Community law textbooks contain 'Tables of Equivalences' to permit correct identification.

2 The TEC has over 300 articles. One of the shortest, art 281 (ex art 210) reads 'The Community shall have legal personality'. One of the longest is art 272 (ex article 203) which extends over two pages.

3 Thus, there may be circumlocutions such as 'point (1)(b) of the first sub-paragraph of Article 63'.

4 The TEC and TEU jointly have 36 Protocols, including specific material such as the Statute of the European Court of Justice (Sixth Protocol), but also others recording the special position of the United Kingdom, Ireland and Denmark who declined to accept certain aspects of freedom of movement of persons (Second to Fifth Protocols).

*Regulations*

Regulations[1] are the principal means by which the Community legislates, and there are thousands made every year[2].

Regulations start with a title in a form exemplified in the following: 'COMMISSION REGULATION (EEC) No 417/85 of 19 December 1985 on the application of Article 85(3) of the Treaty to categories of specialization agreements'. There follows a preamble opening with the name of the initiating institution and closing with the formula indicating enactment, for example, 'THE COMMISSION OF THE EUROPEAN COMMUNITIES ... HAS ADOPTED THIS REGULATION'. These two items are separated by a recital of the treaty provisions giving authority for the regulation to be made, the consultative procedure followed, and the reasoning which has produced the proposal, in a series of statements, possibly covering more than a page, and beginning 'Having regard to ... ' or 'Whereas ... '.

This lengthy preliminary exists because article 253 (ex article 190) requires legislative acts of the Community to state the reasons on which they are based and to refer to any proposals or opinions required by the relevant treaty to be obtained. This in turn allows the European Court of Justice to review the validity of them[3].

The actual provisions of the regulation follow in numbered articles, often grouped into sections or titles, in much the same fashion as in the treaties. The last article usually declares the date on which the regulation comes into force, but if there is no declaration, then by virtue of article 254 (ex article 191) it comes into force on the twentieth day following publication in the *Official Journal*. Unless a regulation stipulates that it is to cease having effect on a certain date, it continues in force until amended or repealed.

After the body of the text, a regulation has the formula: 'This Regulation shall be binding in its entirety and directly applicable in

---

1 The name regulation is also given to one type of United Kingdom delegated legislation. The two should not be confused.

2 In 2002 there were nearly 2,500 regulations.

3 Regulation (EC) 3595/85 concerned tariff preferences for developed countries. In Case 45/86 *Council v Commission* [1987] ECR 1493 (the 'Generalised Tariffs case'), the European Court of Justice annulled the Regulation because the recital was insufficiently concise, clear and relevant on the relevant issues of law and fact. Directive (EC) 86/113 concerned minimum sizes for battery hens' cages. Community officials altered the reasons recited after the Council of Ministers had approved it. The United Kingdom successfully challenged the validity of the directive on this ground in Case 131/86 *United Kingdom v EC Council* [1988] 2 CMLR 364.

all Member States', which reproduces part of article 249 (ex article 189), and indicates its direct effect. Regulations terminate with a statement of the place and date of its making, and the name of the Commissioner responsible.

## Directives

Directives, which are much less frequent than regulations[1] (but no less important), were originally intended to be policy statements delivered by Community institutions to a member state government or member state governments generally. However, they may be drafted to leave little discretion to the member state and, as a result of creative adjudication by the European Court of Justice, the distinction between regulations and directives is now blurred.

The form of a directive is much the same as that of a regulation[2]. By virtue of article 249 (ex article 189), directives take effect from the date of notification to the member states, but because they may require action on the part of the member states, a period for implementation, often two years, is allowed. Directives also finish with a different formula from regulations, reflecting their different original purpose, as follows: 'This Directive is addressed to the Member States'.

## Decisions

Decisions (that is, decisions of the Commission or Council of Ministers, not of the European Court of Justice), of which there are hundreds made each year[3], were originally intended to be individualised executive decisions, addressed by Community institutions to member states, companies or individuals. Most are of limited scope and importance, but some have laid down rules rather like regulations so, as with directives, the distinction between them and regulations may be blurred.

The form of decisions is essentially the same as regulations. As with directives, the decision applies only to the addressees, and

---

1 In 2002 there were 100.
2 For example, 'EIGHTH COUNCIL DIRECTIVE of 10 April 1984 based on article 54(3)(g) of the Treaty on the approval of persons responsible for carrying out the statutory audits of accounting documents (85/253/EEC)'. They are sometimes given more memorable colloquial names, such as 'the Equal Treatment Directive' (76/207).
3 In 2002 there were just over 1,000.

takes effect upon notification to the addressee. They usually end with the words 'This Decision is addressed to . . . ', followed by the words 'Member States', or a particular addressee or addressees, such as 'the Federal Republic of Germany and the United Kingdom'.

### Other Community documents

The Commission and Council of Ministers may also, by virtue of article 211 (ex article 155), make recommendations and deliver opinions, but article 249 (ex article 189) makes it clear these are not legislative.

Some other types of document have exceptionally been held to be legislative when the European Court of Justice has sought to further Community aims at the expense of legal exactitude[1].

The content of such documents is sometimes referred to as 'soft law'.

## Legislative powers of the Community and the Community legislative process

Authority to make Community legislation, and the method of legislation, must be found in the treaties. Some articles of the treaties give specific powers to the Commission and Council of Ministers to legislate. For example, article 94 (ex article 100) allows the Council of Ministers, acting on a proposal from the European Commission (and in some cases consulting the European Parliament) to issue directives to achieve approximation of laws of member states.

Other articles impose obligations without expressly giving the power to legislate. For example, article 137 (ex article 118)

---

1 For example, a resolution of the Council of Ministers in Case 22/70 *Commission v Council (the ERTA case)* [1971] ECR 263, [1971] CMLR 335. An interesting example is the United Kingdom 'Declaration' as to who are 'United Kingdom nationals' for the purpose of free movement of workers within the Community. This was appended to the United Kingdom Treaty of Accession. The definition, like the title, was different from any existing form of United Kingdom nationality. The declaration was amended in 1982 to take account of the British Nationality Act 1981 (see OJ C23, 28.1.1983: also Cmnd 9062). It is a unilateral declaration, and not a treaty, nor a United Kingdom statute, nor had parliamentary approval, nor was a decision of a court. However, the European Court of Justice accepted it in *R v Secretary of State for the Home Department, ex parte Manjit Kaur* [2001] ECR I–237, [2001] CMLR 24, [2001] All ER (EC) 250, [2001] INLR 507.

requires the Commission to promote co-operation in employment and other fields. However, the European Court of Justice has held that the obligation implies the power to legislate to fulfil that obligation[1].

In any case, where there is no clear power, article 308 (ex article 235) says that the Council of Ministers, acting according to a certain procedure, can legislate if it is necessary to attain one of the objectives of the Community. Given the breadth of the treaty objectives and the breadth of the interpretation which they have been given, this power is very wide.

The actual legislative process depends upon the treaty provision giving the power to legislate, and varies with the type of legislation, but is always complicated.

*Basic legislative procedure*

In basic form, the idea for legislation comes from within the Commission. Its staff draft a proposal in consultation with interested parties, including member states. As those drafting are not necessarily lawyers, and drafts are translated into all Community languages, the possibility of misunderstanding is high.

The proposal is sent to the Council of Ministers, which passes it on to the European Parliament. The European Parliament remits the proposal to one of its committees for a report, which may contain suggested amendments, upon which the Parliament votes. Members of the Commission may appear in order to explain the proposal. The European Parliament's views are sent back to the Council of Ministers, which passes them on to one of its working groups, co-ordinated by COREPER, comprising national civil servants who examine it in the light of individual national interests.

COREPER's aim is to produce a version acceptable to all. If this is achieved, the Council of Ministers rubber stamps the proposal. If it is not, the Council of Ministers seeks a compromise which is voted on (by a complicated weighted voting system), or refers the matter back to COREPER. Thus, the final version is that agreed by the Council of Ministers, rather than that desired by the Commission, or that which the European Parliament would accept. Indeed, despite its name, the powers of the European Parliament are not great, and it is certainly not the Community legislature[2].

---

1 Cases 218, 283–285/85 and 287/85 *Germany v Commission* [1988] CMLR 11.
2 Where its opinion is required, failure to obtain it invalidates the legislation, however: Case 138/79 *SA Roquette Freres v Council* [1980] ECR 3333.

*'Co-operation procedure'*

The Single European Act introduced for certain purposes a yet more complicated 'co-operation procedure' (alias 'article 252 (ex article 189c) procedure')[1], which increases the power of the European Parliament to amend proposals. After the existing consultation procedure with the European Parliament (the 'first reading'), the Council produces a 'common position'. The Parliament may (in the 'second reading') accept this (by an absolute majority); it may reject it, in which case it can be adopted only by a unanimous vote of the Council; or it may (by an absolute majority), seek amendment which the Council (by a qualified majority) may accept or reject.

*'Co-decision procedure'*

The Treaty on European Union further increased the European Parliament's power through a more successful 'co-decision procedure' (alias 'article 251 (ex article 189b) procedure' and modified by the Treaty of Amsterdam) in some situations. In simplified form, it operates as follows: the Commission's proposal, after initial consultation, is submitted to the Council and European Parliament simultaneously. If the Parliament (by an absolute majority) rejects it, the Council may convene a Conciliation Committee of equal numbers of representatives of Council and Parliament, assisted by the Commission, with a view to agreeing within six weeks a text acceptable to the Council (by a qualified majority) and to Parliament (by an absolute majority). If it fails, the proposal falls unless the Council adopts its original position, or as amended by the Parliament, within a further six weeks. However, the Parliament by an absolute majority may veto this within six months.

*'Assent procedure'*

The Single European Act also introduced a simple procedure which maximises the European Parliament's power by essentially giving it a veto, which applies since the Treaty on European Union only to a narrow range of issues, such as those under article 49 (ex article O) on membership of the European Union.

---

1 This unfortunately uses the terms 'First' and 'Second Reading', which have a very different technical meaning in United Kingdom legislative procedure.

*Popular accountability*

What is clear is that, despite the increased role of the European Parliament, the Community legislative process has little direct accountability to the electors of the member states. It is an example of the Community's 'democratic deficit'.

## The role of the European Court of Justice[1]

The European Court of Justice may hear an enforcement action brought by the Commission against a member state appearing not to be fulfilling its Community obligations (for example, in failing to implement a directive[2]). It may also hear a preliminary reference under article 234 (ex article 177) from a national court or tribunal with a view to ensuring consistent decisions on validity and interpretation throughout the Community and some other types of action.

The full importance of article 234 (ex article 177) depends upon the principle of direct effect of Community law.

## The relationship of Community law and national systems in general[3]

The treaties give remarkably little explicit guidance on the effect Community legislation is to have on member states' own law.

---

1  For the composition and powers of the European Court of Justice, see ch 3.
2  For instance, art 141 (ex art 119) requires sexual equality in employment, and the Equal Pay Directive (Council Directive 75/117), furthering that policy, was made in 1976. The Commission considered that the Equal Pay Act 1970 did not fulfil the requirements of Community law, and successfully brought enforcement proceedings (Case 61/81 *Commission v United Kingdom* [1982] ECR 2601, [1982] ICR 578). As a result, the 1970 Act was amended by the Equal Pay (Amendment) Regulations 1983, SI 1983/1794. (These were United Kingdom delegated legislation regulations, not Community regulations.) However, the Commission considered that the United Kingdom legislation did not fulfil the requirements of the Equal Treatment Directive (76/207) either and brought further successful enforcement proceedings (Case 165/82 *Commission v United Kingdom* [1984] 1 CMLR 44, [1984] ICR 192, [1984] 1 All ER 353, [1984] IRLR 29). These resulted in the Sex Discrimination Act 1986.
3  It should be recalled that 'Community law' is possible only under the EC Treaty, within 'the Community' and not under the second and third 'pillars' of the European Union, despite the partial incorporation of the third 'pillar' into the 'first'.

*Direct applicability, primacy and direct effect*

Nothing is said about the treaties' own effects in member states' law. Regulations are said in article 249 (ex article 189) to be 'binding' and 'directly applicable'. This was intended to mean that they should be incorporated into national law without national legislation, unlike directives (which though 'binding upon member states' were intended to be incorporated by way of national legislation), and unlike decisions (which are 'binding upon those to whom [they] are addressed').

However, certain ideas were implicit in the structure of Community law, and the European Court of Justice has ingeniously built upon them in various decisions[1]. Primacy is thus regarded as a basic principle, that is, that Community law is intended to supersede national law where the two conflict.

Further, Community legislation is intended, provided that certain conditions are fulfilled, to have 'direct effect'. This term does not appear in any of the treaties, but is hallowed by usage. It means that individuals may bring and defend cases in court on the basis of legislation if it has that characteristic.

These ideas taken together involve that, at least in Community law terms:

(a) Community legislation can be law in every member state;
(b) it may be so without the need for national legislation;
(c) it may therefore be so against the wishes of the national legislature;
(d) such Community legislation supersedes any contrary national law;
(e) the existence of such Community law prevents a national legislature from passing valid contrary legislation in future;
(f) Community legislation is applied by the ordinary courts and tribunals of the member state;
(g) the ordinary national courts of the member state must apply such Community legislation even if there is contrary national law;
(h) such Community legislation may, under appropriate circumstances, be invoked before national courts by individuals and companies against other individuals and companies, and against member states.

1 Chiefly Case 26/62 *Van Gend en Loos* [1963] ECR 1, [1963] CMLR 105; Case 6/64 *Costa v ENEL* [1964] ECR 585, [1964] CMLR 425; Case 11/70 *Internationale Handelsgesellschaft* [1970] ECR 1125, [1972] CMLR 255; and Case 106/77 *Simmenthal (No 2)* [1978] ECR 629, [1978] 3 CMLR 263.

These conclusions can be exemplified by Case 26/62 *Van Gend en Loos* [1963] ECR 1, [1963] CMLR 105. Community law, in the form of article 25 (ex article 12) obliged member states not to raise existing customs duties. However, the Dutch government altered the law to raise them in respect of certain chemicals. Van Gend en Loos was a company which had to pay the higher rate. It therefore sued the Dutch government. On an article 234 (ex article 177) preliminary reference, the question of the relationship of national law (here Dutch) and Community law went to the European Court of Justice. It decided that article 25 (ex article 12), being clear and unconditional, had direct effect and that the treaty provision took precedence over Dutch law. Thus, the Dutch tax tribunal hearing the case had to ignore Dutch law, and apply Community law instead.

In practice, national courts may apply Community law without the rigour the European Court of Justice would like. On the other hand, the Court has not yet exhausted its ingenuity, as the *Francovich* and other decisions (discussed below) show.

*Vertical and horizontal direct effect*

Direct effect is complicated by a division into 'vertical' and 'horizontal', worked out by the European Court of Justice in relation to directives.

Community law may place an obligation with direct effect upon a member state. If it does, but the obligation is not fulfilled, a person or company which suffers as a result can sue the member state. This (on the assumption that the member state is 'above' the person or company) is described as 'vertical direct effect', and *Van Gend en Loos* is an example.

Community law may place an obligation with direct effect upon a person or company. If it does, but the obligation is not fulfilled, another person or company which suffers as a result can sue the first one. This is referred to as 'horizontal direct effect' (on the assumption that the individuals or companies are on the same level). An example is Case 43/75 *Defrenne v Sabena* [1976] ECR 455, [1976] 2 CMLR 98. Article 141 (ex article 119) requires equal pay between the sexes. Defrenne was an air stewardess employed by Sabena, the Belgian airline. She discovered she was being paid less than the male stewards, so sued Sabena. On an article 234 (ex article 177) preliminary reference, the European Court of Justice held that article 141 (ex article 119) (as well as being vertically directly effective) was directly effective as between persons and companies (that is, horizontally directly effective).

*Direct effect and different types of Community legislation*

The conditions under which Community legislation has direct effect are not explicitly laid down in the treaties (nor whether it be vertical, horizontal, or both), but must be inferred from the decisions of the European Court of Justice.

Broadly, there are two conditions necessary to create direct effect. Firstly, the legislation must be clearly and specifically enough drafted for a court to be able to apply it[1]. Secondly, it must create an unqualified right or duty and not require action by some other body before a court can apply it.

**Direct effect and the treaties.** The treaties are binding upon the signatory member states. However, certain articles of the treaties also have direct effect. The *Van Gend en Loos* case decided that article 25 (ex article 12) had direct effect, although the EEC Treaty itself made no mention of its effect, and article 25 (ex article 12) itself certainly did not say that an aggrieved person could sue a member state for breach of it. Where a treaty article has direct effect, it is likely to be both vertical and horizontal.

**Direct effect and regulations.** Regulations were undoubtedly intended to have direct effect (at least if the conditions were fulfilled). Article 249 (ex article 189) describes a regulation as having 'general application' and 'being binding in its entirety and directly applicable in all Member States'. Occasionally, however, a regulation is drafted in unspecific language, or requires action by another body before a court could apply it, so is not directly effective[2].

**Direct effect and directives.** Directives are in a more complicated and uncertain position. Article 249 (ex article 189) says they are 'binding as to the result to be achieved, upon each Member State to which [they] are addressed, but shall leave to the national authorities the choice of form and methods', and time for implementation (perhaps two years) is given. As this implies, originally they were not intended to be directly effective, for they apparently

---

1 Thus, for example, in Case 126/86 *Gimenez Zaera* [1987] ECR 3697, art 2 (which remains art 2) was found to impose insufficiently precise obligations to create direct effect.
2 Case C–403/98 *Azienda Agricola Monte Arosu Srl v Regione Autonoma della Sardegna* [2001] ECR I–103, [2002] 2 CMLR 14.

require action by some other body (the national authorities) before a court could apply them.

However, member states have a poor record of compliance with them, and the European Court of Justice, in a number of major cases in the 1970s such as Case 41/74 *Van Duyn* [1974] ECR 1337[1], inventively reinterpreted the law to give them direct effect in certain circumstances. Directives are now regarded as directly effective provided they are sufficiently clear and specific, require no specific action by another body, and the time limit for implementation has expired.

But because directives are addressed to member states, they have been held only vertically directly effective, and not horizontally. This was settled in Case 152/84 *Marshall v Southampton and South West Area Health Authority* [1986] ECR 723, [1986] 1 CMLR 688. Marshall was a dietician employed by the health authority. She was required to retire at the age of 62, although men were not required to do so until the age of 65. National legislation, the Sex Discrimination Act 1975, s 6(2), expressly permitted this discrimination. A directive, the Equal Treatment Directive (76/207), did not. The European Court of Justice, on an article 234 (ex article 177) preliminary reference, held the differential breached the directive, and that where the employee was employed by a public body, she was employed by the member state (to which the directive was addressed). It was therefore in breach of Community law and could be sued. However, a private employer cannot breach a directive, because it is addressed to, and therefore binding only upon, member states[2]. Thus, in general terms, an individual or

---

1 Free movement of workers between member states is a fundamental principle of the Community, enshrined in arts 39–41 (ex arts 48–50), and given flesh by regulations and directives. Directive 64/221 allowed a member state to limit this free movement on grounds of public policy if the personal conduct of the individual warranted it. Van Duyn was a Dutch Scientologist. Scientology is a quasi-religious cult employing pseudo-scientific learning, invented by L Ron Hubbard, an American science-fiction writer. The Home Office wished to discourage Scientology without banning it, and refused van Duyn leave to enter. She sued the United Kingdom government to vindicate her right to free movement. The European Court of Justice (on an art 234 (ex art 177) preliminary reference) upheld her argument, declaring the directive directly effective, and therefore nullifying any contrary United Kingdom law.

2 A question remains as to what organisations are part of the member state for this purpose. In Case C–188/89 *Foster v British Gas* [1991] QB 405, [1990] IRLR 353, the European Court of Justice decided (and the House of Lords therefore held) that British Gas, when still nationalised, was so. The English Court of Appeal, applying the test laid down by the ECJ in *Doughty v Rolls-Royce plc* [1992] 1 CMLR 1045, CA, held that Rolls-Royce, when in form a commercial company, but wholly owned by the government, was not. What of universities?

ordinary commercial company cannot be sued for breach of a directive.

However, in Cases C–6/90 and C–9/90 *Francovich v Italy* [1991] ECR I–5357, [1992] IRLR 84, the court was again inventive and decided that where a member state has failed to implement a directive, it may be liable to pay compensation to individuals harmed by non-implementation. Directive 80/987 required member states to approximate laws guaranteeing the protection of employees' unpaid remuneration upon insolvency of the employer. The European Court of Justice held that the directive was unspecific as to who was responsible for fulfilling the guarantees, therefore it was not directly effective. However, it also decided that the TEC, in particular article 10 (ex article 5)[1], made member states liable for injury caused by their own infringements of Community law, provided that three conditions are fulfilled. They are: that the directive gives rights to the individual; that the content of those rights can be identified from the directive; and that it was the non-implementation which caused the harm complained of. This reduces the importance of the vertical/horizontal distinction, and provides possible enforcement even where a directive has no direct effect. Indeed, yet further cases have blurred the very distinction between 'vertical' and 'horizontal' direct effect.

In addition, in another line of cases including Case 14/83 *Von Colson & Kamann v Land Nordrhein-Westfalen* [1984] ECR 1891 (*'Van Colson'*) and Case C–106/89 *Marleasing SA v La Comercial Internacionale de Alimentacion SA* [1990] ECR I–1435 (*'Marleasing'*), the European Court of Justice was developing another principle. This is that, because directives were addressed to states, they were addressed to all organs of the state. Courts, as one such organ, should therefore decide cases 'in the light of directives', even if the directives were unimplemented. This is sometimes called 'indirect effect' because it falls between having direct effect and not having direct effect.

**Direct effect and decisions.** Decisions were originally intended to be essentially executive decisions. Article 249 (ex article 189) declares a decision to be 'binding in its entirety upon those to whom it is addressed'. Nevertheless, in Case 9/70 *Grad v Finanzamt Traunstein* [1970] ECR 825, [1971] CMLR 1, the European Court of Justice declared a decision directly effective.

---

1 'Member States shall take all appropriate measures, whether general or particular, to ensure fulfilment of the obligations arising out of this Treaty . . . '

The position of decisions is probably the same as that of regulations.

## The relationship between Community legislation and legislation of any legislature in the United Kingdom

The issues in the relationship of Community legislation and national systems described above operate in relation to all member states. Their operation raises particular questions in the case of the United Kingdom, however. These are described below, save for the way in which statutory interpretation is affected, which is dealt with later.

### Community legislation with direct effect and United Kingdom law

Community law did not become directly effective (let alone achieve primacy) in the United Kingdom as a result of the United Kingdom joining the Community by signing the Treaty of Accession in 1972. In United Kingdom law, treaties have no effect in national law[1]. Legislation was required.

That legislation was supplied by the European Communities Act 1972 (as amended). The most important provision is s 2(1), which is unfortunately drafted in turgid and dense language. The gist of it is, however, clear. It provides that all directly effective Community legislation (already made or to be made, and whether in treaty, regulation, directive or decision form), creates 'enforceable Community rights', that is, it has direct effect in the United Kingdom, and will be enforced by courts and tribunals, and that United Kingdom law is to be applied subject to it. Devolution to Scotland and elsewhere has made no difference to this.

These central provisions are supported by s 3(1) and (2). These provide firstly that judges are to be presumed to know the content and significance of the treaties, of the *Official Journal of the European Union*[2] (in which the other legislation is published), and of decisions of the European Court of Justice. Secondly, they provide that questions of the validity and interpretation of Community law, if not actually sent to the European Court of

---

1 *The Parlement Belge* (1879) 4 PD 129; *Attorney-General for Canada v Attorney-General for Ontario* [1937] AC 326; *British Airways v Laker Airways* [1984] 3 All ER 39. For the special position of the European Convention on Human Rights, see above.

2 Previously *Official Journal of the European Community*.

Justice for an article 234 (ex article 177) preliminary reference, must be decided in accordance with the decisions of the court and the principles laid down by it.

In a long series of cases over the following years United Kingdom courts, chiefly the English Court of Appeal, struggled to take on board the full implications of the legislation[1].

Full acceptance of the implications of s 2(1) of the European Communities Act 1972 seems to be shown in the *Factortame* cases[2]. These cases concerned 'quota-hopping' under the Community's fisheries policy. Spanish vessels were registered in the United Kingdom to enable them to fish the United Kingdom national quota. Parliament passed legislation introduced by the government (the Merchant Shipping Act 1988) which, together with delegated legislation under it (the Merchant Shipping (Registration of Fishing Vessels) Regulations 1988, SI 1988/1926), imposed a nationality condition upon registration. The Spanish companies adversely affected sued the United Kingdom government for breach of articles 12 (ex article 6) (non-discrimination on grounds of nationality) and 48 (ex article 58) (right to establish a business) of the EEC treaty. Proceedings were lengthy and complicated, involving two preliminary references under article 234 (ex article 177), and appeals as far as the House of Lords. There were also separate enforcement proceedings by the Commission[3].

The outcome, however, was that the House of Lords accepted that an Act of Parliament contradicting, and passed after, certain Community legislation, could not be enforced by United Kingdom courts. Moreover, because Community law had to be enforced, courts were entitled to issue orders carrying it out, even though national law gave no such right. This was revolutionary in that it appears to have abandoned the principle of parliamentary

---

1 See, for example, *Bulmer (HP) Ltd v Bollinger (J) SA* [1974] Ch 401; *Schorsch Meier GmbH v Hennin* [1975] QB 416; *Felixstowe Docks v BT Docks Board* [1976] 2 CMLR 655; *Shields v E Coomes (Holdings) Ltd* [1979] 1 All ER 456; *Macarthys v Smith* [1979] ICR 785. The various postures of Lord Denning (who as Master of the Rolls, president of the Court of Appeal, had a pivotal role) are interesting.

2 *R v Secretary of State for Transport, ex parte Factortame* [1990] 2 AC 85, [1989] 2 WLR 997, [1989] 2 All ER 692, [1989] 3 CMLR 1 (HL); Case 213/89 *R v Secretary of State for Transport, ex parte Factortame (No 2)* [1991] 1 AC 603, [1990] 3 WLR 818, [1991] 1 All ER 70, [1990] 3 CMLR 375 (ECJ); Case C- 48/93 *R v Secretary of State, ex parte Factortame (No 4)* joined with *Brasserie du Pêcheur SA v Federal Republic of Germany* [1996] QB 404, [1996] 2 WLR 505, [1996] All ER (EC) 301, [1996] 1 CMLR 889 (ECJ); and *R v Secretary of State for Transport, ex parte Factortame (No 5)* [2000] 1 AC 524.

3 Case C–246/89 *Commission v UK* [1991] ECR I–4585).

supremacy. Nevertheless, if Parliament decided to withdraw the UK from the EC, or explicitly and clearly passed legislation in defiance of Community law, the judges would probably still apply Parliament's expressed will in preference to Community law.

**Article 234 (ex article 177) references.** United Kingdom courts have the same power and obligation as courts in any member state to refer questions of the validity or interpretation of Community law to the European Court of Justice under article 234 (ex article 177), and reference is usually discretionary. Scottish devolution has made no difference to this. When the choice exists there is no clear authority from any United Kingdom court on when it is appropriate to refer. In an English case on Great Britain legislation, *Garland v British Rail Engineering Ltd* [1983] 2 AC 751, [1982] 2 WLR 918, [1982] 2 All ER 402, [1982] 2 CMLR 174, the House of Lords suggested there should be reference where a novel point of law arose, or where there is no constant series of decisions from the European Court of Justice.

There have been few references from Scotland. In *Walkingshaw v Marshall* 1992 SLT 1167, concerning illegal fishing, the High Court of Justiciary, on appeal from the sheriff court, made a reference. In *Westwater v Thomson* 1992 SCCR 624, also concerning illegal fishing, the High Court of Justiciary held that the point at issue was too plain to require a reference to the European Court of Justice. In *Brown v Rentokil Ltd* 1996 SLT 839 a previous decision of the court made a reference unnecessary.

*Community legislation without direct effect and United Kingdom law*

Not all Community legislation has direct effect, but it is nevertheless intended to apply within all member states. Directives, for example, are intended to be implemented by the member state (although they may acquire direct effect if they are not).

Implementation may be by Act of the UK Parliament or the Scottish Parliament. For instance, the Consumer Protection Act 1987 implements Directive 85/347, the Products Liability Directive. However, the European Communities Act 1972 (as amended), in addition to providing that direct effect should operate in the United Kingdom, also provides in s 2(2) a short-cut method of implementation of legislation which does not have direct effect. The provision is almost as difficult to understand as s 2(1). However, again, the gist is clear, for s 2(2) delegated from the UK Parliament to the UK government the power to implement any Community right or obligation by statutory instrument[1]. Thus, the UK government can implement a directive without an Act of Parliament and the statutory instrument is the 'form and method' chosen to implement the directive. This power has been widely used. An example is the Equal Pay (Amendment) Regulations 1983, SI 1983/1794, which were designed to amend the Equal Pay Act 1970 to conform to the Equal Pay Directive 75/117, after the enforcement proceedings in Case 61/81 *Commission v United Kingdom* [1982] ICR 578.

The restrictions upon the use of s 2(2), found in s 2(4) and Sch 2, are that the power may not be used to: impose or increase taxation; make retrospective legislation; allow further delegation (unless for the making of procedural rules for courts and tribunals); or create criminal offences carrying greater than a certain penalty. Thus, any directive requiring any of these things to be done would require an Act.

The Scotland Act 1998, by s 53, transfers to the Scottish Ministers functions in relation to observing and implementing obligations under Community law, with respect to devolved functions. However, there is a reserve power in s 57(1) enabling ministers of the UK government to exercise these functions too, presumably to avoid the possibility that a failure of the Scottish Ministers to act would put the UK in breach of its Community obligations.

*Direct effect, parliamentary supremacy and the role of the United Kingdom Parliament*

The primacy and direct effect of Community legislation appears irreconcilable with the parliamentary supremacy traditionally professed by the United Kingdom Parliament. (No such problem arises with the Scottish Parliament which does not profess parliamentary supremacy.) In Community law terms the UK Parliament irrevocably gave up parliamentary supremacy in the 1972 Act, and the United Kingdom judges' reaction in the *Factortame* cases appears to acknowledge that. In United Kingdom constitutional terms it is less clear for, despite *Factortame*, there can be little doubt that the United Kingdom judges would give effect to conscious and explicit repeal of the European Communities Act 1972, and thus to the removal of direct effect, whatever the Community law position.

---

1 For the meaning and significance of the term 'statutory instrument', see below.

In respect of legislation with direct effect, neither the UK Parliament nor the Scottish Parliament has in formal terms a role, for all national legislatures are bypassed in such cases, and Community institutions do not necessarily, or as a matter of course, even keep them informed.

In respect of legislation without direct effect, the UK Parliament and, with respect to devolved (i e non-reserved) functions, the Scottish Parliament, have roles in that either a statute or a piece of subordinate legislation is required to implement the obligation under the European Communities Act 1972. However, 'executive dominance of the legislature' means that the government or executive can normally get through the legislation it wants.

There are two committees of the United Kingdom Parliament directly concerned with Community matters. The House of Commons European Scrutiny Committee[1] looks at Community documents (including legislation and legislative proposals), seeks to monitor the activities of UK ministers in the Council of the Union, and keeps EU developments under review generally. It can form sub-committees, take evidence, and it has a number of expert advisers. It can recommend a proposal be debated on the grounds of its legal or political significance, in which case it normally will be, and the government will not normally assent to the proposal in the Council of Ministers until it has been. However, while the Committee produces reports on various subjects (such as the Common Fisheries Policy, Greenhouse Gas Emissions in the Community and 'European Scrutiny'[2]) and generates discussion, it is not clear that it makes much difference, given the quantity of documents and the secrecy of Commission and Council proceedings, the fact that its views are not part of the input into Community legislation, and related reasons.

The House of Lords Select Committee on the European Union[3] has broader terms of reference, and is more powerful. It has half a dozen sub-committees examining different aspects of the EU[4]. Its reports (on, for example, a Common Policy on Illegal

1 Formerly called the House of Commons Select Committee on European Legislation.
2 House of Commons European Scrutiny Committee Session 2001–02 Thirtieth Report *Euroepan Scrutiny* HC Paper (2001–02) no 152.
3 Formerly called the House of Lords Select Committee on the European Communities.
4 I e, Economic and Financial Affairs, Trade and External Relations; Energy, Industry and Transport; Common Foreign and Security Policy, International Development and External Relations; Environment, Agriculture, Public Health and Consumer Protection; Law and Institutions; and Social Affairs, Education and Home Affairs.

Immigration, the Convention on the Future of Europe and 'the Scrutiny of European Legislation'[1]) are useful and robust, but again are not part of the formal input into Community legislation.

Other Committees may consider such questions as they arise during consideration of other matters[2].

In respect of Community legislation, the UK Parliament is thus primarily in the position of a well-informed pressure group upon the UK government and European Commmission.

The Scottish Parliament has a European and External Relations Committee. Its terms of reference are: to consider and report on proposals for European Community legislation, the implementation of such legislation, and any other European Union issue (as well as questions of other links the Scottish Administration has with other countries and territories). It has produced reports such as those on Scotland's Representation in Europe, the Enlargement of the European Union, and scrutiny of European documents[3]. It also produces 'Europe Matters', an electronic newsletter available on its website[4].

## Publication and citation of Community legislation

The Community publishes the *Official Journal of the European Union*[5]. Certain legislative material must be published in it, and it is the main means of publishing all official information. The *Official Journal* appears in three parallel series. One is the 'L' (for 'Legislation') series, and contains two sections, 'Acts whose publication is obligatory' (for material required to be promulgated through the *Official Journal*), and 'Acts whose publication is not obligatory'. The second is the 'C' (for 'Communication') series, and contains Council of Ministers and Merger Decisions, European Parliament minutes and resolutions, Court of Auditors reports, and European Court of Justice and Court of First Instance

---

1 House of Lords Select Committee on the European Communities Session 2002–03 First Report *Review of Scrutiny of European Legislation* HL Paper (2002–03) no 15

2 E g, the House of Commons Select Committee on Modernisation of the House Session 1997–98 Seventh Report *The Scrutiny of European Business* HC Paper (1997–98) no 791.

3 E g, Scottish Parliament European and External Relations Committee First Report 1999 (EU/99/R1) *Report on Scrutiny of European Documents: covering 18 August 1999 to 19 October 1999.*

4 I e www.scottishparliament.uk/official_report/ctee/Europe.htm.

5 Formerly *Official Journal of the European Communities*.

judgments. The C series has an electronic section called the 'C E' series which contains documents only published only electronically. The third is the 'S' (for 'Supplement') series, which contains tenders and awards for public works and supply contracts. Debates of the European Parliament are published as an Annex to the *Official Journal* up to May 1989, after which they appear online only (see below).

The *Official Journal* is officially distributed, on subscription, by EUR-OP, the Office for Official Publications of the European Communities in Luxembourg[1]. The *Official Journal* 'L' and 'C' series appear daily on paper in numbered issues, and are also available on a hybrid CD-ROM/Internet version monthly, with an annual cumulative version from 1999. There is a monthly and annual (cumulative) alphabetical and methodological index published in arrears. It is accompanied by a twice-yearly, two-volume, *Directory of European Community Legislation in Force* compiled from the CELEX database (see below). The monthly and annual index, and the *Directory*, are included in the subscription to the *Official Journal*. The 'S' series is available in a twice-weekly CD-ROM format, or online on the TED (Tenders Electronic Daily) database[2] and no longer on paper.

Single copies of the *Official Journal* can be purchased from The Stationery Office, the UK government's publishing agency. Two multi-volume 'Special Edition' series of the *Official Journal* (one for 'Acts whose publication is obligatory', one for the rest) were produced upon United Kingdom accession, containing an authentic English language text of the legislation then in force. Much of this is still in force.

However, Community legislation and related documents are readily available online (on subscription) through the European Union's official database CELEX[3], or the much more user-friendly free-access EUR-lex[4]. EUR-lex gives access to draft legislative texts from the Prelex[5] and OEIL[6] databases, which help track the legislative progress of proposals.

An item in the *Official Journal* 'L' series is conventionally cited in the following form: 'OJ L180, 13.7.90, p 26', (or occasionally [1990] OJ L180, 13.7.90) that is, the item on page 26 of the 180th

---

1 The Office for Official Publications website is at http://publications.eu.int/.
2 I e http://ted.publications.eu.int/static/home/en/homepage.ini.
3 See http://europa.eu.int/celex/htm_en.htm.
4 See http://europa.eu.int/eur-lex/index.html.
5 I e, http://europa.eu.int/prelex/apcnet.cfm?CL=net.
6 I e, http://wwwdb.europarl.eu.int/dors/oeil/eu/default.htm.

issue of the L series, which was published on 13 July 1990. This is in fact the citation of a directive on the rights of workers exercising their rights of free movement within the Community. The 'C' series is commonly referred to by a different convention, for example 'OJ C80/1, 10.3.01', that is, series/issue/page/date (or even the more ambiguous '01/C 80/01', that is, year/series/issue/page number). This is the Treaty of Nice. Citations of items in the Special Edition include the abbreviation 'S Edn'.

The *Official Journal* and commercial derivatives, can be found in any of the 44 European Documentation Centres in universities throughout the UK, or in the European Information Points in the Public Information Relays (PIRs) within public libraries.

## Treaties

Treaties often bear a long official title, but an abbreviated form is usually used[1]. References to the EC treaty ('TEC') are commonly given in the form 'article 234 EC'. Because of the numbering of articles in the TEC and TEU effected by the Treaty of Amsterdam, the form is now commonly 'article 234 (ex article 177)'.

**Community publication.** The relevant treaties are published by the Community. New treaties are published in the *Official Journal* 'C' series. A consolidated version of the TEC, incorporating the amendments made by the Treaty on European Union, the Treaty of Amsterdam and the Treaty of Nice, and the TEU, incorporating the Amsterdam and Nice amendments, has been published there, now constituting the official source[2]. Treaties are also likely to be published as a separate document by EUR-OP[3].

EUR-OP has also published several compilations. These include *Treaties Establishing the European Communities: Abridged Edition*, up to date to 1 July 1987 'for reference purposes only and . . . not

---

1 For example, the Treaty Establishing the European Economic Community (Rome, 25 March 1957) is usually referred to as the 'EEC Treaty', and by many others as the 'Treaty of Rome'. It is now amended to become the Treaty Establishing the European Community, which is usually referred to as the 'EC Treaty' or 'TEC'.

2 The Treaty Establishing the European Community at OJ C325/33, 24.14.02, and the Treaty on European Union at OJ C325/5, 24.12.02. The Treaty of Amsterdam is at OJ C340/1, 10.11.87 and the Treaty of Nice at C80/1, 10.3.01.

3 For example, the Treaty on Political Union (the 'Maastricht Treaty') was so published in 1992.

binding upon the Community institutions'; and *Treaties Establishing the European Communities: Treaties Amending These Treaties: Documents Concerning Accession*, which is up to date to 1 July 1978 only. Following the Treaty on European Union (the 'Maastricht Treaty') the European Community published a small volume of 'Selected Instruments from the Treaties [Book 1 Volume 1] in 1993. A new two-volume edition was published in 1995 to incorporate the provisions relating to the accession of Austria, Finland and Sweden. This was updated to January 1999 in a further edition. These compilations are also not legally binding, and are for reference only. EUR-OP also publishes the *Collection of Agreements Concluded by the European Communities*.

However, the treaties can be readily found through CELEX or EUR-lex (see above).

**United Kingdom official publication.** The United Kingdom government, through The Stationery Office, publishes the treaties as Command Papers[1]. These include, for example, the Treaty concerning the Accession of ... the United Kingdom ... to the European Economic Community (Brussels, 22 January 1972; Cmnd 7460–7463, 1979) (UKTS Nos 15–18). It also produced European Communities Treaties and Related Documents in ten volumes up to date to 1972. Although reliable, these are not authoritative in Community law terms and are oudated.

**United Kingdom commercial publication.** Some commercial publishers produce compilations of the treaties, which, although not authoritative, are in practice more useful as they may be consolidated and annotated (that is, showing the current version, with amendments, and comment). These include the multi-volume loose-leaf and CD-ROM *European Union Law Library* (Sweet & Maxwell), which contains the treaties and many associated documents. Foster *Blackstone's EC Legislation* (Blackstone, 12th edn, 2001) also gives the texts up to date of publication. Texts of relevant parts of the treaties may be found in encyclopaedias and

---

1 Command Papers are formal government policy documents and the like, produced 'by Command of Her Majesty'. They are numbered up to 9,999, so new series are commenced every few years. Different series are distinguished by preceding initials. Currently these are 'Cm'; for the previous series they were 'Cmnd'; before that 'Cmd'. Some sets of Command Papers are published or republished in subordinate series, such as the United Kingdom Treaty Series (UKTS).

textbooks on subjects with a significant Community law dimension[1] and extracts in 'cases and materials' books, such as Craig and de Búrca *EU Law: texts, cases and materials* (Oxford University Press, 3rd edn, 2003).

There are also several online subscription services such as WESTLAW, and others based on CELEX.

*Regulations, directives and decisions – 'secondary legislation'*

**Community publication.** Regulations bear a title, but are usually cited in the following form: 'Council Regulation 1251/70/EEC', or simply 'Regulation 1251/70/EEC'[2], which refers to the 1,251st Regulation of 1970, initiated by the Council of Ministers of the EEC (now the 'Council of the Union'). It is useful to cite them by the *Official Journal* reference as well (in this case 'OJ L124, 30.6.70, p 24 (S Edn 1970 (II), p 402)').

Directives and decisions also bear little-used titles and are cited with the abbreviated year preceding the sequential number, for example 'Council Directive 90/364/EEC (OJ L180, 13.7.90, p26)'. Because the series are now published in separate sequences, with the same 'year/number' citation, the simple form '90/364' is ambiguous, making the correct *Official Journal* citation vital. Directives are sometimes given semi-official names, such as 'First Directive on Company Law Harmonisation' (Cl Dir 68/151/EEC); popular names, such as 'the Equal Pay Directive' (Cl Dir 75/117/EEC); or at least abbreviated names, for example 'the Directive on Animal Semen' (Cl Dir 87/328/EEC). Commonly, however, indication of the initiating body is dropped, as in 'Dir 64/221' (which contains the 'public policy proviso' exception to the free movement of workers), giving no hint that it was initiated by the Council of Ministers.

Regulations must be published in the *Official Journal*, as 'Acts whose publication is obligatory'. Although article 253 (ex article 191) EC only requires directives and decisions to be notified to their addressees, in practice they appear in the section 'Acts whose publication is not obligatory', so are available generally. Up-to-date texts, containing amendments and excluding repeals, are not offi-

---

1 For example, *Butterworths Immigration Law Service*, a looseleaf encyclopaedia on immigration law, contains Community legislation relevant to the subject, and is continuously updated. Macdonald and Webber (eds) *Macdonald's Immigration Law and Practice* (5th edn, 2001), a textbook, contains similar material, updated to the date of publication.
2 The form '1251/70' is too ambiguous and unhelpful.

cially produced, unless there is consolidating legislation, but the EUR-OP *Directory of European Community Legislation in Force* also provides the means of updating. The CELEX database covers all regulations, directives and decisions, and other relevant material, including preparatory documents, and provides the means of updating.

Again, however, secondary legislation is readily found online through CELEX or EUR-lex (see above).

**United Kingdom official publication.** HMSO produced *Secondary Legislation of the European Communities: Subject Edition*, a multi-volume version of the texts, digested into subject headings, but this has not been updated since 1979, so is of limited value.

**United Kingdom commercial publication.** Commercial publications are therefore, as with the treaties, in practice the most useful compilations. These include the multi-volume loose-leaf *Encyclopaedia of European Community Law* (Sweet & Maxwell) which contains most Community legislation, gives annotations and is continually updated, and works such as Foster *Blackstone's EC Legislation* (Blackstone, 13th edn, 2002) and Rudden and Wyatt *Basic Community Laws* (7th edn, 1999). Also, as in the case of the treaties, encyclopaedias and textbooks on subjects with a significant Community law dimension may contain texts of relevant regulations etc, as may 'cases and materials' books.

The online subscription services such as WESTLAW and those based on CELEX also contain the secondary legislation.

*Other related materials published by the Community*

The Community also publishes an enormous quantity of information relating to its legislative and other activities. This includes the annual *General Report on the Activities of the Unions* and monthly *Bulletin of the European Union*. The latter contains an account of current proposals and other material, and has supplements containing details of some legislative proposals and reports. The 'COM' series of Commission documents includes proposals and discussion papers from the European Commission on CELEX or EUR-lex, and there are very many regular and ad hoc publications. The European Parliament also published its *Working Documents* on paper form to 1990 and on microfiche to 1997, since when they can be found only online.

## PART 3: UNITED KINGDOM PARLIAMENTARY LEGISLATION

### Parliamentary legislation, human rights, Community law and devolution

Acts of Parliament, often referred to as statutes, are usually regarded as the normal form of legislation in the United Kingdom[1]. The United Kingdom is a state, and does not exist in order to fulfill certain specified policies but, rather, to run the country in all its complexity, so Acts of Parliament range over many subjects and touch on almost every aspect of life. On the other hand, such Acts rarely deal in fundamental principle, for the underlying principles of the legal system are found in the common law. The lack of a written constitution underlines the point. Legislation is thus principally a means of changing the law, and of stating new law in detail, and it may change direction or policy with changing political priorities of different governments. As noted in Chapters 3 and 4, traditionally, there has been argued to be 'parliamentary supremacy', that is, no legal boundaries to Parliament's legislative power, only political prudence and the morality of its members. In law, it may pass any Act to any effect.

Parliament may therefore legislate on 'human rights' issues, and has. However, 'human rights' has come to be seen as a means of limiting the ability of legislatures to enact laws (as well as the ability of executives to take decisions). The European Convention on Human Rights (ECHR) is thus such a limit, indeed is the principal source of such limits in the United Kingdom context. The nature of the ECHR and its institutions are discussed in Chapter 3, the relationship between the ECHR, the Human Rights Act 1998 and Acts of Parliament sketched in Chapter 4, and considered in detail in Part 1 of this chapter, but it should be recalled that the Human Rights Act 1998 is intended to limit, while preserving, parliamentary supremacy.

The European Community exists for relatively specific (albeit evolving) purposes. It therefore includes statements of underlying principles and relatively constant (if evolving) policies. On the other hand, such relative constancy is in part because Community institutions are much less answerable to any electorate. Also, because it exists for relatively specific purposes, the range of Community legislation is narrower than that of parliamentary

---

1 In terms of sheer quantity, however, delegated legislation is much more important: see Part 5 of this chapter below.

legislation. The nature of the European Community and its institutions was also discussed in Chapter 3, its relationship with Acts of Parliament sketched in Chapter 4, and they were considered in detail in Part 2 of this chapter (including how far parliamentary supremacy is compromised).

The introduction of devolution means that the devolved legislatures are taking over responsibilities within their competencies. Thus, in relation to Scotland, Acts of the Scottish Parliament will gradually take over the role of normal legislation in those areas not reserved to Westminster (although in the early years of devolution a remarkably large proportion of legislation applying to Scotland has continued to be made at Westminster[1]). The nature of devolution and its institutions was also discussed in Chapter 3, and the relationship with Acts of Parliament again sketched in Chapter 4 and they will be considered in detail in Part 4 of this chapter (including the parliamentary supremacy is clearly preserved).

## United Kingdom Acts of Parliament, their types and form

Most statutes are technically 'public, general' statutes, and discussion in this chapter relates exclusively to such statutes unless otherwise stated. 'Local', 'personal', 'private' and 'hybrid' legislation (which are not 'public, general') and particular types of public general Acts are discussed below under 'Special cases'.

There are on average some 50 Acts of Parliament passed in a year[2]. Many Acts repeal or amend existing legislation, so the annual increase is not as great as this rate of production suggests. Acts also vary enormously in length. Effectively, the shortest possible is two sections. Recent examples include the Census (Amendment) (Scotland) Act 2001, the Criminal Defence Service (Advice and Assistance) Act 2001 and the Civil Defence (Grants) Act 2002. There is no theoretical maximum, and many have hundreds of sections, for example the Enterprise Act 2001 with 281 sections, the Capital Allowances Act 2001 with 581 sections, and by far the longest so far is the Income and Corporation Taxes Act 1988, which approaches 1,500 sections (though, as a consolidating statute, it is not typical). The average length of statutes is probably increasing.

---

1 The United Kingdom Parliament may, of course, continue to legislate in devolved areas if it chooses: Scotland Act 1998, s 28(7).

2 In 1997 there were 69 and in 2001 only 25. These represent the extremes in recent years.

Statutes also vary enormously in age. The great majority of Acts in force are relatively modern, but there are still many older ones, and even a few dating from the Parliaments of Scotland and England, which ceased to exist in 1707[1], and the Parliament of Great Britain which lasted from 1707 to 1801.

There is a conventional structure to a modern UK Act of Parliament, described in the following paragraphs[2].

*Short title, chapter number and arrangement of sections*

UK Acts commence with a short title, for example the 'Scotland Act 1998'. The short title is a 19th-century invention, but all earlier statutes still in force have been given them retrospectively by the Short Titles Act 1896 and the Statute Law Revision (Scotland) Act 1964. It is the relatively brief name almost invariably used to identify the Act. Short titles include the year of enactment, which may be important as Acts of similar short title may be passed in different years and may be in force at the same time[3]. When a series of related Acts exists, the last may give a collective title, for example the 'Official Secrets Acts 1911–89'[4] or simply 'the Immigration Acts'[5]. On the other hand, reflecting the ad hoc nature of legislation in a common law or mixed system, Acts on similar topics may have dissimilar names, for example, those concerned with statute law[6]. Short titles often incorporate brackets, and almost all pre-

1 See below in relation to Acts of the original, pre-1707, Parliament of Scotland.

2 Section 19 of the Human Rights Act 1998 requires a minister introducing a Bill into Parliament to state whether or not it conforms to the requirements of that Act. However, there is no requirement that this statement, or an amended form of it, appear on the face of the Act.

3 For example, the British Nationality Acts of 1948, 1958, 1964 (two Acts) and 1965 were all in force at the same time, and required reference to the British Nationality Act 1914. All were repealed by the British Nationality Act 1981 (itself now amended, though by, e g, the Nationality, Immigration and Asylum Act 2002, and not by another Act of identical name).

4 Official Secrets Act 1989, s 16(2).

5 I e the Immigration Act 1971, Immigration Act 1988, Asylum and Immigration Appeals Acts 1993, Asylum and Immigration Act 1996, Immigration and Asylum Act 1999, and Nationality, Immigration and Asylum Act 2002 (but not the Special Immigration Appeals Commission Act 1997): Nationality, Immigration and Asylum Act 2002, s 158.

6 The principal ones include the Acts of Parliament (Commencement) Act 1793; Short Titles Act 1896; Parliament Act 1911; Consolidation of Enactments (Procedure) Act 1949; Acts of Parliament Numbering and Citation Act 1962; Royal Assent Act 1967; and Interpretation Act 1978.

devolution Acts applying only to Scotland are indicated in this way[1], though there are exceptions[2]. Other common uses of brackets are '(Amendment)', and '(Miscellaneous Provisions)'. An Act's short title is officially given to it by a short title provision towards the end of the Act.

As well as a short title, Acts of the UK Parliament have a chapter number which denotes the sequential number of that Act in the year, rendered variously as, for example, 'chapter 15', 'ch 15', 'cap 15', or 'chap 15'[3]. Taken with the year of enactment, it provides a unique reference number of that Act, known as the citation. Thus, the citation '1998 c46' refers uniquely to the Scotland Act 1998[4].

An Act of greater length than a couple of sections is officially printed with an arrangement of sections, which is a contents list of sections and schedules and their marginal notes.

## Long title, date of Royal Assent and preamble

In addition to short titles, UK Acts have long titles. These were used long before short titles. In practice they may be brief or lengthy[5]. Their function is to indicate and delimit the subject matter of the Bill introduced into Parliament, and they may be an aid to interpretation of a statute. At the end of the long title the date of royal assent, that is, the date on which the Act is actually enacted, is given in square brackets[6]. However, while this is the date of enactment, confusingly, it is not necessarily (or indeed, generally) the date or dates on which the Act comes into force, for which, see below in relation to 'Commencement'.

1 E g Criminal Procedure (Scotland) Act 1995. What will happen post-devolution is unclear, but see transitional examples of the Scottish Enterprise Act 1999 and the Mental Health (Scotland) Act 1999. A parallel convention applies to Northern Ireland legislation. Curiously, none applies to legislation applying only in England.

2 Modern examples include the Scotland Acts 1978 and 1998 (and there is the transitional example of the Scottish Enterprise Act 1999.

3 In medieval English constitutional theory, a parliament passed only one statute, so, if it covered different topics, each was distinguished as a 'chapter' (in Latin 'caput').

4 But see below 'Publication and citation of parliamentary legislation: Acts of the Parliaments of Great Britain and the United Kingdom'.

5 The long title of the Official Secrets Act 1989 runs to 20 words and reads 'An Act to replace section 2 of the Official Secrets Act 1911 by provisions protecting more limited classes of official information'. That of the Water Act 1989 runs to some 200 words.

6 Thus, for example, after the long titles of the Official Secrets Act 1989 and Water Act 1989 appear '[11th May 1989]' and '[6th July 1989]' respectively.

Preambles to Acts were formerly used to show their purpose. Very occasionally, a modern Act may have a preamble, commencing with the word 'Whereas ... ', and outlining the reasons for it[1]. This precedes the long title.

## The enacting formula

UK Acts of Parliament do not have lengthy recitals of their origins at the beginning, as Community legislation does. They do have an enacting formula immediately before the actual substantive provisions. It is a validating incantation, recording enactment. There are four forms of it: one is the basic, the others are used in taxation legislation, government expenditure legislation, and legislation under the Parliament Act 1911, respectively[2].

## Sections, marginal notes and marginal references

The basic unit of a UK Act is the section, and sections are numbered sequentially throughout the Act. Draftsmen aim at exactitude (in 'fixed verbal form': see Appendix 1), rather than comprehensibility. They break down the content into sub-sections and the like as necessary[3], and use typographical devices to express grammatical, and thus logical, structure. This use of numbers, letters and indentation typifies statutory language. The principal convention on nomenclature and labelling is as follows (although

---

1 The Welsh Language Act 1967 has the following: 'Whereas it is proper that the Welsh language should be freely used by those who so desire in the hearing of legal proceedings in Wales and Monmouthshire; that further provision should be made for the use of that language, with like effect as English, in the conduct of other official or public business there; and that Wales should be distinguished from England in the interpretation of future Acts of Parliament ... '. Private Bills always have a preamble: see, for example, the British Railways Act 1992.
2 Its basic form, reflecting the relationship of the three parts of Parliament until the 19th century, reads 'Be it enacted by the Queen's most Excellent Majesty, by and with the advice and consent of the Lords Spiritual and Temporal, and Commons, in this Parliament assembled, and by authority of the same as follows ... '. Amusingly, the Finance Acts, which permit taxation, refer to taxes 'freely and voluntarily given', and the Consolidated Fund and Appropriation Acts, which permit government expenditure, to funds 'cheerfully granted'. Legislation under the Parliament Acts omits reference to the Lords but inserts 'in accordance with the provisions of the Parliament Act 1911'.
3 In grammatical terms, the sentence contained in the section is broken into its constituent clauses and phrases. The main clause is likely to start or finish the section. The subordinate clauses form the various sub-sections etc, reflecting their relationship with the main clause.

the sub-section level is sometimes omitted in a short but sub-divided section, so that the draftsman goes straight from section to paragraph):

| section | **1** | (emboldened) |
|---|---|---|
| sub-section | (1) | |
| paragraph | (a) | |
| sub-paragraph | (i) | |

As well as assisting in exact expression of meaning, this convention allows precise identification of provisions, for example, 'Race Relations Act 1976, s 1(1)(b)(iii)', that is, 'section 1, sub-section 1, paragraph b, sub-paragraph ii' (or, where the draftsman has gone straight to paragraphs, 'Nationality, Immigration and Asylum Act 2002, s 5(b)', that is, 'section 5, paragraph b').

Where an amending Act inserts a whole new section, it is identified by a capital letter after the preceding number. A new section after s 1 would be s 1A, and its sub-sections would be rendered 's 1A(1)' etc[1]. Thus, the Immigration and Asylum Act 1999, ss 128–139 inserted 11 new sections between ss 28 and 29 of the Immigration Act 1971, which therefore appear as ss 28A–29K of the 1971 Act. A similar principle applies to inserted sub-sections etc. Thus, the Nationality, Immigration and Asylum Act 2002, s140(3) inserted a new paragraph between s 87(3)(e) and (f) of the Immigration and Asylum Act 1999, which therefore appears as s 87(3)(ea) of the 1999 Act.

Every section has a marginal note. This is a signpost rather than a description, and is the form of words used in the relevant entry in the arrangement of sections.

Where a section in one Act refers to another Act, for instance to amend it, an abbreviated citation to that other Act may given in the margin. For example, the Immigration and Asylum Act 1999, s 22 affects the Asylum and Immigration Act 1996, so, in the margin of the former, next to s 22, appears '1996 c49', the citation of the earlier Act. However, the practice also exists of giving short title, year and chapter number in the text itself.

These conventions are used in official editions of UK Acts. Usage may vary somewhat in commercially produced ones or in textbooks. For example, marginal notes may not be in the margin, but follow the section number; marginal references may not appear

---

1 It follows that s 1(a) and s 1A would be entirely separate provisions. Indeed, there might be a s1(a) and a s 1A(a).

at all; 'section' is usually abbreviated to 's' ('ss' in the plural); and the brackets round the sub-section number are removed.

## Headings

A variety of headings may be used in the text of an Act. Groups of sections may be collectively labelled as Parts, with capital roman numerals and centred capitalised names. For example, ss 1–31 of the Immigration and Asylum Act 1999 are labelled 'Part I' and 'IMMIGRATION: GENERAL', while ss 32–43 are labeled 'Part II' and 'CARRIERS' LIABILITY' and so on. Occasionally, Parts are divided into 'titles' or even 'chapters'[1].

Whether or not an Act has Parts, smaller groups of sections are likely to be labelled by a cross-heading, centred and italicised. For example, within Part 1 of the Immigration and Nationality Act 1999, ss 1–5 are cross-headed '*Leave to enter, or remain in, the United Kingdom*', ss 6–8 '*Exemption from immigration control*' and ss 9–15 '*Removal from the United Kingdom*', and so on. A common usage is to label as '*Supplementary*' or '*Miscellaneous and Supplemental*' the last few sections, which contain a number of operating instructions for the Act, such as the interpretation section, repeals and amendment provisions, and others described below.

## Interpretation sections

Interpretation sections (usually identified by the marginal note), may appear anywhere in a UK Act, but commonly at the end. They specify meanings of words and phrases for the purposes of the Act. This may be necessary because the words are inherently vague, or because they are used in an unusual sense, or because they have been invented for the purpose. For example, the Immigration Act 1971, s 33 stipulates that '"aircraft" includes hovercraft, "airport" includes hoverport, and "port" includes airport', and also that '"Convention adoption" has the same meaning as in the Adoption Act 1976 and the Adoption (Scotland) Act 1978'. The meanings assigned may not actually be definitions, for sometimes the section stipulates that one term 'means' something, sometimes that it 'includes' something, and occasionally that it 'does not include' something. The opening words of the section commonly, but unhelpfully, assign meanings 'unless the context otherwise

---

1 An extreme example is the Capital Allowances Act 2001, which has 12 Parts, divided into 10, 20, 12, 6, 7, 5, 3, 5, 0, 8, 2 and 6 Chapters respectively.

requires'. Section 127 of the Scotland Act 1998 usefully gives a list of some 60 expressions used in the Act (such as 'cross-border authority', 'open power' and 'Scots private law') and in which sections their definition can be found[1].

*Repeals and amendments*

UK Acts of Parliament continue in force unless repealed or amended, subject to two exceptions. Firstly, a provision in the Act may specify a terminal date, as did s 27 of the Prevention of Terrorism (Temporary Provisions) Act 1989 (and its predecessors), though this is rare[2]. Secondly, an Act of the Parliament of Scotland may fall into 'desuetude', that is, lapse through the growth of contrary practice[3].

UK Acts, therefore, commonly repeal or amend earlier Acts, and no special process is required (and amendment is not restricted to Acts with '(Amendment)' in the short title). This follows from the doctrine of parliamentary supremacy, although the direct effect of Community law would appear to have limited this freedom.

Moreover, delegated legislation (for which, see Part 5 of this chapter, below) may repeal or amend an Act of Parliament, provided that Parliament has delegated that power.

Two methods of amendment may be employed[4]. The textual or direct method simply substitutes a new provision for the old, a 'scissors and paste' process. It is generally preferred by the users of statutes as it shows the final form clearly. The referential or indirect method leaves the original text, but describes how it should be changed. It is preferred by Parliament as it shows what changes are proposed.

Repealing and amending provisions may appear anywhere in an Act, but commonly do so in a specific section at the end of the Act. Where there are numerous repeals and amendments, they are usually detailed in a schedule, for example Sch 9 to the Social Security Act 1989 lists 18 Acts which it repeals to various degrees.

---

1 A similar provision in Sch 1, Part 2 of the Capital Allowances Act 2001 lists 130 such expressions.
2 The Murder (Abolition of Death Penalty) Act 1965, most unusually, provided that 'This Act shall continue in force until the thirty first day of July nineteen hundred and seventy, and shall then expire unless Parliament by affirmative resolution of both Houses otherwise determines'. Such an affirmative resolution was forthcoming.
3 See *The Laws of Scotland: Stair Memorial Encyclopaedia* vol 22, para 129.
4 Miers and Page *Legislation* (2nd edn, 1990) p 195, n 6 suggests that ss 60 and 61 of the Wildlife and Countryside Act 1981 are paradigm cases.

Indeed, where chiefly one Act is amended, and there are many amendments to other Acts, there may be two schedules, as in the British Nationality Act 1981, Schs 4 (Amendments of the Immigration Act 1981) and 7 (Consequential Amendments).

Occasionally, Statute Law Revision Acts and Statute Law (Repeal) Acts have been passed, which remove from the statute book obsolete and unnecessary legislation, which inevitably accumulates in a system in which legislation is generally ad hoc. These are discussed under 'Special cases' below.

### Transitional provisions

When a UK Act is repealed or amended, transitional difficulties may arise, for instance in relation to litigation which is in progress. Transitional provisions, usually found at the end of an Act, provide a solution, and the detail is often put in a schedule. For example, s 169(2) of the Immigration and Asylum Act 1999 reads 'Schedule 15 contains transitional provisions and savings'.

### Commencement provisions

By virtue of the Acts of Parliament (Commencement) Act 1793, a UK Act comes into force on the date of royal assent, unless it specifies otherwise[1]. They often so specify in a commencement section normally found at the end of the Act. The simplest form of commencement section gives a specific date for commencement[2]. A rare variant is to declare that the Act comes into force at the same time as another Act[3], and a common one that it does so at a specific period after royal assent, typically three months[4]. A very common method nowadays is to delegate the power to the government to bring the Act into force, to be exercised through a statutory instrument known as a 'commencement order'. An Act may have different sections brought into force on different days, and

---

1 The British Nationality Act 1958 (not specifying otherwise) came into force on the date of royal assent (20 February 1958).
2 Section 34(2) of the British Nationality Act 1948 stipulated that it come into force 'on the first day of January nineteen hundred and forty-nine'.
3 Section 25 of the Company Directors Disqualification Act 1986 stipulates that it come into force on commencement of the Insolvency Act 1986.
4 Section 3(3) of the British Nationality Act 1964 stipulated that it come into force 'at the expiration of two months beginning with the date on which it is passed'.

use a mixture of commencement methods[1], and more than one commencement order, some of which may be years after the enactment which can make it difficult to discover if a particular provision is in force or not[2].

## Short title provision

A provision at the end of a UK Act officially gives it its short title (for which, see above) by stating 'This Act may be cited as . . .'. No chapter number is given, for this cannot be known until enactment.

## Extent provisions

Because Acts of the UK Parliament do not necessarily apply to the whole of the United Kingdom there are commonly extent provisions, stipulating to which law areas they do apply. Such provisions can be complicated[3].

Acts may extend beyond the United Kingdom to dependencies. Commonly such Acts are extended to the Channel Islands and Isle of Man (which are not part of the United Kingdom), and to colonies, as, for example, by s 53(5), does the British Nationality Act 1981.

An Act may even apply to activities by certain people outwith the territorial extent of the United Kingdom and its dependencies. For instance, the Official Secrets Act 1989 extends to the United Kingdom but, by s 15, also applies to specified acts done by British citizens and Crown servants abroad. Acts concerned with the security of the state and terrorism may extend and apply very broadly,

1 Section 53(3) of the British Nationality Act 1981 stipulates that 'section 49 and this section shall come into force on the passing of this Act' (30 October 1981), and s 53(2) that the rest of the Act 'shall come into force on such day as the Secretary of State may by order made by statutory instrument appoint'. That power was exercised in the British Nationality 1981 (Commencement) Order 1982, SI 1982/933, which appointed 1 January 1983.
2 The Control of Pollution Act 1974 has had 20 commencement orders and is still not completely in force. The record is thought to be held by the Easter Act 1928 which is still not in force.
3 The Water Act 1989, s 194(6) specified that Schs 2 and 5, ss 4, 13 and 23 'so far as relating to any scheme under either of those Schedules', s 95 and certain repeals extend to the United Kingdom. Section 194(7) specifies that certain other sections and schedules extend, or extend in part, to Great Britain. Section 194(8) specified that yet other provisions apply only to Scotland, and s 194(9) that yet further provisions extend only to England and Wales.

usually by international agreement. The Taking of Hostages Act 1982, s 1 (which followed the International Convention Against Taking Hostages of 1979) declares 'A person, whatever his nationality, who, being in the United Kingdom or elsewhere' takes hostages contrary to the terms of the Act, commits an offence in the United Kingdom. The Criminal Justice (Terrorism and Conspiracy) Act 1998 was co-ordinated with similar legislation in the Republic of Ireland and by s 5 enabled prosecutions in the UK of conspiracies to commit illegal acts in territories outside the UK.

The most extreme example appears to be the Outer Space Act 1986, which stipulates in s 1 that 'This Act applies to the following activities whether carried out in the United Kingdom or elsewhere ... (c) any action in outer space'. 'Outer space' is defined, strangely, to include the moon.

## Schedules

Many UK Acts have schedules, which are specifically incorporated into the Act by a section. They are appendices, containing detailed matter too complicated for the body of the text, such as lists, tables and incidental rules. The British Nationality Act 1981, for example, has nine schedules[1].

Schedules may have Parts and cross-headings as the body of an Act does, and are usually drafted in broadly the same manner as sections. The conventional labelling and nomenclature are as follows:

| | | |
|---|---|---|
| schedule | 1 | (unemboldened) |
| paragraph | (1) | |
| sub-paragraph | (a) | |
| sub-sub-paragraph | (i) | |

Repeal and amendment schedules are often in tabular form[2].

---

1 Respectively: Requirements for Naturalisation; Provisions for Reducing Statelessness; Countries whose Citizens are Commonwealth Citizens; Amendments of the Immigration Act 1971; Form of Oath of Allegiance; British Dependent Territories; Consequential Amendments; Transitional Provisions; and Repeals. The Enterprise Act 2002 achieved 36 schedules, and the Finance Act 2000 managed 40, but financial legislation is atypical.
2 Typically, a repeal schedule is in the form of a table of three columns, headed respectively 'chapter' (listing the citations of the Acts repealed); 'short title'; and 'extent of repeal' (which may be from a single word to 'The whole Act').

*Explanatory Notes*

Since 1999, for almost every Act[1], 'Explanatory Notes' have been produced by the sponsoring Government department. They are an attempt to explain in lay language what each provision of the Act does. They have, however, no official status, although as a result of Pepper v Hart [1993] AC 593, [1993] 1 All ER 42 (discussed in relation to statutory interpretation below) they may presumably be used in statutory interpretation.

## The United Kingdom Parliament enactment procedure

The proposal for legislation which is presented to the Parliament is called a Bill. Any Bill is itself the result of a lengthy process. Indeed, commonly the changes imposed by the parliamentary process are small compared with what a proposal has already undergone.

*Who seeks legislation and why?*

The government's role in the initiation of legislation is central in the United Kingdom constitution. It is expected to legislate, and has something approaching a monopoly of the initiation of parliamentary legislation. Initiation by others is dealt with below under 'Special cases'.

Some government legislation is party political 'manifesto legislation', for example the community charge or poll tax, imposed by the Abolition of Domestic Rates (Scotland) Act 1987, or the introduction of 'human rights' and devolution in the Human Rights Act 1998 and Scotland Act 1998. Such legislation may be of enormous importance, but represents only a small proportion of all legislation[2]. Other legislation emerges as reaction to events. The Dangerous Dogs Act 1991 was a reaction to public pressure over a number of attacks by dogs, the Anti-Terrorism, Crime and Security Act 2001 was a reaction to the events of 11 September that year, and much legislation in relation to asylum-seeking, in a number of Acts over several years (most recently the Nationality,

1 Technically, with every public general Act (for which see below) introduced by the government, and with at least some introduced as private members' Bills.
2 Rose *Do Parties Make a Difference?* (2nd edn, 1984) pp 72–73 concluded that only 8% of the Bills of the Conservative government 1970–72 were 'manifesto Bills', and only 13% of those of the Labour government of 1974–79. For a more recent analysis on somewhat different lines, see Drewry (1989) 10 Stat LR 200.

Immigration and Asylum Act 2002) is a reaction to increased asylum-seeking, particularly following the opening of the Channel Tunnel. Such legislation may on occasion be symbolic as much as instrumental, but in any case represents only a small proportion of all legislation[1].

The great majority of Bills originate in the normal processes of government. The constitution requires annual legislation to allow the government to raise and spend money. It also now requires the government to produce legislation to put into effect Community policy when Community institutions require it (although this is principally done by delegated legislation). Most legislation emerges from the departments of government, however. As they administer their responsibilities, they discover that the law is not having the desired effect, so legislation to change it is promoted. An important category of this is statute law revision and repeal and consolidation.

*Pre-parliamentary stages of United Kingdom parliamentary legislation*[2]

The pre-parliamentary stages of UK parliamentary legislation are of the utmost importance. It is then that the government decides what legislation it wishes, consults with interested parties, formulates specific proposals, and has them drafted by the Parliamentary draftsman into the Bill which will be presented to Parliament. Because the government has invested considerable resources into producing the Bill, it will be loath to accept amendments to it (though it may introduce amendments itself, reflecting second thoughts or the pressure the draftsman was under) and, given executive dominance of the legislature, it will almost always get the Bill through Parliament in a form it wants, though often at a cost. Also, there is a limited amount of parliamentary time available for legislation, and governments would like to introduce much more legislation than there is parliamentary time for. In consequence, there is a Queen's Speech and Future Legislation Committee of the Cabinet to rank proposals for the coming parliamentary session.

Consultation is a major part of the pre-parliamentary stages. (This topic is dealt with in more detail in Chapter 8.) Advice is

---

1 See Rose *Do Parties Make a Difference?* (2nd edn, 1984).
2 For a fuller, readable account, if now a little dated, see Miers and Page *Legislation* (2nd edn, 1990) chs 4 and 5.

obtained from ad hoc or specialised bodies in highly institution-alised ways. Royal Commissions, composed of disinterested members of the great and good, were once a common method of investigating problems and suggesting solutions, but have largely fallen out of favour[1]. Committees of inquiry, which are less high-powered, and departmental and inter-departmental committees and working parties of civil servants and others are much more common[2]. The Law Commissions are of considerable importance in relation to certain types of legislation[3].

In addition, departments of government have continuing relations with a variety of interest and pressure groups, and it is in the dialogue with them that, within the government's priorities and predilections, proposals are formulated.

Consultation may be in part public. UK governments sometimes issue Green Papers or other consultative documents[4], outlining options and soliciting comment (and sometimes also White Papers, that is, statements of firm policy[5], though some have 'green edges'). Indeed, now some Bills are published in draft, which allows greater scrutiny.

Drafting is done by barristers and a few advocates employed as civil servants, and known collectively as Parliamentary Counsel. They are technically within the Treasury as the Parliamentary Counsel's Office. At any time several will be on loan to the Law Commission, however. Several draftsmen have been transferred to Edinburgh to draft Bills of the Scottish Administration.

Their role in legislation is pivotal. A UK government department, when its proposed Bill has a place in the queue, tells its own lawyers the policy the Bill is to promote, and these lawyers draft instructions for Parliamentary Counsel. United Kingdom or Great

---

1 A major example was the Wheatley Commission, chaired by the then Lord Justice-Clerk, which reported in 1969 (Cmnd 4150), and resulted in the Local Government (Scotland) Act 1973 which set up a new local government structure in Scotland. Another is the Kilbrandon Commission, chaired by a Scottish House of Lords judge, which reported on devolution in 1973 (Cmnd 5460), but ultimately produced no change. However in 1998–99 a Royal Commission chaired by Lord Wakeham sat to make recommendations on the reform of the House of Lords, and consideration of such reform continues.

2 The Carnworth Report (*Enforcing Planning Control*) in 1989 led to the Planning and Compensation Act 1991. The North Report (*Road Traffic Law Review*) in 1988 led to the Road Traffic Act 1991.

3 Especially statute law revision and repeal, and consolidation. See also ch 8.

4 *Quality and Choice: a decent home for all* (DETR 2001) preceded the Homelessness Act 2002

5 *Smoking Kills* (Cm 1477) preceded the Tobacco Advertising and Promotion Act 2002.

Britain Bills go to Parliamentary Counsel, who produce the initial draft which is sent then to the Lord Advocate's office.

A team of three Parliamentary Counsel draft the Bill in liaison with the sponsoring department. This may continue for months, or be hurried, depending upon the parliamentary legislative timetable. It has been suggested that there are five steps to drafting: understanding; analysis; design; composition; and revision[1]: also, that the minister has the last word on matters of substance, the draftsman on matters of form.

The draftsman works under considerable constraints. Firstly, the instructions must be put into legislative form so as to satisfy the government. This may require deliberate vagueness or ambiguity on occasion. Secondly, the Bill must be legally effective and fit within the existing law without producing unintended contradictions. Thirdly, the Bill must be competent for the UK Parliament. Fourthly, the Bill must fit into the parliamentary timetable, and shortage of time may lead to bad drafting and consequent need for extensive amendment in Parliament, requiring more of the draftsman's time. Fifthly, draftsmen see themselves as an elite, employing craft skills, which leads to a certain conservatism in form and expression.

## Parliamentary stages of United Kingdom parliamentary legislation

The enacting formula of an Act records that the three parts of the UK Parliament have agreed. To pass these three parts several stages must be gone through.

A Bill may be introduced into either House of Parliament first by any MP or peer. However, most Bills are government Bills (that is Bills introduced by a member of the government), and most Bills (and certainly controversial Bills and those concerning taxation and expenditure) are introduced into the Commons first.

The stages in each House are called first and second readings[2], committee stage, report stage and third reading. After a Bill has gone through all those stages in both Houses, there is a process of consideration by the House in which the Bill was introduced of the other House's amendments, to produce an agreed version. The royal assent follows.

---

1 Thornton *Legislative Drafting* (3rd edn, 1987) pp 112–13.
2 Unfortunately the 'co-operation procedure' for the European Community legislative procedure has adopted these titles for very different processes: see above.

The whole process suffers from the fact that executive dominance of the legislature normally ensures that the Bill is largely unaltered (although hundreds of amendments may have been unsuccessfully moved) or only altered as the government wishes. Parliament therefore largely rubber-stamps the government's proposals and, at least in the House of Commons, the legislative process often becomes a forum for the opposition to harry the government instead. To ensure that the current legislation gets through despite the opposition's efforts to thwart it there is a Legislation Committee of the Cabinet, operating through the Whips, that is members of the government whose job is to maintain party discipline and convey to the government the concerns of backbenchers.

The first reading is purely formal, but permits the Bill, usually hitherto confidential, to be published. Before the second reading, s 19 of the Human Rights Act 1998 requires the minister in charge of a Bill to make a written statement that, in his view, the provisions of the Bill are compatible with the 'Convention rights' under that Act (for which, see Chapter 3) or, if he cannot do so, state that the government wishes to proceed with the Bill nevertheless[1]. This is one of several devices designed to seek compatibility of legislation with those rights (see Chapter 3 and Part 1 of this chapter). The second reading, perhaps two weeks later, is designed as a debate on the principle of the Bill. Most second readings are unopposed, but a government will almost always win a vote, because it is government by virtue of having a majority in the House of Commons (and the House of Lords will not normally attempt to veto legislation which the majority in the Commons favours). The committee stage, which will often extend over several weeks, is usually taken by a standing committee reflecting the party balance in the Commons[2], and a Committee of the Whole House in the Lords. This stage is designed to examine the Bill in detail to see if it achieves its purpose, and is the chief stage to put amendments. It may allow such examination on an uncontroversial Bill, but in other cases it may be political theatre, possibly with proceedings 'guillotined', that is terminated at a certain point, whether or not

1 This was done in respect to the Anti-Terrorism, Crime & Security Act 2001, which contained provisions incompatible with the Convention right to liberty and security of persons, because it permitted indefinite detention of certain persons. (It also, therefore, required derogation from that part of the European Convention on Human Rights itself: see ch 3 below.)
2 It may be taken by a Committee of the Whole House, as the European Communities (Amendment) Bill 1992–93 (incorporating changes wrought by the Treaty on European Union) was; or by a Select Committee, which can take evidence. However, these committees are rarely used.

discussion has finished. In this case many clauses of the Bill will not be discussed at all. Also, increasingly, governments propose amendments to their own Bills ('legislating on the hoof'), which suggests that they have been ill-drafted, possibly through lack of time. The report stage is for the committee to report its amendments to the Whole House, although further amendments may be put. The third reading gives approval to the House's final formulation of the Bill. Because the first House to take any Bill has not approved any amendments made by the second, there is a process of consideration of the other House's amendments. The House of Lords will usually concede to the reiterated opinion of the Commons. The royal assent has been purely formal for generations, but makes the Bill an Act (although it may come into force only later[1]).

A question raised by parliamentary legislative procedure is whether the unelected House of Lords should have a role. One possible justification is that much legislation is not properly discussed in the Commons, so the Lords provides, in effect, a proper committee stage. This view has been prominent in discussions on House of Lords reform, and tends to characterise the Lords as a 'revising chamber' for legislation. Another is that it provides a sheet anchor to limit the wilder excesses of the Commons, which is dominated by the government of the day. This has not figured largely in these discussions.

### Enactment, the 'Sewel convention' and 'Sewel motions'

As noted above, and in Chapter 3, there is still a remarkable amount of legislation being enacted in relation to Scotland, and within the devolved legislative competence of the Scottish Parliament, but by the United Kingdom Parliament.

This is largely because of the existence of 'Sewel' motions. In brief, during the passage of the Scotland Act 1998, the government, through Lord Sewel, its spokesman in the House of Lords, indicated the expectation that a convention of the constitution would arise. This would be that, while the United Kingdom Parliament had power to legislate within the devolved competence of the Scottish Parliament, it would do so rarely and only with the consent of the Scottish Parliament.

However, the Scottish Parliament has in fact passed a large number of motions invoking the exception. As a result, in the first

---

1 See 'Commencement provisions' above.

couple of years of its existence, the Scottish Parliament passed roughly as many 'Sewel motions' as it passed Acts. Thus, arguably, as much Scots law was changed by Westminster as by Holyrood[1].

It may make sense by including Scotland in reforms applying to the rest of the United Kingdom, applying international obligations, and so on. Nevertheless, this was completely unexpected. The phenomenon shows strong centripetal United Kingdom tendencies in tension with notions of solutions tailored to Scottish wishes, the more remarkable for being at least cheerfully acquiesced in by the Scottish Executive and Scottish Parliament. These centripetal tendencies may flow from a desire for uniformity, caused by electoral expectations, a reliance on UK administrative bodies, the need to avoid inconsistency, and a feeling that diversity should not be sought for its own sake. Moreover, there may be other reasons for not using the Scottish Parliament, such as doubt over the boundaries of devolution, impetus for reform coming from Westminster, a desire to avoid dislocation of the Scottish Parliament's legislative programme, avoidance of challenge, and simple economy of effort. Also, there remain Scottish MPs in Westminster to take care of Scottish interests.

Nevertheless, if all that the Scottish Parliament does is to pass a motion, with limited debate, accepting a Westminster Bill, it loses all control over what happens to the Bill thereafter. One of the problems devolution was set up to solve was Westminster passing legislation which applies to Scotland but is ill-suited to it. Perhaps this problem has been re-invented.

*Special cases*

There are a number of special cases of legislation which must be examined.

**Financial legislation.** The UK constitution requires that there be annual financial legislation. Thus, annual Finance Acts permit taxation and Consolidated Fund and Appropriation Acts permit government expenditure. The legislative procedure for these (which takes up much parliamentary legislative time) differs

---

1 Clearly, one cannot simply compare number of Acts, as they vary in significance (and length), but the point is well made. For an analysis of 'Sewel motions' in the first few years of the Scottish Parliament, see Page and Batey *Scotland's Other Parliament; Westminster legislation about devolved matters in Scotland* [2002] PL 501–23. The following text relies heavily on that analysis.

somewhat from the usual. It does not provide effective control over taxation and expenditure by government, however, and in any case control is increasingly shared with the European Community. The Scottish Parliament receives a block grant which is paid into the Scottish Consolidated Fund along with any other payments. Out of it the Scottish Administration pays all authorised expenditure. The Scottish Parliament has power to vary by resolution the basic rate of income tax by not more than 3 pence in the pound up or down (though the power was not used in its first four years).

**Legislation under the Parliament Acts 1911 and 1949.** The legislative powers of the House of Lords are constrained by the Parliament Acts 1911 and 1949. Firstly, Bills introduced into the UK Parliament which are certified by the Speaker as 'money Bills' (such as taxation and expenditure Bills) can be delayed by the Lords for one month, after which they are deemed to have agreed to them. Secondly, other Bills (unless they fall into the third category) can be delayed for two sessions of Parliament, after which they are deemed to be agreed. Thirdly, Bills to extend the life of the Parliament, and any private legislation, are unaffected by the legislation.

The Parliament Acts have rarely been formally invoked. However, the Lords did reject the War Crimes Bill in 1990, and again when it was reintroduced in 1991. The Bill was thus deemed to have been passed and became law as the War Crimes Act 1991[1].

**Statute law revision and statute law repeal legislation.** Legislation in a common law or mixed jurisdiction is *ad hoc*, and grows by accretion. Legislation on a topic may thus be widely scattered, and may become obsolete. While Acts of the pre-1707 Scots Parliament may fall into desuetude, others are considered immortal unless repealed. Later Acts of the UK Parliament may repeal all or part of earlier ones, but may do so implicitly.

After occasional initiatives over several centuries, in the early years of the 20th century (but somewhat earlier in England) serious attempts at weeding out were undertaken by the Statute Law Committee and others. They produced a number of Statute Law Revision Acts, for example the Statute Law Revision (Scotland) Act 1906. A simplified parliamentary procedure, using a Joint Committee of both Houses for the committee stage, and

---

1 The Higher Education Act 1998 did not use the procedure, but was passed only after the government agreed to review the matter in dispute.

permitting no subsequent amendments, later stages being 'on the nod', was created for them. These Acts collectively repealed thousands of Acts considered no longer in force or obsolete.

Responsibility for such activities was given to the Law Commissions when they were created in 1965. They have produced at the time of writing some ten Statute Law Repeal Acts, most recently in 1998, repealing hundreds more old Acts by the accelerated parliamentary procedure[1]. These Acts repeal Acts considered no longer of practical utility, a somewhat more inclusive definition than used before.

**Consolidation legislation.** In conjunction with the weeding-out process, there have been attempts at consolidation, that is, at placing all provisions on a topic in a single coherent Act, and a large number of consolidating Acts were passed in the 19th century. However, the process of rendering provisions from a variety of Acts into a single coherent whole is difficult without at least marginally altering those provisions, in other words, without incidentally altering the law. Thus, although the same simplified legislative process as for statute law revision was made available, parliamentary jealousy meant it was little used. The Enactments (Procedure) Act 1949 permitted corrections and minor improvements (as defined in the Act) through the accelerated procedure.

The Law Commissions took principal responsibility for consolidation as well as statute law revision. Their initial hopes of large-scale consolidation were not fulfilled before devolution. It may be that the Scottish Parliament will be able to realise them through a simplified procedure. Nevertheless, even before devolution the Scottish Law Commission had generated more than 20 consolidation Acts applying solely to Scotland, for example the Prisons (Scotland) Act 1989. It has also joined with the (English and Welsh) Law Commission on many more applying to Great Britain or the United Kingdom, including the massive Income and Corporation Taxes Act 1988. Those consolidation measures recommended by the Law Commissions undergo a version of the

---

1 Thus, its Schedule contained 10 Parts, each concerned with a different subject matter, e g Part I, Administration of Justice; Part II, Ecclesiastical Law; Part III, Education, and so on. Part VII concerned Scottish Local Acts (for 'local Acts' see below), and repealed some 75 Acts from the Edinburgh Poor Relief Act 1800 to the Zetland Masonic Sick and Widows and Orphans Fund Order Confirmation Act 1900, by way of the Mussel Fishery (Cockenzie) Order Confirmation Act 1894, the Dundee Gas Order Confirmation Act 1921 and the Merchants House (Crematorium) Order 1950.

accelerated legislative procedure even if their incidental amendments go beyond those permitted by the 1949 Act (although the enormous consolidating Companies Act 1985 used an ad hoc procedure laid down in the Companies Act 1981).

In addition, any government department may promote its own consolidating Bill, usually as a result of a report by a committee of inquiry, departmental committee or the like, for example the Highways Act 1959 which followed the ad hoc departmental *Report of the Committee on the Consolidation of Highway Law* (Cmnd 630).

There are thus several means of introducing consolidation Bills, and it has been calculated that about a third of all UK legislation since the Law Commissions were set up has been consolidating.

Consolidation is not a panacea. Firstly, an area of law may be large enough to require several consolidating statutes. The consolidation of customs and excise law in 1979 produced seven Acts. In any case, statutes never stand alone, and must cross-refer. Secondly, a consolidating Act will soon be amended, and may require reconsolidation later. The consolidating Companies Act 1985 was probably amended more in the following six years than the preceding consolidating Companies Act 1949 was in 36. Thirdly, consolidation deals only with statute law, not common law.

**Codification.** Codification, in the sense of a single statute incorporating all the law on the subject from all the sources, has been sought in some areas of law. There are a few late 19th-century United Kingdom examples such as the Bills of Exchange Act 1882 all passed by ordinary legislative procedure. These Acts, however, suffer from similar problems to those of consolidating Acts. The law continues to develop and is only comprehensible in the light of judicial interpretation of the Act, so the codification becomes outdated.

Such codifying statutes must not be confused with the 'codes properly so-called' found in civil law countries. These, taking Justinian's codification of Roman law as their model, not only reduce the entire law on a subject to a single mega-statute, but set it out in reasoned, encyclopaedic form, from first principles. They are the ultimate authority, changed only rarely and then with difficulty.

It is difficult to imagine such a code in a common law or mixed system. The whole grain of such systems runs against comprehensive, final, authoritative statements which reduce the judge's role to a mere mouthpiece.

**Private members' legislation.** Although most Bills in the UK Parliament are introduced by the government, any MP or peer can do so, and such legislation is called private members' legislation. However, as governments and oppositions (as 'governments in waiting') have carved up parliamentary time, there is little left for private members.

Private members may introduce Bills by two special methods. Firstly, the 'ten-minute rule' allows a private member on certain occasions to introduce a Bill and speak in favour of it for ten minutes, after which another can oppose for ten minutes and a vote is taken. This procedure is usually used simply to air a grievance, rather than seriously to propose legislation.

Secondly, the private members' ballot is a device for prioritising between private members' Bills. Participants give in their names, and 20 are drawn from a hat. Standing Orders of the House of Commons allow up to a dozen Fridays for private members' Bills only and procedural rules make it easy to dispose of a Bill undebated, by filibustering. Only those with high places in the private members' ballot are likely to receive enough time. In any case, the government's voting power ensures that no Bill it dislikes will get through Parliament, and private members have little access to Parliamentary Draftsmen.

Thus, private members' legislation is not a large proportion of all United Kingdom legislation, though it has been as much as a third in the recent past. This proportion is misleading, however, for what is ostensibly private members' legislation may be covert government legislation, including Law Commission proposals, which has received drafting and other help. The Age of Legal Capacity (Scotland) Act 1991, introduced by Sir Nicholas Fairbairn (Perth and Kinross), is an example. Private members coming high in the ballot are likely to be inundated with requests from interest groups to adopt their Bill. The Solicitors (Scotland) Act 1991, introduced by Alistair Darling (Edinburgh Central), was a measure sought by the Law Society of Scotland, for example.

Private members' Bills provide a continuing trickle of important legislation, perhaps half-covert government Bills, rarely party politically sensitive, but sometimes on campaigning issues which the government is at worst indifferent to or, as with the Abortion Act 1967, may favour without wishing to be seen to promote.

**Local, personal, private and hybrid legislation.** The public/private distinction is extremely complicated but, broadly, it is used in two separate ways.

Firstly, it is used to refer to the public nature of the contents of an Act. The Interpretation Act 1978, s 3 stipulates that every Act is a 'public Act' unless it otherwise states, and that this means that when cited in court it does not have to be proved to be the law, but can be taken as read. Only personal Acts, discussed below, are private in this sense, and given their rarity and limited effect; in practice this is an unimportant distinction.

Secondly, it is used to refer to the parliamentary procedure a Bill goes through. Public Bill procedure is used for legislation promoted by a member of either House, which will commonly be general in its application, but might apply to a locality only (though if it does, it might be hybrid), or even, rarely, to an individual. Private Bill procedure is used for UK legislation promoted by persons outwith Parliament, such as local authorities, who petition Parliament for legislation. This procedure involves a quasi-judicial procedure, in which promoters and objectors give evidence. Such a private Act in practice will always be 'local', or 'personal', not 'general'. Such legislation was common until in the 19th century promotion of legislation came to be seen as a function of government. It generally sought only to create exceptions to the law. Thus, for example, local authorities might seek exceptional powers through local private Acts, and individuals might seek naturalisation (and, in England, divorce) through personal private Acts. It is in this sense that the public/private distinction is usually made.

Personal private legislation is extremely rare nowadays (though there were a few marriage enabling examples in the 1980s, such as the George Donald Evans and Deborah Jane Evans (Marriage Enabling) Act 1987), for individuals may now achieve naturalisation and divorce through quasi-judicial administrative procedures. Local private legislation still occurs every year, however (for example, the River Humber (Upper Pyewipe Outfall) Act 1992 and the United Reformed Church Act 2000), though most of the need for it has gone as local authorities now have most of their powers given under public general legislation, such as the Local Government (Scotland) Act 1973, s 201 (which gives powers to write by-laws). In any case, accelerated private legislation procedures have been invented to save parliamentary time. The chief one is provisional order procedure under the Private Legislation Procedure (Scotland) Act 1936. This largely delegates the consideration of evidence to commissioners, and the decision to the Secretary of State. If he makes the provisional order requested by the promoters, there must be a confirmation Bill (for example, the Pittenweem Harbour Order Confirmation Act 1992 and the Scottish Borders Council (Jim Clark Memorial Rally) Order Confirmation Act 1996) but it employs an accelerated procedure.

There is also a special parliamentary procedure under the Statutory Orders (Special Procedure) Act 1945, which requires no confirmation Bill, but appears never to have been used.

The Scotland Act 1998 continues the Private Legislation Procedure (Scotland) Act 1936 but, by Sch 8, para 5 it cannot be used where the subject-matter is wholly within the competence of the Scottish Parliament. Thus, there was a Comhairle nan Eilan Siar (Eriskay Causeway) Order Confirmation Act 2000 and Railtrack (Waverley Station) Order Confirmation Act 2000.

Hybrid legislation is that which is partly public general, partly private (and local or personal). The Maplin Development Act 1973 was hybrid. It gave powers to the Secretary of State to acquire land for an airport, but did so in relation to a specific area, thus directly affecting individual interests. Hybrid Bills go through a modified public Bill procedure. Thus, the Maplin Development Act took its place in the Public General Act series as 1973 c64.

## Publication and citation of GB and UK parliamentary legislation

*Acts of the Parliaments of Great Britain and the United Kingdom*

Acts of the Parliaments of Great Britain and the United Kingdom (often bound with those of England) appear in a great variety of editions.

**Chronological series.** Public general Acts of the United Kingdom Parliament are printed and sold by The Stationery Office in single copies, and bound up in several volumes annually in a series called *Public General Acts and Measures*[1], which commenced in 1831. For almost all purposes, these can be taken as authoritative[2].

Most earlier legislation is of historical interest only. Diverse editions of earlier Acts were produced by various publishers, such as various editions of *Statutes at Large* up to 1869 (for example, Ruffhead's, covering English legislation 1215–1707 and Great Britain legislation 1707–1800), and *Statutes of the Realm 1225–1713*, published by the Record Commissioners. These also

---

1 The 'Measures' are legislation of the Church of England, which, for some reason, are bound in the same volume.
2 See, however, Rankine 'Errors in Acts' (1987) 8 Stat LR 53.

contain English, but not Scots, Acts and some older editions are inaccurate.

*Public General Statutes Affecting Scotland 1707–1847* ('Blackwood's Acts') were continued annually until 1946, and *Statutes Revised*, published in 1948, contains Great Britain and United Kingdom (and English) Acts still in force at that date.

All chronological series contain the original unamended text. This is useful for some purposes, but has the disadvantage that it is impossible to tell whether the provision has been repealed (and if so by what), or amended (and if so how).

**Encyclopaedic series.** *Statutes in Force* was published as a loose-leaf encyclopaedia, continually updated by the Statute Law Committee through the Statutory Publications Office. It attempted to provide the text actually in force of all public general Acts in force (with minor exceptions). These were digested into 131 groups and sub-groups. A list of groups and Acts appears in the first volume.

New Acts were inserted, repealed ones removed, and amendments incorporated. An annual cumulative supplement noted amendments and repeals, and the text of heavily amended Acts was replaced from time to time. Unfortunately, the series was not easy to use, and has not been updated since 1991, because it was thought that the Statute Law Data Base, produced by the Lord Chancellor's Department, would be made generally available.

**Commercially produced reprints.** *Current Law Statutes Annotated* (called *Scottish Current Law Statutes Annotated* until 1990) has been published since 1948 by W Green and Sweet & Maxwell. The series reproduces all public general statutes chronologically with annotations. These include citation of parliamentary debates and sometimes lengthy and useful commentaries upon each section. Acts of the current year appear in a loose-leaf service file, and each year's Acts are bound into an annual volume or volumes.

*Halsbury's Statutes* (Butterworths) contains all United Kingdom Acts save those applying only to Scotland. This is unfortunate, as they are digested into subjects, well annotated, and updated through cumulative supplement, current statute service, and noter-up volumes.

There are also reprints of all, or most, statutes on a particular area, such as commercial law and family law. *The Parliament House Book* (W Green) is a four-volume loose-leaf encyclopaedia of information useful to practising Scots lawyers, including reprints of

Acts of particular interest, in amended form. Acts included are also sold separately as *Parliament House Statutes Reprints.* There are also a number of specific area encyclopaedias, such as *Simon's Taxes* (Butterworths). Unfortunately, not all of these contain the Scots law on the subject.

Textbooks and monographs may contain Acts of Parliament, or parts of them, relevant to their subject-matter. For example, Macdonald and Webber *Immigration Law and Practice in the United Kingdom* (5th edn, 2001) contains most of the relevant legislation, amended to the date of publication. Annotated Acts from the *Current Law* series are also sometimes published as books, as, for example, Himsworth and Munro *The Scotland Act 1998.*

**Indexes etc.** Each volume of *Public General Acts* contains alphabetical and chronological lists of the Acts included, and an index to them. The final volume for each year also contains a table of derivations and destinations for consolidation Acts (that is, tables showing the relationship of original and consolidated provisions) although it has no official status; a table of effects of legislation (that is, of repeals and amendments effected during the year); and a table of amendments to Acts effected by statutory instruments.

The Stationery Office also publishes the *Chronological Table of Statutes* approximately annually[1]. The former lists chronologically all Scots, Great Britain and United Kingdom (and English) legislation to date, and indicates repeals and amendments. The latter indexes all those Acts still in force under subject headings.

*(Scottish) Current Law Statutes Annotated* volumes are individually indexed, and the loose-leaf 'Service File' indexes the whole series in various ways.

*Halsbury's Statutes* has a companion volume entitled *Is It In Force?*, also issued with the updating service to *The Laws of Scotland: Stair Memorial Encyclopaedia.* Each annual edition records, in respect of all sections of all statutes for the preceding 25 years[2], whether they are yet in force, and to what extent.

**Computerised retrieval of public general Acts.** Acts of the UK Parliament since the first Act of 1988[3] are available in their original form (i e unamended or unrepealed where appropriate) at the HMSO website in full text, as are the Explanatory Notes on

---

1 Until 1990, it produced an *Index to the Statutes* as well.
2 This is thus a rolling 25 years.
3 As at early 2003. It is possible that the series will be extended backwards further.

government Bills[1]. Bills currently before the UK Parliament can be found in full text at the Parliament website[2].

The WESTLAW database includes all public general Acts in force, in their amended form as appropriate. The BAILII database contains all such Acts but for recent years only. The LexisNexis database includes all Acts applying to the United Kingdom and to England and Wales only, but not those applying to Scotland only.

JUSTIS UK Statutes contains the full text of all Acts of Parliament, including Acts of the (pre-1707) Parliament of Scotland, on CD–ROM.

**Local, personal and private Acts.** The Stationery Office publishes single copies of local and personal Acts and there is an *Index to Local and Personal Acts 1850–1995*, a *Chronological Table of Local Legislation 1797–1994* (4 volumes) and *Chronological Table of Private and Personal Acts 1539–1997* (1 volume, containing all such legislation passed by Parliaments in Westminster). *Public General Statutes* also contains an alphabetical list of local and personal Acts.

Local Acts have often been published in local compilations, for instance, *Dundee Water Acts 1845–82, Dundee Municipal Statutes 1872–98, Dundee Gas and Corporation Acts 1868–1901,* and *Dundee Harbour Acts 1811–1912.*

From 1992 private Acts are published in *(Scottish) Current Law Statutes Annotated.*

**Computerised retrieval of local, personal and private Acts.** Local Acts since the first Act of 1988 can also be found in their original form (i e unamended or unrepealed where appropriate) in full text on the HMSO website[3]. Private and personal ones are also listed, but no text is available.

**Citation of Acts.** Before 1963 public general Acts were cited by the extraordinarily complicated regnal year method which the English Parliament used. In this, as well as (or instead of) the reference to the calendar year of enactment, there was reference to the Parliament that passed it, identified by the year or years of the reign of the contemporary Sovereign, calculated from the date of accession. Thus, the Prevention of Damage By Rabbits Act 1939 was

---

1 The HMSO website is at www.hmso.gov.uk.
2 The Westminster Parliament website is at www.parliament.uk.
3 The HMSO website is at www.hmso.gov.uk. HMSO is extending coverage back in time.

correctly cited as '2 & 3 Geo 6 c44', that is, the 44th Act of the Parliament which started in the second year of George VI's reign, and ended in the third.

There were further complications. Until 1940 statutes were bound in volumes for each Parliament although this did not coincide with any calendar year. For example, the session 22 & 23 Geo 5 straddled 1932 and 1933. Thereafter until 1963 the statutes were bound in annual volumes, although these did not coincide with any parliamentary year. For example, the volume for 1945 contained 8 & 9 Geo 6 c4 to c44 and 9 & 10 Geo 6 c1 to c21.

Since 1963, however, they have been cited in essentially the same fashion as used for Acts of the (original) Parliament of Scotland, by short title, year and chapter number, for example 'Criminal Procedure (Scotland) Act 1987 c46'.

Local and personal Acts are cited in the same form as public general, save that local Acts use lower case roman numerals (for example, the Price's Patent Candle Co Ltd Act 1992 cxvii), and personal Acts, italic numerals (for example, the Valerie Mary Hill and Alan Monk (Marriage Enabling) Act 1985 *c1*).

## PART 4: ACTS OF THE SCOTTISH PARLIAMENT

As noted in relation to Acts of the United Kingdom Parliament, a few Acts of the original pre-1707 Parliament of Scotland are still in force with, effectively, the same status as those of the United Kingdom Parliament[1]. However, this section concerns Acts of the post-1998 Scottish Parliament.

Devolution is making Acts of the Scottish Parliament the normal method of legislating for Scotland (though existing Acts of the United Kingdom will remain the principal source for some time, and a surprising amount of law for Scotland continues to be enacted at Westminster, for reasons considered above in relation to Acts of the United Kingdom Parliament[2]). The 'legislative competence' of the Scottish Parliament was considered in Chapter 3, and its breadth noted, for, in respect of Scotland, all legislative powers that are not specifically reserved to the United Kingdom

1   Though subject to the 'doctrine of desuetude', that is, that they can cease to have effect without explicit or implicit repeal by a later Act, if they have been ignored for a lengthy period, and there is evidence of contrary practice. The oldest Act of the Parliament of Scotland still in force is the Royal Mines Act 1424.

2   I e through the use of 'Sewel motions': also, as with the United Kingdom as a whole, the sheer quantity of (sub)delegated legislation (see Part 5 of this chapter below) far outstrips the quantity of parliamentary legislation.

Parliament are devolved to the Scottish Parliament. So the Scottish Parliament has a plenitude of law-making power (and much greater than if it had been set up under the abortive Scotland Act 1978, which specified the powers to be devolved)[1]. The range of topics for legislation is thus wide. Indeed, as also noted in Chapter 3, in its first four years, the Scottish Parliament passed 62 Acts on topics as diverse as abolition of feudal land-holding and fox-hunting, the appointment of judges and reform of the Scottish Qualifications Agency. The range may also include legislation on Convention rights and Community law[2].

The very concept of 'legislative competence' indicates that Acts of the Scottish Parliament are 'subordinate' or 'delegated legisla-tion' and this is expressly recognised in some legislation[3]. They are delegated legislation as they are made under powers delegated by the sovereign United Kingdom Parliament in the Scotland Act 1998. However, it must be noted that their style of expression is the same as that used by the United Kingdom Parliament. Also, they often make provision for areas such as criminal justice and land law which, until devolution, were dealt with in Acts of the United Kingdom Parliament, rather than in delegated legislation.

Pre- and post-enactment checks, described below, police those limits to legislative competence, and the Scottish Parliament is subject to the ultra vires doctrine (discussed above in relation to human rights and Community legislation, and below in the rela-tion to other delegated legislation). In any case, power to override the Scottish Parliament still rests at Westminster for, as s 28(7) of the Scotland Act 1998 explicitly declares, 'This section does not affect the power of the Parliament of the United Kingdom to make laws for Scotland'.

Nevertheless, the powers of the Scottish Parliament are of such inherent significance, and the breadth of delegation so

1  The position is further complicated in that the Acts of the Scottish Parliament may further delegate powers to the Scottish Executive and others, just as Acts of the Westminster Parliament may so delegate. Exercises of such powers by the Scottish Ministers, whether sub-delegated under Holyrood powers or delegated under Westminster powers, are called 'Scottish Statutory Instruments'. They are considered with other delegated legislation in the next section of this chapter.

2  Thus, for example, the Convention Rights (Compliance) (Scotland) Act 2001 was passed specifically to make Scots law conform to the European Convention on Human Rights.

3  See, e g Human Rights Act 1998, s 21(1).

remarkable, as to justify separate treatment from other delegated legislation[1].

## Acts of the Scottish Parliament, their types and form

The types and forms of Acts of the Scottish Parliament are modelled upon those of United Kingdom Acts (to which reference should be made: see Part 3 of this chapter above). Most are 'public'[2], and all are 'general'[3] in the sense that Acts of the United Kingdom Parliament are, and special types of Act are considered below. It is too early to say what the normal legislative output will be but, in the first three full years, there were 12, 15 and 17 Acts respectively (and a further 17 in the three months of 2003 before the Scottish Parliament was dissolved preparatory to its second election), and they varied considerably in length. The very first Act of the Scottish Parliament had but three sections, and those in the first four years varied from two sections (University of St Andrews (Postgraduate Medical Degrees) Act 2002) to 100 sections (Land Reform (Scotland) Act 2003). Clearly, they do not yet vary much in age (though the continuation in force of Acts of the original Scottish Parliament should not be forgotten).

*Short title, 'asp number' and contents list*

Acts of the Scottish Parliament commence with a short title, normally containing brackets embracing the word '(Scotland)'[4],

---

1 In *Adams v Scottish Ministers* 2003 SLT 366, 2002 SCLR 881, at 385 J, K, Lord Nimmo Smith observed that '. . . despite the reference in the Human Rights Act to Acts of the Scottish Parliament being subordinate legislation, such Acts have, in my opinion, far more in common with public general statutes of the United Kingdom Parliament than with subordinate legislation as it is commonly understood. Indeed, the definition of "subordinate legislation" in the Scotland Act makes this distinction clear. The Parliament is a democratically elected body . . . An Act of the Scottish Parliament, once passed, requires Royal Assent to become law . . . [I]t might be better to regard it as *sui generis*'.

2 I e they go through the normal process of enactment unless they fall into the 'Private Bill' category: Standing Orders of the Scottish Parliament, r 9.17.1

3 I e they are 'judicially noticed' so do not require proving in court: Scotland Act 1998, s 28(6).

4 But not invariably, for example, if the title is otherwise unequivocal: see e g Scottish Public Services Ombudsman Act 2002. Note also that Acts of the Westminster Parliament exclusively concerning Scotland were usually identified by the parenthetic '(Scotland)' in the past (the last pre-devolution Act of the United Kingdom Parliament which applied exclusively to Scotland was the Mental Health (Amendment) (Scotland) Act 1999) and so no doubt will any in the future.

for example, the 'International Criminal Court (Scotland) Act 2001' (and may contain other bracketed words, as does the 'Mental Health (Public Safety and Appeals) (Scotland) Act 1999'). They also bear an 'asp' ('Act of the Scottish Parliament') number, that is, a sequential number which, with the year of enactment, identifies the Act, for example, 'asp 10'. Thus '2002 asp 10' was the Fur Farming (Prohibition) (Scotland) Act 2002[1].

All but the shortest Acts have an official 'Contents' list of sections with their numbers and their marginal notes.

*Statement of enactment*

Unlike Acts of the United Kingdom Parliament, there is no incantatory 'Enacting formula', but each Act has a statement indicating its parliamentary passage in the form 'The Bill for this Act of the Scottish Parliament was passed by Parliament on 6th March 2002 and received Royal Assent on 11th April 2002'.

*Long title and preamble*

Acts of the Scottish Parliament also have a long title, delimiting the scope of the Bill introduced into the Parliament. Thus, the Fur Farming (Prohibition) (Scotland) Act 2002 has the long title 'An Act of the Scottish Parliament to prohibit the keeping of animals solely or primarily for slaughter for the value of their fur; to provide for the making of payments in respect of the related closure of certain businesses; and for connected purposes'.

*Sections, marginal notes*

The section is the basic unit of Acts of the Scottish Parliament, and they are numbered sequentially through the Act. They may be broken into sub-sections, paragraphs and sub-paragraphs for, as with Acts of the United Kingdom Parliament, the draftsmen aim at exactitude (in 'fixed verbal form') rather than comprehensibility, and use typographical devices to express the logic of the section. This also allows precise and unequivocal identification of

---

1 Short titles and asp numbers were required by the Scotland Act 1998 (Transitory and Transitional Provisions) (Publication and Interpretation etc of Acts of the Scottish Parliament) Order 1999, SI 1999/1379, arts 4, 5.

provisions, for example 'Debt Arrangement and Attachment (Scotland) Act 2002, s 2(3)(a)(iii)'.

The United Kingdom convention of numbering a new section or sub-section inserted by an amending Act is employed. Thus the Criminal Procedure (Amendment) (Scotland) Act 2002, s 1(1) inserts new sub-sections 150(3A) and (3B) between the existing sub-sections 150(3) and (4) of the Criminal Procedure (Scotland) Act 1995[1].

Marginal references to legislation referred to in the text have not been used, the draftsman preferring to reproduce short title, year and chapter number or asp number in the text.

### Headings

Groups of sections, as in the United Kingdom convention, may be grouped under 'cross-headings', and into Parts and even Chapters. For example, the Land Reform (Scotland) Act 2003 has its 100 sections divided into 4 Parts, with 6, 2, 7 and 5 Chapters respectively.

No doubt 'Titles' will also be used if considered necessary.

### Interpretation sections

Where words or phrases are inherently vague, or are used in an unusual sense, or have been invented for the purpose, in interpretation section may provide a meaning. Thus, the Abolition of Feudal Tenure (Scotland) Act 2000, s 72 defines, among other things 'land'[2].

### Repeal and amendment

The standard United Kingdom conventions apply to Acts of the Scottish Parliament, that is, that Acts continue in force unless repealed or amended and no special process of repeal is necessary,

---

1 This is an example of an Act of the Scottish Parliament amending an Act of the United Kingdom Parliament (both, however, identified by the parenthetic '(Scotland)')

2 The Scotland Act 1998 (Transitory and Transitional Provisions) (Publication and Interpretation, etc of Acts of the Scottish Parliament) Order 1999, SI 1999/1379, Sch 2 contained a list of 'General Definitions' (including one of 'land') to be applied to Acts of the Scottish Parliament.

so 'implicit repeal' is possible[1]. Also, while repeals and amendments may appear anywhere in the Act, commonly, a specific section at the end effects them, often in conjunction with a schedule. For example, the Adults with Incapacity (Scotland) Act 2000, Sch 6 is headed 'Repeals' and contains a table indicating what provisions are repealed, and to what extent, and the Housing (Scotland) Act 2001, Sch 10, headed 'Modification of Enactments', contains a long list of repeals and amendments.

However, in the case of Acts of the Scottish Parliament, because of their delegated status, particular considerations concerning repeal and amendment should be noted. Firstly, because of the general possibility that they may be found to be outwith the Parliament's 'legislative competence', s 107 of the Scotland Act 1998 gives the United Kingdom government, in such cases, the power to make 'necessary or expedient' provision by ordinary delegated legislation (see Part 5 of this chapter below). This clearly includes the power to repeal or amend. And, secondly, in any case, as s 28(7) reiterates, the United Kingdom Parliament retains the power to legislate for Scotland which even more clearly includes the power to repeal or amend Acts of the Scottish Parliament. (Indeed, the continued use of the United Kingdom Parliament to legislate for Scotland through 'Sewel motions', considered above in relation to Acts of the UK Parliament, means that such legislation is in fact a frequent and regular occurrence.) Thus, repeal or amendment of Acts of the Scottish Parliament may well be by means other than further Acts of the Scottish Parliament.

*Transitional, commencement, short title and extent provisions*

In broad terms these operate, or will operate, in the same fashion as with United Kingdom statutes, save that the difficulty which extent provisions deal with does not arise, as legislating outwith Scotland is beyond the Scottish Parliament's legislative competence. Thus, the University of St Andrews (Postgraduate Medical Degrees) Act 2002, s 2 states that it may be so cited, but contains no reference to commencement, so came into force on the date of royal assent[2], while the Scottish Qualifications Authority Act 2002, s 6, declares that it may be so cited, but that (other than s 6 itself)

---

1 On the effects of repeal, see SI 1999/1379 (see previous note), Sch 1, paras 11–14. In principle, repeals are not retrospective and repeals of repeals do not revive the original provision.
2 30 July 2002 is indicated in the 'Statement of enactment' (see above).

it comes into force 'on such day as the Scottish Ministers may by order appoint'[1].

*Schedules*

Schedules are attached to Acts of the Scottish Parliament in the same fashion, and for the same purposes, as to Acts of the United Kingdom Parliament. Thus, the Water Environment and Water Services (Scotland) Act 2002 has four schedules, two split into two Parts each[2].

*Explanatory Notes*

Almost every Act has accompanying 'Explanatory Notes' (as United Kingdom Acts have since 1999), produced by the sponsoring government department and attempting to explain in lay language what each provision of the Act does. As with United Kingdom legislation, they nevertheless have no official status, although, as a result of Pepper v Hart [1993] AC 593, [1993] 1 All ER 42 (discussed in relation to statutory interpretation below), they may presumably be used in statutory interpretation.

**Scottish Parliament enactment procedure**

Proposed Acts of the Scottish Parliament, by s 28(2) of the Scotland Act 1998, 'shall be known as Bills' and are the product of a lengthy process, as are Acts of the Untied Kingdom Parliament (for which, see above), though with certain specialities.

*Who seeks legislation and why?*

The role of legislation in Scotland under devolution is intended to be, and likely to be, very much as is its role in the United Kingdom

---

1  Its royal assent was obtained on 6 June 2002. The Scottish Ministers, under s 6 of the Act, appointed 19 August 2002 for s 1(7)(a)(iii), (8), (9), by the Scottish Qualifications Authority Act 2002 (Commencement No 1) Order 2002, SSI/335, art 3(2). Thus, at that time, s 1(1)–(6), (7)(a)(i),(ii), (b) and ss 2–5 had not been brought into force.

2  'Matters to be included in river basin management plans' (split into 'Matters to be included in every plan' and 'Additional matters to be included in revised plans'); 'Controlled activities regulations' (split into 'List of purposes' and 'Supplementary provisions'); 'Sustainable urban drainage systems: further amendments'; and 'Modifications of Part III of the 1980 Act', respectively.

as a whole. Thus, most legislation comes from the Scottish Executive. This may be 'manifesto legislation' promised by the party forming (or forming part of) the Scottish Executive, for example the Abolition of Feudal Tenure, Etc (Scotland) Act 2000. One sort of legislation that was expected to figure largely in the early years (indeed, the expectation of which was part of the justification for devolution), was uncontentious reform for which the United Kingdom had failed to find time. There have been examples, such as the Adults with Incapacity (Scotland) Act 2000.

However, legislation may be a reaction to events, as was the very first Act of the Scottish Parliament, the Mental Health (Public Safety and Appeals) (Scotland) Act 1999. A person had been convicted of culpable homicide some years earlier, and was detained in the State Mental Hospital at Carstairs. Such detention was, under the relevant legislation, competent only where there was treatment capable of alleviating the subject's condition or preventing further decline. It was agreed that, on the facts, this person's treatment could not have this effect. As a result, a sheriff concluded that the detention was unlawful. The 1999 Act was designed to reverse this result.

The Bail, Judicial Appointments, Etc (Scotland) Act 2000 and the Convention Rights (Compliance) (Scotland) Act 2001 could also be seen in this light, but perhaps fall into the most common class of legislation, that is, legislation which simply emerges from the processes of government. In the early years of the Scottish Parliament, some of this is legislation simply setting up new institutions and procedures, such as the Public Finance and Accountability (Scotland) Act 2000, instituting governmental financial controls.

### Pre-parliamentary stages of Scottish parliamentary legislation

As with United Kingdom legislation, the procedures before a Bill even appears are critical, for it is then that the Scottish Executive consults and decides what legislation it wishes to bring forward. This is discussed further in Chapter 8, though it may be remarked that the Scottish Parliament was set up with the intention of being more open to the population, and less bound by party political considerations, than is the United Kingdom Parliament[1].

---

1 See *Shaping Scotland's Parliament; report of the Consultative Steering Group on the Scottish Parliament* (Scottish Office 1998), section 3.6 'Access and Information'. One specific example of this is the common use of Draft Bills, published for consultation.

The Scottish Executive has been a coalition of two political parties, which puts additional strain upon the process of deciding what legislation to propose. There is no Queen's Speech in the Scottish Parliament, and the practice in the first Parliament was for the Scottish Executive to outline its intended legislative programme in September. However, in the second, proposals were published from shortly after the election.

*Parliamentary stages of Scottish parliamentary legislation and 'pre-enactment checks' on legislative competence*

Any member of the Scottish Parliament may introduce a Bill and, when a Bill is introduced, s 31 of the Scotland Act 1998 requires the person introducing it to state that it is within the Scottish Parliament's 'legislative competence' (discussed above in Chapter 3), and the Presiding Officer to decide separately whether or not this is the case (and he is required to give reasons where he decides a provision is not). These are the first two 'pre-enactment checks' on legislative competence. Since legislation incompatible with the 'Convention rights' under the Human Rights Act 1998 (for which, see Chapter 3) is not permitted, this is also one of the devices used to seek compatibility between legislation and those rights (see Part 1 of this chapter and Chapter 3).

The Bill is also required by the Standing Orders of the Scottish Parliament to have 'accompanying documents', that is, a Financial Memorandum giving best estimates of administrative, compliance and other costs, and (unless it is a 'Member's Bill': see below) 'Explanatory Notes' summarising the provisions and giving other necessary information, and a 'Policy Memorandum' giving the policy objectives of the Bill, describing why the Bill took the approach it did, the consultation which was undertaken, and an assessment of its effects on a somewhat mixed bag of factors, including equal opportunities, human rights, island communities, local government, sustainable development and any other relevant matter.

The Statement of Enactment records the date the Bill was introduced, and the date it received the royal assent, but is silent on what passes on and between those dates. However, s 36 of the Scotland Act 1998 lays down a procedure for enactment similar to that of the United Kingdom Parliament, though by no means identical[1]. One difference is clearly that there is no equivalent of the

---

1 The procedures of other small countries and devolved legislatures were studied before the final procedure was fixed.

House of Lords. Another is that the various subject-based Committees of Parliament such as Education, and Justice (see Chapter 3) are more involved, and involved earlier.

Thus, s 36 requires (subject to exceptions) that standing orders include provision for:

—  a general debate (referred to as 'Stage 1', and equivalent to the second reading);
—  a consideration of, and the opportunity for members to vote on, the details of a Bill (referred to as 'Stage 2' and equivalent to the committee stage);
—  a final stage at which a Bill can be passed or rejected (referred to as 'Stage 3' and equivalent to the third reading).

The Standing Orders of the Scottish Parliament fill in the detail.

Stage 1 effectively falls into two parts. In the first, the Bill is referred immediately to the relevant Parliamentary Committee (the 'lead committee') which considers and reports on the general principles to the Parliament as a whole, and any Policy Memorandum. (Where the Bill straddles the interests of more than one Committee, there is still a 'lead committee', but the other may also consider them, and in any case, the Subordinate Legislation Committee may also consider matters of delegated legislation: see below.) During this consideration, there can be public taking of evidence.

In the second part, the Parliament debates the general principles in the light of the Committee report, and may refer it back for a further report. If the Parliament disagrees with the general principles, the Bill fails. If it agrees, the Bill is remitted to the lead committee, or another committee, or a Committee of the Whole House, for Stage 2.

Stage 2, which must be at least two weeks later, considers each provision of the Bill, which must be agreed to, amended or rejected (though provisions concerning delegated legislation may be referred to the Subordinate Legislation Committee).

Stage 3, which must be at least two further weeks later if there have been amendments, may permit further amendments, and indeed may involve remitting the Bill back to Stage 2, but is essentially the decision as to whether to pass the Bill, as amended in Stage 2. If the decision is pushed to a vote, there is a quorum of one quarter of all MSPs.

Royal assent is required by s 32, but s 33 gives to certain officials, in the four weeks following Stage 3, the right to refer a Bill to the Judicial Committee of the Privy Council (the final authority on disputes on the Scotland Act: see Chapter 3) for a decision as to whether Bill is within the Parliament's legislative competence. These officials are the Advocate General for Scotland (the Scottish law officer of the Westminster government: see Chapter 3) or the Attorney-General (of England and Wales: see Chapter 3), either of whom might be concerned about an encroachment on Westminster's reserved powers, and even the Lord Advocate (the Scottish Executive's principal law officer: see Chapter 3), who, though a member of the Scottish Executive, might be unhappy with the form the Bill finally took. The Bill may not be presented for royal assent during this period. This is the third 'pre-enactment' check on legislative competence and, like the others, operates as another of the devices seeking to ensure compatibility between legislation and 'Convention rights' under the Human Rights Act 1998.

There is a fourth 'pre-enactment check' in that the Secretary of State (in other words, the United Kingdom government) may issue an order under s 35, forbidding the Presiding Officer from submitting a Bill for royal assent. This is different in kind from the other 'pre-enactment checks', for it is not in the hands of an official exercising a quasi-judicial function, but in those of a clearly party political person. However, the Secretary of State may take this grave step only if he believes on reasonable grounds that the Bill will transgress some international obligation (which would include a breach of the European Convention on Human Rights, or of Community law) or with the interests of defence or national security, or that, in modifying the law on reserved matters, it will have an adverse effect on them.

In addition to the 'pre-enactment checks', there are the 'post-enactment checks' considered in Chapter 3, whereby in any litigation concerning legislation which is in force, a 'devolution issue' may arise.

*Special cases*

**Financial legislation.** As noted in relation to legislation of the UK Parliament, financial legislation has a particular constitutional status, and taxation is in any case a reserved matter. However, Part IV of the Scotland Act 1998 gives the Scottish Parliament the power to raise or lower the basic rate of income tax by 3p in the pound. Therefore, if this power is exercised, it must be by means of a 'Tax-Varying Resolution' of the Scottish Parliament, rather than an Act. Following UK constitutional convention, such Resolution would have to be annual.

Tax-spending powers (and any tax-raising powers other than varying the basic rate of income tax), can be exercised only through legislation, following UK constitutional convention. Thus, any such legislation requires a 'Financial Resolution' before Stage 2 can be taken. Respecting the constitutional convention requiring annual Acts authorising expenditure, there has been an annual 'Budget (Scotland) Act'.

**Consolidation, statute law repeal and statute law revision legislation.** 'Consolidation' etc are discussed above as special examples of United Kingdom legislation. Although there is insufficient legislation from the Scottish Parliament for these procedures to be needed in respect of it, the Scottish Parliament is, of course, entitled to seek to simplify the statute book by consolidating United Kingdom Parliament legislation within its legislative competence, and there are simplified procedures in the Standing Orders of the Scottish Parliament[1].

**Members' legislation.** Most legislation is introduced by government but, as noted in relation to the UK Parliament, any MSP may do so. The 1998 Act does not specifically refer to such private members' legislation, but the Standing Orders of the Scottish Parliament anticipate it, under the description 'Member's Bills'. Indeed, there have been some such Member's Bills[2], some of which have been enacted, though it is too early to conclude what role such Bills will usually fulfill.

**Committee legislation.** In addition, in an interesting innovation, committees themselves may introduce Bills on matters which they have enquired into, provided the Parliament agrees (and in

---

1 These powers have been exercised. In 2003, following the Scottish Law Commission Report 'Report on the Consolidation of Certain Enactments concerning Salmon and Freshwater Fisheries' (Scot Law Com 188), the Salmon and Freshwater Fisheries (Consolidation) (Scotland) Act consolidated one Act of the Scottish Parliament (the Theft Act 1607), 23 Acts of the United Kingdom Parliament (the oldest dating from 1804) and four pieces of delegated legislation.
2 In 2003, these included the Council of the Law Society Bill (introduced by David McLetchie MSP), the Dog Fouling (Scotland) Bill (introduced by Keith Harding MSP) and the Gaelic Language Bill (introduced by Mike Russell MSP). The first two were successful; the third was not.

which case the first part of Stage 1 is dispensed with). Again, it is too early to see how this innovation will develop[1].

**Local, personal, private and hybrid legislation.** Existing forms of private Bill procedure are retained for those matters not within the competence of the Scottish Parliament. Thus, for reserved matters (which include oil and gas and most transport matters), the Private Legislation Procedure (Scotland) Act 1936 (discussed above in relation to UK private, personal etc legislation), continues unchanged, still requiring the decision of the Secretary of State and a UK Parliament Confirmation Act. The alternative procedure under the Statutory Orders (Special Procedure) Act 1945, which is partly devolved, also remains (though it appears never to have been used in Scotland, even before devolution).

However, for fully devolved matters, the public/private distinction applies to legislation of the Scottish Parliament as it does to the United Kingdom Parliament. There is provision in the Standing Orders of the Scottish Parliament for 'private' legislation in this sense, that is, for Bills introduced by a promoter who is an individual person, a corporate body (such as a local authority or a trading company) or an unincorporated association (such as a club, society or trust which was not incorporated) for the purpose of obtaining particular powers or benefits in excess of, or in conflict with, the general law. This includes Bills relating to 'estate, property, status or style or otherwise relating to the personal affairs of the promoter'. In such case, the lead committee requires the promoter to deposit documents, give notice, deposit copies of the Bill for public inspection, give notice to interested parties and invite objections[2]

1 In 2003, the Commissioner for Children and Young People (Scotland) Bill was a Committee Bill, following the Education, Culture and Sport Committee's Report 'An Inquiry into the Need for a Children's Commissioner in Scotland' (2nd Report of 2002, SP Paper 508, 14 February 2002) and 'Report on the proposed Commissioner for Children and Young Persons Bill' (11th Report of 2002, SP Paper 617, 3 July 2002): the proposal was accepted by the Parliament on 25 September 2002 and introduced on 4 December 2002, and was successfully enacted 26 March 2003, receiving its royal assent on 1 May 2003.
2 The only private Bills until early 2003 were the Robin Rigg Offshore Wind Farm (Navigation and Fishing) (Scotland) Bill promoted by Offshore Energy Resources Ltd and Solway Offshore Ltd, and designed to allow them to interfere with public rights of navigation and fishing in order to construct and maintain the wind farm and the Stirling-Alloa-Kincardine Railway and Linked Improvements Bill promised by Clackmannanshire Council and designed to construct a rail connection to Longannet Power Station and related works, including closing level crossings and roads, and purchasing land compulsorily.

**Emergency legislation.** There is special provision for 'emergency Bills' in the Standing Orders of the Scottish Parliament providing rapid enactment. No definition of 'emergency' is attempted[1].

*Enactment, the 'Sewel convention' and 'Sewel motions'*

As noted above in relation to Acts of the United Kingdom Parliament, and in Chapter 3, the amount of legislation being enacted in relation to Scotland, and within the devolved competence of the Scottish Parliament, but by the United Kingdom Parliament, is remarkable, largely because of the existence of 'Sewel motions'.

## Publication and citation of Acts of the Scottish Parliament

*Acts of the pre-1707 Parliament of Scotland*

Acts of the original Parliament of Scotland, a few of which are still in force, are printed in a number of modern series. The *Acts of the Parliament of Scotland* 1124–1707 (alias the Record Edition) was published in the 19th century by the Commissioners of Public Records[2]. Acts and related documents, such as Charters, from 1135 are published in the several volumes of *Regesta Regum Scottorum* (Edinburgh University Press) which commenced in 1960. Each deals with the output during the reign of a monarch.

Those Acts still in force in 1964 appear in an HMSO reprint also called *Acts of the Parliaments of Scotland 1424–1707*.

Acts of the Parliament of Scotland are usually cited by short title and year, for example the 'Union with England Act 1706'. Different editions do not always agree on the chapter number[3] but,

---

1 However, the Criminal Procedure (Amendment) (Scotland) Act 2002, designed to overturn a particularly awkward decision on criminal procedure, *Reynolds v Dyer* 2002 SLT 295, 2002 SCCR 322, was passed by this means. The court decision was on 14 February, and the Bill was drafted by, and passed all its stages, on 27 February 2002. The learned annotator in the *Current Law* volume containing the Acts justly remarked that it is unlikely that the Westminster Parliament would have reacted that quickly.

2 Earlier editions include the *Laws and Acts of Parliament 1424–1681*, published by Sir Thomas Murray of Glendook (Glendook's Edition), itself based on those published a century earlier by Skene.

3 The Royal Mines Act 1424, the oldest Scots Act still in force, is described by the Record Edition as c13, but by Glendook's Edition as c12.

as so few are still in force, it is possible to omit it. In historical contexts they are sometimes cited by reference to the volume and page of the Record Edition, for example 'APS [i e Acts of the Parliament of Scotland] VIII, 80'.

## Acts of the Scottish Parliament

Acts of the Scottish Parliament are cited by short title, year and 'asp' number, for example 'Regulation of Care (Scotland) Act 2001 asp 8.

**Chronological series.** Acts of the Scottish Parliament are printed and sold in individual copies by The Stationery Office and are bound into annual volumes so entitled[1], and these can be taken as authoritative.

In addition, the *Passage of Bills* series published by The Stationery Office most usefully contain all relevant accompanying documents, including Scottish parliamentary debates, and indeed the Bill as amended at different stages, with the Act itself in final form.

**Encyclopaedic series.** It is understood that there are no plans to produce an encyclopaedic series.

**Commercial produced reprints.** *Current Law Statutes Annotated* reproduces all Acts of the Scottish Parliament, including private legislation.

No doubt *The Parliament House Book* and *Parliament House Statutes Reprints* will include relevant Acts of the Scottish Parliament, and text-books and monographs will do likewise.

**Indexes etc.** Annual volumes of *Acts of the Scottish Parliament* are indexed, but no indexes as such have yet been published.

**Computerised retrieval of Acts of the Scottish Parliament.** Acts of the Scottish are available in their original form (i e unamended or unrepealed where appropriate) at the HMSO website in full text, as are the Explanatory Notes[2]. Bills currently before the Scottish Parliament can be found in full text, and with

---

1 In early 2003, only the single Act of 1999 and those of 2000 had been so published, but those of 2001 and 2002 were expected soon.
2 The HMSO website is at www.hmso.gov.uk.

links to 'accompanying documents' and 'policy memoranda' and references to the relevant Committees, at the Scottish Parliament website[1].

The WESTLAW database includes all Acts of the Scottish Parliament in force, in their amended form as appropriate, with sophisticated search facilities. The BAILII database also contains all such Acts.

## PART 5A: OTHER DELEGATED LEGISLATION

### The nature of delegated legislation

*The origins and purpose of delegated legislation*

Delegated legislation is legislation made by a body other than the United Kingdom Parliament, under powers delegated to it by that Parliament. It is not a novel phenomenon. Its modern use dates from the early 19th-century Parliaments' reforming zeal, and it has proliferated in the last 50 years.

The reasons for having delegated legislation are various and interlocking, but can be summed up as speed and flexibility, and use of expertise. Parliamentary time is overburdened, so delegating power to legislate bypasses the bottleneck. Moreover, much legislation requires frequent minor change, and it is a lot easier to amend delegated legislation. Much legislation is also complicated, concerning subjects such as nuclear safety or teachers' superannuation, and Parliament has no collective expertise in most such areas. Therefore, delegation to experts, typically civil servants, but usually in consultation with outside interests affected by the proposals, may be sensible. One particular form of expertise is local knowledge, implying delegation to local authorities[2]. Other benefits said to accrue from delegation, for example its use for emergency powers, are usually variations upon those mentioned. One other advantage for a government (which already dominates Parliament and thus the legislative process) is said, cynically, to be further reduction in parliamentary control. Consultation with interested parties before and during drafting is as important with delegated legislation as with parliamentary, and because it is less

---

1 The Scottish Parliament website is at www.scottish.parliament.uk/.
2 For example, whether drinking alcoholic beverages in public in the centre of cities should be controlled or not is probably best left to local decision: see for example, the City of Dundee District Bylaws for Prohibiting the Consumption of Alcohol in Designated Places 1995 and equivalents elsewhere.

often drafted against the clock, the standard of draftsmanship is often thought to be higher than for Acts.

Overall, delegated legislation can be seen as a means by which the modern administrative machinery of government is reconciled (satisfactorily or otherwise) with democratic control. It also demonstrates the common characteristic of modern law, that is, that much of it is a form of procedural guide to officials and incomprehensible to the uninitiated, rather like a guide to computer software.

Delegated legislation is sometimes referred to as 'subordinate legislation'[1] or even 'secondary legislation', which implies that it is less powerful than other forms. This is misleading for, provided the exercise of the delegated power is within the boundaries of the delegation and not ultra vires, legislation under delegated powers is as powerful as an Act of the United Kingdom Parliament. As illustrated below, it can be used to amend or even repeal Acts of Parliament

Not all grants of powers in Acts of Parliament are delegations of legislative powers, that is, of powers to write laws. They may be grants of executive or administrative powers, that is, powers to take decisions. For example, powers are granted by the Immigration and Asylum Act 1999, s 83(1),(2) to the Secretary of State to appoint (after consultation with the Lord Chancellor and the Scottish Ministers) an Immigration Services Commissioner with a duty to operate a register of persons qualified to provide immigration advice and services, and by s 85(3) and Sch 6 powers are granted to the Commissioner himself to determine whether a person is competent to provide such advice and services and, if so, to register that person as so qualified.

### Nature and uses of delegated legislation

Delegated legislation, as noted above, is legislation made by a body other than the United Kingdom Parliament, under powers delegated to it by that Parliament. Such a delegate is not itself a source of law, so cannot legislate without such an act of delegation by that Parliament. There must therefore be a 'parent Act', as it is commonly called. In practice, most Acts are 'parent Acts', though many have only few progeny.

In principle, delegation might be to any body, although commonly it is to 'the Secretary of State', that is, the government.

---

1 The Scotland Act 1998 does so, for instance: see e g s 104.

In principle, delegated legislation may cover the same enormous range of subjects as do Acts of Parliament[1], although there are conventions which tend to restrict its use to, broadly speaking, more detailed matters, leaving the principles to the parent Act.

**Standard uses of delegated legislation.** Much detailed domestic regulation is thus made by delegated legislation, for example the rules requiring headlamps of a certain size and power on cars, and the like[2], and speed limits[3]. Delegated legislation is often used to bring Acts of Parliament into force[4]. Much, however, is of minor significance, for example fixing fees for various services which may require frequent amendment[5].

Some delegated legislation is of major importance, however. Constitutions of newly independent ex-colonies were habitually

1 Statutory instruments (the principal form of delegated legislation) in 2002 concerned subjects as diverse as the Aggregates Levy and zoos, by way of architects, business names, chiropractors, the continental shelf, electricity, and so on: 'Statutory Instruments Statistics' on Her Majesty's Stationery Office website (www.legislation.hmso.gov.uk). This indicates that, unsurprisingly, in that year some of the most common subjects were education, the National Health Service and social security. Among the first half-dozen statutory instruments of 2002 were the Landfill Tax (Amendment) Regulations 2002, the Import and Export Restrictions (Foot & Mouth Disease) Regulations 2002, the Immigration and Asylum Act 1999 (Part V Exemptions: Relevant Employers) Order 2002, the Tax Credits (Miscellaneous Amendments) Regulations 2002, and the Retained Organs Commission (Amendment) Regulations 2002. The frequency of the word 'amendment' is not misleading.
2 For example, Road Vehicles (Construction and Use) Regulations 1986, SI 1986/1078 (as amended); Motor Vehicles (Authorisation of Special Types) General Order 1979, SI 1979/1198) (as amended); Motor Vehicles (Tests) Regulations 1981, SI 1981/1694 (as amended) etc; and even the Pedal Cycles (Construction and Use) Regulations 1983, SI 1983/1176, made under various powers, now chiefly the Road Traffic Act 1988.
3 Chiefly the Motor Vehicle (Variation of Speed Limits) Regulations 1947, SR&O 1947/2192; Motorway Traffic (Speed Limit) Regulations 1974, SI 1974/502; 70mph, 60mph and 50mph (Temporary Speed Limit) Order 1977 and Temporary Speed Limit (Continuation) Order 1978, SI 1978/1548; and Motor Vehicle (Variation of Speed Limits) Regulations 1986, SI 1986/1175, made under various powers, chiefly now the Road Traffic Regulation Act 1984.
4 In other words, although the Act is law, having passed through Parliament, it has no effect until a further piece of legislation, the power to make which was delegated by the Act (typically to the government), is exercised: see 'Commencement provisions' above and, for example, the Scotland Act 1998 (Commencement) Order 1998, SI 1998/3178.
5 For example, the Consular Fees (No 2) Order 1999, SI 1999/3132, made under the Consular Fees Act 1980 s 1(1), fixes fees for visas.

laid down by this means[1]. 'Direct rule' in Northern Ireland operated from the 1970s through delegation of certain 'transferred
powers' to the Secretary of State for Northern Ireland[2]. Much
Community legislation (that which is without direct effect: see
above) takes effect in the United Kingdom by this means[3]. Of more
contemporary interest, Acts of the Scottish Parliament are, strictly
speaking, a form of delegated legislation, for they are made under
powers conferred by the UK Parliament (in the Scotland Act
1998) to a body created by it (the Scottish Parliament)[4]. However,
their significance is such to amply justify its separate consideration
above.

**Controversial uses of delegated legislation.** Some uses of delegated legislation are controversial. Firstly, governments often seek
very wide powers of delegation, and may even propose 'skeleton
Acts', that is, bare frameworks, the detail all to be provided by delegated legislation. Framework Acts, with clear principles, may not
be objectionable. However, at some point, the provisions of the Act
become too skeletal. An example of an Act which is controversial
on this point is the Education (Student Loans) Act 1990. This has
but four sections and two fairly brief schedules, and can be
summed up in s 1(1) which reads 'The Secretary of State may
make arrangements for enabling eligible students to receive loans
towards their maintenance ... '. The term 'eligible students' is
partly defined in s 1(2)(a), and various other terms are defined
elsewhere, but s 1(2)(b) permits the Secretary of State to impose
on eligible students 'such other conditions as may be prescribed by
regulations made by him' and Sch 2 permits regulations to
prescribe the maximum annual loan, the timing and manner of
repayment, deferment or cancellation of liability etc, with few

---

1 For example, the original constitution of Zambia is in Sch 2 to the Zambia
  Independence Order 1964, SI 1964/1652, made under powers delegated to the
  government by the Foreign Jurisdiction Act 1890 and the Zambia Independence
  Act 1964.
2 Northern Ireland Act 1974, s 1(3), (4), and Sch 1(1)(b), read with the Northern
  Ireland Constitution Act 1973, ss 2, 3. The Northern Ireland Act 1988 replaced
  this with a new form of devolution, but in early 2003 it was not clear whether
  these arrangements would succeed.
3 See 'Community legislation without direct effect and United Kingdom law'
  above.
4 Delegation by Acts of the Scottish Parliament itself (technically, therefore, sub-
  delegation) is dealt with below.

restrictions. Thus, the actual scheme is to be found, not in the Act, but almost entirely in delegated legislation[1].

Secondly, delegated legislation may be used to amend Acts of Parliament. This may be restricted to a power to amend earlier Acts in 'Transitional Provisions' (see above)[2], though it has been used to permit more major change, and indeed, even future amendment of the very Act giving the delegated powers[3]. Such uses have been termed 'Henry VIII clauses'.

**Recent remarkable examples of the use of delegated legislation.** There have been several examples of very wide delegation in recent years[4]. One of the most extraordinary is the Regulatory Reform Act 2001 (amending the Deregulation and Contracting Out Act 1994) which allows the United Kingdom government, by means of a 'regulatory reform order', to amend or repeal any Act which it considers imposes unjustifiable administrative or bureaucratic burdens on individuals, companies or voluntary organisations and either to remove that burden or to replace it with a lesser one, provided that this is done within two years of the Act being passed. This almost amounts to extending the legislative process for two years after royal assent and, as any amended Act will be one the government itself sponsored, invites carelessness in framing the original proposals.

Another remarkable example is the Scotland Act[5], which includes (however inappropriately titled in dynastic terms) 'Henry VIII clauses'. Thus, for example, s 30(2) allows Schs 4 and 5 to the Act itself to be amended; s 89 allows modification of the functions of cross-border public authorities set up by the Act if 'necessary or expedient'; s 104 allows any provision to be made which is 'necessary or expedient' in consequence of the Scotland Act or delegated legislation under it; s 105 allows modifications to legislation made before the Scotland Act which are 'necessary or expedient' in consequence of the Scotland Act; s 106 allows modification of the functions exercisable by the government which is 'appropriate' to enable it to be transferred to the Scottish Executive; s 107 allows 'necessary and expedient' amendments to be made in consequence

---

1 In early 2003, there were 34 sets of such regulations in force.
2 Eg the Education Reform Act 1988, s 231.
3 Eg the Sex Discrimination Act 1975, s 80(1) permits amendment to listed provisions of the Act itself, and s 80(3) allows that list itself to be amended!
4 See eg the European Communities Act 1972, s 2(2) and the Human Rights Act 1988, s 10.
5 Delegation to Scottish authorities, including 'Scottish Statutory Instruments', are considered below, as such.

of ultra vires legislation by the Scottish Parliament or action by the Scottish Executive; and so on, all by means of delegated legislation. Moreover, s 113 extends the scope of all these, and other powers to make delegated legislation, in various ways. And s 114 allows amendment by delegated legislation of some of those very provisions which give the power to amend by delegated legislation. No doubt this can be justified in so far as the draftsmen could plead that it was impossible for them, or the Members of Parliament, to foresee all the necessary provisions. Certainly, some of these powers have been used extensively.

**Control of uses of delegated powers.** Concern about parliamentary control over delegation of powers to legislate produced what is now the House of Lords Select Committee on Delegated Powers and Regulatory Reform which takes evidence and reports on whether a Bill 'inappropriately delegate[s] power or whether [proposes] an inappropriate level of parliamentary scrutiny', and reports to the House[1].

## Types of United Kingdom delegated legislation and their form

UK delegated legislation is very common. The total number of all forms of statutory instrument, the main type, rose from about 2,000 each year in the mid-1980s to nearly 4,000 in 2002[2]. Some apply only in Scotland, some only in Wales, some only in England, some only in Great Britain, and others in the whole United Kingdom[3].

---

1 In 2001–02, it made 29 reports on delegations and on the other part of its remit in relation to 'regulatory reform proposals' (discussed below). In early 2003, the recent reports on delegations included consideration of the Patient (Assisted Dying) Bill (a private member's Bill containing a 'Henry VIII clause' which the Committee found acceptable, and another in relation to which it suggested amendment); the Electricity (Miscellaneous Provisions) Bill (also containing a 'Henry VIII clause' which was acceptable, but another which it thought deserved 'affirmative resolution procedure'). See also below in relation to 'Classification by degree of UK Parliamentary and governmental control and publicity'.

2 The highest number ever, 4,642, was in 2001, but this is attributable to several hundred relating to the outbreak of Foot and Mouth Disease: see 'Statutory Instrument Statistics' on Her Majesty's Stationery Office website (see above).

3 Thus, there were 575 Scottish Statutory Instruments (see below) in 2002 (and over 300 Welsh ones): 'Statutory Instrument Statistics' (see previous note). Those applying only to England (or England and Wales) are not separately numbered, and those applying only in Northern Ireland raise other issues. Devolution has clearly increased the number of statutory instruments made.

Many have a limited life, and many others replace or amend earlier ones, often marginally, so (as with Acts of the UK Parliament) the actual quantity in force is not rising so steeply. They also vary enormously in length, from one page to (on occasion) hundreds. There may be an increasing propensity to delegate, and to delegate more important matters. For example, the Social Security Act 1986, s 20 created income support, but most of the detail of this benefit is found in a lengthy statutory instruments[1].

The form of delegated legislation varies with the type, although all mimic parliamentary legislation. There are two ways of classifying UK delegated legislation: by delegate and name; and by degree of parliamentary and governmental control and publicity.

Legislation delegated by the Scottish Parliament (technically sub-delegated, since delegated by Acts of the Scottish Parliament, themselves technically delegated legislation) can be fitted into this analysis, but deserves separate treatment, which follows. It should also be noted that, rather confusingly, the term 'Scottish Statutory Instruments' is used to refer to such legislation applying exclusively to Scotland whether made under powers (sub-)delegated by the Scottish Parliament, or under powers directly delegated by the United Kingdom Parliament.

*Classification by delegate and name*

In principle, the United Kingdom Parliament can delegate to any body (subject to any restrictions that Convention rights and Community law may impose). In practice, delegation is largely to four types of delegate: the government[2]; local government; the courts; and statutory bodies.

**Delegation to government: orders, regulations, rules, etc.**
Most delegation is to the Secretary of State[3] or other minister, in other words, to government. It is of course the civil servants in the relevant department who actually draft the legislation. The

---

1  Income Support (General) Regulations 1987, SI 1987/1967 (now amended).
2  For the difference between Parliament and government, see ch 3.
3  The title 'Secretary of State' is attached to most Cabinet ministers in charge of departments. There may therefore be nearly a dozen Secretaries of State. In principle, any Secretary of State could exercise powers so delegated. Commonly, one is clearly the relevant one. Before devolution, in a number of cases the function was carried out in Scotland by the Scottish Secretary, and in England by another. This can still occur, however.

resulting legislation may be termed 'order' (for example, the European Communities (Designation) Order 2002, SI 2002/248); 'order in council' (for example, the Scotland Act 1998 (Transfer of Functions to the Scottish Ministers, etc) Order 1999, SI 1999/1750); 'regulations' (for example, the Statutory Maternity Pay (Compensation of Employers) Amendment Regulations 2002, SI 2002/225); or 'rules' (for example, the Immigration and Asylum Appeals (Procedure) Rules 2000, SI 2000/2333). Other titles are occasionally used, as, for example, with the Injuries in War (Shore Employment) Compensation (Amendment) Scheme 1990, SI 1990/1946, the British Gas Corporation (Disposal of Wytch Farm Oilfield Interest) Directions 1981, SI 1981/1459 and the Foreign Compensation (People's Republic of China) Rules Approval Instrument, SI 1988/153.

There is no clear policy on which title to use, but rules are usually procedural rules; regulations of general application; and orders brief. Confusion is possible with orders in council, where the nominal delegate is the Privy Council[1]. The title is usually used for delegated legislation of constitutional significance, but the same title is used for some prerogative (therefore not delegated) legislation[2]. The name 'regulation' is also the name used for the principal form of Community legislation.

**UK delegation to local authorities: by-laws and management rules.** Delegation to local authorities is common, giving powers to write laws for the good government and suppression of nuisance in their areas, for example, by requiring licensing of abattoirs, public houses, and taxi operations, and prohibiting ball games in parks. Such legislation is usually in the form of by-laws. The power to make by-laws is delegated by a variety of Acts relating to public health, transport etc, but most importantly by the Local Government (Scotland) Act 1973, ss 201–203 (as amended, chiefly by the Civic Government (Scotland) Act 1982). Breach of a by-law is commonly a criminal offence.

In addition to by-laws, local authorities may make less formal 'management rules' under the Civic Government (Scotland) Act 1982, s 112 for the control of their premises. Breach of them is not

---

1 In origin, the Privy Council was the forerunner of the Cabinet. It is, in this context, a dignified and mystifying title for the government, and is recipient on occasion of substantial delegated powers, for example to amend unilaterally (albeit after consultation) the constitutions of universities, under ss 202–208 of the Education Reform Act 1988. Cabinet Ministers, Bishops and other worthies are appointed Privy Councillors as a form of honour.

2 See ch 4.

of itself criminal, but may lead to ejection and (after a hearing) an exclusion order, breach of which may be criminal. Since local government is a devolved responsibility, no doubt in time this legislation will be replaced by Acts of the Scottish Parliament which will delegate powers to local authorities.

**UK delegation to courts: Acts of Sederunt and Acts of Adjournal.** Courts have delegated powers to make rules for their own organisation and procedure. The Lord President and other judges of the Court of Session are delegated such powers in respect of the Court of Session by the Administration of Justice (Scotland) Act 1933, s 16, and the legislation they produce is called Acts of Sederunt, for example the Act of Sederunt (Rules of Court) (Consolidation and Amendment) 1965, SI 1965/321. They are granted similar powers under the Sheriff Courts (Scotland) Act 1971 in relation to the sheriff court, exercised, for example, in the Act of Sederunt (Ordinary Cause Rules) (Sheriff Court) 1993, SI 1993/1956.

The same judges in criminal guise are given parallel powers in respect of the High Court by the Criminal Procedure (Scotland) Act 1995, s 305, exercised in Acts of Adjournal, for example the Act of Adjournal (Criminal Procedure Rules) 1996, SI 1996/513[1].

However, this delegated legislation now appears in 'Scottish Statutory Instrument' form (discussed below).

**UK delegation to public corporations, statutory bodies and utilities: by-laws.** Some public corporations, statutory bodies and privatised utilities may be granted the power to make law. The Railways Act 1993, s 129 gives 'independent railway operating companies' power to make by-laws to regulate the use and working of railways. Smoking in a non-smoking carriage is a criminal offence by virtue of a rail operating company by-law which is invested with legal force by a delegation of law-making power by the United Kingdom Parliament under s 129(2)(c) of that Act[2].

**UK delegation to other bodies.** There are many examples of delegated legislation which do not fit easily into the above four

---

1 In the 16th and 17th centuries courts were regarded as having inherent powers to produce such legislation, and did so upon subjects far removed from administration and procedure. See *Introduction to Scottish Legal History* p 28.
2 '. . . an independent railway operator may . . . make bye-laws [*sic*] . . . with respect to the smoking of tobacco in railway carriages . . .'

categories, for example the powers given by the Immigration and Asylum Act 1999, s 83(4) and Sch 5, Pt 1 to the Immigration Services Commissioner to make rules regulating the professional practice, conduct and discipline of those qualified to provide immigration advice and services, exercised in the 'Commissioner's Rules' published by the Commissioner[1]. These standards may appear to be internal professional rules rather than laws, and breach of them is not criminal. However, they are created under powers granted by Parliament, and breach can lead to professional disciplinary proceedings under a statutory procedure. Such proceedings could result in various penalties, including expulsion from the profession (and provision of such services by an expelled person would be criminal)[2].

*Classification by degree of parliamentary and governmental control and publicity*

The UK Parliament has control over delegated legislation in so far as a parent Act is always required. Thus, the Bill which will become the parent Act is subject to such scrutiny as Parliament provides[3]. Firstly, therefore, Parliament accepts that the Bill should delegate at all. Most Bills delegate to a limited extent (for example, in relation to Commencement Orders: see above). Secondly, the Parliament accepts the Bill's intended delegate. Thus, delegation under the Local Government (Scotland) Act 1973, s 201(1) (as amended) is to councils, and under the Solicitors (Scotland) Act 1980, s 34 to the Law Society of Scotland. Thirdly, Parliament accepts that the Bill makes the delegation as wide or as narrow as the draftsman has drafted it. Thus, delegation to the government under s 2(2) of the European Communities Act 1972 is solely for the purpose of putting into effect Community legislation, and then subject to certain exclusions. Fourthly, Parliament may require any procedure it likes by the delegate before exercise of the delegated powers. Thus, delegation to the government under the Social Security Act 1980 to produce certain social security regulations is, by ss 9 and 10 and Sch 3, to be exercised only after consultation with the Social Security Advisory Committee. Such consultation requirements are very common, although those required to be

1 Available at the Immigration Services Commissioner's website at www.oisc.org.uk.
2 As to Scottish solicitors, see ch 7 below.
3 See above in relation to the House of Lords Select Committee on Delegated Powers and Regulatory Reform.

consulted may not be closely specified. Fifthly, the Parliament may require a degree of publicity for the resulting rules, and sixthly, it may impose the possibility of a veto upon such legislation. These last two requirements are generally fulfilled either by requiring the delegated legislation to be in statutory instrument form when the government is the delegate, or by separately delegating control to the government as 'confirming authority' when others are the delegates, as discussed below.

Thus, the most familiar classification of delegated legislation, that is, into statutory instruments and non-statutory instruments, is produced by the degree of parliamentary control[1]. This in turn draws attention to the less familiar classification of by-laws into those subject to various types of confirmation.

**The United Kingdom Parliament and statutory instruments.** There is a complicated definition of 'statutory instrument' in the Statutory Instruments Act 1946 but, in essence, it is simple. A piece of delegated legislation is a statutory instrument if the parent Act says it must be. Thus, for example, the Immigration Act 1971, s 4(3) says that 'The Secretary of State may by regulations made by statutory instrument . . . make provision for' certain things, including a requirement upon aliens to register with the police. The power was therefore exercised in a statutory instrument, the Immigration (Registration with Police) Regulations 1972, SI 1972/1758, and subsequent amending instruments. Legislative powers delegated to the government are usually required to be in statutory instrument form.

United Kingdom statutory instruments (with the exception of certain ones of only local or temporary effect[2]) are required by the Statutory Instruments Act 1946, ss 2, 3 and 4 to be dated, numbered, printed, published and sold. This may sound mundane,

---

1 The picture is complicated by a common propensity to assume, inaccurately, that 'delegated legislation' and 'statutory instruments' are synonyms. The inaccuracy of this is exemplified by the 'Commissioner's Rules' under the powers given to the Immigration Services Commissioner by the Immigration and Asylum Act 1999, s 83(4) and Sch 5, Pt 1 to make rules regulating the professional practice, conduct and discipline of those qualified to provide immigration advice and services. These are not required to be in statutory instrument form, even though breach of them could result in removal of a person from the register of people qualified to give immigration advice and services, but they must be published by the Commissioner.

2 For example, the Dundee–Aberdeen Trunk Road (A94) (Stracathro Junction) (Prohibition of Specified Turn) Order 1990, SI 1990/1829.

but if they were not numbered etc, how would one even know they existed?[1]

Statutory instruments are also usually subject to certain parliamentary procedures principally laid down in ss 4–7 of the Statutory Instruments Act 1946 and designed to allow Parliament to be informed of their existence, and apply a veto if it wishes. (It cannot, however, amend other than in certain exceptional cases.)

Firstly, statutory instruments may be required to be laid before the Parliament (that is, made available to any MP) three weeks before coming into effect, showing the dates when it was made, when it was laid, and when it is intended to come into force. (In some cases they must be laid in draft, in some cases in final form.)

Secondly, statutory instruments may be examined by the Joint (i e Commons and Lords) Committee on Statutory Instruments[2], which concerns itself with 'technical scrutiny' of statutory instruments, that is, whether they are properly made and do not purport to do something constitutionally inappropriate. The Joint Committee cannot reject instruments, but may refer them to either House on any of nine extensive grounds (such as that the instrument is defectively drafted, or appears ultra vires). Such referral is, in fact, rare, but when it occurs, the statutory instrument may be debated (but still not amended). The Joint Committee also produces general reports on specific topics such as the consolidation of delegated legislation.

Thirdly, statutory instruments may be subject to a parliamentary vote. Briefly put, this may be either a 'negative' or 'affirmative' resolution procedure in one or both Houses of Parliament (or in a delegated legislation standing committee of one). The 'negative resolution procedure', which is common, means the statutory instrument may be negatived by the parliamentary vote. The 'affirmative resolution procedure' means the statutory instrument does not come into force unless affirmed by a parliamentary vote. In neither case, however, may they be amended. This is the stage at which 'the merits' may be considered, that is, Parliament decides if it wants a statutory instrument which does what this one proposes

1 The Statutory Instruments Act 1946, s 3(2) created a special defence to prosecution for an offence laid down in a statutory instrument, that is, that it had not been issued by HMSO, nor reasonable steps taken to bring it to the notice of those likely to be affected.
2 Not to be confused with the House of Lords Select Committee on Delegated Powers and Regulatory Reform, for which, see above. There is a House of Commons Select Committee on Statutory Instruments, comprising the Commons members of the Joint Committee, for those SIs which require only House of Commons approval.

to do (and does so possibly with the assistance of a report from the House of Lords Select Committee on Delegated Powers and Regulatory Reform, noted above).

Other Acts of Parliament may impose their own specific approval regimes. The European Communities Act 1972 requires statutory instruments made under s 2(2)[1] to undergo a negative resolution by either House unless there has been an affirmative approval of a draft instrument by each House. The Regulatory Reform Act 2001[2] requires the 'regulatory reform orders' it permits to be laid before Parliament in draft for 60 days for the House of Lords Select Committee on Delegated Powers and Regulatory Reform, and the House of Commons Regulatory Reform [Select] Committee to report, after which the government must seek approval of both Houses of an amended or unamended form[3]. Controls over powers of delegation under the Scotland Act are of considerable complication. Such legislation must be in statutory instrument form, but parliamentary approval is required in one of eleven different ways from 'Type A' (draft instrument has been laid before, and approved by resolution of, each House of the UK Parliament and laid before and approved by resolution of the Scottish Parliament) to 'Type K' (instrument subject to annulment by a resolution of the House of Commons)[4].

Parliamentary controls are, of course, subject to the fact of executive dominance of the legislature. Governments are therefore free to draft Bills delegating powers and making delegated powers subject to such procedures, safe in the knowledge that normally their majority removes any likelihood of the controls being effective. The House of Lords rejected the Southern Rhodesia (United Nations Sanctions) Order 1968 but, after a threat to extend the Parliament Acts 1911 and 1949 to delegated legislation, passed an identical order a month later. The Joint Committee, however, is thought to have raised the standard of drafting.

**Confirming authorities and by-laws etc.** Local authority and public corporation by-laws are generally subject to approval by a 'confirming authority', the powers of which may be very wide, including powers to modify or reject on various grounds. The

---

1 That is, ones bringing into force Community law without direct effect.
2 Which allows the United Kingdom government to amend or repeal any Act which it considers imposes an unjustifiable administrative or bureaucratic burden and either remove or replace it with a lesser one within two years.
3 This has been called a 'super-affirmative resolution procedure'.
4 Scotland Act 1998, s 115, Sch 7.

confirming authority is commonly stated in pre-devolution legislation to be the Secretary of State, that is, the UK government, but this is now commonly devolved to the Scottish Ministers in relation to Scotland by the 'general transfer of functions' under the Scotland Act 1998, s 53.

Thus the Secretary of State, as such, is confirming authority for independent railway operators' by-laws under the Transport Act 1962, s 67 (as amended) and the Railways Act 1993, for provision and regulation of railway services is a retained matter. However, the First Minister is now, under the Local Government (Scotland) Act 1973 (as amended), confirming authority for local authority by-laws (s 201(2)) after public consultation (s 202(4)–(7)), for local government is devolved. Again, under the Law Reform (Miscellaneous Provisions) (Scotland) Act 1990 the Secretary of State was (after consultation with the Director General of Fair Trading) the confirming authority for rules written by the Scottish Conveyancing and Executry Services Board setting standards of conduct for qualified conveyancers and executry practitioners because regulation of the professions is devolved (save for architects, health professions and auditors).

Local authorities are required by the Local Government (Scotland) Act 1973, s 202 (as amended by the Civic Government (Scotland) Act 1982, s 110) to publish, make available and sell copies of their by-laws, and by s 202A, required to review their by-laws every ten years. Independent railway operators are subject to similar requirements under the Transport Act 1962, s 67 (as amended).

Local authority management rules are, by virtue of the Civic Government (Scotland) Act 1982, ss 114 and 115, required to be displayed on the relevant premises and made available for inspection and sale.

Other rules made under a confirming authority procedure may not be subject to a requirement to be published.

## The form of United Kingdom delegated legislation

In their form, statutory instruments and other forms of delegated legislation mimic parliamentary legislation, though the details vary according to the type in question.

**Citation.** Statutory instruments commence with their citation in the form of a year and sequential number, for example '2002 No 3204' (commonly abbreviated to 'SI 2002/3204'). This may be followed by brackets enclosing a further reference number preceded by 'S', 'W' or 'Cy', 'NI', 'C', or 'L'. These indicate respectively that the instrument applies only in Scotland (as do some each year even after devolution[1]); applies only in Wales, alias Cymru (as do some also after devolution); applies only in Northern Ireland; is a Commencement Order (see above[2]); or is a procedural instrument applying solely in England and Wales[3]. Thus, 'S13' would indicate the instrument is the 13th of that year applying solely to Scotland. However, while these conventions remain, since devolution, Scottish and Welsh statutory instruments are published in separate sequences (as considered below).

Before the Statutory Instruments Act 1946, the equivalent class of delegated legislation was called 'statutory rules and orders', cited as 'SR&O'.

**Name.** In official editions of statutory instruments, after the citation, appear one or two headings, for example, 'FOOD' followed by 'MILK AND DAIRIES'. These are not part of the name but a guide to the subject-matter.

The name, equivalent to an Act's short title, is given thereafter, for example 'The Milk (Special Designations) (Scotland) Order 1988' or 'The Advice and Assistance (Scotland) (Prospective Cost) (No 3) Regulations'[4]. Brackets are much favoured, enclosing 'Scotland', 'Amendment', 'Variation' and other things[5], including numerical sequences, as where an Act has several commencement orders[6].

---

1  In 2002, there were 13, from the Scotland Act 1998 (Agency Arrangements) (Specification) Order 2002, SI 2002/261 (S1) to the Race Relations Act 1976 (General Statutory Duty: Code of Practice) (Scotland) Order 2002, SO 2002/3111 (S13).
2  In 2002, there were 109.
3  In 2002, there were 18.
4  There is a good deal of innocent amusement to be had in discovering the most unusual statutory instrument name.
5  For example, the Town and Country Planning (Determination of Appeals by Appointed Persons) (Prescribed Classes) (Scotland) Amendment Regulations 1989, SI 1989/577. It is surprising that 'Amendment' is not bracketed.
6  For example, by early 2003, the commencement orders for the Immigration and Asylum Act 1999 ran from the Immigration and Asylum Act 1999 (Commencement No 1) Order 1999, SI 1999/3190 to the Immigration and Asylum Act 1999 (Commencement No 12) Order 2003, SI 2003/2, without the whole Act yet being in force. Indeed, that twelfth Commencement Order actually followed the Nationality, Immigration and Asylum Act 2002 (Commencement (No 1) Order 2002, SI 2003/1, starting to bring into force the next major piece of immigration legislation.

**Dates.** After the name, statutory instruments list three dates, those of making, laying before Parliament, and of coming into force (unless the instrument is not required to be laid before Parliament).

**Arrangement of regulations, articles or rules.** A statutory instrument of more than a few provisions is likely to have contents list, that is, an 'arrangement of regulations' (articles or rules) at the beginning. But the titles used there reappear as shoulder headings to the actual provisions.

**Recital of delegated powers.** By definition, the legislation is delegated, and each statutory instrument contains a recital of the powers under which it is delegated (and possibly of consultation carried out), for example, 'The Secretary of State, in exercise of the powers conferred on him by sections 37(1)(b), 38(1) and 143(1) of the Roads (Scotland) Act 1984 and of all other powers enabling him in that behalf, and after consultation with representative organisations in accordance with sections 37(6) and 38(2) of that Act, hereby makes the following Regulations ...'. This bears on the question of ultra vires, but its significance is reduced by the common use of 'and all other powers in that behalf'.

**The substantive provisions – regulations, articles and rules etc.** The name of the basic unit of a statutory instrument varies with whether it is called regulations (regulation), an order (article), or rules (rule). Structure is in the same form as an Act, but subdivisions of the basic unit are always called paragraphs, sub-paragraphs (and even sub-sub-paragraphs).

In an instrument of any length, there are shoulder headings to each regulation, rather like the marginal notes in an Act. Parts and Part headings are used in much the same way as in Acts.

Operating instructions such as interpretation, amending and repealing (known in statutory instruments as 'revoking') provisions may appear and, while most are placed at the end, as with Acts, interpretation paragraphs are usually placed at the beginning.

Schedules are common.

**The explanatory note.** Invariably, official editions of statutory instruments have an explanatory note appended. This is declared 'not part of' the instrument and they seldom provide any useful explanation.

## Ultra vires and judicial control of United Kingdom delegated legislation

Law appearing in delegated legislation is as powerful as law appearing in Acts of Parliament, and therefore (subject to any requirements of Community law) cannot be struck down by the court. There is an important exception, however, in the ultra vires doctrine, a form of judicial control.

Judicial control of delegated legislation interlocks with parliamentary control. In practice, Parliament always limits delegation. Parent Acts delegate specific powers to specific persons, for specific purposes, to be exercised through specific procedures, possibly subject to specific publicity requirements and a veto.

If those limits are exceeded, the purported laws are ultra vires, that is, 'beyond the powers' which were delegated. In this case a court may strike them down. For example, *Malloch v Aberdeen Corporation* 1974 SLT 253 turned on the Education (Scotland) Act 1962 which delegated to the Secretary of State certain powers to make regulations for certain purposes. Under these powers he made a regulation, the Teachers (Education, Training and Certification) (Scotland) Regulations 1967, SI 1967/1162, among other things purportedly requiring teachers retrospectively to register with the General Teaching Council for Scotland[1]. Malloch, a teacher employed by Aberdeen Corporation, was dismissed for failure to register. He sued the Corporation, and the Inner House upheld his claim that the 1962 Act did not delegate the power to make such regulations, so that they were ultra vires[2].

In practice such striking down is rare. This is for several reasons. Firstly, the delegation may in practice be very wide, and give discre-

---

1 There was considerable related litigation, in part of which Mr Malloch most remarkably appeared as a litigant in person, in other words without benefit of legal representation, in the House of Lords: see 1973 SLT (Notes) 5.

2 See also *Marshall v Clark* 1957 JC 68 and *Magistrates of Ayr v Lord Advocate* 1950 SLT 102. An interesting English case is *Bugg v Director of Public Prosecutions* [1993] QB 473, [1993] 2 WLR 628, [1993] 2 All ER 815. RAF Alconbury By-laws 1985 and HMS Forest Moor and Menwith Hill Station By-laws 1986, made by the Secretary of State under Pt II of the Military Lands Act 1892, purported to exclude the public from certain military sites. Bugg was convicted of the offence of entering a place protected by the by-laws without permission, and convicted. On appeal, the Divisional Court of Queen's Bench held that there were two types of invalidity, substantive (where the by-law was invalid on its face because ultra vires or unreasonable) and procedural (where a procedural requirement, such as consultation, had not been followed). In the instant case, neither by-law set out with sufficient clarity the area it covered, and the Alconbury by-laws covered the area within a perimeter fence, but the fence had been moved in an attempt unilaterally to extend the area.

tion to the delegate[1]. Secondly, the courts have regarded some procedural requirements as merely directory rather than mandatory, that is they are required, but failure to follow them does not annul the regulations[2]. Thirdly, there may be attempts to oust the jurisdiction of the courts, that is, prevent the courts from pronouncing on the validity of the delegated legislation. For example, the Education (Scotland) Act 1980, s 114(2) (as amended by the Education (Scotland) Act 1981, Sch 6, para 13) provided that an instrument giving effect to a scheme under Part IV of the Act was to be conclusive proof that the scheme was not ultra vires.

## Publication and citation of United Kingdom delegated legislation

### Chronological series of statutory instruments

Statutory instruments of general effect (and, since 1989, important local ones) are printed and published by The Stationery Office, sold as individual copies and bound up in several annual vòlumes entitled *Statutory Instruments*. The volumes are grouped into 'Parts' and 'Sections' but, as the instruments are printed chronologically, and sequence of instruments in each volume is printed on its spine, these names can be ignored.

### Encyclopaedic series of United Kingdom statutory instruments

*Halsbury's Statutory Instruments* (Butterworths) is a multi-volume encyclopaedia. It covers instruments in force in the whole United Kingdom (or solely in England and Wales) under a large number of subject headings, but does not cover those instruments which apply solely in Scotland.

The full text of the more important instruments it covers is given. Others are outlined, and there are brief descriptions of the general effect of instruments on various topics.

1 An extreme example was the Finance (No 2) Act 1940 which purported to give powers to the Commissioners of Customs and Excise to make such rules 'as appear to them necessary' in relation to deciding tax liability in the absence of a tax return. However, this was successfully challenged in an English case *Commissioners of Customs and Excise v Cure and Deeley Ltd* [1962] 1 QB 340, [1961] 3 All ER 641.
2 In English cases, requirements for publication were held directory in *Sheer Metalcraft Ltd* [1954] 1 QB 114, but requirements for consultation were mandatory in *Agricultural Training Board v Aylesbury Mushrooms Ltd* [1972] 1 WLR 190.

*Other commercially produced reprints of statutory instruments*

Acts of Sederunt and Acts of Adjournal are reprinted in *The Parliament House Book* (referred to above in relation to commercially produced reprints of Acts) arranged by broad subject-matter, and until 1990 also in *(Scottish) Current Law Statutes Annotated*. (These now appear as 'Scottish statutory instruments': see below.) Other subject-area encyclopaedias may contain relevant instruments. For example, Butterworths *Immigration Law Service* reprints all statutory instruments in force relevant to its subject-matter, updated as necessary, and the various editions of the principal textbook on the subject, Macdonald and Webber (eds) *United Kingdom Nationality Law and Practice* (5th edn, 2001, updated by supplement) have reprinted all those in force at the time of publication.

Commencement orders (and a numerical list of statutory instruments) are, since 1992, reprinted in *(Scottish) Current Law Statutes Annotated* (W Green and Sweet & Maxwell).

*Indexes of statutory instruments*

Each volume of *Statutory Instruments* contains an index, numerical list and table of effects.

The Stationery Office also publishes the *Table of Government Orders* annually and *Index to Government Orders* every two years, parallel to the chronological *Table and Index of Statutes* respectively. There is also a monthly and annual *List of Statutory Instruments* with alphabetical and chronological tables.

*Computerised retrieval of United Kingdom statutory instruments*

All statutory instruments since 1 January 1997 are available in full text at The Stationery Office website[1] and JUSTIS UK Statutory Instruments contains full text of all statutory instruments published by The Stationery Office from 1 January 1987 on CD-ROM.

The LexisNexis computer database includes all statutory instruments in force, incorporating amendments except, unfortunately, those applying only in Scotland.

---

1  I e http://www.hmso.gov.uk.

*Delegated legislation which is not in statutory instrument form*

There are no general requirements for publication of delegated legislation which is not in statutory instrument form, but the requirements of publicity of by-laws and local management rules mean that they are likely to be reasonably available in the area to which they apply.

## PART 5B: OTHER DELEGATED LEGISLATION IN SCOTLAND

### Delegation, the Scotland Act 1998 and Acts of the Scottish Parliament

It is worth recalling initially that devolution itself involves a massive delegation, for the Scotland Act 1998 delegated to the Scottish Parliament and Scottish Executive all powers, legislative and executive, outwith the 'reserved matters'[1].

Acts of the Scottish Parliament are thus technically delegated legislation, because the United Kingdom Parliament set up the Scottish Parliament by statute, and delegated to that new Parliament some of its power to legislate for Scotland[2]. Devolution itself, and Acts of the Scottish Parliament, are fully discussed above, and such Acts are not 'Other delegated legislation' in the sense of this section, though their status has to be borne in mind.

The Scotland Act 1998 did, of course, give the United Kingdom Government very wide powers to make delegated legislation to make consequential changes to the law, including to the Scotland Act itself[3].

### Delegated legislation in Scotland and devolution

The principles which apply to United Kingdom delegated legislation also apply to delegated legislation in relation to Scotland.

---

1 For 'reserved matters', see ch 3.
2 This is made explicit in the Human Rights Act 1998, s 21(1), *sub voc.* 'subordinate legislation'.
3 The HMSO website (www.hmso.gov.uk) has a useful list of Links to the Scotland Act 1998 and associated legislation which contains, int. al., the delegated legislation under that Act.

It might be thought that the position is therefore simple, and that, since devolution, all that happens is that the Scottish Parliament delegates to the Scottish Executive, which produces a new breed of delegated legislation replacing the earlier UK delegated legislation.

There is indeed a new breed of 'Scottish statutory instrument' ('SSI'), made by the Scottish Ministers and in some sense replacing UK statutory instruments ('(UK) SIs') made by the UK government, but the position has considerable complexities which need carefully disentangling, and produce some surprising conclusions[1].

## Delegated legislation and 'reserved matters'[2]

Acts of the UK Parliament delegate powers to the UK government and other bodies in relation to 'reserved matters'. This was, of course, the position before devolution, and continues to be so since. The delegated legislation so produced was normally in the usual UK form of statutory instrument or by-law (as appropriate) before devolution, and will normally continue to be so since. Such delegated legislation, both pre- and post-devolution, will continue to apply in Scotland[3], unaffected by devolution, subject to a particular complication[4].

The complication is that, as noted in Chapter 3, some functions within the 'reserved matters' can in fact be devolved by the UK government to the Scottish Ministers by the process known as 'executive devolution', under powers in the Scotland Act 1998, and others, while not transferred, can be used by Scottish

---

1 The authors are grateful for the assistance derived from Himsworth 'Subordinate legislation in the Scottish Parliament' (2002) 6 ELR 356–379, Reid 'Who Makes Scotland's Law: delegated legislation under the devolution arrangements' (2002) 6 ELR 380–384 and Reid 'The Limits of Devolved Legislative Power; subordinate legislation in Scotland' (*Statute Law Review:* forthcoming).

2 See ch 3.

3 Mostly, this will be legislation applying to the whole UK, or GB, but occasionally includes legislation applying solely to Scotland, typically because it concerns devolution: see e g Scottish Parliament (Disqualification) Order 2002, SI 2003/409 (S4) which specifies persons disqualified from being MSPs.

4 The HMSO website (www.hmso.gov.uk) has a useful list of Acts of the UK Parliament and UK Statutory Instruments which apply exclusively or primarily to Scotland.

Ministers under an 'agency agreement' with the UK government, also under powers in the Scotland Act 1998[1].

## Delegated legislation and 'devolved matters'[2]

*Existing delegated legislation on devolved matters*

Acts of the UK Parliament, of course, also delegated powers before devolution concerning what have become 'devolved matters', to the Secretary of State for Scotland, Scottish local authorities, Scottish courts and other persons and bodies within Scotland[3]. The delegated legislation so produced was also normally in the usual UK form of statutory instrument or by-law (as appropriate) before devolution. However, devolution did not remove this delegated legislation at a stroke. Thus, most of it is still in force. Indeed, it remains in force unless and until replaced.

However, that does not mean that such existing legislation is unchanged by devolution. As noted in Chapter 3, basic provisions of the Scotland Act 1998 perform a 'general transfer of functions' from UK government to the Scottish Ministers in relation to Scotland. Thus, they confer upon the Scottish Ministers the governmental functions previously granted to the Secretary of State and other members of the UK government in so far as they apply to Scotland[4]. Thus, where such delegated legislation gave powers and responsibilities to the Secretary of State, it must now

---

1 E g the Scotland Act 1998 (Transfer of Functions to the Scottish Ministers) Order 1999, SI 1999/1750, which provided for the transfer of an enormous number of disparate functions of the UK government, so far as exercisable in relation to Scotland by the Scottish Ministers, or still by the UK government but with the agreement of the Scottish Ministers, and the Scotland Act 1998 (Agency Arrangements) Order 2002, SI 2002/261 (S1) which allows the Scottish Ministers to make arrangements on behalf of the UK government in preparing an emissions trading scheme for the implementing of the UK's obligations under the Kyoto Protocol on Climate Change.

2 For 'devolved matters', see ch 3. Note that the Scotland Act 1998 does not define 'devolved matters', as they are simply all matters which are not 'reserved matters'.

3 Obvious examples delegation of powers to the Scottish courts to write their own procedures include Acts of Sederunt (e g Act of Sederunt) (Rules of Court) (Consolidation and Amendment) 1965, SI 1965/321, made under the Administration of Justice (Scotland) Act 1933, s 16) and Acts of Adjournal (e g Act of Adjournal (Criminal Procedure Rules) 1996, SI 1996/513, made under the Criminal Procedure (Scotland) Act 1995, s 305).

4 Or rather, within the 'devolved competence' of the Scottish Ministers.

be read as giving them to the Scottish Ministers[1]. So, where previously, the Secretary of State might be given the power to take a decision, or the responsibility for carrying out a duty, it is now the Scottish Ministers who may, or must, do so[2].

### New delegated legislation on devolved matters

The devolution settlement envisages that the existing (UK) SIs will be replaced by SSIs in relation to devolved matters but, briefly put, the replacement occurs in three separate ways which require to be distinguished.

Firstly, it occurs by means of the Scottish Ministers exercising powers under existing UK legislation. The basic provisions of the Scotland Act 1998 just referred to, conferring upon the Scottish Ministers the functions previously granted to the Secretary of State, include not just powers to take decisions but also powers to make delegated legislation. Thus, where the UK government used to exercise these powers under UK Acts of Parliament, now the Scottish Ministers do, but they do so by means of SSIs rather than (UK) SIs[3]. At least in the short term, this way of replacing (UK) SIs with SSIs is to be expected, simply because the Scottish Parliament has not had time to replace such UK legislation. However, it also includes examples which are by no means interim ones, for example conferring upon the Scottish Ministers the power to effect Community law which does not have direct effect[4].

Secondly, it occurs by means of the Scottish Ministers exercising

---

1 In the event that powers to make delegated legislation on subjects which are now devolved matters were delegated to any person or body other than the UK government, such delegation would be unaffected.

2 Thus, for example, the Police (Scotland) Act 1967, s 4 requires that a police authority obtain the approval of the Secretary of State before appointing a new Chief Constable. This now means they must obtain the approval of the Scottish Ministers.

3 Thus, for example, the pre-devolution Land Registration (Scotland) Act 1979 (Commencement No 12) Order 1998, made under powers in the Land Registration (Scotland) Act 1979, s 30(2), was issued by the Secretary of State for Scotland and was an SI (SI 1998/2980), while the post-devolution Land Registration (Scotland) Act 1979 (Commencement No 13) Order 1999 made under precisely the same powers was issued by the Scottish Ministers and is an SSI (SSI 1999/111).

4 Under the European Communities Act 1972, s 2(2): e g the very first SSI, i e the Environmental Impact Assessment (Scotland) Regulations 1999, SSI 1999/1 (implementing an EC Directive).

powers to make delegated legislation delegated to them by Acts of the Scottish Parliament as such Acts gradually replace the existing UK legislation which delegates such powers[1]. Again, they do so by means of SSIs, and this means of replacement can be expected to increase in significance as the Scottish Parliament passes more Acts replacing UK legislation.

However, this process of replacement of UK legislation by Scottish legislation is slower than was expected because the Scottish Parliament has in its early years used 'Sewel motions' (discussed above) remarkably frequently, in effect handing back its delegated powers on certain topics to the UK Parliament. Thus, the third method of replacement is that where this happens, there is new UK legislation (whether as a result of 'Sewel motions' or not) which delegates powers to make delegated legislation to the Scottish Ministers. Again, however, they do so by means of SSIs, rather than (UK) SIs[2].

Note, however, that where the delegate is a local authority, or in some other cases, the delegated legislation was not in SI form before devolution, so is not to be replaced by SSIs[3].

## Controls over delegation of legislative powers and Scotland

### (UK) SIs and SSIs

As explained above, statutory instruments ('SIs') will continue to apply in Scotland, unless and until replaced. This is the case whether the SI concerns a reserved matter or a devolved matter.

However, where a power to make delegated legislation by SI is given to the Scottish Ministers (or any other Scottish public

---

1 Such delegated legislation is technically sub-delegated, since Acts of the Scottish Parliament are technically delegated legislation.

2 Thus, for instance, the Tobacco Advertising (Commencement) (Scotland) Order 2002, SSI 2002/512 (C26), Tobacco Advertising (Commencement No 4) (Scotland) (Amendment and Transitional Provisions) Order 2003, SSI 2003/80 (C3) and Tobacco Advertising and Promotions Act 2002 (Commencement No 5) (Scotland) Order 2003, SSI 2003/11 (C5), all made by the by the Scottish Ministers under the Tobacco Advertising and Promotion Act 2002, s 22(1) (which gives 'the appropriate Minister' the power to do so) read with s 21 (which defines 'appropriate Minister in relation to Scotland as 'the Scottish Ministers'), brought that Act, a UK Act of Parliament passed in relation to Scotland by means of a 'Sewel motion', into force.

3 Thus, by-laws made by Scottish local authorities under the Local Government (Scotland ) Act 1973, ss 201–203 (as amended) remain by-laws.

authority, such as the Scottish courts[1]), it is to be exercised by a Scottish statutory instrument ('SSI')[2]. This is also the case whether the delegation is within the 'devolved competence' of the Scottish Ministers or within one of the examples of 'executive devolution' of 'reserved matters', and whether the power is in an existing UK Act of Parliament, an Act of the Scottish Parliament, or any new UK Act of Parliament[3].

*Controls over (UK) SIs*

(UK) SIs in existence were, of course, subject to the usual controls over SIs, discussed above when they were made, and any future ones can be expected to be so too.

*Controls over SSIs*

The significance of the concept of SSI is three-fold. Firstly, SSIs must be in a form broadly equivalent to (UK) SIs. Thus, SSIs must be numbered, printed and sold[4].

Secondly, where the power is in an existing UK Act of Parliament, then the requirement for laying before Parliament, and for 'affirmative' or 'negative resolution procedure', is a requirement in relation to the Scottish Parliament instead of the UK Parliament (or either House of it)[5].

Thirdly, where the power is in an Act of the Scottish Parliament, controls modeled on, but not identical with, those for (UK) SIs are imposed. Thus, there is a Subordinate Legislation Committee of the Scottish Parliament which combines the relevant roles of the House of Lords Select Committee on Delegated Legislation and

---

1 Or, within the devolved competence, some other body. Thus the Act of Sederunt (Rules of the Court of Session Amendment No 7) (Miscellaneous) 1999, made by the Lord President of the Court of Session, is an SSI (SSI 1999/109). All previous Acts of Sederunt in modern times were SIs.

2 Scotland Act 1998 (Transitory and Transitional Provisions) (Statutory Instruments) Order 1999, SI 1999/1096, arts 2(1) *sub voc.* 'Scottish statutory instrument', read with art 4(2). Those made jointly with a member of the UK government are exceptions and there are some other exceptions. As this is an SSI made under a UK Act of Parliament (the Scotland Act 1998), it will no doubt in time be amended and even replaced by an SSI made under an Act of the Scottish Parliament: see below.

3 Unless such future Act decides otherwise.

4 Scotland Act 1998 (Transitory and Transitional Provisions) (Statutory Instruments) Order 1999, SI 1999/1096, arts 5–8.

5 Scotland Act, s 118.

Regulatory Reform to consider the powers granted in Acts, and of the Joint [Select] Committee on Statutory Instruments to provide technical scrutiny of the delegated legislation actually produced. In the former role, it may be involved in the enactment of Bills (as described above under the heading 'Acts of the Scottish Parliament'). In the latter role, it may be involved in the procedure for approval of the exercise of delegated legislation.

This procedure, laid down in the Standing Orders of the Scottish Parliament, has provision for laying the delegated legislation before the Parliament, and possible discussion of it by the 'lead committee' (that is, the subject committee most concerned with the subject matter, which is likely to have been the lead committee for the enactment of the Act containing the powers) on the merits of the delegated legislation, and the Subordinate Legislation Committee on technical scrutiny on grounds similar to those used by the United Kingdom Joint Committee of Delegated Legislation (and the Parliament itself if either Committee refers a matter to it). It also has provision for equivalents to 'negative' and 'affirmative' resolution procedures.

In the first four years of devolution, the Subordinate Legislation Committee raised a significant number of issues, though no delegated legislation was rejected. One area in which issues were raised was whether certain SSIs breached the Convention rights (see Chapter 3 and above), in particular, the art 6 right to a fair trial. Interestingly, this was not in relation to criminal trials, which have been the overwhelmingly frequent source of art 6 challenges to Scottish Executive action (see Chapter 3), but to a variety of matters including planning, pollution control, agricultural grants and appointments to official panels[1]. Another area in which issues were raised was compatibility with Community law. The division between reserved matters and devolved ones did not produce much difficulty (though the question of whether the 'graduate endowment' for Scottish university students was a tax, and thus 'reserved', did arise in parliamentary debates).

*Controls over by-laws*

Controls over by-laws remain as they were before devolution, unless and until replaced, subject to the fact that where the Secretary of State was the confirming authority, it will now be the

---

1 See Reid 'The Limits of Devolved Legislation Power; subordinate legislation in Scotland' (*Statute Law Review:* forthcoming).

Scottish Ministers, by operation of the 'general transfer of functions'.

## Use of delegated legislative powers in Scotland

There are hundreds of Scottish statutory instruments every year so, as with the United Kingdom as a whole, it is a much more fecund source of law than Acts of Parliament[1]. They cover the expectedly wide range of topics, though concentrating on certain areas. In 2001, for example, three large groups dealing with the particular current issues of Foot and Mouth Disease, shellfish poisoning and National Health Service reforms constituted almost third, and another fifth were local traffic orders. Other significant areas were fisheries and food, legal aid, the courts, the National Health Service (other than in relation to the specific reforms) and education, with a variety of quantitatively minor matters including adults with incapacity, housing, public finance, sports grounds, partnerships and wrecks[2].

The range of topics, it must be recalled, is not limited by the legislative competence of the Scottish Parliament, for SSIs may be made under powers granted to the Scottish Ministers and others by Acts of the United Kingdom Parliament, and may do so in connection with functions transferred to them which are within 'reserved matters' (see Chapter 3)[3]. Indeed, the commonest single parent Act was not an Act of the Scottish Parliament. This is perhaps not surprising, as the Scottish Parliament had been in operation for such a short time. What is surprising is that it was the European Communities Act 1972, which permits Community law without direct effect to be put into effect in the United Kingdom (see Chapter 3). Relations with the European Community is clearly a reserved matter, so the Scottish Ministers were exercising their power outside their normal devolved competence, under s 57 of the Scotland Act. A fifth of the SSIs, largely concerning agriculture and food, were made under that authority.

---

1 In the first four calendar years of the devolution, there were 203, 453, 494 and 570 respectively. This compares with 1, 12, 15 and 17 Acts of the Scottish Parliament.
2 See Reid 'Who Makes Scotlands Law?' (2002) 6 ELR 380–384 at 381.
3 Delegated legislation made under Acts of Parliament extending to Scotland by means of a 'Sewel motion' (for which, see above) will relate to devolved matters, and the legislation will normally be in SSI form.

But, beyond SSIs, it must also be remembered that much delegated legislation made in England continues to apply in Scotland, and indeed there may be more SIs than SSIs each year applying to Scotland[1]. This includes not only delegated legislation on reserved matters, for there is also delegated legislation on devolved matters. This is possible because the United Kingdom Parliament retains its power to legislate for Scotland on those matters which it might exercise by delegating in SI form, and in any case, certain powers (for example, to make delegated legislation to carry out obligations of Community law) are shared between the United Kingdom government and the Scottish Ministers.

### Form and citation of delegated legislation in Scotland

Delegated legislation made under Acts of the United Kingdom Parliament continue to be in the familiar form, even when applying to Scotland. Delegated legislation under Acts of the Scottish Parliament is in essentially the same form[2]. The only particularity worthy of remark is that SSIs are cited in a year-and-number manner, parallel to that of (United Kingdom) statutory instruments, but commencing with the abbreviation 'SSI', for example 'SSI 2003/143', and use the 'C' abbreviation and sub-sequence of numbers for Commencement Orders. No distinction is made on the face of the instrument to distinguish those made under Acts of the United Kingdom and those made under Acts of the Scottish Parliament.

### Ultra vires and judicial control of delegated legislation in Scotland

The same issues arise as with United Kingdom delegated legislation. However, two points require emphasis. Delegated legislation made in Scotland is as powerful as that made elsewhere, therefore it may amend Acts of the United Kingdom, even if it was made under an Act of the Scottish Parliament. On the other hand, the limits upon the Scottish Ministers are more exiguous, for the delegated legislation must be within the devolved competence, or an extension of it where the Scottish Ministers may exercise powers relating to reserved matters (see Chapter 3 and above: and *mutatis*

---

1 Figures produced by Reid 'Who Makes Scotlands Law?' (2002) 6 ELR at 380–384, suggest as many as a quarter of all SIs, say, 1,000 a year.
2 Scotland Act 1998 (Transitory and Transitional) (Statutory Instruments) order 1999, SI 1999/1096, art 5.

*mutandis* in relation to other delegates), and not breach Convention rights or Community law.

### Publication of delegated legislation in Scotland

Scottish Statutory Instruments of general effect are printed and published by The Stationery Office, as are (United Kingdom) statutory instruments, and bound up in annual volumes[1].

No encylopaedic series yet exists, nor commercially produced reprints.

All SSIs are available in full text at the HMSO website.

## PART 6: APPLICATION OF LEGISLATION – STATUTORY INTERPRETATION

### The need for application

Legislation is not self-applying: it must be applied by someone. This is regularly done by a variety of people, especially officials such as civil servants, local government officers and the police, as well as by lawyers. The way officials construe and interpret legislation is enormously important. The decisions of, say, local council planning officers on the application of planning legislation affect the way that planning law operates in practice.

However, legal attention is usually directed exclusively at the way judges apply the law. There is good reason for this. Firstly, judges work from the authentic legislative texts and not from simplified guides, or explanatory material. Secondly, it is a central part of the judges' job and, by virtue of their experience, they have acquired expertise in it. Thirdly, judges give reasoned, public decisions published in the law reports. Fourthly, judges' decisions are impartial as between the parties. Fifthly, and most importantly, judges' decisions are uniquely authoritative, for they are signals to officials, including civil servants, local government officers, the police, tax inspectors, company secretaries, personnel managers, and the public at large, as to the correct view on the application of the legislation in question.

Much effort goes into the preparation and production of legislation, so it might be thought that it is easy to apply. Often this is the case, but by no means invariably, and there are remarkably few attempts to analyse what problems the application of legislation

1 Scotland Act 1998 (Transitory and Transitional) (Statutory Instruments) Order 1999, SI 1999/1096, arts 8, 9. In early 2003 only the volume for 1999 had been published, but those for 2000, 2001 and 2002 were expected shortly.

involves. The reasons for the problems probably lie in the interplay of several factors. Some are inherent: rules concerning complicated matters will be complicated; no language is an instrument of complete precision; no draftsman can foresee all eventualities, and sometimes they make mistakes. Others are not: the United Kingdom tradition in drafting is to seek to cover all possibilities, at the expense of comprehensibility, while the Community law tradition involves looser drafting, giving more discretion to those applying it; the legislation may be an unhappy compromise, or it may be deliberately obscure[1]; much parliamentary legislation is ill-discussed because of the pressures upon parliamentary time; modern legislation is often a set of technical instructions to officials, and is not designed to be understood by lay people; frequent amendment may make comprehension difficult; United Kingdom or Great Britain legislation applying to Scotland has in the past often been a modified version of that drafted for England and Wales[2]. It may be that the Scottish Parliament will be able to adopt a drafting style which avoids these pitfalls, though the drafting style is essentially the same.

These difficulties produce various problems. Complexity may make legislation very resistant to comprehension. The legislative text may be unclear on its face, typically through numerous conditions and exceptions, exacerbated by frequent cross-reference, but also through ambiguity. Or it may be clear on its face but produce a result which seems absurd, for example by apparently failing to cover certain situations (there is a *lacuna* or *casus omissus*). Further, sometimes it may reasonably be disputed whether the text is clear or not; or if it is clear, whether it produces an absurd result or not. To compound the problem, no synthesised approach to a solution has been developed, but rather a series of disparate and potentially competing solutions, expressed in principles not 'in fixed verbal form', and vague, in consequence of which broad and not always acknowledged notions of public policy and morality tend to influence outcomes. This is therefore an unsatisfying area of law. Various reforms have been proposed in recent decades, but have come to nothing, possibly because, while academic commentators

1 The Equal Pay (Amendment) Regulations 1983, SI 1983/1794 were widely regarded as an unwilling response to the demands of Community law, drafted in obscure fashion, and involving a tortuous procedure in order to deter those seeking a remedy under them.
2 While devolution may have cured that defect, note the frequent use of 'Sewel motions', discussed above in relation to Acts of the United Kingdom and Scottish Parliaments, means that it may not.

and students are dissatisfied, the major players, Parliament and the judges, are not.

The area is usually called statutory interpretation, but arguably it involves two processes. Firstly, there is 'construing' the rule, that is working out what the rule is from what the draftsman wrote. This is rather like working out from a word-processing software manual the procedure for altering the margins of a document, or inserting footnotes, and has to be done whenever legislation is applied. Secondly, there is 'interpreting' the rule, that is working out what the rule means in relation to the facts of a case when it is unclear. This is rather like trying to work out what the software manual means when it uses incomprehensible terms, or appears to leave out important stages from the instruction. The two processes are not easy to distinguish, and they overlap. Also, terminology is not constant, 'construction' and 'interpretation' often being used interchangeably. Both processes are separate from the finding of facts, however. Indeed, interpretation assumes that the facts have been admitted or proved.

*The idea of construction*

The construction of legislation has received less attention than the interpretation. Nevertheless, it may in practice cause difficulty more often for it is unavoidable, while interpretation is usually only necessary where the meaning of the legislation is unclear.

Legislation must be written, so there is always a text from which it may be extracted. The text must express the logic of the rule in its grammar and syntax. This is particularly obvious in the United Kingdom drafting tradition because it seeks exactitude, and expresses the logic through typographical devices such as indentations as well as by division into sections, sub-sections etc.

A useful approach to construing legislation is therefore to remember that rules can be seen as 'if . . . then' statements, that is, may be analysed into *protasis* and *apodosis*[1]; extract the facts of the *protasis* (which are likely to be separated into sub-sections or paragraphs within a sub-section) and determine their relationship, and distinguish the *apodosis* (which may be in head-words before any sub-divisions of the section, or in tail-words after them).

One commentator, an experienced former Parliamentary Draftsman[2], has taken this process further, and suggests that

1 See Appendix 1.
2 *Bennion on Statutory Law* (3rd edn, 1990): see also *Understanding Common Law Legislation* (2001).

legislative provisions can be analysed into five aspects: case, condition, subject, declaration and exception. In slightly modified form, his example, taken from the legislative provision on the production of driving licences, is as follows:

(a) Case – where a person is in charge of a motor vehicle (who is under consideration?).
(b) Condition – if so required by a constable (what must be true before the obligation or right applies?).
(c) Subject – that person (on whom does the obligation or right fall?).
(d) Declaration – shall produce his licence (what is the obligation or right created?).
(e) Exception – unless he is exempt from holding a licence (when does the obligation or right not apply?).

In straightforward cases, such analysis is done intuitively, but many cases are not straightforward. They are complicated by amendment; by cross-reference within the legislation (such as to interpretation sections); by cross-reference between pieces of legislation (particularly, in the United Kingdom context, between Acts of Parliament and delegated legislation); and by use of 'referential' rather than 'textual' amendment. Thus, for example, s 289E(2) of the (now repealed) Criminal Procedure (Scotland) Act 1975 (itself inserted by the Criminal Justice Act 1982) read:

'Where the penalty or maximum penalty for an offence to which s 457A(1)(b) of this Act applies has not been altered by any enactment passed or made after 29th July 1977 (the date of the passing of the Criminal Law Act 1977), this section applies as if the amount referred to in subsection (5)(a) below were the greatest amount to which a person would have been liable on any conviction before that date'.

There is no law to assist on the construction of such complex rules. Patience and diligence are required, and analysis in the terms offered above is suggested[1].

### The idea of interpretation

Construing legislation may leave open a number of interpretive questions in actual cases; in other words, situations for which the

1 See also Twining and Miers *How To Do Things with Rules* (4th edn, 1999), especially App 2, which offers analysis in terms of algorithms.

draftsman appears not to have provided. What does a phrase like 'in charge of a motor vehicle' actually mean? Is a person alone in the front passenger seat 'in charge'? This sort of problem has received much attention.

For example, the Race Relations Act 1976 makes it unlawful in certain situations to discriminate against people on the ground of their 'colour, race, nationality or ethnic or national origins' (in the words of s 3(1)). In *Mandla v Lee* [1983] AC 548 the question was whether discrimination against a Sikh was on this ground. The House of Lords finally decided that it was. Sikhs constitute an ethnic group, so discrimination against them is on the grounds of their '... ethnic ... origins'. In *Nyazi v Ryman Conran* [1988] Race Discrimination Law Reports 85 the same question arose in relation to Muslims, and it was decided that it was not unlawful discrimination. Muslims are a religious group, so discrimination against them is not on the grounds of their 'colour, race ... [etc]'. Thus, legislation requires to be interpreted in respect of any set of facts, which may show the precise meaning is unclear, so has to be resolved by the courts.

### Modes of constructing and interpreting legislation

So far as the United Kingdom is concerned, there is more than one mode of construction and interpretation. These are not Scottish and English modes, however, for there appears to be no significant difference between their approaches.

It is possible that one will develop with the growth of Acts of the Scottish Parliament, but this seems unlikely for several reasons. Firstly, much United Kingdom legislation (both in the forms of Acts of the United Kingdom Parliament and of delegated legislation), will remain in force in Scotland. Secondly, the propensity for this is willingly reinforced by the Parliament's use of 'Sewel motions': see above). Thirdly, in any case, the Scottish Parliament seems to be adopting United Kingdom drafting approaches. And fourthly, the centripetal effects of the House of Lords as final court of appeal are not diminished by devolution (and such effects are in fact increased by the use of the Judicial Committee of the Privy Council as final court of appeal in devolution cases).

Thus, the modes are, rather, the traditional mode which evolved over a lengthy period in the United Kingdom, without reference to other legal systems (save those of the common law family, which were largely seen as daughter systems of English law), and a 'Community law mode' (which reflects the pre-occupations of civil law systems), introduced through accession to the European Community, and the obligation to apply Community law (with or without direct effect).

It may be that a synthesis is emerging for, as noted above, the latter is having a marked influence upon the former. In any case, modifications have been imposed upon the mixture by the explicit requirements of the Human Rights Act 1998 (which reflects strong civil law influence in the case law of the European Court of Human Rights) and of the Scotland Act 1998 (which is clearly affected by some of the results of the mixing process). These will be addressed in turn.

## The traditional mode of construction and interpretation of legislation by United Kingdom courts

There appear not to be separate Scottish and English traditions of construction and interpretation of legislation. Indeed, as the House of Lords is final civil appeal court for both jurisdictions and much legislation covers both, it would be surprising if there were[1]. In the field of criminal law, however, where the House of Lords has no jurisdiction in Scotland, occasionally Scottish and English courts give different interpretations to statutes which apply in both jurisdictions, as in *Ritchie v Petrie* 1972 JC 7 (concerning drunk driving) and *Kelly v MacKinnon* 1982 SCCR 205 (concerning possession of firearms). One effect of the lack of different traditions is that writers on the subject in Scotland cite English cases without remark.

Most discussions revolve around the interpretation of Acts of Parliament but, *mutatis mutandis*, the principles apply to delegated legislation as well. The important characteristics of United Kingdom legislation from the point of view of the application of legislation can be summed up in the phrase 'the intention of Parliament'.

### 'The intention of Parliament'

Courts commonly state that they seek to apply 'the intention of Parliament'. This appears unhelpful in that the UK Parliament comprises 659 MPs and approximately as many peers, many of whom may have voted against the legislation in question, and that

1 See *Dalgleish v Glasgow Corporation* 1976 SC 32.

legislation usually closely reflects the government's wishes. But, in so far as draftsmen seek exactitude couched in fixed verbal form, Parliament's intention has traditionally meant the intention expressed in the text approved by Parliament[1].

This has constitutional significance. With statutory interpretation, the (unelected) judge is not making the law he is applying that made by the (partly elected) Parliament. The point is expressed in a well-known exchange in the English case of *Magor and St Mellons RDC v Newport Corporation* [1952] AC 189 (HL), [1950] 2 All ER 1226 (CA). Lord Denning (famous for his lack of respect for orthodoxy) said in the Court of Appeal (at 1236) that he had 'no patience with an ultra legalistic interpretation which would deprive [the plaintiffs] of their rights altogether'. On appeal to the House of Lords, Lord Simonds said (at 191) 'The duty of the court is to interpret the words that the legislature has used; those words may be ambiguous but, even if they are, the power and duty of the court to travel outside them on a voyage of discovery are strictly limited', and referred to Lord Denning's 'naked usurpation of the legislative function under the thin disguise of interpretation'.

However, while courts still say that they seek to apply the intention of Parliament, the way they do it has changed significantly in recent years, in part under the influence of Community law, the Human Rights Act 1998 and the Scotland Act 1998, and they are now closer to Lord Denning's attitude than Lord Simonds'.

*Materials considered by United Kingdom courts in construing and interpreting legislation*

The principal material the court considers is the legislative text itself and, although it may be crumbling, the orthodoxy has been that it considers no other text. It is applying the intention of Parliament as expressed in that text (in fixed verbal form). This renders other texts not so much useless as irrelevant. The difference of tradition with the European Court of Justice is obvious.

**The legislative text.** In so far as interpretation of legislation is a problem only where the meaning of the Act is unclear, a rule

---

1 The intention is that to be taken from the text at the time of enactment. This principle is referred to *contemporanea expositio*: see, for example, *Montrose Peerage Case* (1853) 1 Macq 401. Curiously, there is some authority rejecting the principle in relation to modern statutes: see *Scottish Cinema and Variety Theatres v Ritchie* 1929 SC 350, 1929 SLT 323. Ancient statutes are expressed in style and vocabulary very different from today's.

requiring first, and possibly last, resort to the unclear text seems paradoxical. However, reference to the legislation means reference to the whole legislative text in order to interpret the unclear word or phrase.

(a) *The Act as a whole.* Thus, an Act is a legislative unity which gives a context to any word or phrase. For example, the Race Relations Act 1968, s 3(1) made discrimination unlawful on the grounds of, among other things, 'national origins'. In *Ealing London Borough v Race Relations Board* [1972] AC 342, [1971] 2 WLR 71 the House of Lords considered whether this included discrimination against those not British subjects. The majority decided, on the basis of the general intent of the Act as a whole, that 'national origins' referred to the ineradicable characteristic of belonging to a 'nation', and not to holding a particular legal nationality, which was alterable.

(b) *Differences within the Act.* However, in some cases, courts have found the same phrase to mean different things in different parts of the same legislation. For example, the English Court of Appeal found that the word 'discrimination' bore different meanings in ss 1 and 4 of the Sex Discrimination Act 1975 (a Great Britain statute). On the other hand, Lord Justice-General Balfour in *Jacobs v Hart* (1900) 2 F(J) 33 at 37–38, concerning the Summary Procedure (Scotland) Act 1864, considered that schedules, although annexed to Acts, could not alter the clear meaning of words in the body of the Act.

(c) *Interpretation sections and the like.* United Kingdom legislation also contains certain specific features which may assist in interpretation of legislation. Legislation is likely to have interpretation provisions. Thus, vague or unusual terms may be explained, for example 'racial discrimination', 'racial grounds' and 'racial groups' in the Race Relations Act 1976, s 3(3). There may be also lists and examples. Section 20 of the Race Relations Act 1976 makes discrimination unlawful in the provision of 'facilities and services'. Those terms are not defined, but s 20(2) says 'The following are examples of the facilities and services mentioned in subsection 1 ...'. However, interpretation provisions can only assist where the draftsman has foreseen the difficulty, are usually preceded by the words 'unless the context otherwise requires', and may not be applicable to other Acts[1].

(d) *Titles and preambles.* Long and short titles are found in all United Kingdom Acts. Long titles may be used to remove doubts, but not to raise them if a provision is otherwise clear, as held in

1 See references to legislation '*in pari materia*', p 198 below.

*Kelly v Nuttal & Sons Ltd* 1965 SC 427 (see, for instance, Lord Wheatley at 438). In practice, they are rarely useful. There seems to be no Scottish authority on short titles, but English authority declares that as 'statutory nicknames' they cannot be used at all[1]. Preambles can be used[2], but are very rare (except in private legislation).

(e) *Marginal notes, headings etc.* Marginal notes, cross-headings and the like are sometimes described as the 'unenacted' parts of an Act because they are not discussed in Parliament. In *Farqharson v White* (1886) 13 R(J) 29 (concerning the word 'month' in the Game Act 1773) and *Magistrates of Buckie v Dowager Countess of Seafield's Trustees* 1928 SC 525, 1928 SLT 362 (concerning the phrase 'any other place' in the Burgh Police (Scotland) Act 1892, s 90), the Inner House held such parts to be in the same position as the long title. Unenacted parts were also discussed by the House of Lords in *DPP v Schildkamp* [1971] AC 1, an English case on the Companies Act 1948, a Great Britain statute. The court resolved an ambiguity by reference to a cross-heading. No clear principle emerged, but the remarks of Lord Reid, a notable Scottish judge, are usually taken to indicate and confirm the position arrived at in the earlier Scottish cases, and it was subsequently applied in *Hill v Orkney Islands Council* 1983 SLT (Lands Tr) 2, concerning the Tenants' Rights Etc Act 1980.

**Other texts.** The broad rule applied by United Kingdom courts is that only the legislative text approved by the UK Parliament is to be considered. A distinction has nevertheless been drawn between looking at other documents to discover the general background to the case (that is, for the 'mischief' referred to in the 'mischief rule'; see below) on the one hand, and looking at them to find Parliament's intention on the other. The former is permissible and, on occasion, freely done. The latter is not permissible. However, even to this exclusionary rule there are important exceptions, and the very rule is being eroded.

(a) *Earlier judicial decisions on the legislation and legislation 'in pari materia' ('about similar things').* It is the legislation which

---

1 *Vacher & Sons v London Society of Compositors* [1913] AC 107; *R v Boaler* [1915] 1 KB 21.
2 *Anderson v Jenkins Express Removals Ltd,* reported in *James Kemp (Leslie) Ltd v Robertson* 1967 SC 229 at 233–234 per Lord Mackintosh. The *locus classicus* is the English House of Lords case of *A-G v Prince Ernest Augustus of Hanover* [1957] AC 436, especially per Lord Normand (a Scottish judge), although the role of Scots law was overlooked in that case.

determines the meaning, not other judges' views[1]. However, earlier cases interpreting the same legislation may be used to extract its meaning and only a bold judge would depart from a series of similar decisions interpreting an Act, or even from a single decision of a higher court[2]. Previous interpretations are difficult to avoid as a means of seeking meaning, and are one of the most commonly used. They operate as precedents in essentially the same way as in the common law[3], as the Inner House decided, albeit with some difficulty, in *Dalgleish v Glasgow Corporation* 1976 SC 32. However, as the Inner House also decided, in *AIB Finance Ltd v Bank of Scotland* 1995 SLT 2, subsequent legislation amending cannot be so used, as it cannot shed light on the intention of Parliament at the time of enactment of the legislation which is to be interpreted.

Other legislation concerning the same subject may also sometimes be used to interpret, as it can be assumed Parliament meant the same thing if it used the same words. In some cases, an Act specifically stipulates that it is 'to be construed with' another. That is also implied where Acts are given collective short titles. In general, however, this principle means that cases concerning the legislation *in pari materia* can be used as precedents. Reinforcing this is a presumption, based on the House of Lords' decision in *Barras v Aberdeen Steam Trawling and Fishing Co Ltd* 1933 SC(HL) 21, 1933 SLT 338, of statutory endorsement. If a word or phrase has received a particular interpretation by the courts, and it is incorporated in subsequent statutes, then it may be assumed that Parliament was endorsing that interpretation. However, some doubt was cast upon this by the High Court in *Kelly v MacKinnon* 1982 SCCR 205. Consolidation Acts are a special case of legislation *in pari materia* with the Acts consolidated. They re-enact, though may do so with minor amendment.

There are exceptions and limits to the *pari materia* principle. In particular, there is the question of how '*pari*' the '*materia*' must be.

---

1 In the English case of *Farrell v Alexander* [1977] AC 59 at 97, [1976] 2 All ER 721 at 746, Lord Edmund-Davies in the House of Lords approved the remark of Lord Denning in the Court of Appeal [1976] QB 345 at 359, [1976] 1 All ER 129 at 137 that 'where there is a conflict between a plain statute and a previous decision, the statute must prevail'.

2 In *Nicol's Trustees v Sutherland* 1951 SC(HL) 21 at 32, 1951 SLT 201 at 207 Lord Normand said 'A construction which recommended itself to Lord President Inglis [and a series of other notable judges] could only be rejected if on consideration by [the House of Lords] it appeared an inescapable conclusion that the words of the statute were plain beyond doubt and that they had been repeatedly misunderstood by Judges who were not usually prone to such error'.

3 See ch 6.

For example, the Sex Discrimination Act 1975 and Race Relations Act 1976 concern different subjects but are drafted in large measure identically. Cross-reference to one is therefore sometimes made by the courts in order to interpret the other, as, for example, the English Court of Appeal did in *Singh v West Midlands Passenger Transport Executive* [1988] IRLR 186. On the other hand, Acts on the same subject may have differing interpretation provisions, as observed by the Inner House in *Lord Advocate v Sprot's Trustees* (1901) 3 F 440, (1901) 8 SLT 403 (IH).

There is also difficulty with delegated legislation, since it is not written for, nor normally expressly approved by, Parliament. In *Hanlon v Law Society* [1981] AC 124, an English case before the House of Lords on the English legal aid legislation, Lord Lowry (a Northern Irish judge) suggested (at 193–194) half a dozen principles to apply. These indicate that delegated legislation can be used to interpret its parent Act or related Acts, provided those Acts are ambiguous, or provided it can amend them. In the former case, they cannot control the meaning of the Act but, if consistent, can confirm an interpretation, and are particularly reliable if they flesh out a skeleton Act. In the latter case (and if they are to have effect as if enacted in the Act), they are a clear guide.

(b) *The Interpretation Act 1978, dictionaries and textbooks.* The Interpretation Act 1978 gives certain standard definitions, such as that 'words importing the masculine gender include the feminine' and vice versa; that references to time are references to Greenwich Mean Time or British Summer Time, as appropriate; and the like. While useful, its application is limited, and the definitions are subject to the legislation expressing a contrary intention[1].

Dictionaries have always been admitted to find the ordinary meaning of words. However, they are not often helpful[2]. Textbooks on law are sometimes referred to, but they are evidence of what commentators thought, rather than guides to Parliament's intention. *The Laws of Scotland: Stair Memorial Encyclopaedia*

---

1 For an example of which, see Lord Chancellor Loreburn and Lord Robertson in *Nairn v St Andrews and Edinburgh University Courts* 1909 SC(HL) 10 at 13 and 15–16 respectively.
2 In *Mandla v Lee* [1983] QB 1 at 9–10 Lord Denning in the English Court of Appeal relied upon three dictionaries to assign a meaning to 'ethnic' in the Race Relations Act 1976. His interpretation, relying heavily upon etymology, was roundly rejected as absurd by Lord Fraser of Tullybelton on appeal to the House of Lords [1983] AC 548 at 560–565. In *Mandla v Lee* (see above), Lord Denning also sought to rely on anthropological works. In *Reed International v IRC* [1976] AC 336 at 359 Lord Wilberforce, having found Dr Johnson's *Dictionary* unhelpful, referred to Palgrave's *Dictionary of Political Economy* of 1896.

(Butterworths) has created a great new source of information and argument.

(c) *International treaties*. International treaties may be incorporated into Scots law, and this is becoming more important with an increasing number of multilateral treaties directly affecting individuals. Typically, they apply by express enactment in an Act of Parliament. For example, the Child Abduction and Custody Act 1985 incorporates the Convention on the Civil Aspects of International Child Abduction (and another treaty), and in *Viola v Viola* 1988 SLT 7 (OH) the judgment rests almost entirely upon the terms of the Convention. However, where there is express enactment, and certainly where the treaty is incorporated into a schedule, as in this instance, the treaty is not an external aid at all.

English courts have in some cases considered that they might look at other, unincorporated versions of the treaty; commentaries on it (which might involve translation); and even the treaty's *travaux préparatoires*[1]. Indeed, there is Scottish authority in *Gatoil International v Arkwright-Boston Manufacturers Mutual Insurance* 1985 SC(HL) 1 (especially Lord Wilberforce at 10 and 11 and Lord Keith of Kinkell at 16). This concerned the Administration of Justice Act 1956 and the Brussels Convention Relating to the Arrest of Seagoing Ships. It suggested that even where the treaty is not expressly incorporated, so is external to the Act, it can be examined, and so possibly could some of its *travaux préparatoires*.

Such practice may be justified by the need for consistent interpretation in different countries (as is required of Community law). Treaties are, however, always aids to be used at the judges' discretion to interpret the legislative text and are not the text itself. Changes in attitude to treaties have been influenced by use of Community law in United Kingdom courts.

The European Convention on Human Rights has long been regarded as an exceptional case among treaties, and its position is considered separately below in relation to the effects of the Human Rights Act 1998

(d) *Hansard and government documents*. *Hansard*, the verbatim account of proceedings in Parliament, provides the obvious *travaux préparatoires* for Acts of Parliament. Traditionally, there has been a complete rejection of its use, following directly from the principle that the Act forms Parliament's final words which the judges must loyally apply. This was frequently and emphatically

---

1 *James Buchanan & Co Ltd v Babco Forwarding and Shipping (UK) Ltd* [1978] AC 141; *Fothergill v Monarch Airlines Ltd* [1981] AC 251, [1980] 2 All ER 696.

reiterated in the 1970s and 1980s by the House of Lords in the face of attempts by Lord Denning to alter the rule. The reasons for the exclusionary rule in relation to *Hansard* were summed up by the Law Commissions as relevance, reliability and availability[1]. In other words, it is unlikely that the precise question before the court was discussed; parliamentary debates are commonly attempts to persuade rather than to examine dispassionately, and contradictory statements may be made on any topic[2], and *Hansard* is available in few libraries (though all parliamentary debates are now available on the Parliament website[3]. Occasional exceptions to the rule nevertheless were discovered, as noted below, in relation to Community legislation, most notably in *Litster v Forth Dry Dock and Engineering Co Ltd* 1989 SLT 540, [1990] AC 546.

Arguments for excluding government documents such as White Papers, Royal Commission and other reports overlap those in relation to *Hansard*, and are even stronger. They cannot be evidence of Parliament's intention. This position was taken in an English case on United Kingdom legislation before the House of Lords, *Assam Railways and Trading Co Ltd v IRC* [1935] AC 445 (see Lord Wright at 457–458) and in a Scottish case, *Inglis v British Airports Authority* 1978 SLT (Lands Tr) 30. However, while in a complicated judgment in another English case the House of Lords preserved the rule in *Black-Clawson International Ltd v Papierwerke Waldhof Aschaffenburg AG* [1975] AC 591, [1975] 1 All ER 810, some of its members were prepared to accept that in certain circumstances a draft Bill attached to a report, and possibly other documents, might be considered.

A major change in the exclusionary rule, prefigured by cases like *Litster*, occurred, however, in *Pepper v Hart* [1993] AC 593, which concerned the Finance Act 1976. In a majority decision of the House of Lords, Lord Browne-Wilkinson's leading judgment reiterated the reasons for excluding Hansard in terms of constitutional proprieties, practical difficulties and the need for a definite text. However, on the grounds that the courts' job is to apply the intention of Parliament, that Parliament cannot have intended an

---

1 *The Interpretation of Statutes* (1969) Sco Law Com 1, Law Com 21, paras 53–62.
2 Lord Diplock in *Hadmor Productions v Hamilton* [1983] 1 AC 191 at 232, [1981] 2 All ER 724 observed that 'Lord Denning . . . sought to justify the construction he placed on s 17(8) by referring to the report in Hansard of a speech made by a peer, who is a distinguished academic lawyer, Lord Wedderburn, when moving an opposition amendment (which was defeated) to delete the subsection from the Bill'.
3 I e www.parliament.uk.

ambiguity, and the exclusionary rule thwarted the attempt to find the true meaning, a 'limited modification' to the existing rule was introduced. That modification is that where a statute is ambiguous, obscure or leads to an absurdity, statements by a minister or other promoter of the Bill may be referred to, if necessary with other parliamentary material, provided they are clear. The Lord Chancellor dissented, rehearsing the familiar arguments for the rule[1].

*Pepper v Hart* was applied in *Short's Trustee v Keeper of the Registers of Scotland* 1994 SLT 65. In this conveyancing case the Reid and Henry Reports which preceded legislation on the registration of titles, as well as aspects of the parliamentary process, were referred to in the Outer and Inner House and found in the latter court to be 'of limited assistance'. But in *AIB Finance v Bank of Scotland* 1995 SLT 2 and in *Customs and Excise Comrs v Robert Gordon's College* 1995 SLT 1139 the *Pepper v Hart* exception was not utilised since no ambiguity or obscurity could be found in the relevant statutes.

The modification refers explicitly to statements in Parliament, but if the views of the promoters of a Bill are to be considered, there seems no reason not to permit other governmental statements. However, in *Melluish v Fitzroy Finance* [1996] 1 AC 454 it was observed that the range of materials which might be looked at should not be widened.

(e) *The Reports of the Scottish Law Commission.* These are a special instance where there is a case for invoking materials beyond the legislation in question for these reports now customarily rehearse the law before the legislation, identify its defects and offer a remedy in the form of a draft Bill with supporting arguments. If Parliament has in all material respects enacted the Bill as drafted by the Commission, its Report would seem a useful means of discovering the meaning of the Act. In *McWilliams v Lord Advocate* 1992 SLT 1045 Lord Morton made full use of two Commission reports on the question whether a child had a right of action for injuries sustained before birth. However, the more common attitude of the judges, as exemplified in *Barratt Scotland Ltd v Keith* 1994 SLT 1343, has been to restrict reference to Law Commission

---

1 See Bates 'Judicial Application of *Pepper v Hart*' 1993 JLSS 251; Walker 'Discovering the Intention of Parliament' 1993 SLT (News) 121, Bates 'The Contemporary Use of Legislative History in the United Kingdom' [1995] Camb LJ 127.

publications to cases of ambiguity or other doubts. But, as has been pointed out[1], statutory language is neither clear nor unclear in the abstract. It depends on the context and part of that context is the 'mischief' for which the Commission recommended a remedy. In *MacDonald v HM Advocate* 1999 SLT 533 it sufficed that it would be 'helpful' to refer to a Commission report.

*Techniques employed by United Kingdom courts in construing and interpreting legislation*

The techniques employed by the United Kingdom courts are usefully divided into presumptions and rules, although there are problems with this classification, and an attempted synthesis is suggested.

**Presumptions.** There are a number of presumptions. These operate unless explicitly or implicitly excluded. In general they apply when there is doubt as to the meaning of the legislation, though some are so strong as to displace an apparently clear meaning. There is no exhaustive or official list of any of them, and they may contradict each other.

(a) *Legal presumptions.* Firstly, there are certain legal presumptions. They are so various as to defy easy classification, and different authorities give different examples[2]. These differences can be reconciled by regarding them as examples of three broad overlapping presumptions, that is: against unclear alteration of settled law; against absurd results; and against injustice. Clearly, a judge is

---

1 Maher 'Statutory Interpretation and Scottish Law Commission Reports' 1992 SLT (News) 277.
2 Compare, for example, the list in *The Laws of Scotland: Stair Memorial Encyclopaedia* vol 12 'The Interpretation of Statute' paras 1126–1133 (against changing existing law, ousting or adding to courts' jurisdiction, taking away rights or imposing burdens, technical constructions of legislation, incorrect usage, and also against injustice, interpreting legislation to render it invalid, and absurdity) with that of 'principal' ones in DM Walker *The Scottish Legal System* (8th edn, 2001) pp 428–430 (against binding the Crown, altering fundamental principles of law, infringing international law, altering the jurisdiction of courts, rendering the legislation inoperable, retrospective operation, interfering with individual liberty, dispensing with *mens rea*, taking property without compensation, imposing a tax, altering rights of appeal, using precedents interpreting legislation now re-enacted, preventing a person from opting out of benefits etc). Compare further the 'judicial principles' referred to by Paterson, Bates and Poustie *The Legal System of Scotland: cases and materials* (4th edn, 2001) pp 384–386, and the 'presumptions of general application' and 'presumptions for use in doubtful cases' in Cross *Statutory Interpretation* (3rd edn, 1995) ch 7.

thus given considerable discretion as to whether there is in fact doubt as to the meaning of the legislation; as to whether (if there is doubt) any presumption applies to the particular situation before him; and as to whether (if it does apply to it) it is strong enough to displace any alternative interpretation. This discretion must also be seen against two background facts. Firstly, legislation is generally ad hoc and provides few broad principles, which must therefore be sought in the common law. Secondly, the operation of presumptions depends heavily upon the prevailing moral and political atmosphere.

A commonly cited example of a legal presumption fitting readily into one or more of the suggested three categories is that against the creation of offences not requiring *mens rea* (that is, roughly, a guilty mind). It is well illustrated by *Sweet v Parsley* [1970] AC 132, an English case on a United Kingdom statute, the Dangerous Drugs Act 1965. Section 5 created the offence of 'being the occupier' or 'concerned in the management' of premises used for the offence of 'smoking of cannabis resin'. It was silent on whether such a person committed the offence if unaware of the smoking by others. Sweet, a non-resident landlord, wholly ignorant of the actual smoking, was convicted. The House of Lords quashed the conviction on appeal, deciding that only the clearest words could exclude *mens rea* from such an offence, and that mere silence was insufficient. Lord Reid, a notable Scottish judge, observed (at 148) that 'there has for centuries been a presumption that Parliament did not intend to make criminals of persons who were in no way blameworthy . . . '.

Nevertheless, there are many deliberately created (but usually merely regulatory) offences of strict liability, requiring no *mens rea*, for example speeding. Parliament may deliberately override any other presumption, such as that against retrospective legislation, which again clearly fits in one or more of the three suggested categories, as it did in both the War Damage Act 1965 and the War Crimes Act 1991.

An example of a legal presumption showing the effect of the prevailing mores is *Nairn v St Andrews and Edinburgh University Courts* 1909 SC(HL) 10, 16 SLT 619. The Representation of the People (Scotland) Act 1868 gave graduates the right to vote for parliamentary seats representing their universities, in addition to their normal votes. The Universities (Scotland) Act 1889 permitted universities to allow women to graduate. The two Acts taken together appeared to give women graduates the vote for university seats. However, at that time, women did not have the vote. The House of Lords decided that male franchise was a fundamental constitutional provision, and it could be presumed that Parliament would only have altered it explicitly, not incidentally. This readily fitted into the suggested three broad categories of presumption in the early 20th century, but not in the early 21st.

(b) *Linguistic presumptions.* Secondly, there are certain linguistic presumptions[1]. Legislation in the United Kingdom is in English, and what are regarded as the standard grammatical and semantic rules of that language apply. There is a vast unsatisfactory case law on their application, however, including little Scottish authority, and these presumptions are rarely of help in practice.

Three such presumptions, tricked out in Latin, are orthodox to cite, and certain word usages deserve mention. *Noscitur a sociis* means, roughly, 'a thing is known by its context' ('words of a feather flock together'), and *eiusdem generis* ('of the same kind') is a special case of it. *Expressio unius, exclusio alterius* means 'if you don't say it, you don't mean it' (which might contradict a legal presumption such as that against injustice, as in *Sweet v Parsley*). One example of the second of this trio (*eiusdem generis*) will suffice. The presumption applies to a common statutory formulation, 'Any A, B, C, or other X'. This strongly implies that X is the genus of which A, B, and C are species. Thus, s 11 of the Representation of the People (Scotland) Act 1832 referred to 'any house, warehouse, counting house, shop, or other building'. In *Duncan v Jackson* (1905) 8 F 323, 13 SLT 932, the Inner House held that the genus expressed by 'or other building' was delimited by the species expressed by the words 'any house . . .' etc. The genus was thus 'residential, commercial and agricultural premises'. It did not include a structure which, though a building in common parlance, and large, and made of stone and brick, was built to house a gas meter.

The words 'shall', 'may', 'and' and 'or' deserve attention. 'It shall be an offence . . . ', a common formulation, means 'It is an offence . . . ' emphasising obligation rather than futurity. Also, used in relation to a procedure, 'shall' generally makes it mandatory (that is, obligatory) rather than directory (that is, recommended), so failure

1 In this context, *The Laws of Scotland: Stair Memorial Encyclopaedia* vol 12, paras 1165–1174, especially 1169–1170, using somewhat different criteria, lists several relevant 'subsidiary principles of construction', and also refers under 'mandatory, directory and permissive enactments'; Cross *Statutory Interpretation* (3rd edn, 1995) pp 134–141 uses the term 'rules of language'; Paterson, Bates and Poustie *The Legal System of Scotland* (4th edn, 2001) pp 392–393 refer to 'the grammatical context' as part of the general context in which a statute must be construed; DM Walker *The Scottish Legal System* (8th edn, 2001) p 420 uses the term 'reference to context'.

to follow the procedure invalidates the outcome, as held by the House of Lords in *London and Clydeside Estates v Aberdeen District Council* 1980 SC(HL) 1, 1980 SLT 81 (which concerned a planning appeal procedure under the Town and Country Planning (General Development) (Scotland) Order 1959, SI 1959/1361). However, the presumption can be rebutted, as, for example, in *HM Advocate v Graham* 1985 SLT 498 (which concerned the lodging of copy indictments under the Criminal Procedure (Scotland) Act 1975). Where legislation says someone 'shall' do something, it also implies he is given the power to do so. 'May' in legislative discourse generally denotes power or permission, but not an obligation to use it, as held, for example, in *Patmor Ltd v City of Edinburgh District Licensing Board* 1988 SLT 850 (concerning gaming licences under the Gaming Act 1968). On occasion, however, permissive words have been interpreted as obligatory, as, for example, in *Gray v St Andrews and Cupar District Committees of Fife County Council* 1911 SC 266, (1910) 2 SLT 354 (concerning the Highways (Scotland) Act 1771). The words 'and' and 'or' appear unambiguous, but 'and' may in practice mean 'and/or'[1].

**'Rules'.** Traditionally, three 'rules' of statutory interpretation have been said to exist: the 'mischief rule', the 'literal rule' and the 'golden rule'. All are based on English cases, but have been applied without comment in Scotland.

(a) The *'mischief rule'*. The mischief rule dates from the English *Heydon's Case* (1584) 3 Co Rep 7a. It is usually said to mean that if a provision is unclear, the judge should look to the 'mischief' the Act was designed to overcome, and interpret it in order to 'suppress the mischief and advance the remedy'. Although it is often seen as a warrant for judges to rewrite legislation in a fashion they find more palatable, it has been suggested that it was actually developed as a means of compelling judges to focus on what Parliament intended[2]. The rule has been explicitly applied in Scotland. For example, the Tweed Fishing Act 1859, s 10 allowed a court, where salmon had been poached, to order forfeit any 'boat, cart, basket or package' used to carry it. In *Leadbetter v Hutcheson* 1934 JC 70 the High Court interpreted 'cart' to include a motorcycle combination, in the words of Lord Morison (at 73) 'so as to cope with the mischief'.

---

1 It is curious that no major European language appears to have a word expressing the common and useful idea of 'and/or', and that the phrase became widespread only with the spread of computers.

2 Miers and Page *Legislation* (2nd edn, 1990) p 171.

(b) The *'literal rule'*. The literal rule emerged later, with the growth of the practice of drafting legislation 'in fixed verbal form'. The crystallisation of the idea is that Parliament is the law-maker *par excellence*, and judges simply apply that law. It asserts that the judge should apply the literal meaning of the legislation, but the title is best reserved for the principle that it should be applied even if the result is absurd, or at least something common sense suggests Parliament did not intend, and probably overriding one of the presumptions. For example, the Finance Act 1933 taxed certain 'profits'. In *Ayrshire Employers Mutual Insurance v IRC* 1946 SC(HL) 1, 1946 SLT 235, the House of Lords considered whether this included the 'surpluses' generated by mutual insurance companies. Even though reasonably sure that the government, the draftsman and Parliament all intended the legislation to tax them, it held that such surpluses were not regarded as profits elsewhere in the law, and it applied a literal interpretation, thereby excluding them. In another example, the Misuse of Drugs Act 1971, s 5 made it an offence to possess cannabis resin. In *Keane v Gallagher* 1980 SLT 144, the High Court decided to apply 'the plain unqualified words' to uphold conviction of possessing a minute quantity (totalling 11 milligrams), too small to be usable.

(c) The *'golden rule'*. The golden rule implies that the literal meaning should be applied unless it produces, in Lord Blackburn's classical exposition of the rule in *River Wear Commissioners v Adamson* (1877) 2 App Cas 743 (reiterating an earlier version), 'an inconsistency, or an absurdity, or inconvenience so great as to convince the court' that the intention of Parliament must have been different. Such an outcome will justify the court in applying another meaning which the words will bear[1]. For example, in *Caledonian Railway Co v North British Railway Co* (1881) 8 R (HL) 23 at 25, the Lord Chancellor, Lord Selborne, observed:

'The more literal construction ought not to prevail if . . . it is opposed to the intention of the legislature as apparent by the statute, and if the words are sufficiently flexible to admit of some other construction by which that intention will be better effectuated.'

In another example, the Prevention of Crimes Act 1871 distinguished between (more serious) 'crimes' and (less serious) 'offences'. Under s 7, it was a crime in itself for a person, within

---

1 A weaker version of the golden rule might indicate simply a presumption that, where legislation is ambiguous, a 'sensible' interpretation is to be preferred to any other.

seven days of conviction of an earlier crime, to be found in such circumstances as to satisfy the court that he was going to commit an 'offence'. It did not expressly refer to those going to commit 'crimes'. In Strathern v Padden 1926 JC 9, the High Court (ignoring any relevant presumptions) rejected the interpretation that s 7 did not apply to those going to commit 'crimes', because that would be, in Lord Justice-General Clyde's words (at 13) 'absurd and irrational'. In K v Craig 1997 SLT 748, a case involving the discharge of a mental patient into community care, the court held that the reclaimer's contention that the literal wording of the Act required that a person who did not need to be detained must be released would 'lead to an absurd result'.

**Problems with the rules.** The problem for the mischief rule is that, given the exclusion of most documents save the legislative text itself, it is not clear how Parliament intended to overcome the mischief. That for the literal rule is that it denies there is any problem, and it is no help where the difficulty is ambiguous legislation. That with the golden rule is that reasonable people can disagree on whether an outcome is absurd or sufficiently inconvenient.

The problem with all three rules is that they are clearly alternatives, but there is no clue as to which should be preferred and when, thus giving the impression that they may be fig-leaves to cover the embarrassment of conclusions arrived at by other means. In any case, commonly judges do not refer explicitly to any rule and, when they do, sometimes it is to explain that fortunately all point in the same direction. Academic commentators tend to explain the rules with examples promiscuously chosen from different judges, in different periods, in different courts, in different jurisdictions. The rules may thus appear mere talismans, arcane precepts extrapolated from certain cases of unknown representativeness, designed to render decisions beyond criticism.

It is, however, too cynical to dismiss the rules completely. Probably they are insufficiently subtle explanations of the complicated processes which judges employ to resolve the tension among the principle that the legislator is entitled to have his will carried out; the fact that this will cannot be exactly expressed and is frequently ill-expressed; the judges' impatience with ill-expressed legislation; their knowledge that legislation provides a poor reservoir of principle compared with the common law; and perhaps their residual reluctance to relinquish the overwhelming primacy in expounding the law that they once enjoyed.

Some commentators have suggested that the rules should be

seen as examples of two alternative approaches. One, a literal approach, regards the language of the text as primary, and tries to apply the actual words of the legislation, come what may. The other, purposive approach assumes that the legislator had a purpose which has to be applied, and that the words of the legislation are one piece of evidence of that purpose.

**An attempted synthesis of the techniques employed by United Kingdom courts in construing and interpreting legislation.** One respected academic commentator argued[1] that there is a single 'basic rule' with five parts. This view was developed exclusively from English cases, but separate Scottish and English traditions have not existed in modern times, and the learned author of the entry on the interpretation of statute in the *Stair Encyclopaedia* seems to take a consonant view[2].

This basic rule is:

(a) the judge must give effect to the grammatical and ordinary or, where appropriate, technical meaning of words, given their context;

(b) if the result is absurd, or contrary to the purpose of the statute, he may apply a secondary meaning;

(c) if necessary, the judge can read in missing words implied by words which are present and, to a limited extent, add to, ignore or alter words to prevent unintelligibility, absurdity, complete unreasonability, unworkability, or irreconcilability with the rest of the statute;

(d) in applying the above rules, the judge may have resort to the various materials and presumptions available;

(e) the judge must interpret a statute so as to give effect to directly applicable EC law.

This view does provide a more satisfying rule of thumb synthesised from judicial practice. However, it is not the orthodoxy. Nor does it appear to take account of the fact that, under the influence of Community law, and specific requirements of the Human Rights Act 1998 and the Scotland Act 1998, courts are nowadays taking a more purposive view of the construction and interpretation of legislation.

---

1  Cross *Statutory Interpretation* (3rd edn, 1995) p 49.
2  See also Wilson 'Trials and Try-Ons: Modes of Interpretation' 1992 Stat LR 1.

## Construction and interpretation of legislation by United Kingdom courts under the influence of Community law

As noted above, since the accession of the United Kingdom to the European Community, and the obligation to apply Community law (with or without direct effect), another mode of construction and interpretation of legislation has been introduced. United Kingdom courts have therefore been faced with a problem in the interpretation of legislation with a Community law element. Their solution to the problem has had consequential effects upon interpretation of other legislation.

It is useful to commence with consideration of the European Court of Justice, however

### *Construction and interpretation by the European Court of Justice*

The European Court of Justice applies legislation in a manner closer to that employed in civil law countries than to that in common law countries, although the differences can be exaggerated.

Community legislation has been suggested to have four characteristics relevant to application of legislation[1]. Firstly, the treaties exist for certain purposes, which they set out. Secondly, Community legislation is a single, separate, legal system, so must be uniformly applied in all member states. Thirdly, Community legislation is written in several different languages, all equally authentic, so literal interpretations may have to be discounted. Fourthly, the form of Community legislation is subject to certain requirements, in particular, article 253 (ex article 190) which says that all secondary legislation must have a preamble outlining its origins. Collectively, these indicate that Community legislation may not be regarded as 'in fixed verbal form'.

**Materials considered by the European Court of Justice in construing and interpreting Community legislation.** The European Court of Justice looks, of course, at the legislative text itself. However, Community legislation is not always drafted with as great a degree of detail as United Kingdom legislation usually is, and there are not usually interpretation sections. For example, article 39(1) (ex article 48(1)) declares that 'Free movement of

---

1 Millett 'Rules of Interpretation of EEC Legislation' [1987] Stat LR 163.

workers shall be secured . . . ', but does not define 'worker'. A definition had to be worked out through a series of decisions.

This apparent vagueness may be unavoidable with many equally authentic texts in different languages, which are often the result of political bargaining[1]. Clear differences of meaning can occur, and may indeed be used to throw light upon meaning, as for instance in Case 29/69 *Stauder v City of Ulm* [1969] ECR 419 (where there was a difference between Dutch and German texts on the one hand, and French and Italian on the other). It may also be desirable, in that the concepts described are ones of Community law, not of any national system.

The court also looks at other materials as well. The lengthy recitals at the beginning of secondary legislation required by article 253 (ex article 190) contain a list of the treaty provisions under which they are made, the legislative history of proposals and opinions ('having regard to . . .'), and a statement of the reasons for the provision itself ('whereas . . .')[2]. This expressly directs the court's attention to certain other documents (which are sometimes referred to as *travaux préparatoires*).

Indeed, the court tends to look at any piece of legislation as part of a general scheme containing a reservoir of principles expressed in various legislative texts, rather than as a single free-standing text in fixed verbal form. For example, in Case 283/81 *CILFIT Srl v Ministry of Health* [1982] ECR 3415 at 3430, [1983] 1 CMLR 472 at 491, the court said 'every provision of Community law must be placed in its context and interpreted in the light of the provisions of Community law as a whole, regard being had to the objectives

---

1 In Case 136/79 *National Panasonic (UK) Ltd v Commission* [1980] ECR 2033 at 2066, the Advocate General observed that 'what members of the Council [of the Union] do when they adopt regulation is to agree upon a text. They do not necessarily all have the same views as to its meaning'.

2 For example, Council Directive 64/221 (25/2/64) OJ 1964 p 850 (S Edn 1963–4) p 117, which contains the 'public policy proviso' permitting member states to limit free movement, commences ' . . . Having regard to the Treaty . . . especially Article 56(2), . . . the Council Regulation 15 of August 16, 1964 on initial measures, . . . the Council Directive of August 16, 1964 on administrative procedures . . . governing entry . . . of workers, . . . the General Programmes for Abolition of restrictions on freedom of establishment . . . the Council Directive of February 25, 1964 on abolition of restrictions upon movement, . . . the proposal from the Commission . . . the opinion of the European Parliament . . . the opinion of the Economic and Social Committee . . . ', and continues 'Whereas co-ordination of provision . . . which provides for special treatment of foreign nationals on grounds of public policy . . . should . . . deal with the conditions of entry . . . of nationals of Member States moving within the Community . . . to pursue activities as employed or self-employed person . . . [etc]'.

thereof and to its state of evolution at the date on which the provision in question is to be applied'. The last words imply that interpretation can change over time.

Not all *travaux préparatoires* are examined. Those of the treaties themselves, and the proceedings of the Commission and Council, are not published. Debates of the European Parliament, though published, are rarely referred to. The opinions of individual members of the Commission, Council or Parliament or of their staff are not admissible according to the Advocate General's opinion in Case 136/79 *National Panasonic (UK) Ltd v Commission* [1980] ECR 2033 at 2066, even if they negotiated or prepared the text in question.

As well as *travaux préparatoires*, decisions of the court and opinions of the Advocates General are often cited in argument, though rarely in judgments. The court usually follows its previous decisions, though it does so tacitly, and a series of consistent decisions produces a lasting interpretation. It is not bound by any previous decision, however, and occasionally contradicts itself, without formally overruling the previous decision, as it did in Case 25/62 *Plaumann & Co v Commission* [1963] ECR 95.

The court has also drawn on the constitutions of member states, and national courts' interpretations of them, and on international treaties, in particular the European Convention on Human Rights, to produce 'general principles of law common to all Member States' such as certainty and proportionality, which it has applied in some cases, for example Case 63/83 *R v Kirk* [1984] ECR 2689, and Case 222/84 *Johnston v Chief Constable of the RUC* [1986] 3 CMLR 240. While it would be unusual to regard this as a form of Community common law, generated by precedent, it is difficult to regard it otherwise than as a source of Community law additional to Community legislation.

**Techniques employed by the European Court of Justice in construing and interpreting Community legislation.** The European Court of Justice seeks to apply not the literal meaning of the text before it, but what it considers the purpose of the legislation, as extracted from the legislation in question, related legislation, *travaux préparatoires*, its own previous decisions, and elsewhere.

It has been suggested that three techniques, termed 'teleological', 'schematic' and 'literal', are employed, although in practice they intertwine, and are complementary, not alternative[1], and

---

1 See Millett 'Rules of Interpretation of EEC Legislation' [1987] Stat LR 163, also Miers and Page *Legislation* (2nd edn, 1990) pp 184–190.

application is in the light of the 'general principles of law common to Member States' it has extracted from the European Convention on Human Rights and elsewhere.

The 'teleological' technique means that the court considers the general objective of the authors of the treaties, as revealed by the materials examined. The 'schematic' places the provision in question within a general legislative scheme, discovered from the materials examined, for implementation of those objectives. The 'literal' considers the text itself, but in a broad and naturalistic way[1]. Because no single technique is sufficient, a clear and unambiguous textual meaning can be rejected if the other techniques suggest something different. In Case 9/70 *Grad* [1970] ECR 825 at 839, for example, the court said 'It is true that a literal interpretation of . . . Article 4 . . . might lead to the view that this provision refers to [a certain date]. However, such an interpretation would not correspond to the aim of the directives in question . . . '.

This purposive approach, probably inevitable in its setting, has been reinforced by the fact that the court has been very '*communautaire*'. It has seen its role as pushing the Community forward when member states have dragged their feet. This is evident in the court's inventiveness in generating the 'general principles of law common to all Member States', and in a number of decisions which have been frankly legislative, such as Case 41/74 *Van Duyn v Home Office* [1974] ECR 1337, in which the court decided directives might be directly effective, despite the apparently contrary wording of article 189 and intention of the treaty itself.

At least on occasion, therefore, the court fairly explicitly decides cases on the basis of what it thinks the law should be rather than what it is.

*Construction and interpretation by United Kingdom courts where there is a Community law element*

Community law may bear on any legal issue in one of two ways. Firstly, Community law may have direct effect, in which case it should be applied irrespective of existing Scots law. Secondly, Community law not of direct effect is to be implemented by United Kingdom legislation. In either case, the court is required

---

1 It is unfortunate that this is described as 'literal' for, in United Kingdom practice on statutory interpretation, 'literal' is used to describe the approach which applies the literal meaning of a text, even if absurd, and without reference to any other consideration.

expressly or impliedly by the European Communities Act 1972, to interpret the law in the same fashion as the European Court of Justice would. This would seem to involve consulting various other texts, in particular *travaux préparatoires*, and adopting a purposive approach.

There are a few examples in the area of Community law and related treaties of United Kingdom legislation expressly referring to a specific other text. The Civil Jurisdiction and Judgments Act 1982, s 3(3) specifically requires that it be interpreted in the manner laid down in the European Communities Act 1972, and that regard be had to reports by named individuals on a relevant Convention and the United Kingdom Accession Treaty. A marginal reference (not reproduced in *Scottish Current Law Statutes Annotated*) gives the citation of these reports in the *Official Journal*. The Consumer Protection Act 1987, s 1 specifically requires that Part I of the Act be interpreted in accordance with a directive.

As the following sections show, United Kingdom courts are likely to seek to act more like the European Court of Justice when applying Community law with direct effect, or United Kingdom legislation implementing Community law. This, as noted, is having an effect upon the interpretation of United Kingdom legislation with no Community element.

However, how far lower-level United Kingdom courts will be able to cope with the possibility of *travaux préparatoires* in order to find the inferred purpose of the legislation may be questioned. Also, the United Kingdom tradition of lengthy judgments, with a wide possibility of dissent, and lack of Advocates General, all within a common law tradition, mean that there is unlikely to be complete conformity of practice. There is also the question of what, or whose, purpose a purposive interpretation seeks.

**Construction and interpretation by United Kingdom courts of Community law with direct effect.** Community legislation with direct effect is to be applied by United Kingdom courts. The great majority of cases where United Kingdom courts have applied Community legislation with direct effect appear to have raised no problems. Many cases have in fact been heard by tribunals, such as those heard by Social Security Commissioners (previously National Insurance Commissioners) on the application of Regulation 1408/71 on social security rights of those exercising their right of free movement between member states. Any problem has been reduced by the ready propensity in England (though less in Scotland) to resort to article 234 (ex article 177) preliminary references, which removes from the United Kingdom court the need to interpret.

Section 3(1) of the European Communities Act 1972 requires United Kingdom courts, where they do not send such a question to the European Court of Justice, to interpret Community law in the same way as that court would. There are, however, examples in early cases of United Kingdom courts applying severely traditional interpretive methods to Community law with direct effect, as, for example, the English Court of Appeal did in *R v Henn & Darby* [1978] 3 All ER 1190. Article 28 (ex article 30) prohibits quantitative restrictions upon imports between member states and 'all measures having equivalent effect'. The Lord Chief Justice, Lord Widgery, argued that a total prohibition was not a quantitative restriction as no quantity was mentioned[1].

Cases where there is United Kingdom legislation and directly effective Community legislation on the same topic have caused difficulty. The courts often argued that they were applying the United Kingdom legislation but, striving to avoid a conflict, interpreted it to conform to Community legislation. The English Court of Appeal did this, for example, in *Macarthys v Smith* [1979] ICR 785, [1979] 3 All ER 325 (but did also make an article 234 (ex article 177) reference). This approach did not necessarily involve the United Kingdom courts in formally adopting the European Court of Justice's approach, but did do violence to the traditional United Kingdom methods of interpretation, and implicitly required a more purposive approach.

However, since the *Factortame* cases[2] the House of Lords appears to have fully accepted the implications of direct effect (subject always to the question of explicit repeal of the European Communities Act 1972), and it seems likely that United Kingdom courts will consciously adopt interpretive styles closer to those of the European Court of Justice in the interpretation of Community law with direct effect.

**Construction and interpretation by United Kingdom courts of United Kingdom legislation which implements Community legislation without direct effect.** Community law

---

1 On appeal to the House of Lords ([1981] AC 850, [1981] 2 All ER 166), there was an art 177 (now art 234) preliminary reference, and the European Court of Justice interpreted the provision differently.

2 Case C–213 *R v Secretary of State for Transport, ex parte Factortame* [1990] 2 AC 85, [1989] 2 WLR 997, [1989] 2 All ER 692, [1989] 3 CMLR 1; Case C–213/89 *R v Secretary of State for Transport, ex parte Factortame* [1991] 1 AC 603, [1990] 3 WLR 818, [1991] 1 All ER 70, [1990] 3 CMLR 375. See p 131.

without direct effect is not applied as such by United Kingdom courts, but where such law has been implemented by United Kingdom legislation, that must be applied. This is also now very common, for example, in the application of the VAT legislation by the VAT Tribunal, and otherwise.

No preliminary reference under article 234 (ex article 177) is possible in such a case, nor does the European Communities Act 1972 expressly require such legislation to be interpreted as the European Court of Justice would. However, while United Kingdom courts might regard such legislation as to be interpreted in the light of the intention of Parliament, clearly it is intended by Community law that such national legislation be interpreted in the fashion of the European Court of Justice, and the European Court of Justice so held in Case 14/83 *Von Colson and Kamann v Land Nordrhein-Westfalen* [1984] ECR 1891, [1986] 2 CMLR 430.

Lord Diplock in *Garland v British Rail Engineering Ltd* [1983] AC 751, an English case on Great Britain legislation, asserted (at 770–771) a similar view. However, for many years United Kingdom courts generally took the traditional line. In *Duke v Reliance Ltd* [1988] AC 359, [1988] 2 WLR 359, [1988] 1 All ER 626, [1988] ICR 339, the House of Lords was again applying Great Britain legislation, the Sex Discrimination Act 1975, in an English appeal. Although this Act had been passed shortly before Directive 76/207 (the Equal Treatment Directive), it was known that the Act was intended to implement it, and that the draft directive was available to Parliament. Nevertheless, Lord Templeman said that to interpret the 1975 Act in the light of the 1976 directive would 'distort' its meaning, and the House decided to ignore the directive.

Shortly afterwards, however, in *Pickstone v Freemans plc* [1989] AC 66, [1988] 2 All ER 803, [1988] ICR 697, a closely parallel English case, the House of Lords took a different view. It concerned s 1(2)(c) of the Equal Pay Act 1970, which had been added to that Act by a statutory instrument (the Equal Pay (Amendment) Regulations 1983, SI 1983/1794) made under s 2(2) of the European Communities Act 1972 expressly to implement Directive 75/177 (the Equal Pay Directive), which the United Kingdom had been found (in Case 61/82 *Commission v United Kingdom* [1982] ECR 2601) to be breaching. The House of Lords consulted parliamentary materials to discover if the legislation had been introduced by the government in order to implement Community law and Lord Templeman said (at 121) 'the explanations of Government and the criticisms voiced by Members of Parliament in the debates which led to approval of the draft Regulations provide some indications of the intention of Parliament'.

The change of heart was yet plainer in a Scottish appeal to the House of Lords, *Litster v Forth Dry Dock and Engineering Co Ltd* [1990] AC 546, 1989 SLT 540. Directive 77/187 required rights of employees to compensation for unfair dismissal to be preserved when their employing company was taken over. This policy was implemented in the Transfer of Undertakings (Protection of Employment) Regulations 1981, SI 1981/1794 in respect of those employed immediately before the takeover. Certain employees were dismissed one hour before the transfer of ownership of the employing company, apparently with a view to evading the regulations. The House of Lords held that United Kingdom courts should give a purposive interpretation to the regulations because they were designed to implement Community obligations, and that this might involve departing from the strict and literal meaning of the words of the legislation.

Arguably there was no ambiguity in the regulations under consideration. However, Lord Oliver, giving the leading judgment, referred to the recital ('whereas . . . ') at the beginning of the directive (at 1989 SLT 545), and briefly to the French version of it (at 1989 SLT 549). He said (at 1989 SLT 545):

'If the legislation can reasonably be construed as to conform with [Community obligations] – obligations which are to be ascertained not only from the wording of the relevant Directive, but also from the interpretation placed on it by the European Court of Justice . . . – such a purposive construction will be applied even though, perhaps, it may involve some departure from the strict and literal application of the words the legislature has elected to use.'

This still leaves open to doubt the position if the United Kingdom legislation cannot 'reasonably be construed to conform with' them, although the House of Lords was prepared to read in words which were not in the text in *Litster*. Lord Templeman went even further, saying that United Kingdom courts are under 'an obligation to follow the practice of the European Court of Justice by giving a purposive construction to Directives and Regulations [*scil* statutory instruments] issued for the purpose of complying with Directives'. Both Scottish judges (Lord Keith and Lord Jauncey) concurred[1].

---

1 Nevertheless, in *Stirling District Council v Allan* 1995 SLT 1255 at 1259 D–E the Inner House observed *obiter* that 'The [terms of the very same Directive] cannot affect the construction of the [the very same statutory instrument] except to the extent that there may be an ambiguity which may be resolved by reference to the Directive'.

## Modification of construction and interpretation of legislation by United Kingdom courts through the Human Rights Act 1998

### Statutory interpretation and the European Convention on Human Rights

The Scottish courts initially took the view that, as the Convention was not part of the law of Scotland, but merely an international treaty, they were not entitled to have regard to it, even as an aid in interpreting United Kingdom legislation[1]. However, in *T, Petitioner* 1997 SLT 724 at 733 Lord President Hope stated that where there was an ambiguity in United Kingdom legislation it would be appropriate to look at the European Convention so as to produce an interpretation in conformity with it[2]. He pointed out that under European Community law, to which the Scots courts were bound to give effect, 'general principles of law' included fundamental human rights. In *McLeod, Petitioner* 1998 SLT 233, on the recovery by the defence of police statements in the hands of the Crown, the High Court thought it prudent, in view of the impending enactment of the Human Rights Bill, to have regard to the case of *Edwards v UK* (1992) 15 EHRR 417 and found the judgment of the European Court in line with Scottish authority. English courts, incidentally, were much more ready to use the ECHR to assist in interpreting the law[3]. The position has now in any case been overtaken by enactment of the Human Rights Act 1998.

### Statutory interpretation of legislation under the Human Rights Act 1998, and the concept of 'incompatibility'

By s 2 of the Human Rights Act 1998, any court or tribunal in deciding a question in connection with a Convention right must take into account 'any judgment, decision, declaration or advisory opinion' of European Court of Human Rights, that is to say, its

---

1 See *Kaur v Lord Advocate* 1980 SC 319, 1981 SLT 322 per Lord Ross, approved in *Moore v Secretary of State for Scotland* 1985 SLT 38.
2 Following House of Lords decisions such as *R v Secretary of State for the Home Department, ex parte Brind* [1991] AC 696. See also *Anderson v HM Advocate* 1996 JC 29
3 As, for example, in *Ex parte Brind* (see previous note). It was this dissonance which encouraged Lord Hope to take a new line in *T, Petitioner.*

case law[1]. Thus, a common interpretation among signatories of the ECHR is encouraged, and it is a noticeable feature of most cases involving human rights issues, at least on appeal, that they quote decisions of the European Court of Human Rights, courts in other European countries discussing the ECHR, and indeed courts of yet other countries concerning other human rights conventions[2].

Further, by s 3(1), all legislation from whatever source 'must so far as is possible be read and given effect to in a way that is compatible with Convention rights'. There is a question as to what this means. Clearly, it means that where legislation is of uncertain meaning, it is to be interpreted to achieve compatibility. However, it may also mean that where the legislation is of apparently clear meaning, a court may add qualifications or exceptions to achieve compatibility. So far, there is a certain parallel with the treatment of Community law.

But what is the result of incompatibility? Delegated legislation (including Acts of the Scottish Parliament) found to be incompatible is thereby invalid, so has no effect. However, Acts of the United Kingdom ('primary legislation') are not so affected and continue in force unabated because s 3(2) declares that the duty to interpret compatibly 'does not affect the validity, continuing operation or enforcement of any incompatible primary legislation'. This is a fundamental difference from the treatment of Community law.

By s 4, if the Court of Session or the High Court (sitting as an appeal court) considers that a provision of such 'primary' legislation is incompatible with a Convention right, it can make a 'declaration of incompatibility'. (It can also make such a declaration with regard to a provision of delegated legislation if there is primary legislation which prevents removal of the incompatibility.) The Crown is by s 5 entitled to be given notice of any intended declaration, so that it (including a member of the Scottish Executive) can intervene and make submissions.

So what is the result of a declaration of incompatibility? Such a declaration does not affect the validity of the provision at all. Nor does it bind the parties to the proceedings. It simply puts the government on notice that there is a conflict, in the opinion of the court, between a statutory provision and a Convention right,

1 Also the opinions of the European Commission on Human Rights and the Committee of Ministers of the Council of Europe under the earlier ECHR procedure (for which, see ch 3).
2 E g in *Starrs v Ruxton* 2000 JC 208, 2000 SLT 42, over 30 cases were cited, half of them from the European Court of Human Rights, or, in a few cases, elsewhere, such as Canada.

though it may also thereby create an expectation that the Westminster Parliament will take steps to remove the incompatibility. This could be done by normal legislative activity but, by s 10 and Sch 2, the appropriate Minister of the Crown may, 'where there are compelling reasons', use a special short-cut delegated legislation procedure (subject to the approval of both Houses of Parliament), to make a 'remedial order' amending the provision. Such a remedial order can operate retrospectively, though not so as to make a person guilty of an offence. The difference from the treatment of Community law is underlined.

These provisions are clearly framed so as to stress that the 'parliamentary supremacy' of Westminster (in so far as it has survived the 'direct effect' of Community law) is preserved, both as regards United Kingdom legislation encapsulating the content of the ECHR and Scottish parliamentary legislation.

## Modification of construction and interpretation of legislation by United Kingdom courts through the Scotland Act 1998

Not only does the Human Rights Act 1998 impose a special requirement upon courts interpreting its terms, so does the Scotland Act 1998. Section 101 applies to any provision of an Act of the Scottish Parliament which could be read in such a way as to be outside the Parliament's legislative competence, and to any legislation made under powers delegated to the Scottish Ministers by the Act itself which could be read in such a way as to be outside the powers so delegated[1].

In such a case, s 101 stipulates that it 'be read as narrowly as is required for it to be within competence, if such reading is possible'. If such reading is not possible, clearly the legislation is ultra vires, so void[2], however, the aim is equally clearly to preserve the provision from this fate if at all possible.

The drafting is different from that of s 3 of the similar Human Rights Act 1998, considered above. Firstly, it requires an ambiguity before the rule is invoked, which might suggest that this

---

1 This provision is somewhat obscurely drafted, but seems to mean that s 101 applies not only to legislation made by Scottish Ministers under powers delegated to Scottish Ministers by the Scottish Parliament, but also all those made by them under powers devolved to them by the United Kingdom Parliament (and whether within their 'devolved competence' or not: for which, see ch 3).

2 Indeed, if it is a provision of an Act of the Scottish Parliament, it is specifically stated in s 29 to be 'not law'.

rule is not intended to operate on clear provisions, unlike the provision under the Human Rights Act. Secondly, it specifically enjoins a narrow interpretation which might have the effect of preserving provisions more readily that the provision under the Human Rights Act. Thirdly, s 29(3) of the Act requires that, on a question of whether a provision concerns a reserved matter, this is to be determined by reference to its purpose. There is also the question, since the Scotland Act s 57(2) requires the Scottish Ministers not to act incompatibly with Convention rights, as to whether in interpreting any provision, both the Human Rights Act, s 3(1) and the Scotland Act, s 101 appear to apply, but produce different answers.

However, all conclusions are speculative, and we must wait for the courts to decide these matters[1].

1 In early 2003, no court was reported as having had to consider the meaning of s 101.

# 6. Precedent

## PRECEDENT AS A SOURCE OF LAW

Precedent is a formal source of law[1]. It emerges from the justifications that judges provide for their judgments. As such it has an existence independent of legislation. It can be distinguished from the role of judges in the construction and interpretation of statute. There the judges are not making law on their own, but seeking to find out and apply the intention of the legislature.

Rules of law created by precedent are not explicitly created as Acts of Parliament are, written down in a single authentic text. They are created by judges in the course of deciding cases, primarily to justify their decisions, and have to be extracted from their written judgments. These judges may be reasonably explicit in explaining the rule they are applying, but they may not. In either case, they are not laying down a rule 'in fixed verbal form', and their words are not designed precisely to encapsulate the rule, but principally to describe its operation upon the facts of the case being decided. Usually they are only extending an existing rule, but it is not always clear what the historical source (see Chapter 4) of the rule is. It may come from custom, the judge's sense of morality, or elsewhere.

Thus, reasonable people may disagree on what rule has actually been laid down, and how it might apply to another case. The rule may have to be inferred from the decision. Indeed, it may only be possible to make this inference with confidence when a series of decisions on the same topic has been given; in other words, only from a series of precedents. This means, incidentally, that what look like hard and fast rules when written in a textbook may be the author's view, with the benefit of hindsight, of what the court found the more persuasive of two alternative propositions of law,

1 See ch 4.

both plausible enough to cause the parties to spend time, money and energy in litigating.

As a formal source of law, precedent carries its own authority. Lawyers and other users of the law will respect it as genuine law. Courts in the same judicial structure will hear arguments based on similar cases already decided and are obliged, or at least encouraged, to follow the rule that seems to emerge from an earlier case with similar facts. Why should this be so? The main reason is that there is a deep-seated sense which everyone to some extent possesses that like cases should be treated alike. It is perhaps the most basic meaning of 'justice'. When two people have been found guilty of the same offence and one for no apparent reason receives a heavier sentence than the other, the resultant outcry testifies that the popular sense of justice has been outraged. Following past rules of law helps to prevent such criticism. Moreover, if a rule contained in a past case has been written about in law books and has been quoted by the legal profession or other regular users of law and come to be relied upon, then there would be at least a sense of annoyance if the rule were not applied by a court. These considerations are strengthened where the courts are arranged in a clear hierarchy. Respect will be felt for the more senior judges. If, as appellate judges, they have the power to overrule the decision of a lower court, the judge there will only reject the rule on some strong ground, such as that new social conditions have rendered the rule unworkable or out of date.

Not all systems of law accept precedent as a formal source (and acceptance or non-acceptance of precedent is an essential differ-ence between common law and civil law countries, as discussed below). Scots law did not accept it until the early 19th century (again, as discussed below)[1], but precedent is an important formal source of law today. Many fundamental areas of law were largely created by precedent (albeit sometimes building upon the work of the institutional writers), and may still be developed by this means. Contract, delict and criminal law, for example, are of this nature. Their basic rules are not to be found written in Acts of Parliament, but have to be extracted from precedents. Thus, the basic rules on what contract is, how a contract is made, what the effect on it is of error by one party as to any of the terms, and so on, are found in, or inferred from, precedents. Acts of Parliament, such as those

---

1 Indeed, the assertion that Scots law relies on principle rather than precedent implies a continuing doubt as to the role of precedent.

relating to the sale of goods and consumer credit, may be regarded as making modifications to this basic structure[1].

A problem about precedent is that the law can only develop if there are new precedents, and that depends upon litigants bringing cases to court in the areas needing development[2]. As Scotland has a population about one-tenth that of England and Wales, the potential for elaborating the law by means of judicial decisions is that much less. By the same token, the development of the law through cases requires that there be people with the resources and the determination to have their disputes settled by courts.

### Nobile officium and declaratory power

Two exceptional exercises of legislative power by the courts require special mention, that is, the *nobile officium* and the declaratory power. The *nobile officium* is an exceptional equitable power exercised by the Court of Session and High Court of Justiciary to provide a remedy where none exists but the court feels it should. In the Court of Session, the power goes back to at least the time of Stair, at the end of the 17th century. He mentions in his *Institutions* at IV, 3, 2 seven miscellaneous exercises of it. That varied character has continued to the present day. A modern, much cited description of that is by Lord President Emslie: 'It may be exercised in highly special or unforeseen circumstances to prevent injustice or oppression. It cannot however be invoked in such a way as to defeat a statutory intention, express or implied, or to extend the scope of an Act of Parliament'[3]. Petitions are heard by three judges of the Inner House[4].

On the criminal side the *nobile officium* (not always so described) is referred to by Alison in his *Practice* of 1833 as used 'in

---

1 'The common law is a canvas on which a picture is being painted. The cloth may be obscured by layers of pigment, but it is ever apt to show through and without it the whole image crumbles', McBryde *The Law of Contract in Scotland* (2nd edn, 2001) para 1–15.
2 On the social limitations on Scottish case law, see Willock 'Making Law and Keeping to the Law' 1982 JR 237 at 250.
3 *Humphries, Petr* 1982 SLT 481, applied in *L v Kennedy* 1993 SCLR 693, *Sloan, Petr* 1991 SLT 527 and *H, Petrs* 1997 SLT 3 (all Children's Hearings cases). Other modern examples include *Royal Bank of Scotland v Gillies* 1987 SLT 54 (reduction of decree obtained by petitioners).
4 *Institute of Chartered Accountants in Scotland, Petr* 2002 SLT 921.

circumstances unforeseen for which the law makes no provision'. The Crown may seek its exercise as well as an accused[1]. Modern criminal instances of this power do tend to emphasise the avoidance of injustice or oppression as a justification for its use[2]. Examples of the absence of a remedy as such injustice or oppression include *Wylie v HM Advocate*, where the then lack of provisions on sentencing for contempt of court was held to justify invoking the *nobile officium*[3].

The declaratory power is an exceptional power held by the High Court of Justiciary to declare behaviour which it considers morally wrong to be a criminal offence, although it was not, or not unequivocally, regarded as criminal before. This could be a wide and unpredictable power, and was so used in the formative years of Scots criminal law[4]. It is now very rarely invoked, and only in cases closely analogous to existing crimes, and is difficult to distinguish from the application of existing vague offences to new circumstances, as for example in *Khaliq v HM Advocate* 1984 JC 23 which rendered criminal the selling of glue-sniffing kits as the wilful supply of potentially noxious substances[5].

---

1  E g *Bryceland, Petr* 2003 SLT 54, 2002 SCLR 995.

2  See e g *Perrie, Petr* 1992 SLT 655; *Windsor, Petr* 1994 SCCR 59; *Beglan, Petr* 2002 SLT 1175.

3  1996 SLT 149. For another absence of statutory provision case, see *Wan Ping Nam v German Federal Republic Minister of Justice* 1972 JC 43, 1972 SLT 220. The Extradition Act 1870 allowed *habeas corpus* and no other remedy for review of a decision to extradite someone. A person arrested in Scotland and whose extradition to Germany was requested sought *habeas corpus* from the High Court. This was refused on the ground that it was a remedy unknown in Scotland. Nevertheless, looking at the intention of the Act, the court exercised the *nobile officium* and was prepared in principle to liberate the person if he could show good cause.

4  As such it was justified by Hume, the institutional writer on criminal law. In *Greenhuff* (1838) 2 Swin 236 its advantages and disadvantages were set out by the majority and the one dissenting judge Lord Cockburn. Its existence bears out the criticism of Bentham, the great political and legal philosopher of two centuries ago, that the common law operates as you train a dog. You wait till it does what you dislike, then you punish it. Any broad exercise of the declaratory power is liable to contravene art 7 of the European Convention on Human Rights which forbids retrospectivity in crimes and punishments.

5  See also *Ulhaq v HM Advocate* 1991 SLT 614. The offence does not seem to cover the supply of other noxious substances such as tobacco, but it is in the nature of the common law and the use of the declaratory power that it is not possible precisely to define what is prohibited.

## Precedent and the common law

Precedent and common law are intertwined. Originally, at least in England[1], 'common law' meant custom which was common to the whole country, rather than purely local. Now, however, custom having crystallised into law through the decisions of judges, the basic meaning has come to be law which has been made by precedent, and this English law-based meaning has largely displaced any others. In a slightly extended form, the phrase refers to the minor sources as well, in other words, to all law that is not legislation. In both these meanings common law is contrasted with statute law.

Systems of law which accept precedent as a formal source are known as common law systems. They are widespread because English law, the original common law system, was exported to most British colonies (not least those which later formed the United States of America). Thus, there is said to be a family of common law systems. It is contrasted with the family of civil law[2] systems, that is, those which claim Roman law as their intellectual progenitor and which, generally speaking, do not recognise precedent as a formal source of law. This family includes most European states, and countries formerly their colonies (such as the whole of South America).

Scots law is said to be one of a few 'mixed' or 'hybrid' systems, because it claims some Roman ancestry like the civil law systems), but now uses precedent (like the common law systems). Other such systems are Louisiana, Quebec, South Africa and Sri Lanka.

European Community law, because it has been created largely in a milieu of civil law countries, operates essentially as a civil law system, with limited reliance upon precedent. 'Human rights law',

---

1 Originally in Scotland, the term 'common law' was used as a translation of the Latin *'ius commune'* and referred to canon law, that is, the law of the Christian church. In this sense there was a 'common law of Europe', as canon law was applied by courts throughout Christendom as a subsidiary source to 'municipal law', that is, national law. It was supported by Roman law, and the plural of *'ius commune'*, that is, *'jura communia'*, translated into Scots as 'the commoune lawis of the realme', was often used here and (translated into other languages) elsewhere, to describe canon law plus Roman law: see Dolezalek 'The Court of Session as a *Ius Commune* Court – witnessed by "Sinclair's Practicks", 1540–1549' in McQueen (ed) *Miscellany IV* (Stair Society, 2002). Modern Continental European lawyers sometimes use the phrase *'ius commune'* to refer to common principles of European civil law systems, seen as increasingly expressed through Community law.

2 It has been argued that this is a misleading term, used by English lawyers, and that the *'ius commune'* is better: see previous note.

as expressed in decisions of the European Court of Human Rights, also bears evidence of civil law reasoning.

There are other uses of the term 'common law'[1]. For example, in English law, it has a technical meaning more restricted than the basic meaning. For centuries in England there were two parallel sets of courts. The basic common law courts generated common law in this most restricted sense. The supplementary courts of Chancery generated equity. The two court systems were amalgamated in the 1870s, and English courts are now both common law and equity courts, but common law and equity are still said to be separate sets of rules or principles. Also, histories and theories of the common law (in any of its senses) are usually histories and theories of English law, and thus the common law is sometimes taken to mean English law.

## Precedent and Scots law

Before the 19th century, Scottish courts were applying customary law (native and feudal), fortified by concepts of canon law and Roman law (the 'common law' in the original Scots sense[2]), reinforced and modified by statute, and consolidated by legal writers (Scottish, French, German and other), including, as time went on, those later regarded as 'institutional'[3].

Precedents were recorded in the *Practicks* which judges created for their own use from the earliest days of the Court of Session, and which were later published by them and others in collections.

---

1 Some phrases using the term 'common law' which have entered the popular language are misleading. 'Common law wife', referring to an unmarried partner, has no more meaning legal meaning than does 'bidie-in' or 'kippie-uppie'. Civil law also has several meanings, including 'non-criminal law' and Roman law. These meanings are also etymologically linked.

2 See previous notes. McQueen 'Two Visitors in the Session, 1629 and 1639' in McQueen (ed) *Miscellany IV* (Stair Society, 2002) recounts that an English visitor (Sir C Lowther) remarked that '[m]uch of their law is Acts of Parliament and Regiam Majestatem', presumably in contrast to the common law (English style) with which he was familiar in English courts. ('Regiam Majestatem' is a medieval collection of laws: see ch 1).

3 Lord Cockburn, in his *Memorials of His Times* (1856, reprinted 1971), critically examining the intellectual rigour of the preceding generation, recorded Lord Hermand, a judge appointed in 1799, as 'very apt to say "My Laards, I feel my law – here my Laards" striking his heart'. However, although well disposed towards Hermand on a personal level, Cockburn was a Whig, strongly opposed to the Tory dominance of Scotland of the time, manifested in the law by Hermand and others. For the 'instituional writers', see ch 4.

Such precedents were cited in court and Stair cited many in his *Institutions*. However, they were not the formal source of the law, but merely evidence of what it was. Indeed, the way the *Practicks* and early series of law reports were edited meant that nothing like the modern system of precedent could operate. For example, cases were commonly recorded without giving the judges' reasoning[1]. It can be very unclear, therefore, what rule or principle the judges considered they were applying.

In the 19th century reliance on institutional works did not wane, but reliance on precedent increased, and it became recognised as another, alternative, formal source of law. This reflected a number of factors, including change in the perception of the nature of law[2], and the reorganisation of the Court of Session[3]. It has also been orthodox to blame the availability of appeal to the House of Lords (then very common) for various ills, including the descent from grace involved in abandoning Roman law and adopting precedent, although recent research has suggested otherwise[4]. The growth of

---

1 Lord Cockburn (above at pp 164–165) also related of early law reporting that 'It had never [before the 19th century] been the practice to give any full and exact account of what passed on the Bench, but only results . . . [T]heir Lordships were very jealous of this pretension [to full law reporting]. They considered it a contempt . . . aggravated by the accuracy of the report. Mr Robert Bell . . . was the first who advertised an independence in this matter . . . This design was no sooner disclosed than he met with many threatening hints, and as much obstruction as could be given in open court. The hated but excellent volume at last appeared [*Bell's Cases*, in 1790], and . . . he was actually called into the robing room, and admonished to beware. [Lord] Eskgrove's objection was "the fellow taks down ma' very words" '.

2 Legislation in its modern guise emerged at this time, and the creation of a distinct class of institutional writers, with Stair pre-eminent, occurred: see *The Laws of Scotland: Stair Memorial Encyclopaedia* vol 22, para 256 and Blackie 'Stair's Later Reputation as a Jurist' in *Stair Tercentenary Studies* (ed Walker) (Stair Society, vol 33, 1981). Law was seen less as immemorial custom, and rather as the expression of Sovereign will. A parallel change in the status of precedent was also occurring in England: see *The Laws of Scotland: Stair Memorial Encyclopaedia* vol 22, para 252.

3 The Court of Session sat as the unwieldy 'Haill Fifteen', with essentially written procedures from its foundation in 1532 to the Court of Session Acts of 1808, 1810, 1825 and 1830. (Lord Cockburn in his *Journal* vol I (1874) pp 221–222 referred to it as 'a mob of fifteen judges, meeting without previous consultation, and each impatient for independent eminence'. As indicated above, Cockburn's remarks cannot be taken as unbiased, however there is other evidence. The Court of Session Acts gave it its present structure and the basis of its present procedure. These reforms made possible inconsistent judgments by different judges, Divisions or Houses, created a hierarchy and thus posed questions of relative authority.

4 *The Laws of Scotland: Stair Memorial Encyclopaedia* vol 22, para 255.

law reporting in the modern form seems more likely to be a result than a cause of the growth of precedent, but the existence of full clear reports can only have encouraged recourse to precedent[1]. The Faculty of Advocates attempted, unsuccessfully, to introduce better reports than the *Practicks* from the early 18th century, but modern law reporting started with *Shaw's Reports* in 1821, which commenced the series now appearing as *Session Cases*. In the earlier reports precedents and references to the institutional writers appear in the reported arguments of counsel rather than in the judgments themselves, but in the course of the 19th century fully reasoned judgments became reported. This allowed the operation of precedent in the contemporary sense, although only in the second half of the 20th century did explicit reliance upon precedent become a major feature, and Scots law clearly, in part at least, a common law system.

## How do rules emerge from precedents? – precedent and adjudication

Precedents are cases which are assumed to be capable of laying down rules or principles, or extending existing ones. Although this assumption is central to the operation of a common law or mixed legal system, there is not complete agreement about how the process occurs. Indeed, it is the central mystery of such a system, both in the sense of an obscure process and in the older sense of a jealously guarded trade skill.

The orthodoxy is as follows. There are many ways of resolving disputes. Violence is common in international affairs, spinning a coin in some other situations. What distinguishes court-based dispute resolution, and thus the operation of precedent, is adjudication. Precedents are created by judges in courts deciding disputes brought before them as cases, by means of adjudication.

Adjudication can be described as dispute resolution where a third party imposes a solution upon the disputants, whether they agree to his decision or not. This solution is not a compromise (so there are winners and losers), and is justified by reference to a rule

---

1 Lord Cockburn in his *Memorials of His Times* (1856, reprinted 1971) attributed the rise in accurate reporting to the fact that '[T]he public, or at least the independent proportion of the legal profession, had begun to require something more [than the reporting of merely the results of cases]'.

of general application (rather than personal preference[1] or some random method). The decision must therefore fit into the matrix of previous similar cases. By the same token it is capable of use as a precedent in later cases of similar type. The decisions therefore form a more or less coherent system, and are not 'a wilderness of single instances'[2]. Adjudication also implies that the decision is taken by a judge, that is, someone professionally employed by the state to resolve disputes in this way[3].

Other methods of non-violent (and non-random) dispute resolution exist, such as conciliation, mediation and arbitration and other forms of 'alternative dispute resolution'. Some of them may be employed by courts from time to time. But they do not have all the features of adjudication, so do not generate precedents.

Because every case adjudicated is decided according to a rule or principle, the decision must reflect that rule or principle, which must therefore be discoverable from the judgment itself. This rule or principle is referred to as the *ratio decidendi*[4] (often abbreviated simply to *ratio*). *Ratios*[5], being law, bind later judges under certain circumstances, that is, under these circumstances, later judges must apply them whether they wish to or not. In other circumstances, *ratios* are simply more or less persuasive, that is, may or may not be applied at the discretion of the later judges, depending upon whether they are persuaded by them. The principle that *ratios* may bind is called *stare decisis*[6].

This orthodoxy is made more comprehensible by viewing the central mystery in the light of the ideas of rules not 'in fixed verbal form', and of analysis of rules in terms of *protasis* and *apodosis*[7].

1 'Why does the judge not make his reason explicit by granting Mrs McTavish her divorce just because she has a ravishingly pert retroussé nose? Because such are not accepted as good reasons within the system for ... granting divorces', MacCormick *Legal Reasoning and Legal Theory* (1978) p 15. Lord Atkin is believed to have consulted his young children before deciding *Donoghue v Stevenson* 1932 SC(HL) 31, however.

2 'Mastering the lawless science of law/ That codeless myriad of precedent/ That wilderness of single instances/ Through which a few by wit or fortune led/ May beat a path to wealth and fame', Tennyson *Aylmer's Field* 1, 436.

3 An interesting and accessible account of the theory of precedent by a leading contemporary commentator is MacCormick *Legal Reasoning and Legal Theory* (1978).

4 The first word is pronounced 'ray-she-oh' or 'rah-tea-oh', the second 'dess-ee-dend-aye'.

5 The plural in Latin would be *rationes decidendi* but this is rarely used.

6 Usually pronounced 'star-ray dee-sigh-sis'.

7 See Appendix 1.

## *RATIO DECIDENDI* AND *OBITER DICTA*

Commentators have often observed that defining the idea of the *ratio*, and identifying one in an actual case, are separate problems.

### Defining '*ratio decidendi*'

A direct translation of '*ratio decidendi*' ('the reason for deciding') is unanimously agreed to be misleading, but there is no unanimity on a better one[1]. This is partly because commentators use the phrase to refer to slightly different things, partly because of lack of complete agreement on what the phenomenon actually is[2]. Also, usage is said to differ as between Scotland and England. This is important as most of the academic discussion has centred on English law[3], but it is noticeable that most commentators describe the concept and its operation using Scottish and English cases indifferently.

For present purposes an adequate interpretation is 'the rule or principle of law for which a competent observer considers the case to be authority'[4]. There are, however, four riders to be added.

Firstly, no *ratio* stands alone. It can only make sense within the matrix of other relevant precedents (that is, within the matrix of the common law). It is the reasoning adopted by a judge to decide the specific issue before him and justify his decision, and the judge must presume, and rely on, the surrounding law which it is not open to him to change. However, some cases which raise very wide issues go before appeal courts, giving them the opportunity to pronounce a rule or principle over a broad area.

Secondly, because of the way *ratios* are constructed, competent

---

1 Walker *The Scottish Legal System* (8th edn, 2001) p 462 refers to seven possible translations.
2 Some argue that the phrase refers to the reasons advanced by the judge in the case; others that it is what later judges make of those reasons; yet others, that it is a combination of both: see, for example, *The Laws of Scotland: Stair Memorial Encyclopaedia* vol 22, para 335; MacCormick, *Legal Reasoning and Legal Theory* (1978) pp 86 and 215; Willock 'Judges at Work: Making Law and Keeping to the Law' 1982 JR 237, 246.
3 However, perhaps the leading commentator is MacCormick (see previous note), whose Scots credentials are impeccable.
4 MacCormick *Legal Reasoning and Legal Theory* (1978) p 215 suggests that it is 'the ruling expressly or impliedly given by a judge which is sufficient to settle a point of law put in issue by the parties' arguments in a case, being a point on which a ruling was necessary to his justification (or one of his alternative justifications) of the decision in the case'.

observers may genuinely differ as to what rule or principle is laid down. Common law rules are not 'in fixed verbal form', so that, although an authentic version of the judges' words is available, there is no single authentic version of the actual rule or principle. Moreover, judges may not even be very explicit as to what rule or principle they consider they are laying down. Thus, there may be 'wide' (more inclusive) and 'narrow' (less inclusive) versions of any *ratio*.

Thirdly, later judges and other commentators must interpret the apparent *ratio* of a case. This flows inevitably from the first and second riders, and from the fact that new cases appear all the time. It is an important truth that a precedent is what later judges say it is, and they decide upon the width of the *ratio*. All the judge actually laying down the precedent can do is to restrict the range of possibilities.

Fourthly, any *ratio* may nevertheless be regarded as wrong by other judges and commentators. A *ratio* can only be understood in the light of other *ratios*, and the law generally, and a judge is constrained to decide consistently with them. If he fails to do so, his decision does not properly fit into the matrix of the common law, by which token it is wrong. Whether the later judges can put the error right, however, depends upon whether it is binding upon them or not. Even if they cannot, they may still be able to avoid its effects by 'restrictive distinguishing' and other devices. These questions are dealt with below, in relation to *stare decisis*.

This interpretation and its riders are best understood by recalling the nature of the process of adjudication. A judge is required to decide the case before him according to some rule or principle (rather than by compromise, personal preference, or some random method). The judge may find the existing rules and principles, discoverable from the *ratios* of existing precedents, are clear enough to indicate the decision. In such a case, the judge's *ratio* in the new case adds nothing but another illustration to the existing law. However, the rules and principles may not be so clear, in which case the judge has the opportunity and duty to extend or restrict existing rules and principles, or lay down some new ones to decide the case, and the *ratio* of the new case will have some novelty. It thus develops the law. In laying down a new rule or principle, however, the judge is severely constrained by the need to fit into the matrix of existing common law, and is aware that the *ratio* may be cited in future as a precedent for other cases. Thus, the common law grows by the accretion of analogous cases.

### Identifying a *ratio decidendi*

While it is the judge or judges in the precedent examined who uttered the words from which a *ratio* is to be extracted, it is later judges who, with the assistance of counsel representing the parties, have to identify it in later cases.

It would be helpful for such identification if judges explicitly identified the relevant rule or principle they consider they are applying. Sometimes they do. However, usually they do not, and even where they appear to do so, the statement must be treated with care, for reasons implicit in the definition of *ratio decidendi* and the riders to it.

Thus, while it is the words of judges which must be considered, it is a mistake to 'dig for buried treasure' by looking for a useful quotation from a judge which, wrenched from its context, provides a memorable and comprehensible but possibly inaccurate statement.

These problems are best approached by considering four things: what the relevant facts are; what their appropriate level of generality is; how multiple *ratios* are to be dealt with; and wide and narrow *ratios* and the development of principles.

### *What are the relevant facts?*

A useful way forward to confirm an apparently clear statement of rule or principle, or to infer a *ratio* where there is no clear statement, is to employ analysis in terms of *protasis* and *apodosis* (although this approach is unorthodox)[1]. If a legal rule comprises a series of facts which (or some of which) must be fulfilled in order for the legal result to occur, then a *ratio* can be sought by identifying those facts the judges stated or implied to be relevant or material, that is, appeared sufficient for him to come to the conclusion he did (and excluding those which he stated or implied were not relevant or material). This approach has been elaborated largely in relation to English law and United States law[2], but is appropriate, if care be taken, in relation to Scots law[3].

1 See Appendix 1.
2 See, for example, Goodhart's 'The *Ratio Decidendi* of a Case' in *Essays in Jurisprudence and Common Law* (1931), and Llewellyn's very readable *The Bramble Bush* (1951) (as well as Twining and Miers *How To Do Things With Rules* (4th edn, 1999)).
3 *The Laws of Scotland: Stair Memorial Encyclopaedia* vol 22, para 344 expresses doubt but, subject to caveats, MacCormick in *Legal Reasoning and Legal Theory* (1978) appears to approve Goodhart's approach. Perhaps in modern conditions the assertion that Scots law relies on principle rather than precedent, while English law does the reverse, means that Scots lawyers are prepared to generalise further.

Thus, for example, to discover what can amount to an offer or an acceptance sufficient to constitute a contract, it is useful to consider what actual communications were considered relevant or material by the judges in the relevant precedents, and what they considered not. In other words, what facts were adequate to allow the judges to decide that they constituted offer and acceptance?

*What is the appropriate level of generality?*

Identifying the right facts still leaves the problem of determining the right level of generality of the facts. If a ginger beer manufacturer is made liable for harm done to the ultimate consumer by noxious substances concealed, through negligence, in ginger beer, is this a liability upon ginger beer manufacturers only, upon manufacturers of any drink, manufacturers of any food or drink, or of anybody distributing anything which might contain hidden noxious substances? The judge who laid down the precedent will have limited the range of possibilities, but it is the later judges who determine the actual level. The rule of thumb is to ask what, in the light of the judges' actual words, and all other precedents, is plausible.

*How are multiple ratios to be dealt with?*

Most discussion of the nature of the *ratio decidendi* assumes that there is one judge in the court. However, in appellate courts there will be more than one. If this is so, they may disagree on the decision (that is, essentially, on who wins), or agree on the decision, but disagree on the reasoning justifying that decision. Increasingly, in Scottish appellate courts, both civil and criminal, a single judgment is issued, usually written by the senior judge (assuming there are no dissenting judges). However, this is not always so and it is not true of the House of Lords[1]. So, both in relation to some

1 A good recent example of the problem is *Macfarlane v Tayside Health Board* 2000 SC(HL)1, [2000] 2 AC 59, [1999] 3 WLR 1301, [1999] 4 All ER 961. A couple with four children, a number they considered sufficient, relied on a negligently inaccurate report of a vasectomy test and produced a fifth. The mother sued for damages for pain and suffering from pregnancy and birth, consequential expenditure, and loss of earnings. The House of Lords held that the claim for pain and suffering was relevant (unanimously); the claim for expenditure consequential upon the pregnancy and birth was relevant (Lords Clyde and Millett dissenting) but that for expenditure consequential upon bringing up the child was not (unanimously); and the claim for loss of earnings consequential upon the pregnancy

contemporary judgments and most older ones, the problem of multiple *ratios* exists. Appellate decisions are always more important than cases at first instance. They come from higher in the hierarchy and send out stronger signals as to what the law is. There are four possibilities to consider.

**Disagreement on the decision – majority decisions.** If the judges do not all agree on the decision, then the majority view prevails, although the problems of multiple *ratios* may arise within the majority. The views of the dissenting minority, while they can bind no-one, may throw light on those of the majority.

**Agreement on the decision where there is an opinion of the court.** Where all judges in a court agree on the decision, they can be assumed to agree on the reasoning producing that outcome. Then no problem arises. But sometimes, and quite commonly in the House of Lords, one full judgment will be given, but the other judges will add a few additional comments or ones which rephrase part of what the leading judge has said[1]. Then it is usually the leading judgment alone which is taken to contain the *ratio*.

**Agreement on the decision where there are separate judgments.** In a significant proportion of House of Lords cases and older Inner House cases, the judges agree on the outcome, but deliver separate judgments. In such cases their reasoning may differ somewhat, or it may be difficult to tell whether they agree completely or not[2], in which case, there may be multiple *ratios*.

---

and birth were relevant (Lords Clyde and Millett again dissenting) but that loss of earnings consequential upon bringing up the child was not (unanimously). In respect of the consequential expenditure claim unanimously held irrelevant, in brief, Lords Slynn and Hope so concluded because they saw it as 'pure economic loss'; Lord Steyn relied on 'principles of distributive justice'; Lord Clyde on 'disproportionality'; and Lord Millett on the benefits of having a child outweighing any detriments. Even on the merely majority issues, there was much variation as between the reasoning of the majority.

1 Lord Carmont (appointed to the Court of Session in 1934, entered the Inner House in 1937, and died in office in 1965), was said to concur so frequently that his motto was 'I came, I saw, I concurred'.

2 In *Manuel v A-G* [1982] 3 All ER 786, an English case before the Chancery Division, Sir Robert Megarry VC (the President of the court), at 798, observed 'During the argument it was not surprisingly suggested to me on this point: (a) there was a majority for Lord Denning's view and that Kerr LJ was in a minority and (b) that there was a majority for the view of Kerr LJ and Lord Denning was in the minority. A third contention was that May LJ was agreeing with Lord Denning in his general view, but with Kerr LJ in his particular application. A variant is that May LJ . . .'.

The question is then posed as to what is the *ratio* of the case as a whole.

It is surprisingly unclear what is supposed to happen in such an eventuality, for there are few precedents explicitly on the question. The vagueness of rules not derived from statute, and the discretion of later judges to determine the *ratio* of precedents sometimes allows the issue to be avoided[1]. Three different situations must be distinguished:

(a) *Leading judgment.* If there is a leading judgment, that is, one more fully argued than the rest, and to which the other judgments merely add variations or emphases, the *ratio* extracted from it is likely to be treated as the *ratio* of the case, especially if that judge is more senior or more respected. The variations to it may be treated as persuasive rather than binding, or simply ignored.

(b) *No leading judgment but consistent reasoning.* If there is no leading judgment, and all judgments are broadly consistent, though not identical, then the *ratio* of the case is likely, according to some Scottish commentators[2], to be taken to be the highest common factor among the judges sitting and other parts of the judgments are ignored. According to a commentator on English law[3], in such circumstances, the *ratio* of the case might be taken to be the sum of all *ratios* of the judges sitting. A third possible view is that the *ratio* is a version of the judgment which fits most neatly into the existing law[4]. In any case, clearly a wide discretion is left to judges in later cases.

(c) *No leading judgment and inconsistent reasoning.* If there is no leading judgment, nor any high degree of overlap in the reasoning of the judges, both the common factor and sum of the *ratios* approaches produce ridiculous results, and it is not possible to fit the decision neatly into the existing law. In this situation, the view cannot be avoided that the judges, though arriving at the same decision, do so by inconsistent reasoning, and there may be said to be no *ratio* for the case at all (or the case described as 'authority only for its own facts').

---

1 Paterson, Bates and Poustie *The Legal System of Scotland: Cases and Materials* (4th edn, 1999) at p 441 remark ' . . . juggling with multiple ratios is one more technique which the wise judge acquires'.

2 Paterson, Bates and Poustie *The Legal System of Scotland: Cases and Materials* (4th edn, 1999) p 440, and *The Laws of Scotland: Stair Memorial Encyclopaedia* vol 22, para 342. No authority is cited.

3 Goodhart in 'Determining the *Ratio Decidendi* of a Case' in *Essays in Jurisprudence and the Common Law* (1931). Examples are given, but no authority cited.

4 *The Laws of Scotland: Stair Memorial Encyclopaedia* vol 22, para 342 describes this procedure as 'dubious'.

Commonly quoted are the words of Lord Dunedin in the English case of *Great Western Railways Co Ltd v Owners of the SS Mostyn* [1928] AC 57 at 73 '. . . if [the *ratio* of a case] is not clear, then I do not think it is part of the tribunal's duty to spell out with great difficulty a *ratio decidendi* in order to be bound by it'.

**Multiple *ratios* and the single judge.** Multiple *ratios* may also arise where a judge gives alternative lines of reasoning. Again, there is little authority as to how it is supposed to be treated, but probably the case then has two alternative, equally valid, *ratios*.

*Wide and narrow* ratios *and the development of principles*

A *ratio* may clearly be wide or narrow, or rather, widely or narrowly expressed. The fewer facts found to be material, and the higher the level of generality considered appropriate (and if the 'common factor' approach to multiple *ratios* be employed), the more inclusive or wider a *ratio* is. Conversely, the more facts, the lower the level of generality (and if the 'sum of all facts' approach to multiple *ratios* be employed), the less inclusive or narrower it is. As noted already in relation to the question of defining the *ratio*, the width can vary. In so far as *ratios* are not fixed and it is later judges who determine what they shall be taken to mean, a *ratio* may get wider or narrower as time passes. This can be shown in relation to *Donoghue v Stevenson* 1932 SC(HL) 31 (bearing in mind the definition of *ratio decidendi* and the riders to it).

*Donoghue v Stevenson* has for decades been cited as authority for certain propositions, and has been the basis of most of the modern law of negligence in Scotland and England. The decision does not stand alone. Like any other precedent, it has to be seen against the background of the earlier law. Before the decision, for example, it was not clear whether a manufacturer was liable to someone with whom he had no contract, and much of the judgment in *Donoghue* is spent reviewing the earlier precedents (different judges coming to different conclusions as to their significance). *Donoghue* settled the question, within limits, in the affirmative. The current view of *Donoghue*, and how far the principle attributed to it goes, equally can only be understood in the light of the numerous later precedents which have developed it.

As is the way with *ratios*, not all those of the judges in *Donoghue* are clear. Lord Atkin, for example, gives two different versions of his. One, most succinctly expressed at 44 (at the risk of falling into the trap of 'digging for buried treasure') is broad, and is his 'neighbour principle'. It includes few facts, and those at a high level of generality, and could be rendered as the following: 'If you act in such a way as to make it reasonably foreseeable that you will injure someone, if that person ought reasonably to be in your contemplation, and if such a person is in fact injured, then you are liable to compensate that other person for the injury suffered'. The other, most succinctly expressed (subject to the same risk) at 57, is narrower. It includes more facts, and at a lower level of generality, and could be rendered as the following: 'If you are a manufacturer of food and drink for consumption by the public, and if you produce such food or drink in sealed containers, then you are liable . . .'.

However, later judges, after initially ignoring the decision, have generally asserted the broader version to be the principle for which the case is authority. This is the more surprising because, firstly, the decision was by a bare majority of 3 to 2; secondly, it is not clear on the face of it that Lord Atkin's is a leading judgment; and thirdly, the other two judges of the majority, Lords Thankerton (especially at 59–60) and Macmillan (at 71), produced principles close to Lord Atkin's narrow version. The way *Donoghue* has been used subsequently by no means supports the 'sum of the facts' approach to the multiple *ratios* problem. It may be consistent with other approaches but, really, Lord Atkin's views have been retrospectively elevated to leading judgment status.

Later judges have used the broad version of *Donoghue* to give compensation for a variety of losses including those caused by negligent misstatements by banks, which were losses of profit rather than physical losses (*Hedley Byrne v Heller & Partners* [1964] AC 465) and losses caused by the escape through negligence of borstal[1] boys (*Dorset Yacht Co v Home Office* [1970] AC 1004). It is far from clear that even Lord Atkin would have accepted all such subsequent developments of his principle, and Lord Thankerton and Lord Macmillan's views are much less commonly considered.

Not all such developments have proved lasting, however. *Donoghue* was used by the House of Lords to justify the liability not only for wrongful acts, but also for the failure to act, in an English case concerning local authority building inspectors, *Anns v Merton Borough Council* [1978] AC 728, only to decide in *Murphy v Brentwood District Council* [1990] 1 AC 398 that they had decided *Anns* wrongly.

---

1 'Name of a town in Kent applied orig. to the system adopted there for reforming "juvenile adult" offenders': *Shorter Oxford English Dictionary*. Thus, effectively, a young offenders' institution.

Thus, the views expressed in *Donoghue v Stevenson* have been a fecund source of principle in a wide area. The potential has been realised in some ways, but pinched off in others, but in all cases at the instance of later judges, and despite the fact that most of these developments could hardly have been foreseen by the original judges.

### Defining and identifying '*obiter dicta*'

*Obiter dicta*[1], usually translated as 'things said by the way' (that is, 'in passing') is the phrase applied to any reasoning of a judge which is not part of his *ratio*. These include other observations upon the law, typically hypothetical examples. The problems of definition and identification of *obiter dicta* thus reflect those of *ratio decidendi*.

*Obiter dicta* have an importance. Although by definition they are never binding upon any court (not being a *ratio*), they may be persuasive, depending upon certain factors[2]. Also, given the difficulty of determining the *ratio* of a case, it may be that there is disagreement as to whether a particular piece of reasoning is *ratio* or *obiter*.

## *STARE DECISIS*

If precedent is a source of law, the *ratios* of precedents must, at least on occasion, bind later courts. In other words, on occasion, they lay down for the later court how a case is to be decided, and the later judge has no choice but to apply the rule or principle laid down. This doctrine is known as *stare decisis*, that is 'to stand by what has been decided'[3]. There are stronger and weaker versions of *stare decisis*, and Scotland is said to employ a weaker.

---

1 '*Obiter dicta*', pronounced as spelt, is plural; the singular is '*obiter dictum*'. A noteworthy remark or remarks by a judge may be referred to as a '*dictum*' or '*dicta*' of his (as in 'Lord Reid's *dictum* in the case of . . .'). Confusingly, this usage does not imply that such *dicta* are *obiter*.
2 Discussed below under '*STARE DECISIS* – persuasiveness'.
3 Also rendered *stare decisis et quieta non movere*. The additional words mean 'and not disturb settled matters'.

## Why have *stare decisis*?

There are several possible reasons for applying a doctrine of *stare decisis*. Some are unworthy, such as a desire on the part of judges to shuffle off responsibility for their decisions, or a form of ancestor worship. Others are less so, such as the efficiency of processing cases, enhanced by removing the need to decide every case anew when similar ones have been decided before. What most justifies *stare decisis*, however, is that it tends to ensure consistency. In other words, like cases should be decided alike, which as we have seen is a basic requirement of justice. Indeed, if like cases were not decided alike, in what sense would there be legal rules? On the other hand, consistency is bought at a price, for it may stultify development, and be seen to work injustice in individual cases.

## What makes a precedent binding?

Not all precedents are binding. The binding nature depends upon two principal factors, that is, firstly, whether or not the *ratio* in question is 'in point', and secondly, upon the relative position in the hierarchy of the court examining the precedent to the court which laid down the precedent. Also, in Scotland it is said that a single precedent cannot bind, only a series of similar decisions, although as a *ratio* must always be seen as part of the matrix of the common law, it is rare for a precedent to be capable of being regarded as standing alone. In some cases it is not clear whether a precedent is binding or not, and there are exceptional cases where an apparently binding precedent is not so.

Precedents which are not binding may be 'persuasive', that is, they do not bind, but may persuade a judge to decide in conformity with them. Persuasiveness is a matter of degree, unlike bindingness, which is categorical.

*'In point', 'follow', 'not follow', 'distinguish', 'explain', and related terms*

A precedent is said to be 'in point'[1] when the issue (or an issue) in that case is the same as the issue (or an issue) in the case to be

1 The term 'on all fours' is also sometimes used.

decided (the 'instant case'). This means that the material facts, at an appropriate level of generality, are the same[1].

Either a case is in point or it is not (although this has to be decided in each instance, and inevitably the decision involves a discretion). If it is in point, then, depending upon the relationship of the two courts, it may be binding (in which case the judge may be said to be required to 'follow' it). If it is not, it cannot be binding, though it may be persuasive (in which case, the judge may choose either to follow it, or not to follow it).

A judge who decides a precedent is not in point is said to 'distinguish' it[2]. There is more than one way of distinguishing. There may be a factor in the rule or principle of the precedent which is absent in the instant case. On the other hand, there may be a significant factor in the instant case which was absent in the precedent. The latter form is sometimes called 'restrictive distinguishing', because its effect may be to restrict the width of the *ratio* of the precedent, whether by creating an exception, or more generally.

In addition to the limited repertoire of basic responses represented by 'follow', 'not follow' and 'distinguish', there are a number of variations such as 'apply', 'approve', 'disapprove', 'doubt', 'consider', and 'overrule'. These are also used by editors of law reports and others. They are broadly self-explanatory, although no official definitions exist[3]. For example, 'disapprove' and 'doubt' fall short of 'overruling' (and might be used where the court in the instant case could not overrule). 'Consider' may imply no particular attitude was taken, or that the person using the term does not wish to commit himself to a view.

'Explain' is of a slightly different nature. It is used where the judge in the instant case thinks the *ratio* of the precedent insufficiently clear, so he cannot decide the appropriate response to it until he has elucidated it. Thus, 'explain' is likely to be used in combination with any other term.

On occasion, judges have certainly resorted to restrictive distinguishing and interpreting a *ratio* in a precedent excessively narrowly to avoid applying a precedent. However, distinguishing is

---

1 Some commentators are keen to insist that it is the issues which are compared, and that material facts are but part of this, for example, *The Laws of Scotland: Stair Memorial Encyclopaedia* vol 22, para 344; DM Walker *The Scottish Legal System* (8th edn, 2001) especially p 465. With respect, this appears to ignore the question of the appropriate level of generality.

2 That is, he finds it distinctly different, not that he finds it an admirable case.

3 See, however, the list of meanings given in each volume of *The Digest* (formerly *English and Empire Digest*) (3rd edn) in relation to English law.

not itself improper. It is an essential part of the operation of
. . . . . . . . . . . .t.

*. . . osition in the hierarchy of courts*

. . . courts are in one triangular hierarchy, and criminal courts in
a similar, separate, one. There is a vertical dimension to these hierarchies in that some courts are 'above' others, and a horizontal one
in that there will be one final court at the apex, but many courts at
lower levels. The vertical dimension is created by the possibility of
appeals and other factors (including special provision for cases of
major importance). This dimension is important because not only
may higher courts be able to overrule lower ones, but also, even
when not overruling, higher courts send out stronger signals to
lower courts and other users of the law as to what the law is on a
given issue. The horizontal dimension is created by the need for
multiple local points of entry to the system but not to have
competing final courts of appeal. This dimension is important
because there are relationships in the hierarchy other than 'above'
and 'below'. There is also a possible relationship between the two
hierarchies, and with courts outside the hierarchy, in other legal
systems.

The hierarchy is not entirely simple. The Court of Session is
above any sheriff court, although their jurisdiction is remarkably
similar. Within the Court of Session, the Inner House is in some
sense above the Outer House, for it hears appeals from it, but the
court is a collegiate court and Courts of Five Judges (or other odd
number) may be convened[1]. It is difficult to say in hierarchical
terms what the relationship between the Outer House and sheriffs
is succinctly. The relationship between the House of Lords and the
Privy Council (newly revivified by devolution) is not entirely clear,
though they have a common membership.

Also, while civil and criminal courts are separate, there may be
cross-reference of precedents. For example, whether a certain
action is theft may depend upon who owned the item, which is a
question of the law of property.

Further, it is difficult to fit the European Court of Human
Rights into the hierarchy at all. By the Human Rights Act 1998,
s 2, courts determining cases involving 'Convention rights' (see

1 As membership of the Divisions of the Inner House was enlarged from four to
  five in 2002, it may be that the smallest augmented court is now a Court of Seven
  Judges.

Chapter 3) must 'take into account' all decisions of that court (and of the former European Commission on Human Rights).

It is equally difficult to fit the European Court of Justice in. It must effectively be seen as above any Scottish court in matters of Community law, for preliminary references to it under article 234 (ex article 177) TEC are binding, and where one is not made, that court's interpretations must be followed.

Further, English cases, which are clearly outside the hierarchy, are frequently cited in Scottish cases.

Nevertheless, for the purposes of *stare decisis*, it can be said that certain courts are above, at the same level, or below, or in a different hierarchy from, certain others.

*The interplay of precedents in point and the hierarchy of courts*

The basic principles can be stated in the following propositions:

(*a*) a precedent which is distinguished cannot bind, regardless of whether it comes from a court above, on the same level or below, and the question of following therefore does not arise;

(*b*) a precedent which is in point, if it comes from a court above (which includes the European Court of Justice and, effectively, the European Court of Human Rights), binds and it must therefore be followed;

(*c*) a precedent which is in point, if it comes from a court at the same level, is effectively binding if both courts are high in the hierarchy, and therefore is very likely to be followed, but does not bind if both courts are low in the hierarchy, and therefore may be followed or not followed, depending upon its persuasiveness;

(*d*) a precedent which is in point, if it comes from a court below (or from any court in another hierarchy), cannot bind, and therefore may be followed or not followed, depending upon its persuasiveness.

In all cases, however, the orthodoxy is that a single precedent cannot bind, only a series of consistent decisions.

*Exceptional cases where a precedent is not binding*

There are exceptional cases where a precedent, although apparently in point and from a higher court (or one of the same level where such a precedent appears to bind) and therefore seemingly binding, will be taken not to be binding.

Firstly, where the precedent has been overtaken by legislation (Community, United Kingdom or Scots), it is no longer to be applied.

Secondly, where the precedent is *'per incuriam'* it is not binding. This means that it was laid down by a court which had not considered all the relevant law, and had therefore come to an erroneous conclusion. Thus, in *Mitchell v Mackersy* (1905) 8 F 198, 13 SLT 570, the Inner House overruled its own decision in *Gray's Trustees v Royal Bank of Scotland* (1895) 23 R 199, 3 SLT 168, on the ground that it had been decided without reference to the House of Lords' decision in *Globe Insurance Co v Mackenzie* (1850) 7 Bell App 296, 22 SJ 625. The *per incuriam* rule is rarely applied, however.

Thirdly, age and defective reporting may render a precedent not binding. It is said that mere age of itself is insufficient, and ancient cases are relied upon from time to time. For example, *William Duncan v Town of Arbroath* (1668) Mor 10075 was explicitly followed in *Jacksons (Edinburgh) v Constructors John Brown* 1965 SLT 37[1]. Indeed, age might demonstrate consistent application and thus the fundamental nature of the principle the case embodies. However, because the doctrine of precedent only grew up in the 19th century, there is something odd about using 18th-century or even earlier cases as precedents (rather than as illustrations of a long consistent principle of law)[2]. In any case, they may disclose no clear *ratio*, and the form of the report of the case may be unclear or its contents suspect. Nevertheless, in *Morgan Guaranty Trust Co v Lothian Regional Council* 1995 SLT 299, cases of 1959 and 1975 were overruled but a case of 1733 (*Stirling v Earl of Lauderdale* Mor 2930) was approved, along with the conclusions of Bankton[3], for the proposition that whether or not money was paid under a mistake of law or of fact, it must be repaid, unless it was a gift. A determined court may go a long way to examine alternative reports and other records of an ancient case, as the House of

---

1 And thus a case about a hirer's liability for damage to a machine decided in part by reference to the Arbroath magistrate's liability for cannon buried in the sand to avoid capture by the English army.
2 See Styles 'Antique Judgments and Modern Judges' 1989 SLT (News) 393, examining *American Express v Royal Bank of Scotland (No 2)* 1989 SLT 650 in which the Lord Ordinary (Dervaird) felt bound to follow a mid-18th century Court of Session decision *Gordon v Murray* (1765) Mor 16818.
3 The institutional writer: see ch 4.

Lords did in *Wills'Trustees v Cairngorm Canoeing and Sailing School Ltd* 1976 SC(HL) 30, 1976 SLT 162, where *Grant v Duke of Gordon* (1781) Mor 12820, 2 Pat 582 was considered.

Fourthly, a precedent may be robbed of authority where a court decides that the maxim *'cessante ratione legis, cessat ipsa lex'* applies. The phrase means 'where the reason for a law ceases to exist, so does the law itself'. Clearly, this could be a device to run a coach and horses through the doctrine of precedent, and its application is in practice limited and rare. Indeed, it has been doubted whether courts ever do apply the maxim, apparent cases being in fact examples of courts' non-binding precedents which failed to persuade, or of common law overruled by legislation, or of *obiter dicta* etc. A clear example of its use, however, is *Commerzbank AG v Large* 1977 SC 375, 1977 SLT 219, in which the Inner House rejected the House of Lords' decision in *Hyslops v Gordon* (1824) Shaw's Appeals 451 that judgments for money must be expressed in sterling. In the opinion of the court, at 328, 'the case of *Hyslops*, decided as it was in the context of conditions which no longer apply, does not now bind this court. We are accordingly free to consider, in the context of the age of floating currencies and rapidly fluctuating exchange rates, the true objectives of our law . . .'.

*Persuasiveness*

Decisions which do not bind may nevertheless be persuasive. In other words, a judge may choose to apply the *ratio* of the precedent, even though he need not. *Obiter dicta* may also be persuasive.

Persuasiveness, unlike bindingness, is not categorical, but is a matter of degree. Various factors, which are difficult to disentangle, influence persuasiveness. The fundamental factor is perhaps how well decided the precedent seems to be: does the rule or principle applied seem a good one, emerging out of the existing law on the subject? This in turn depends on other factors. These include how convincingly the judges in the precedent have expressed themselves, but also upon how well respected those judges are, how high in the hierarchy the decision was taken, whether it was unanimous or not, and the subsequent judicial history of the precedent, that is whether intervening judges have approved it, doubted it, distinguished it, or otherwise.

# THE SYSTEM IN PRACTICE – THE CIVIL COURTS

Subject to the exceptional cases just dealt with, in which an otherwise binding precedent does not bind, *stare decisis* operates in the civil courts as follows.

**Sheriff courts.** Sheriff courts are local civil courts with a local appeal to the sheriff principal. Appeals direct to the Inner House or from appeal to the sheriff principal are possible in many cases, but are rare, and each sheriffdom forms its own small hierarchy. Thus, a sheriff (including a sheriff principal) is bound to follow precedents from: the sheriff principal of his sheriffdom (if he is not sheriff principal); the Inner House, or any Court of Five or more Judges[1]; the Outer House, possibly[2]; the House of Lords; and the Privy Council (on devolution issues). The sheriff court is also bound by preliminary references and the case law of the European Court of Justice in respect of Community law, and s 2 of the Human Rights Act 1998 requiring it to take into account the case law of the European Court of Human Rights in relevant cases.

**The Court of Session.** The Court of Session is a collegiate court. Its judges (and their decisions) are therefore judges (and decisions) of the court as a whole. Appeals from Lords Ordinary to the Inner House are called reclaiming motions, whereby a larger bench reconsiders the decision of the single judge. Questions of difficulty or importance, or ones where (rarely) a Division is equally divided, have traditionally been heard by a Court of Five or more Judges[3] or even the Whole Court, although this is most

---

1 See n 3 below.
2 In *Jessop v Stevenson* 1987 SCCR 655 the High Court of Justiciary decided that a decision of a single High Court judge in a trial bound a sheriff. In *Cromarty Leasing v Turnbull* 1988 SLT (Sh Ct) 62 Sheriff Wilkinson held, by parity of reasoning, that in civil matters an Outer House judge bound a sheriff, and Sheriff Principal Ireland has said 'I have to accept [Jessop] as binding upon me': see 1990 SCLR 388. However, Sheriff Stoddart in *Farrell v Farrell* 1990 SCLR 717 took a different view.
3 As noted above, because the Divisions of the Inner House were expanded from four judges to five in 2002, it may be that the smallest augmented court will now be of 7. Larger courts, sometimes referred to as 'Full' or 'Fuller Courts', of Seven Judges or more (typically one Division with three judges from the other) have been used in the past. For recent examples of Courts of Five Judges before the expansion, see *Cullen v Cullen* 2000 SC 395, 2000 SLT 540 (concerning legal aid) and *MT v DT* 2000 SLT 1442, 2000 SCLR 1057 (concerning child witnesses).

unlikely[1]. There is therefore no straightforward hierarchy. There is also a lack of precedent on how *stare decisis* operates in a number of relationships. Nevertheless, broadly speaking, higher courts bind lower, and larger bind smaller, and the position appears as follows:

(a) a Lord Ordinary is bound to apply precedents from: the Inner House and any Court of Five or more Judges[2]; the House of Lords.

(b) a Division of the Inner House is bound to apply precedents from: either Division of the Inner House in all probability, for although the Inner House has never specifically pronounced on the matter, neither Division has departed from such a precedent for more than 50 years; a Court of Five or more Judges[3]; the House of Lords.

(c) a Court of Five or more Judges is bound by precedents from: another Court of the same or greater number of judges, in all probability[4] the House of Lords.

The Court of Session is also bound by preliminary rulings and the case law of the European Court of Justice in respect of Community law, and the Human Rights Act 1998, s 2 requiring it to take into account the case law of the European Court of Human Rights in relevant cases.

**The House of Lords.** The Appellate Committee of the House of Lords is the apex of the hierarchy of Scottish civil courts, and those of England and Wales, and of Northern Ireland (save, in all cases, in relation to devolution cases[5]). This raises three problems in relation to *stare decisis*, namely: whether a precedent laid down in a case appealed to the House of Lords from one hierarchy binds courts in another; whether the House of Lords binds itself; and what is the relationship between the Appellate Committee of the House of Lords and the Judicial Committee of the Privy Council.

(a) *House of Lords precedents from other United Kingdom hierarchies.* It is unclear how far precedents from one hierarchy in the United Kingdom bind courts in another hierarchy. This is partly because there are nowadays few appeals to the House of Lords

1 The Whole Court has not been convened since *Bell v Bell* 1940 SC 229, and the larger size of the court and greater pressure of business make it unlikely that it will ever be again.
2 See n 3 above.
3 See n 3 above.
4 See *The Laws of Scotland: Stair Memorial Encyclopaedia* vol 22, para 289.
5 Note the impending changes referred to in Appendix Part I to the Preface.

from Scotland so the occasion for pronouncement does not arise, and partly because the vagueness of rules not 'in fixed verbal form' makes it difficult to know what the *ratio* of a case is, and easy to evade taking an unequivocal decision. The House of Lords has in the past shown a propensity to modify Scots law to conform to English[1], and the Scottish courts willingly to acquiesce[2]. Also, it is remarkable how commonly English precedents are cited in Scottish decisions, even in some central areas of law such as delict and how, for example, the law of negligence has developed in common in Scotland and England out of *Donoghue v Stevenson* 1932 SC(HL) 31, 1932 SLT 317.

The matter was discussed by Lord Normand in the House of Lords in *Glasgow Corporation v Central Land Board* 1956 SC(HL) 1, 1956 SLT 41, and by Lord Justice-Clerk Wheatley in the Inner House in *Dalgleish v Glasgow Corporation* 1976 SC 32. Four propositions as to the authority of House of Lords decisions in Scots courts can be distinguished:

(i) Judgments on questions of Scots common law are binding on Scottish courts.

(ii) Judgments upon questions of English (or Northern Irish) common law are not binding upon Scottish courts. However, there are exceptions, dealt with as the third and fourth situations (and there may be further exceptions[3]).

(iii) Judgments upon questions where Scots and English (or Northern Irish) common law are the same, are probably binding on Scottish courts. However, the problem in such cases is likely to be whether the common law is in fact the same[4].

---

1 The most memorable example is the words of Lord Cranworth in *Bartonshill Coal v Reid* (1858) 3 Macq 266 at 285, where he said, apparently without irony, 'But if such be the law of England, on what ground can it be argued not to be the law of Scotland?'.

2 In *Virtue v Commissioners of Police of Alloa* (1874) 1 R 285 a Court of Seven Judges split 4:3 on whether they were bound by House of Lords' decisions in English cases. The majority, including both Lord President Inglis and Lord Justice-Clerk Moncrieff, thought they were. Some of the minority might have agreed, but were of the opinion that the English case could be distinguished, so the issue did not arise for them.

3 See references to the Exchequer jurisdiction in *The Laws of Scotland: Stair Memorial Encyclopaedia* vol 22, para 282.

4 This was part of the problem in the split decision in *Virtue v Commissioners of Police of Alloa* (1874) 1 R 285. See also the history of the law of occupiers' liability, as recounted in Smith 'The Full Circle: the Law of Occupiers' Liability in Scotland' in TB Smith *Studies Critical and Comparative* (1962) p 154.

(vi) Judgments upon questions of the interpretation of Great Britain or United Kingdom legislation are probably binding upon Scottish courts (although the principle may not extend to criminal legislation).

(b) *How far the House of Lords binds itself.* Lower courts do not bind themselves. For example, sheriffs are not bound by other sheriffs (save their own sheriff principal). Higher courts may bind themselves. For example, the Inner House has never explicitly said it is bound to do so, but in practice Divisions follow their own judgments and those of the other Division. If the Inner House is contemplating departing from a judgment of one of its Divisions, then a larger court is convened. The House of Lords is the highest court, and the arguments that it should bind itself are most powerful. As a final court of appeal sending the strongest signals to other courts, it would sow confusion by changing its mind. But also, by virtue of its finality, the conflict between the certainty of precedent and need for justice in the individual case will be most acute.

In the 19th century, the arguments for certainty prevailed. After many years in which it was the undeclared practice, in an English case, *London Street Tramways v London County Council* [1898] AC 375, the House of Lords declared itself bound by its own precedents (subject to an exception in relation to cases decided *per incuriam*, for which, see above), and this has always been taken to apply both to the common law and to the construction and interpretation of statutes. The position was never declared in relation to Scots law. It cannot seriously be doubted to have been the same, however[1].

In the succeeding half of the century, particularly because of the enormous social changes, this position became irksome. In 1966, the Lord Chancellor issued a Practice Direction[2] concerning judicial precedent. This reiterated the desirability of certainty, but admitted that 'too rigid adherence to [it] may lead to injustice in a particular case' and might 'unduly restrict the proper development of the law'. It then declared that their Lordships 'propose to . . . depart from a previous decision when it appears right to do so', but

---

1 See, however, *First Programme of the Scottish Law Commission* (SLC 1, 1976) para 18: *The Laws of Scotland: Stair Memorial Encyclopaedia* vol 22, para 283 suggests it was this publication which precipitated the Practice Direction.
2 [1966] 1 WLR 1234, [1966] 3 All ER 77. A Practice Direction is an administrative rule on the running of the courts. Not the least interesting aspect of this change is that it was effected by a mere Practice Direction.

'would bear in mind the danger of disturbing retrospectively . . . contracts, settlements of property and fiscal arrangements . . .'.

As this guarded wording prefigured, the House of Lords has rarely used its new power. There have been less than a dozen cases, and only one in a Scottish appeal[1], that is, *Dick v Burgh of Falkirk* 1976 SC(HL) 1, where it overruled *Darling v Gray* (1892) 19 R(HL) 31. There is no clear policy behind these few cases, but attempts have been made to isolate relevant factors[2].

Thus, the House of Lords is bound by precedents from the House of Lords itself, subject to its power to depart from them under the 1966 Practice Direction.

(c) *What the relationship between the Appellate Committee of the House of Lords and the Judicial Committee of the Privy Council is.* The Appellate Committee and the Judicial Committee cannot both be at the apex of the hierarchy of courts. Since there is no point in making the Judicial Committee of the Privy Council the ultimate authority on devolution issues if the Appellate Committee of the House of Lords could overrule it, presumably, it will not.

The House of Lords is also bound by preliminary references and the case law of the European Court of Justice in respect of Community law, and s 2 of the Human Rights Act 1998 which requires it to take into account the case law of the European Court of Human Rights in relevant cases.

**Judicial Committee of the Privy Council.** The Judicial Committee of the Privy Council is the final authority on 'devolution issues'[3]. Its decisions on such issues must therefore be binding on all other courts.

Since devolution issues are statutory matter, not common law, and the statute in United Kingdom legislation, there is unlikely to be a problem of using precedents arising in one jurisdiction in another. How far it binds itself is not clear, but since it has not claimed to, and draws upon the same personnel as the Appellate Committee of the House of Lords, it can be expected to take a similar line to that court if the question arises[4]. Since it has the role

---

1 Paterson, Bates and Poustie *Legal System of Scotland: Cases and Materials* (4th edn, 1999) p 431 estimate that, since 1966, it has been asked to reverse one of its precedents once or twice a year and, between 1996 and 1983, actually did so in nine cases (on average about once every three years). Since 1966, the House of Lords has heard over 2,000 cases (though few of them Scottish appeals).

2 See, for example, *The Laws of Scotland: Stair Memorial Encyclopedia* vol 22, para 285.

3 Note the impending changes referred to in Appendix Part I to the Preface.

4 This may not be soon. By early 2003, of the dozen devolution issue cases heard by the Privy Council, only one was not criminal.

of final court of appeal in relation to devolution issues, it cannot be bound by the House of Lords on such an issue.

The Privy Council is bound by preliminary references and the case law of the European Court of Justice in respect of Community law, and s 2 of the Human Rights Act 1998 which requires it to take into account the case law of the European Court of Human Rights in relevant cases.

**Civil courts of special jurisdiction.** Several courts of special jurisdiction exist, such as the Land Court and the Restrictive Practices Court. In general, these courts are not bound by their own precedents (and bind no other court), but are bound by precedents of the Inner House, to which appeals from them go; by those of the House of Lords; and also, in relation to Community law, by preliminary references and the case law of the European Court of Justice, and s 2 of the Human Rights Act 1998 which requires it to take into account the case law of the European Court of Human Rights in relevant cases.

**Precedents from another jurisdiction.** Precedents from English courts are frequently cited in Scottish courts, for instance in cases on delict, where the law is largely common law in both jurisdictions. Those from some other common law jurisdictions such as Australia, Canada, New Zealand and the United States are cited occasionally. Thus, in *Morgan Guaranty Trust Co v Lothian Regional Council* 1995 SLT 299 decisions from superior courts in Australia, Canada, and South Africa were mentioned by Lord President Hope as 'instructive'. Despite the apparent parallel of Scots law with other mixed systems, such as South Africa, precedents from such jurisdictions are not frequent.

All are in the same position in that, coming from a different jurisdiction, they cannot bind Scottish courts (save that decisions of the House of Lords on the construction and interpretation of Great Britain or United Kingdom legislation are likely to be regarded as binding), though they may be persuasive. In any case, in judicial decisions and legal textbooks not only are English cases often cited, but often without specific warning that they do not determine Scots law. The issue is clouded by the complexities of the position of the House of Lords.

In relation to Community law, special considerations arise, as such law with direct effect is intended to have the same meaning throughout the European Community. Thus, decisions of the European Court of Justice and the Court of First Instance bind United Kingdom courts, and decisions of courts in other member states may be cited. However, precedent does not operate in Community law in the way it does in United Kingdom law, and the position of the European Court of Justice is dealt with below.

In relation to 'human rights' cases other special considerations apply, for decisions of the European Court of Human Rights are required to be taken into account, and decisions from courts of other countries applying the European Convention on Human Rights and like documents are inevitably and frequently cited. The position of the European Court of Human Rights is looked at specifically below.

## THE SYSTEM IN PRACTICE – TRIBUNALS

There are many tribunals, such as those for certain employment cases and for immigration cases. Commonly they form small ad hoc hierarchies in order to allow appeal within each tribunal system, for example, from Employment Tribunal to the Employment Appeal Tribunal, and from immigration adjudicator to the Immigration Appeal Tribunal. Tribunals do not bind themselves, but decisions of an appeal tribunal effectively bind the lower tribunal.

From most tribunal systems, there is appeal on a point of law to the Inner House, and thereafter to the House of Lords, (for example, from the Employment Appeal Tribunal). In any case, all tribunals are bound by the law laid down by the Inner House and House of Lords.

Most tribunals operate on a Great Britain or United Kingdom basis (although the Employment Appeal Tribunal sits in Scotland and England separately, with a Scottish or English judge presiding, as appropriate). Most of the law applied by tribunals is common to the whole of Great Britain or the United Kingdom, and many more decisions are taken by them in England and Wales, so decisions of the English Court of Appeal and of the House of Lords in English decisions arising out of tribunal cases are very persuasive[1].

In relation to Community law, tribunals are also bound by preliminary references and the case law of the European Court of

---

1 In *Brown v Rentokil Ltd* 1992 IRLR 302, Lord Mayfield, sitting in the Employment Appeal Tribunal, said 'this court, being part of a United Kingdom body in the field of employment law, would only depart from an opinion of the Court of Appeal on a matter which was purely related to an aspect of Scots law. Accordingly, we find [a certain decision of that court] binding upon us'.

Justice, and s 2 of the Human Rights Act 1998 which requires them to take into account the case law of the European Court of Human Rights in relevant cases.

## THE SYSTEM IN PRACTICE – THE CRIMINAL COURTS

Precedent is considered to apply less rigidly in the criminal courts, in the interests of the individualisation of criminal justice. On the other hand, criminal cases may turn upon civil court precedents. For example, whether or not an act is theft may depend upon ownership and thus the law of property. Subject to these points, and to the exceptional cases in which otherwise binding precedents do not bind, *stare decisis* operates in the criminal courts in the following fashion.

**The district court.** District courts deal with minor local crime. Most cases turn upon the facts, so questions of law rarely arise. Appeal is to the High Court sitting as an appeal court, and there is no further appeal, save to the Privy Council on a devolution issue. District courts are bound by precedents from: a sheriff possibly[1]; the High Court of Justiciary as a trial court probably[2]; the High Court of Justiciary as an appeal court; and the Privy Council on a devolution issue.

In relation to Community law, the district court is also bound by preliminary references and the case law of the European Court of Justice, and s 2 of the Human Rights Act 1998 which requires it to take into account the case law of the European Court of Human Rights in relevant cases.

**The sheriff court.** Sheriff courts are local criminal courts dealing with the middle range of crime. Appeal is to the High Court sitting as an appeal court (called the Court of Criminal Appeal), and there is no further appeal, save to the Privy Council on a devolution issue. It used to be orthodox to say that a sheriff was not bound by the High Court sitting as a trial court (with which it has a considerably overlapping jurisdiction). However, in *Jessop v Stevenson* 1987 SCCR 655, the High Court, sitting as an

---

1 This is asserted by DM Walker *Scottish Legal System* (8th edn, 2001) p 447, but no authority is offered. *The Laws of Scotland: Stair Memorial Encyclopaedia* vol 22 is silent. There is a certain parity of reasoning with the position of the sheriff and the High Court as a trial court.
2 By a parity of reasoning with the position of the sheriff court.

appeal court from a sheriff's decision, held that sheriffs were bound by it sitting as a trial court. This was controversial, but the High Court has taken no steps to retreat from it. Sheriffs are thus bound by precedents from the High Court of Justiciary as a trial court and as an appeal court; and the Privy Council on a devolution issue.

In relation to Community law, the sheriff court is also bound by preliminary references and the case law of the European Court of Justice, and s 2 of the Human Rights Act 1998 which requires it to take into account the case law of the European Court of Human Rights in relevant cases.

**The High Court of Justiciary.** The High Court of Justiciary, like the Court of Session, is a collegiate court, so hierarchy does not work within it in a straightforward way. It sits as a trial court with a single judge, trying major crime from anywhere in the country, with a jury. Appeal is to the High Court of Justiciary sitting as an appeal court (often called, without statutory warrant, the Court of Criminal Appeal) with two judges for sentencing appeals and three, or occasionally more, for appeals against conviction. There is no further appeal, save to the Privy Council on a devolution issue. Thus, the High Court of Justiciary, sitting as a trial court, is bound by precedents from the High Court of Justiciary sitting as an appeal court. The High Court of Justiciary sitting as an appeal court, is bound by precedents from the High Court of Justiciary sitting as an appeal court with a bench of similar size, or larger.

A larger court may be formed to overrule a precedent which has been found unacceptable or otherwise clarify the law. Formerly such occasions were rare. In *Sugden v HM Advocate* 1934 JC 103 and *Kirkwood v HM Advocate* 1939 JC 36, 'Whole Courts' of 12 (the full bench, less the Lord Justice-Clerk) in the former case, and 11 (the full bench, less the Lord Justice-General and Lord Pitman) in the latter were convened[1]. In *Sugden*, they were to overrule a decision of five judges in *HM Advocate v Macgregor* (1773) Mor 11146 that a prosecution could not be raised 20 years after the presumed date of the crime, and in *Kirkwood* they reviewed precedents from smaller benches on the significance for sentencing of a plea of diminished responsibility. Such 'Whole Courts' are unlikely

---

1 The 'Haill Fifteen' of the original Court of Session was reduced to 13 in 1830 (though restored to 15 in 1948, and subsequently more than doubled). Thus, in the 1930s, only 13 judges were available to act as Lords Commissioners of Justiciary.

ever to be convened again, as there are more judges and more pressures on judges' time.

However, smaller augmented courts have become more frequent in recent years[1]. A court of five judges revisited diminished responsibility in *Galbraith v HM Advocate (No 2)* 2001 SLT 953 to consider whether a lengthy period of physical abuse could justify that plea. A court of nine judges was used in *McCutcheon v HM Advocate* 2002 SLT 27 to overrule a decision of seven judges concerning cross-examination in *Morrison v HM Advocate* 1990 JC 299, 1991 SLT 57, 1990 SCCR 235. The request to convene a larger court is the more persuasive if made by counsel for both parties, as in *McFadyen v Annan* 1992 SCCR 186, where counsel for the appellant and the Advocate Depute in a case of oppression requested that the case of *Tudhope v McCarthy* 1985 JC 48 should be reconsidered. The interval between the reviewing and reviewed judgments is usually much less than the 160 years in *Sugden*. An extreme example, though on statutory interpretation, is *Elliott v HM Advocate* 1995 SLT 612 where, on 24 March 1995, five judges met and overruled the decision on 10 February 1995 of three judges in *Church v HM Advocate* 1995 SLT 604.

In relation to Community law, the High Court is bound by preliminary references and by the case law of the European Court of Justice, and s 2 of the Human Rights Act 1998 which requires it to take into account the case law of the European Court of Human Rights in relevant cases.

**Judicial Committee of the Privy Council.** The Judicial Committee of the Privy Council is the final authority on 'devolution issues' in criminal matters, as in civil[2]. Its decisions on such issues must therefore be equally binding on all other courts (subject to the less rigid application of precedent in criminal cases).

As noted in relation to the Privy Council in civil matters, since devolution issues are statutory matter, not common law, and the statute is United Kingdom legislation, there is unlikely to be a problem of using precedents arising in one jurisdiction in another. The question of whether the court binds itself is more of an innovation in criminal matters, for no appeal from the High Court was possible until the Privy Council acquired its devolution issue juris-

---

1 A court of five judges was used in *HM Advocate v Al-Megrahi (No 4)* 2002 JC 99, 2002 SCCR 1433, the appeal from the Lockerbie Trial, but this was a unique occasion, for the trial had been before three judges and no jury.
2 Note the impending changes referred to in Appendix Part I to the Preface.

diction. Nevertheless, no doubt it remains that the court can be expected to take a similar line as the House of Lords does if the question arises.

The Privy Council is bound by preliminary references and the case law of the European Court of Justice in respect of Community law, and s 2 of the Human Rights Act 1998 which requires it to take into account the case law of the European Court of Human Rights in relevant cases.

**Precedents from another jurisdiction.** Precedents from courts in another jurisdiction are essentially in the same position as in relation to civil matters, save that House of Lords' decisions in English cases on the construction and interpretation of legislation are likely to be regarded as persuasive only, as there is no appeal to the House of Lords in criminal cases from Scotland.

## PRECEDENT AND THE EUROPEAN COURT OF JUSTICE

The European Court of Justice and Court of First Instance do not readily fit into the hierarchy of courts. There is no appeal to them from any court, nor appeal from them (although there may be appeal from the CFI to the ECJ).

The ECJ is, however, the guardian of Community law, and by virtue of article 234 (ex article 177) TEC any court may, and final courts of appeal must (subject to the *acte clair*[1] doctrine), remit to it questions of the validity or interpretation of Community law for a preliminary reference. Also, by virtue of s 3 of the European Communities Act 1972, any such question, if not referred under article 234 (ex article 177), must be decided by any United Kingdom court 'in accordance with the principles laid down by and any relevant decision of' the European Court of Justice. This means on the one hand that Scottish courts must in effect follow precedents of that court, and on the other, that a Scottish precedent, in point and otherwise binding, may have to be ignored.

Decisions of the European Court of Justice are, in United Kingdom terms, strictly speaking questions of the construction and interpretation of legislation rather than precedent on the common law model. Firstly, however, a form of precedent operates in relation to the construction and interpretation of legislation, for courts in practice use the decisions of earlier courts as a principal

---

1 Where the Community provision is so clear it does not need interpretation.

means of determining the meaning of legislation, often in preference to the actual words of the legislation. Secondly, the European Court of Justice has developed certain 'general principles of law common to all Member States' which it requires to be applied to any decision on Community law. It has thus generated something approaching a Community law doctrine of precedent, as is evident from cases such as Cases 28–30/62 *Da Costa en Schaake NV and Others v Nederlandse Belastingadministratie* [1963] ECR 31 and Case 283/81 *Srl CILFIT and Another v Ministry of Health* [1982] ECR 4315.

On the other hand, the European Court of Justice has decided, for example, in Case 4/69 *Alfons Lüttike GmbH v EC Commission* [1971] ECR 325, that it is not actually bound by its own decisions. This is because it sees itself as an instrument of the evolution of Community policy. In fact it is sometimes not clear whether the court is following or not following precedent. It does not cite other cases in its judgments, even when relying on them or when consciously rejecting them. The problem is aggravated by the fact that only a single judgment is given, which may reflect a compromise between several lines of reasoning, making it difficult to determine what principles are being applied. The Advocate General's opinion is printed with the judgment, and is able to avoid many of these difficulties. Thus, it is often cited as a form of precedent, though it lacks authority.

There is, in United Kingdom terms, no developed concept of *ratio decidendi* in the operation of Community law, and thus no clear operation of *stare decisis*. Thus, the ECJ and CFI are not bound by precedent in the English and Scottish sense.

## PRECEDENT AND THE EUROPEAN COURT OF HUMAN RIGHTS

The European Court of Human Rights fits even less well into the hierarchy of courts than does the European Court of Justice, for not only is there no appeal to it from United Kingdom courts, nor any appeal from it, there is not even an equivalent of article 234 (ex article 177) TEC for preliminary rulings.

On the other hand, it is the authoritative interpreter of the European Convention on Human Rights, the contents of the ECHR are enacted as 'Convention rights' by the Human Rights Act 1998, and s 2 of that Act requires its decisions to be taken into account by United Kingdom courts when deciding cases on Convention rights. Thus, its decisions in some sense are binding upon the United Kingdom courts. However, there is a notion of 'margin of appreciation'. This means that the Court accepts that the articles of the ECHR cannot be applied mechanically to national situations, and a democratically elected government has some room for manoeuvre in balancing opposing interests and taking account of national conditions. There is not necessarily 'a uniform European conception of morals'[1].

However, while the Court strives for consistency, it cannot be said to bind itself. Indeed, there are a number of complicating factors in determining whether it has actually been consistent. The articles of the ECHR are generally brief[2], and even the most specific is drafted in the form of a principle rather than a rule[3]. In any case, it is expressly asserted that the ECHR is 'a living instrument ... which must be interpreted in the light of present-day conditions'[4], that is, it is (according to taste) either 'dynamic' or simply 'mutable'.

Clearly, the European Court of Human Rights is not bound by precedent in the English and Scottish sense, either.

## LAW REPORTS

Any system of precedent relies upon efficient law reporting. Unless the decisions in at least the most important cases, and the reasoning which produced them, are readily available, no doctrine of *stare decisis* can operate.

Law reporting also exists in civil law countries, where precedent is not, generally speaking, accepted as a formal source of law, and where at most a very weak doctrine of *stare decisis* operates. Its role in these countries is rather to illustrate how a code or other enacted law is being understood and applied. The form of law reports reflects this, being often more laconic, and reasoned in a formal stereotyped way in terms of the enacted law with usually no reference to precedents. The form of law reports of European Community law, or from the European Court of Human Rights are, however, far from laconic, though this may reflect the difficulty of a single opinion from a disparate body in the one case, and

---

1 *Handyside v United Kingdom* (1976) A/24, 1 EHRR 737, para 48.
2 Art 3 is simply 'No one shall be subjected to torture or inhuman or degrading treatment'.
3 See arts 5 and 6.
4 *Tyrer v United Kingdom* (1978) A/26, 2 EHRR, para 31.

allowing broad discussion of principle from a disparate body in the other.

Within any common law system there is now so much legislation that law reports now also perform the function of reporting decisions on the construction and interpretation of legislation. Indeed, in many branches of the law it is nowadays difficult to find a report concerned solely with common law.

## Law reporting in Scotland

There has long been some form of reporting in Scotland, for the *Practicks* date to the mid-16th century, and reports intended for wide publication among the legal profession from the 18th. Modern law reporting, that is, full reporting of the judges' actual words, with a view to their use as precedents, is an early 19th-century development, probably a reaction to the increased reliance upon precedent inherent in the growth of precedent as a formal source of law[1].

Curiously, given the fact that precedent relies upon it, law reporting has not been seen as an obligation of government, and (with a few exceptions[2]) was not done by any governmental body. However, in 1999 the Scottish Court Service introduced a new electronic form of reporting[3], and House of Lords judgments since 1996[4] are so available and Privy Council judgments since 1999 (with some earlier ones)[5]. There are roughly equivalent systems operated by the English[6] and Northern Irish[7] Courts Services.

The most authoritative reports are produced by a non-profit-making semi-official body, the Scottish Council of Law Reporting (and in England by a parallel Incorporated Council of Law Reporting), but most reporting is done by commercial legal publishing companies.

1 See, for example, the prefaces to the first edition, and new and enlarged edition (1834) in vol 1 of Shaw's reports. Compare also an early report, such as *Huntar v Huntar* (1573) Mor 16233, which has 30 words only, as follows: 'The tutor dative is maid and gevin be the King, quha may dispose the samin at his awn plesour to ony persoun be his gift theirof under the quarter seill'.
2 For example, Reports of Patent, Design and Trade Mark Cases and Immigration Appeal Reports, published by HMSO.
3 The Scottish Courts website is at www.scotcourts.gov.uk.
4 Through the parliamentary website at www.parliament.uk.
5 The Privy Council website is at www.privy-council.org.uk.
6 The (English) Court Service website is at www.courtservice.gov.uk.
7 The Northern Irish Court Service website is at www.courtsni.gov.uk.

There are some 70 series of law reports published in the United Kingdom. These are of various types. In addition to concentration on Scots law or English law, some aim at relatively rapid comprehensive coverage (such as the Scots Law Times), some at authoritative reporting of major cases from the principal courts (such as Session Cases), some at significant cases in a particular area of law, irrespective of the court or tribunal giving judgment (such as the Scottish Civil Law Reports and Scottish Criminal Case Reports, or focusing on a smaller area, such as the Industrial Case Reports). Nevertheless, it is only a tiny proportion of cases heard by courts and tribunals which is ever considered worthy of reporting.

Most series of reports are concerned with cases decided in England and Wales. However, because so much law is now in legislation, and so much legislation extends over Great Britain or the United Kingdom, such reports may be of value in Scotland.

## Citation of cases

Precedents, like legislation, have citations, that is, references which identify the case and help find a report of it. So far as Scotland is concerned, unlike the position with legislation, there is no 'official' citation of cases, so citations relate not to the case itself, but to the report of it. Thus, while citations uniquely identify reports, any case may, if reported in more than one series of law reports, have several citations, presenting a forbiddingly prolific combination of names, numbers and letters, for example, *Wilsons and Clyde Coal Co v Scottish Insurance Corporation* 1949 SC(HL) 90, 1949 SLT 230, [1949] AC 462, [1949] LJR 1190, 65 TLR 354, 93 SJ 423, [1949] 1 All ER 1068.

The citation of a report refers to the names of the parties, and to the initial page of the report in the appropriate volume of the relevant series of law reports. Recently, there has been a tendency also to include initials to identify the court which heard the case, such as 'OH' for Outer House. Community law case citations also include a case number.

However, in England and Wales, since 2001, there has been introduced an interesting innovation to accommodate the availability of judgments online, which may not (or may not yet) be reported, and for which page numbering is meaningless[1]. This is,

---

1 The English courts now permit use of a print-out of a case instead of a proper report.

the 'neutral citation' a unique official identifying number for the purposes of citation. It is to be used for precedents cited by judges in their opinions, and is to precede any other form of citation (so the other forms remain). The form of neutral citations is familiar, but indicates the year, the court and the case, rather than year, report and page. Thus '2003 EWCA Civ 1' indicates the first case of 2003 from the (England and Wales) Court of Appeal, Civil Division[1]. Further, every judgment is to have numbered paragraphs (the numbers running through the whole judgment, even if there are several judges). Thus, reference is made to a paragraph rather than a page, in the form '[2001] EWCA Civ 10 at [59]'. The paragraph number is bracketed to avoid confusion with page numbers.

*Names*

Cases are usually known by the names of the parties, for example, *Junior Books Ltd v The Veitchi Company Ltd*[2]. These names are often abbreviated (for example, simply to *Junior Books v Veitchi*, or just *Junior Books*). In a case at first instance the pursuer's name comes first, but if the defender appeals, his name may come first. If the parties are acting in a particular capacity this may be recorded in the citation, such as in *Aitken's Trustees v Aitken*[3].

Community law cases present special problems. Their names may be ambiguous, as in *Commission of the European Communities v United Kingdom of Great Britain and Northern Ireland* for there are several cases of that name. Most Community law case names are not in English (and if translated, are not always consistently trans-

---

1 Practice Direction on the Form of Judgments, Paragraph Marking and Neutral Citation of 11 January 2001 ([2001] 1 WLR 194, [2001] 1 All ER 193) and Practice direction – Neutral Citations of 14 January 2002 ([2002] 1 WLR 346, [2002] 1 All ER 351). The full list of abbreviations used in early 2003 were: 'UKPC' for the judicial Committee of the Privy Council; 'UKHL' for the Appellate Committee of the House of Lords; 'EWCA (Civ)'; 'EWCA (Crim)'; EWHC (Ch)' for the Chancery Division; 'EWHC (Pat)' for the Patents Court; 'EWHC (QB)' for the Queen's Bench Division; 'EWHC (Admin)' for the Administrative Court; 'EWHC (Comm)' for the Commercial Court; 'EWHC (Admlty)' for the Admiralty Court; 'EWHC (TCC)' for the Technology and Construction Court; and 'EWHC (Fam)' for the Family Division.
2 1982 SLT 492.
3 1927 SC 374.

lated), so may have abbreviated names, as in *Van Gend en Loos*[1], or unofficial ones, such as the *Isoglucose* case[2]. In any case they are referred to in Community practice by the case number.

A court lawyers' shibboleth[3] requires that the '*v*' is never pronounced 'versus' or '*v*', but 'against', or sometimes (particularly in England) 'and'. The first named party is not necessarily the pursuer, because if the defender loses at first instance and appeals, the names are reversed. Occasionally there is more than one piece of litigation between two parties, in which case it will be referred to with '*No 2*' after the names, for example, *Weir v Jessop*[4] (concerning search of premises) and *Weir v Jessop (No 2)*[5] (concerning entrapment).

There are variations. Where there are reporting restrictions, as with some cases involving children, initials may be used, as with *E v T*[6]. Where procedure is by petition, as with the *nobile officium*, the case may be referred to in the form *McLachlan, Petitioner* (or *Petr*)[7]. Also, because it has been common in Scottish reports to record a married woman's maiden name as well, both may appear in the citation, at least in English-based sets of reports. Indeed, for this reason in the English series called Appeal Cases *Donoghue v Stevenson* 1932 SC(HL) 31 is cited as *M'Alister*[8] *(or Donoghue) v Stevenson* [1932] AC 562, and *Darling v Gray & Sons* (1892) 19 R(HL) 31, as *Wood v Gray & Sons* [1892] AC 576. The married name is politically incorrectly preceded by 'Mrs'.

---

1 This case appears in the official European Court Reports at [1963] ECR 1 as Case 26/62 *NV Algemene Transport en Expeditie Onderneming van Gend en Loos v Nederlandse Administratie der Belastingen* (which means roughly, '*Ghent and Loos General Transport and Export Co Ltd v Dutch Tax Commission*'). In Common Market Law Reports ([1963] CMLR 105) the respondent appears reported in the table of cases as *Nederlandse Belastingadministratie*, and in the body of the volume as *Nederlandse Tariefcommisie*.

2 *Royal Scholter-Honig v Intervention Board* [1977] 2 CMLR 449.

3 '1. The Hebrew word used by Jephthah as a test-word by which to distinguish the fleeing Ephraimites (who could not pronounce the *sh*) from his own men, the Gileadites (Judges xii 4–6), 2. *transf.* **a.** A word used as a test for detecting foreigners, or persons from another district, by their pronunciation . . . **b.** *loosely* A custom, habit, mode of dress or the like, which distinguishes a particular class or set of persons . . . 3. (*fig*) A catchword or formula adopted by a party or sect, by which their adherents or followers may be discerned, or those not their followers may be excluded': *Shorter Oxford English Dictionary*.

4 1991 SCCR 242.

5 1991 SCCR 636.

6 1949 SLT 411.

7 1987 SCCR 195.

8 'M'', is an old-fashioned version of 'Mc'.

In criminal cases, the names used are those of the nominal prosecutor and the accused. With cases heard by solemn procedure the prosecutor is always nominally 'Her Majesty's Advocate'[1], often abbreviated to 'HM Advocate' or simply 'HMA', for example, *HM Advocate v McPhee*[2]. With cases heard by summary procedure, it is the senior procurator fiscal for the sheriff court district, for example, *English v Smith*[3] (Smith being the regional procurator fiscal for Dundee). If the accused is convicted and appeals, the names are again usually reversed, for example, *Khaliq v HM Advocate*[4]. Older criminal cases are commonly cited only by the name of the accused, for example, *John Ballantyne*[5].

Similar conventions apply to English cases, but three variations are worth noting. Criminal cases are cited as '*R*' (i e *Regina* or *Rex*, that is 'Queen' or 'King' respectively), for example, *R v Dudley and Stephens*[6] (pronounced as 'Queen against Dudley and Stephens'). Judicial review cases (where the court reviews a decision of government or a tribunal) are in England technically brought by the Crown ('*R*') against the relevant person, on behalf of ('*ex parte*') the complainer, so are cited as, for example, *R v Secretary of State for the Home Department, ex parte Zamir*[7]. In proceedings where there is not a straightforward action by one person against another, the name of the principal party or other information is preceded by '*Re*' or '*In re*' (meaning 'concerning'), for example, *In re an Arbitration between Polemis and Another and Furness Withy & Co Ltd*[8] (often abbreviated to *Re Polemis*).

### Reference to page, volume and law report

In principle, reference to the page, volume and law report is simple. Basically, the citation normally gives a year, an abbreviation for a series of reports, and a page number (though paragraph numbers are increasingly used instead of page numbers). If a case is cited in several series, there will be several citations. However, there are numerous complications. These are dealt with in relation to each series of reports discussed below.

1 In civil cases, he is referred to as 'Lord Advocate'.
2 1935 JC 46, 1935 SLT 179.
3 1981 SCCR 143.
4 1984 JC 23, 1984 SLT 137, 1983 SCCR 483.
5 (1859) 3 Irv 352.
6 (1884) 14 QBD 273, 15 Cox CC 624.
7 [1980] AC 930.
8 [1921] 3 KB 560.

## Form and content of law reports

The great variety of modern law reports, Scots, English and United Kingdom, have a broadly similar form and content, as described below. Older ones, and European Community ones, are more dissimilar.

*Names of the parties, their roles, and counsel*

Reports commence with the names of the parties abbreviated (for the purpose of citation) and sometimes repeated in full. Their role in the proceedings, such as pursuer, defender, appellant or reclaimer (i e a person appealing from Outer House to Inner House), is explicitly noted in some reports and the names of their counsel, that is, advocates[1]. (Initials are not given where only one advocate of that name is in practice.) The abbreviations 'QC' and 'AD' mean 'Queen's Counsel' and 'Advocate Depute' respectively.

Thus, for example, the first report in Session Cases for 1986 is headed *Walker v Strathclyde Regional Council* and continues:

> William Stafford Walker and Mrs Rosalind Harriet Sneader or Walker, petitioners *Rodger, QC*
> Strathclyde Regional Council, respondents *McFadyean, QC*

*Case number and date*

Beneath the parties' names or in the margin, the case number and date may be noted, for example, 'No 1' and 'Oct 1 1985'.

*Names of judges and court*

Usually beneath the names of the parties, or in the margin, will be noted the names of the judges and the court hearing the case, for example, 'Outer House' and 'Lord Davidson'.

*Catch words*

Under the names of the parties is a series of brief references to certain facts, terms or concepts and questions, and where any

---

1 For the role of advocates in litigation, see below.

question of the construction or interpretation of legislation arises, to such legislation, for example, *'Contract – Heritable property – Sale – Consensus in idem placitum – Whether consensus reached where purported withdrawal of offer verbally communicated between agents of parties – Whether subsequent formal acceptance of offer resulted in bargain being thereby concluded – Whether probative writ withdrawing offer required'*. They are usually italicised or emboldened, and separated by dashes, and if the case concerns several disparate issues, there may be more than one series. There is no official name for them, but they are often referred to as the catch words. Their function is to show at a glance an idea of what legal issues were raised in the case, and they are inserted by the editor of the reports.

## Headnote

After the catch words appears in continuous prose the headnote (sometimes referred to as the 'rubric'). It will contain in it the word *'Held'* (usually italicised), and should be seen as divided into the part before and the part after that word. The part before is a précis of the facts and general argument in the case. The part after is a précis of the decision ('Held' meaning 'decided'). The latter therefore gives what appears to the editor of the reports to be the *ratio decidendi*. However, a headnote is only a précis of the case, and is written by the editor of the report. It is therefore unwise to rely entirely upon it.

A headnote may contain other italicised words, such as *'aff.'* or *'affirmed'*, followed by the name of the court from which the appeal came, and *'opinion per'* a named judge, which indicates a view expressed by that judge alone. It will also record if any judge dissented, usually by giving his name after the italicised abbreviation *'diss.'*, and possibly with some indication of his reasoning. A headnote may also indicate that a precedent cited has been followed, distinguished, approved or otherwise, and end with the decision, such as 'appeal dismissed'.

Where a case covers more than one distinct set of legal issues, there may be more than one distinct headnote.

## Recital of facts and procedure and argument of counsel

More authoritative reports contain a recital of relevant facts, and of the procedure which brought the case to that court, and an abbreviated account of the arguments deployed by counsel[1]. This may be several pages long, and possibly longer than the actual judgment. It may explain why the dispute took the form it did. For example, one party may have conceded certain issues, which therefore do not have to be argued. Thus, it may throw light upon the breadth of the ratio decidendi or its persuasiveness.

Sometimes the report simply records that the facts are as described by the judge.

## Cases and legislation cited

Some reports list the cases referred to by the judges in their judgments, and sometimes others cited by counsel in argument. Legislation referred to is often quoted in a footnote.

## Opinions

The body of the report is formed by the opinion of the court, or separate opinions, where the judges have delivered them, preceded by their names (sometimes in the form 'Lord Davidson's opinion'). These are in the judges' own words, and are not written by the editor of the reports, as the rest of the report is. Thus, they are that part from which all legal reasoning, including extraction of ratio decidendi and assessment of persuasiveness, chiefly flow.

Not all of an opinion may be reported, however, if the report of the case is concerned with only part of the dispute. Also, a judge's recital of the facts may be omitted if an adequate summary exists, or they are recounted by another judge.

## Disposal

Every piece of litigation must end in a decision. This appears in the opinion of the judge or judges, but may be separately recorded at the end by the editor, for example, 'appeal dismissed'.

## Solicitors and counsel

The names of the firms of solicitors (or the public office, such as Crown Agent, of the person acting as solicitor[2]) acting for the

1 'Counsel' (not 'Council') means advocate (or advocates); see below.
2 For the role of a solicitor in litigation, see below.

parties is given at the end of the report. So may the names of counsel, if not recorded with the parties' names. This appears to be an ancient form of permitted advertising.

## Commentary

Some specialised reports try to put the case in context and explain its implications. A modern development is the appearance of such commentaries in general reports, such as Scottish Criminal Case Reports and Scottish Civil Law Reports.

## Reporter's name or initials

The report may terminate with the name or initials of the reporter, that is, the person responsible for the report of the case. Initials can be decoded from a list of reporters at the beginning of the volume.

## Series of Scottish law reports[1]

### Official reports

As noted above, with minor exceptions, there had never been any official reports of Scottish cases until the Scottish Court Service introduced electronic law reporting in 1999, by making decisions available on its website[2].

The opinions of judges in the Court of Session and High Court from September 1998 are contained on the site. New judgments are added about 2 pm on the date they are published. Important civil judgments from the sheriff courts from September 1998 (and commercial cases from January 1988) and also from Fatal Accident Inquiries from March 1999 are also included.

Also, all judgments of the House of Lords published since 14 November 1996 are available electronically on the day of publication from its website[3], and all Privy Council judgments are likewise available[4].

---

1 Full lists of the Scottish law reports which have existed, the dates they cover, and the abbreviated form of their name used for citation purposes, are to be found in DM Walker *The Scottish Legal System* (8th edn, 2001) p 493.
2 The Scottish Courts website is at www.scotcourts.gov.uk.
3 The House of Lords website is www.parliament.uk/.
4 The Privy Council website is www.privy-council.org.uk.

These are available without catch words or headnotes, which makes them harder to understand, but their rapidity of publication makes them extremely useful for updating and quick reference. (See also 'Electronic reporting and computerised retrieval of law reports' below).

*Other reports*

**Session Cases and the 'nominate' reports.** The principal law reports in Scotland are those produced by W Green, a commercial publisher, on behalf of the Scottish Council of Law Reporting. Although this publication is referred to generically as 'Session Cases', it comprises four parallel series, that is: Privy Council cases on appeal or reference on a devolution issue; House of Lords cases on appeal from the Inner House; High Court of Justiciary cases ('Justiciary Cases'), usually on appeal; and cases, either at first instance or on appeal, heard by the Court of Session ('Session Cases').

Citations of reports in these series are given as 'SC(PC)', 'SC(HL)', 'JC'[1], and 'SC' respectively, with year and page number, for example '1942 SC(HL) 1'. These series have for many years been bound together in a single annual volume, misleadingly marked 'Session Cases' on the spine, the four series being separately paginated within it. Thus, there are separate reports cited '1942 SC(HL) 1' (*Crofter Hand Woven Tweed Co Ltd v Veitch*), '1942 JC 1' (*Duguid v Fraser*), and '1942 SC 1' (*Swaire v Demetriades*) respectively, all in the same volume[2].

The Session Cases series in its present form commenced in 1907. It was, however, the continuation of privately produced reports in broadly the same form, in five sequential series sometimes collectively referred to as the 'nominate reports', but individually known by the name of the five editors. These are Shaw (1821–38), Dunlop (1838–62), Macpherson (1862–73), Rettie (1873–98), and Fraser (1898–1906). Reports are cited by the editor's name or, more commonly, initial ('Dunlop' or 'D' and 'Rettie' or 'R', for example), with the volume number within that series, and page number, the whole preceded by the year which,

---

1 From 1906 to 1916, Justiciary cases were cited 'SC(J)'.
2 Until the revivification of the Privy Council by creation of its devolution issue jurisdiction, there were only the House of Lords Cases, Justiciary Cases and Session Cases series. In 2000, there were House of Lords, but not Privy Council cases reported, and in 2001, there were Privy Council but no House of Lords cases reported, so 2002 is the first in which all four series appeared.

because inessential, is in brackets ('(1875) 2 R 595', for example).

From 1850 (that is, from volume 13 of Dunlop's reports), the series usually contains House of Lords reports as well as Session Cases, bound in the same volume and separately paginated, and such reports are cited 'D(HL)' instead of 'D' etc, for example, '(1850) 13 D(HL)'. From 1874 (that is, from the first volume of Rettie's reports), they also contain Justiciary reports, similarly bound and separately paginated and cited 'R(J)' instead of 'R' (or 'R(HL)'), for example '(1874) 1 R(J) 8'.

The House of Lords and Justiciary cases, usually bound in with Session cases in the nominate reports, are sometimes bound separately. In any case, there used to be separate series of such reports, such as Macqueen's reports of House of Lords cases (1851–1865), and Adam's reports of Justiciary cases (1893–1916). Reports were cited in broadly the same way as in the nominate reports, with name or abbreviation, for example '(1852) 1 Macq 232'. They have not, however, been produced for many years.

**Scottish Criminal Case Reports and Scottish Civil Law Reports.** The Scottish Criminal Case Reports and Scottish Civil Law Reports are two separate series published by the Law Society of Scotland, on a commercial basis, since 1981 and 1987 respectively. Citations of reports are given as 'SCCR' and 'SCLR' respectively, with year and page number, for example '2001 SCLR 26'. They cover cases considered worth reporting from any court in the country, and some have a commentary on them added by the editor or other commentator. The SCLR series contains brief 'Notes' of cases not deserving of a full report, and brief 'Quantum' notes on cases for which the chief interest is the 'quantum' (amount) of damages awarded, or means of its calculation.

These series commenced in part because of the then chronic delays in the production of Session Cases. They are produced in loose parts about six times a year, and bound into an annual volume at the end of each year.

**Scots Law Times.** The Scots Law Times is, like Session Cases, published by W Green, but as a purely commercial enterprise. It contains professional information and articles, but also law reports of devolution cases going to the Privy Council, Scottish appeals (and occasionally English appeals) to the House of Lords, and cases from the Court of Session, High Court of Justiciary, sheriff courts, Scottish Land Court and Lands Tribunal and the Lyon Court.

Citations of reports are given, with year and page number, as

'SLT' or 'SLT (Reps)' (Privy Council, House of Lords, Court of Session and High Court of Justiciary cases), and 'SLT (Sh Ct)', 'SLT (Land Ct)', and 'SLT (Lyon Ct)', for example, '2003 SLT 366[1]. Articles and professional information are cited as 'SLT (News)'.

The Scots Law Times is produced weekly through the year, except when the Court of Session is on vacation. It thus provides rapid publication of reports. From the 1920s to 1990, it was produced in one annual volume, and some editions marked the News, House of Lords reports, Court of Session reports, etc sections by different coloured edges to the page. From 1991, it has been bound into two volumes per annum, one containing Privy Council, House of Lords, Court of Session and High Court of Justiciary reports, the other containing all other reports. The SLT law reports are also available on CD-ROM.

**Greens Weekly Digest.** Greens Weekly Digest has also been produced by W Green since 1986. It contains brief notes, but not a report, upon recently decided cases, under digested headings such as 'agency' and 'contract', and appears in weekly looseleaf parts thus providing rapid, but limited, information. Some libraries bind these into annual volumes. Citation of the notes are given as 'GWD', with the year, issue, and paragraph number, for example, '2002 GWD 2–60'.

**Earlier reports and compilations.** Many other reports than the 'nominate' ones were produced in the 19th century and later, such as the Scottish Jurist (1829–1873) and Scottish Law Reporter (1866–1924). Reports in these series are cited in the same fashion as are the nominate reports, using the abbreviations 'SJ' or 'Sc Jur' and 'SLR' or 'Sc Law Rep'[2] respectively. They sometimes cover cases not found in other reports, or provide alternative reports.

Before the 19th century several major series existed to which reference is made, such as that of Lord Stair (cited, as are the nominate reports, with the unabbreviated name 'Stair'), that of Forbes (cited 'Forbes' in the same fashion) who was the first of a

---

1 Citation of earlier volumes is confusing. The earliest volumes were cited by annual volume number usually preceded by the year in brackets, for example, '15 SLT' or '(1907) 7 SLT'. For some years until 1921, two annual volumes were produced, cited by year, but including the volume number, for example '(1915) 1 SLT'.

2 Thus, avoiding confusion with another later, but overlapping, series called the Scottish Law Review.

number of reporters appointed by the Faculty of Advocates, and the Faculty Collection (cited as 'FC' or 'Fac Col' with the date).

Reference may be made instead to the reports in Morison's Dictionary which, with 'synopses' and 'supplements', covers cases from the 16th to the early 19th centuries in some 40 subject-volumes. Citations of reports in Morison's Dictionary are given to the page numbers, which run continuously throughout all volumes, after the abbreviation 'Mor Dic', 'Mor', 'Mo' or (likely to cause confusion with Macpherson's reports) 'M', the whole often preceded by the year in brackets), for example '(1714) M 14757'. Most of these reports are very short and without reasoned judgments.

Cases in the 15th to 17th centuries are to be found in the *Practicks*, made by judges and others and published later, such as Balfour's *Practicks*, available in a modern edition published by the Stair Society.

Selected cases from Morison's Dictionary, the Faculty Collection, the earlier Session Cases and some other reports were reprinted in 1873 as Scots Revised Reports.

## Series of Community law reports

*Official reports*

Reports of cases before the European Court of Justice and the Court of First Instance, usually called the 'European Court Reports', are produced by the Office of Official Publications of the European Communities.

The form and content of the reports differ somewhat from the common form in the United Kingdom. A summary appears which contains catch words and a précis of the principle applied, instead of a headnote. The opinion of the Advocate General (which has no analogy in United Kingdom practice) is normally included, and usually contains numbered sets of paragraphs, often grouped down into parts dealing with specific topics (such as 'jurisdiction', 'the first question' and 'costs'), and ending with a formal conclusion as to the law. The judgment of the court is given in more formal terms than in United Kingdom practice, specifying the nature of the proceedings and *dramatis personae*, and containing a decision, in numbered paragraphs, likely to be constructed in parts like the Advocate General's. It also ends with a formal conclusion preceded by words such as 'On these grounds . . . '.

The reports are cited by case number (often in round brackets) as well as year in square brackets (as essential, following English practice) and page number, with the abbreviation 'ECR'. Since the Court of First Instance was instituted, the case numbers have been preceded by either 'C–'[1] if it is a case of the court, or 'T–'[2] if it is of the Court of First Instance. Community practice is to put the case number before the parties' names, for example, 'Case 24/62 *Germany v Commission* [1963] ECR 63' (the 24th case commenced in the court in 1962, reported on page 63 of the 1963 volumes of ECR)[3]. United Kingdom practice is to put it after, and in brackets, for example '*Germany v Commission* (Case 24/62) [1963] ECR 63'[4]. This distinction matters, for it is Community practice to index cases by the case number, United Kingdom practice to do so by the parties' names.

There are several numbered parts each year[5], but the bound volumes (several per year) supersede this numbering and, in any case, the pages run as a continuous sequence through all parts. The volumes are sometimes helpfully bound with the pages in each volume marked on the spine.

European Court Reports are the most authoritative reports, but have been slow to appear (although unbound copies of judgments rendered in English may be much faster), and are produced without the editorial assistance of headnotes in the United Kingdom fashion. Thus, the Common Market Law Reports are often preferred.

*Other reports*

**Common Market Law Reports.** The Common Market Law Report series is published by Sweet & Maxwell, on a commercial basis. It has similar but fuller coverage than the European Court Reports, including cases heard before national courts as well as those before the European Court of Justice and Court of First Instance. There are weekly loose parts produced, bound into a

---

1 For 'Court', or perhaps, rather, 'Cour', as in 'Cour de justice': see note 2 below.
2 For 'Tribunal', the CFI having been originally known in English as the 'Tribunal of First Instance' and still known in French as the 'Tribunal de première instance'.
3 Or 'Case C–59/91 *France v Commission*', or 'Case T–70/89 *BBC v Commission*'.
4 Or '*France v Commission* (Case C–59/91)', or '*BBC v Commission* (Case T–70/89)'.
5 E g '2000–1' to '2000–12' (confusingly, *via* not only '2000–5A' and '2000–5B' and also '2000–8/9A' and '2000–8/9B').

number of volumes every year, and reports have headnotes in the United Kingdom fashion.

The form and content are closer to United Kingdom practice than the European Court Reports, as in place of the summary there is usually a fuller précis of the issues, and the facts are more clearly spelled out. However, its basic form is determined by the form of the Advocate General's opinion and the court's judgment. The actual translation of those items into English is not identical to that in European Court Reports.

The reports are cited in the same way as with the European Court Reports, but with the abbreviation 'CMLR' and the number of the volume for that year, for example, '*Clarke v Chief Adjudication Officer* (Case 384/85) [1987] 3 CMLR 277'[1] (a case before United Kingdom tribunal which went to the European Court of Justice on an article 234 (ex article 177) preliminary reference), and '*Pickstone v Freemans plc* [1987] 2 CMLR 572' (a case heard only before United Kingdom courts). The final annual volumes have been a sub-sequence of 'anti-trust' cases for some years.

These reports may be bound in the usual United Kingdom fashion (English variant) with '[2001] 1', '[2001] 2' etc are printed on the spine. However, there is a separate single sequence number running from the first volume which may be used instead so that, for example, the volumes for 2001 are not marked '2001 1', '2001 2' and '2001 3', but '90', '91' and '92' (although also bearing the year).

**All England Law Reports European Cases.** This is an addition to the standard English set of All England Law Reports commercially produced by Butterworths, and contains decisions of the European Court of Justice and Court of First Instance.

The reports are cited by year (in square brackets, as essential), and page number, with the abbreviation 'All ER (EC)', e g '[2002] All ER (EC) 193'.

### Series of 'human rights' reports

*Official reports*

The official reports of the European Court of Human Rights appeared initially as *Publications of the European Court of Human*

---

1 Community practice would render this as 'Case 384/85 *Clarke v Chief Adjudication Officer*'.

*Rights: Series A: Judgments and Decisions* and *Series B; Pleadings, Oral Argument and Decisions.* Judgments of the Court were cited as, for instance, 'Bryan v United Kingdom, judgment of 22 November 1995, Series A no 335–A'. The volumes were numbered but this number was not used. However, the volumes also bore the number of the case or cases contained (in this case '335–338').

From 1996, the 'Series A' and 'B' titles were dropped, so citations were modified to, for instance '*Murray v United Kingdom*, judgment of 8 February 1996, Reports of Judgments and Decisions 1996–I'. Volume numbers now bore the year, and the citation indicated the case within that volume.

From 1999, there has been a single series of volumes, so citation has become, for instance, '*Hay v United Kingdom*, no 41894/99, ECHR 2000–XI'.

## Other reports

**European Human Rights Reports.** The main commercial English language series of law reports on the application of the European Convention of Human Rights is the European Human Rights Reports (EHRR) published by Sweet & Maxwell. It contains full reports of judgments of the Court (and admissibility decisions of the former European Commission on Human Rights).

The annual volumes have a continuous sequence of numbers, so reports are cited in the standard fashion of year (in round brackets, as inessential), volume number and page[1], eg '(2000) 29 EHRR 245'. Sometimes the case number is included, eg '(A/121) (1988) 10 EHRR 29'.

**Butterworths Human Rights Cases.** This is another commercially produced series, related to the All England Law Reports series.

## Other series of specialised reports

A considerable number of specialised law reports are produced, generally on a United Kingdom basis, concentrating upon specific areas of law. These include, for example, Building Law Reports,

---

1 Helpfully, while the sequence of page numbers appears on top left and right of the pages, there is a running title giving the citation of the case, including its starting page number, at the top of every page.

Estates Gazette Law Reports and Immigration Appeal Reports. Some may include comment, as does the Industrial Relations Law Reports. Many professional journals, and certain newspapers, carry brief law reports, sometimes with comment.

Specialised reports are usually cited by the year, the abbreviated name of the reports (such as 'Build LR', 'EGLR', 'Imm AR'), and the page number. In most, the year is essential so, following the English practice, it appears in square brackets, and may be followed by the volume number for that year, for example, '[1990] Imm AR' (Immigration Appeal Reports) and '[1992] 2 LL Rep' (Lloyd's Law Reports). In some cases the year is inessential, so is in round brackets, followed by the sequential number of the volume in the series, for example, '(1991) 94 Crim App R' (Criminal Appeal Reports)[1].

Newspaper reports are usually cited by the name of the newspaper and the date, for example, 'Independent, 11 Feb 2003'.

## Series of English law reports

### Official reports

As noted in respect to Scottish law reporting, there were, with minor exceptions, no official reports until the (English) Court Service made some decisions available on its website[2]. This is roughly equivalent to the Scottish system, for the decisions are without catch words or headnote, but unbeatable for rapid updating. However, only recent decisions are held and reference is made on to 'Casetrack', (see below) provided commercially. As noted in relation to official Scots reports, all recent judgments of the House of Lords are available electronically from its website[3], and all Privy Council judgments from its website[4].

**'The Law Reports'.** The most authoritative English law reports are those produced by the Incorporated Council of Law

---

1 Note that, since the introduction of 'neutral citations' (see below), Criminal Appeal Reports and other Sweet & Maxwell published reports cite by case number, not page number. Thus '(2002) 105 Crim App Rep 2' refers to the second case in that volume, not the second page.

2 The (English) Court Service website is at www.courtservice.gov.uk. The Northern Irish Court Service website is at www.courtsni.gov.uk.

3 The House of Lords website is at www.parliament.uk/.

4 The Privy Council website is at www.privy-council.org.uk.

Reporting. They are commonly, if presumptuously, referred to in England and Wales simply as 'the Law Reports'.

They comprise five series. The first of these is 'Appeal Cases' containing appeals heard by the Judicial Committee of the Privy Council, the Appellate Committee of the House of Lords (including Scottish ones). The second, third and fourth are, respectively, the 'Queen's Bench', 'Chancery' and 'Family' series, containing cases heard by the three divisions of the (English) High Court, and appeals from them to the Court of Appeal. The fifth series is the 'Weekly Law Reports' ('WLR') which produces rapid reports of those cases to be more fully reported later in the other four series (annual volumes 2 and 3), and other cases (annual volume 1). Each of these appears initially in loose parts, bound into one or more volumes per annum.

Citation is given by year in square brackets (because it is essential), volume number for that year, the abbreviated name of the relevant series ('AC', 'QB', 'Ch', 'Fam'[1] and 'WLR'), and page number, for example, *Anns v Merton London Borough Council* [1978] AC 728, [1977] 2 WLR 1024'.

For a period in the 19th century, a similar but more complicated system operated[2]. Before that, there were nominate private reports known by the name of the editor, rather as in Scotland. The more important were collected in various compilations, including the 'English Reports' (cited 'ER'), and 'All England Reports Reprint' (cited 'All ER Rep').

**All England Law Reports.** The All England Law Reports is produced by Butterworths, a commercial legal publisher. It reports all cases considered worth reporting from any court in England and attempts more rapid production than the Law Reports. It is produced in weekly loose parts, bound into several volumes per annum. Citation of reports in the All England Law Reports is in the same fashion as for the Law Reports. *Anns v Merton London Borough Council* is also reported at [1977] 2 All ER 492, for example.

---

1 Until 1971 this was the Probate, Divorce and Admiralty Division, and its reports were so named, and cited as 'PDA'.
2 For details, see Sweet & Maxwell *Guide to Law Reports and Statutes*.

## Electronic reporting and computerised retrieval of law reports

*Official sources*

**The United Kingdom.** Electronic reporting as a new form of official reporting, is discussed above in relation to Scottish, English and Welsh, and Northern Irish 'official' law reporting.

**Community law.** Community law, so far as it emerges from United Kingdom cases, can be accessed from United Kingdom databases. All European Court of Justice cases and Court of First Instance staff cases from June 1997 are available from the European Court of Justice website[1].

**'Human rights' law.** 'Human rights' cases emerging in the United Kingdom can be accessed from United Kingdom databases. All European Court of Human Rights cases are available from the European Court of Human Rights website[2].

*Commercial sources*

It should be noted that where judgments are obtained from official sources, as noted above, they do not contain catch words or headnotes.

**The United Kingdom.** Casetrack, operated by Smith Bernal who are official shorthand writers to the English courts, covers the Court of Appeal and the Administrative Court from April 1996, the High Court as a whole and the Employment Appeal Tribunal from July 1998, and the VAT Tribunal from January 2002.

The LexisNexis computerised database supplied by Butterworths contains all cases reported in Session Cases or the Scots Law Times reported since November 1944; all cases reported in Scottish Criminal Case Reports from January 1986; all cases reported in Scottish Civil Law Reports since February 1986; unreported Inner House cases since January 1982; and unreported Outer House cases since January 1985.

It also contains cases from the (usually English-based) series of specialised United Kingdom law reports, such as the Industrial

1 The European Court of Justice website is at www.curia.int/eu/.
2 The European Court of Human Rights website is at www.echr.coe.int/.

Court Reports and Immigration Appeal Reports, and from the major English law reports ('the Law Reports') and All England Law Reports, as well as innumerable United States reports series.

WESTLAW UK SCOTS LAW, operated by Sweet & Maxwell and W Green, provides all Scots Law Times reports from 1930, and Green's Weekly Digest for updating. WESTLAW, as such, also contains a wide variety of English material.

BAILII covers Court of Session decisions, High Court of Justiciary decisions and significant civil and criminal Sheriff Court decisions, all from, effectively, 1998.

**Community law.** LexisNexis and WESTLAW can be used to access Community law cases including reported European Court of Justice and Court of First Instance cases.

**'Human rights' law.** LexisNexis and WESTLAW can also be used to access 'human rights' cases, including reported (and some unreported) European Court of Human Rights cases.

# 7. Legal services

## THE NEED FOR LEGAL SERVICES

Although much modern law offers some kind of advantage to people, they may miss the benefits if they do not take them up in the right way. And the kind of law that holds out threats over people who do not obey them can easily be abused by the officials wielding the threats – in criminal law, the police, the prosecutors and the penal authorities who actually apply the sentences. In other words, laws may miss their intended objectives.

To avoid this it is important that the subjects of the law should know what the law is – or at least be able to discover it, to find out how it applies to their particular situation, and then to utilise it, if that seems to be in their interests, and comply it with it if it has a penalty attached. They need knowledge, advice and sometimes representation.

In a simple society where the law is largely custom they could probably do all this for themselves. But as law becomes more comprehensive, it becomes less accessible. The sheer bulk of it is intimidating. How to find one's way about it is a problem. Even when one has found what seems to be the right bit of law, the words used may be technical and obscure. The draftsmen of statutes often seem to defeat their own ends; in trying to cover every possible situation, they end up with laws that are beyond the understanding of those who are expected to use them – even the lawyers and officials.

The laws in the statute books may not be enough, for they may have been interpreted in a certain way by senior judges if there has been a similar dispute in the past which has reached the stage of a court hearing. For instance, if a house purchaser claims he was misled by a favourable report by a surveyor instructed by a building society and is entitled to compensation, questions of what actually happened and the terms of contracts, of statute and of case law and the value of his loss will all have to be considered. Then if the claim seems a sound one, it may be pursued by negotiation, arbitration or litigation (in a court). Given that the defenders will be advised by legal experts, the house purchaser would not get very far without the help of a lawyer.

When an individual is on the receiving end of laws, then the need for knowledge, advice and representation is still greater, for there is an inequality between him and the professionals who are doing the job daily. This is especially so in criminal cases where prosecution is usually a rare or unprecedented occasion for the accused and moreover one which may lead to the loss of his liberty.

To meet these needs a class of experts in the law has arisen in all mature systems of law, ones which have reached such a stage of complexity that people cannot make their way through them unaided. They may be called by various titles. In Scotland lawyers come in two classes: advocates and solicitors. No-one can belong to both classes at the same time, though transfers from solicitor to advocate are quite common. In carrying out their functions they all act under law and have various privileges and duties. However, they do not necessarily meet the entire need for legal services and we shall examine later other more informal responses to that need.

# HISTORY OF THE LEGAL PROFESSION

## Advocates

How do we come to have two mutually exclusive categories of lawyer, both enabling people to make the best use of the law? In medieval Scotland, two specific needs for legal services emerged. These were speaking as a 'forspeaker' in a court on behalf of a person called before it, and authenticating the documents which described occurrences under feudal law, upon which the all-important titles to land depended.

It seems very likely that court pleaders, from whom the later profession of advocate emerged, appeared first in the ecclesiastical courts. By the 13th century they had elaborate procedural rules and a largely written procedure which obviously called for literacy. It was not peculiar to Scotland. It derived from the universal canon law of the Catholic Church. Canon law provided until the Reformation the Scots law on marriage and its annulment, legitimacy, succession to items other than land, and contracts supported by an oath. On other matters too its courts were often resorted to, as being impartial and usually free from the influence of local magnates.

Many of the occasional references to lawyers before the 15th century seem to have some connection with church courts. Thus, a Glasgow cleric, Adam Urri, was criticised in 1288 for practising civil law (i e Roman law) for personal profit, but repented before he died[1]. The records of the Great Cause[2] around 1290 over the succession to the throne of Scotland and later those of a long litigation on titles to land in the Court of the Bishop of Aberdeen (as a secular lord) in 1382[3] show that men with a wealth of knowledge of civil in the sense of Roman law and of Canon law were available in Scotland. One such, Baldred Bissett, was a graduate of Bologna and an official or ecclesiastical judge in the Diocese of St Andrews in 1282. Later, in 1301, with two others he was in Rome presenting in legal arguments the Scottish case against Edward I to the Papal Curia[4].

In 1424, when James I returned from captivity in England and set about remodelling the Scottish legal system, there must have been sufficient lawyers around in the royal courts for judges to ensure that, as Parliament enacted, poor persons should have 'a leill and wyse advocate to folow sik pure creaturis causes'[5]. Advocates and forspeakers were also to swear that their cause was a 'gude and leill'(or true) one[6]. By 1455 advocates must have been recognised as professional participants in courts of some formality, for by an Act of that year forspeakers 'for meide' (or reward) were to wear 'habits of grene of the fashion of a tunicle and the sleeves to be open as a tabard'[7]. In 1479 there is the first mention of the King's Advocate, the ancestor of the Executive's chief law officer in Scotland today, the Lord Advocate[8].

When the Court of Session was established about 1532, eight men of 'best name, knawlege and experience' were selected to be 'general procurators', their number not to go above ten[9]. Others

1 *Chronicle of Lanercost for 1288.*

2 DM Walker *A Legal History of Scotland* vol II (1990) p 267; see p 14 above.

3 Stein 'The Influence of Roman Law on the Law of Scotland' 1963 JR 205.

4 DER Watt *A Biographical Dictionary of Scottish Graduates Before 1410.* See generally HL MacQueen *Common Law and Feudal Law* ch 3.

5 APS II, 8.

6 APS II, 19.

7 APS II, 43.

8 APS II, 125 He is simply described as 'the Advocate', which is the manner in which the Lord Advocate is still referred to by the inhabitants of Parliament House. In 1579 he acquired his role as prosecutor of grave criminal offences on behalf of the Crown.

9 See RK Hannay *The College of Justice* p 137. In 1567 an Act narrated the great number of advocates in Edinburgh and restricted the number authorised to appear before the Session to ten, thus releasing others to appear in the other courts of Edinburgh (APS III, 41). See generally Gordon Donaldson 'The Legal Profession in Scottish Society in the 16th and 17th Centuries' 1976 JR 1.

were admitted as individuals to practise before the court on satisfying the judges of their competence. The first sign of an organisation of these advocates is a mention in 1582 of Master John Sharp,
'dene of the advocattis of sessioun'[1]. Gradually they seem to have
acquired a corporate identity and a monopoly of representation in
the Court of Session. Their earliest extant minutes are of 1661[2],
but the Faculty of Advocates had some form of existence as part of
the College of Justice long before then – certainly by 1582, if not
earlier.

## Solicitors

The development of the advocates' profession is fairly simple to
chart, as with the judges they have formed part of the College of
Justice since its creation in 1532 and have thus been based in
Edinburgh. Solicitors on the other hand were and are to be found
throughout Scotland and their corporate existence began as local
societies of lawyers. Many of these still exist, but all practising
solicitors must now be members of the Law Society of Scotland,
which is the creation of statute.

The formation of societies of solicitors in the provincial towns is
not well documented, except in Glasgow and Aberdeen. The term
'solicitor' is a relatively modern one. Lawyers in Glasgow specifically rejected it, preferring to be known as procurators, originally
those who were licensed to appear before the Commissary Courts
of the pre-Reformation Archdiocese of Glasgow. Reborn under a
Charter of Queen Mary in 1563, the Commissary Court of
Glasgow continued to dominate the legal life of the city. Lawyers in
Glasgow, whether or not they regularly practised before the court,
called themselves procurators and belonged to the Royal Faculty of
Procurators in Glasgow, which still exists[3].

In Aberdeen the men of law called themselves advocates and
belonged to the Society of Advocates in Aberdeen, which also still
exists. It traces its origin to 1633 when the Sheriff of Aberdeen
recognised 16 practitioners as being alone qualified to appear
before him, but a list of advocates going back to 1549 survives[4]. A
society was formed in 1685 and it received Royal Charters in 1774,

---

1 RK Hannay *The College of Justice* p 144.
2 See JN Pinkerton *The Minute Book of the Faculty of Advocates* (Stair Society, vols
   29 and 32).
3 See JS Muirhead *The Old Minute Book of the Faculty of Procurators in Glasgow.*
4 See article in (1969) 14 JLSS 325.

1799 and 1862[1]. The Dundee Faculty of Procurators and Solicitors was incorporated by Royal Charter in 1819. The members of none of these bodies, despite their titles, concentrated exclusively on court practice, but it was the right to appear in court that gave them their standing.

At the level of the Supreme Courts in Edinburgh non-advocates were also becoming involved in procedures. Advocates drafted the written pleadings or allegations and arguments on which they were to base their oral representations, but these documents had to be sealed with the Royal Signet. The Clerks of the Signet received fees for this transaction, which continued until 1933. They formed the Society of Writers to the Signet, which is now an organisation of solicitors, mainly in Edinburgh, where it has a fine hall and library. The Society of Solicitors in the Supreme Courts had a less auspicious beginning in the throng of 'agents' as they called themselves who throughout the 17th century crowded the courts offering to help litigants with their cases. The advocates resented their intrusion and obtained several Acts against the agents. Eventually they were tolerated and by the mid-18th century individual agents were formally admitted to assist litigants before the Supreme Courts[2]. As the Society of Solicitors in the Supreme Courts of Scotland they now operate under private Acts of Parliament. They have no special privileges but speak for the interests of many of those solicitors in Edinburgh who regularly instruct advocates to appear on behalf of their clients and those of firms outside Edinburgh.

Another common ancestor of the modern Scottish solicitor is the medieval notary. Notaries were licensed by the Pope or the Holy Roman Emperor (and usually by both) to record transactions of legal significance. Their record was enough to prove that the transaction had taken place as stated. The office of notary was recognised in courts throughout Europe. A supplication to the Pope in 1425 complained that there were few notaries in Scotland, to the detriment of the people, especially when documents had to be authenticated by a notary in order to be sent to the courts in Rome. Six new notaries were then created who might be priests[3]. In 1469 King James III decided to remedy this shortage by taking

---

1 Collected in *Records of the Society of Advocates in Aberdeen* (New Spalding Club); Henderson Begg *Law Agents* p 12.
2 Henderson Begg *Law Agents* p 8.
3 Henderson Begg *Law Agents* p 10.

powers as, in effect, Emperor of Scotland to create notaries to operate within Scotland[1].

Notaries kept copies of all the deeds they drew up in what were called Protocol Books. These were preserved after the notary's death and formed a kind of public register and a safeguard against loss of or alterations to the originals. The many surviving ones give a vivid account of the variety of a notary's work[2]. The conveyancing and drafting side of the solicitor's work has its origin in the work of the notary. Their deeds still have international recognition. Until 1896 the office of notary was an additional qualification which many solicitors sought. Since 1896 only enrolled solicitors have been eligible to become notaries. Most solicitors now do so[3].

There are thus two historic strands in the background of the present-day solicitor: admission by judges to provide services in their courts and the power to create authentic documents. Both of these privileges were sought by individuals. But there was no means of checking on the qualifications of those who applied and no means of training them. A first step towards remedying this deficiency was taken in 1825 when the Court of Session decreed that anyone seeking admission as a procurator before any court must first have served an apprenticeship for three years with a procurator, writer to the signet or solicitor.

There was still a lack of a prescribed curriculum and a means of testing proficiency in it. This was remedied in the Procurators Act 1865, which provided an easy means by which lawyers in every county could form an incorporated society. Having done so they were to hold examinations in general knowledge and law, with the approval of the local sheriff. But as the users of the law began to include companies and other organisations which operated nationally or in many localities, it was plainly unsatisfactory that the qualifications of new lawyers should be left to the initia tive and variable competence of local societies. So, following a Royal Commission Report, their training and admission were closely regulated in the Law Agents Act 1873. Applicants for admission to a local society had to have served a five-year apprenticeship under a registered indenture or three years if they

---

1 DM Walker *A Legal History of Scotland* vol II (1990) p 272.
2 See, e g, *Selkirk Protocol Books 1511–1547* (Stair Society, vol 40).
3 The admission and regulation of notaries public is now controlled by the Solicitors (Scotland) Act 1980, Pt V, as amended by the Law Reform (Miscellaneous Provisions) (Scotland) Act 1990, s 37. On the history of notaries in Scotland, see John C Murray *The Law of Scotland Relating to Notaries Public* ch 1.

held a degree in arts or law. The Court of Session would nominate examiners to hold examinations in general knowledge and law. A registrar was appointed to keep a roll of enrolled law agents. The universities which had played little part in the education of lawyers were now given a role, in that applicants, whether or not graduates, must have attended the classes of Scots law and conveyancing in a Scottish university.

The law agents as a whole had no voice. Having no collective say on who should be admitted to their number they were lacking in one of the essential indicators of a profession, which in the early 20th century they aspired to be. In 1933 by the Solicitors (Scotland) Act (giving official recognition to their now usual name) a General Council of Solicitors in Scotland was created, to be elected by all their local societies. It had power to hold examinations and to regulate the admission and enrolment of solicitors. It also made nominations to the Solicitors' Discipline (Scotland) Committee. In 1949, when a system of civil legal aid to help finance court actions was about to be introduced, it was decided that the legal profession should operate the scheme on behalf of the government. Yet the existing structure which did not represent all solicitors was felt to be inadequate. So a Law Society of Scotland was created by the Legal Aid and Solicitors (Scotland) Act 1949 to replace the General Council and exercise its powers and more. All solicitors wishing to practise as such must now hold a current practising certificate from it. The present law concerning solicitors is to be found in the Solicitors (Scotland) Act 1980, as amended by the Solicitors (Scotland) Act 1988, the Law Reform (Miscellaneous Provisions) (Scotland) Act 1990 and the Council of the Law Society of Scotland (Scotland) Act 2003.

Thus, their separate histories explain the existence of two branches of the legal profession in Scotland. But they do not necessarily justify it. The advent of solicitor-advocates in the 1990s is one example of the drawing together of the two branches (see below).

## LEGAL PROFESSIONS?

From the standpoint of the state the main purveyors of legal services in Scotland are regarded as a single profession. The title of the Conservative Government's Consultation Paper of 1989 on the supply of legal services is *The Legal Profession in Scotland*, which it states 'comprises both solicitors and advocates'. In their responses to this document, which challenged many of their assumptions, the

Faculty of Advocates and the Council of the Law Society of Scotland (speaking for solicitors) agreed that their members formed two branches of the one profession.

But what is a profession? What justifies the use of this traditional label? Sociologists who range over the whole world in their scrutiny of societies find the term problematical, to the point of admitting defeat in trying to encapsulate the term in one meaning. But we can single out certain features of a profession as the term is habitually used in Scotland (and England too).

For our purposes a profession is taken to comprise those who possess a specialised body of knowledge and skills related to it. It sustains an organisation which enables it to define with greater precision that knowledge and those skills; to admit to its membership those who possess them to a sufficient degree; to impose on its members certain standards of behaviour; and to discipline those who fail to maintain them. The maintenance of these standards is regarded as a matter of such public benefit that the organisation is by law conceded certain privileges to be enjoyed by its members.

We shall examine each of these characteristics in turn, in relation to advocates and solicitors, and then look at the internal stresses and strains and the external pressures to which the legal profession is subject.

## ORGANISATION OF THE LEGAL PROFESSION

### Advocates

The Faculty of Advocates consists of those who have been admitted by the judges of the Court of Session to practise before it. They thereby have access to the other superior courts of Scotland, most importantly the High Court of Justiciary, in London to the House of Lords and Judicial Committee of the Privy Council and in Luxembourg to the Court of Justice of the European Union. They can also appear before all the lower courts of Scotland, but they share that right of access with solicitors. Certain solicitors may also appear in the superior courts[1].

The Faculty is in law a corporation, that is, it has a legal existence separate from that of its individual members. But it enjoys that status by custom. No statute created it. Nor does it have a written constitution. The conduct of its members was a matter of

1 See p 274 below.

unwritten custom. But the Royal Commission on Legal Services in Scotland in its report in 1980 urged that the Faculty 'should promulgate an authoritative written guide to the professional conduct expected of advocates'. The Faculty responded in 1988 with the *Guide to the Professional Conduct of Advocates*, which, being available to the public, enables breaches of that conduct to be complained of. In 2003 it was undergoing revision.

There are about 450 advocates in practice as such. Each practises on his or her own. Partnerships are not permitted. Practising advocates are either seniors or juniors. They enter as juniors and after about 12 to 15 years of successful practice they may apply through the Lord President to be appointed by the Queen to the Roll of Queen's Counsel in Scotland, which, following English custom, was formed in 1897. As a QC or senior an advocate is entitled to require that he be accompanied by a junior to assist him in the conduct of a case, but he may choose not to be. Until 1977 a senior was invariably supported in court by one or more juniors, but this practice was adversely commented on by the Monopolies and Mergers Commission and then abandoned.

Advocates are to be found in and around the Advocates' Library in Parliament House, Edinburgh, where consulting rooms are available. They do not share accommodation, as do English barristers in 'chambers'. But they share the services of one of twelve clerks, through whom they are approached and who keep their diaries. Negotiations on fees are also conducted by the clerks. Fees are unregulated, except by statutory instrument in civil and criminal legal aid cases, where it is the state that pays. But they should be 'reasonable'. All practising advocates belong to a company called Faculty Services Ltd formed in 1971, which issues a note of the proposed fee to the instructing solicitor and if it is not disputed receives payment.

It is unlawful for an advocate (or solicitor) to enter an agreement to be paid a proportion of, and out of, the proceeds of an action. This is widely used in the United States where it is known as a contingency fee. However, it is permissible for an advocate or solicitor to agree to give his services on the basis that he will be paid only if the action is successful; but there must be a reasonable prospect of success[1]. This is called a speculative action[2]. Because of

---

1 *X Insurance Co Ltd v A and B* 1936 SC 225 at 239.
2 See Faculty of Advocates *Guide to the Professional Conduct of Advocates* (1988) 5.10, 9.6; McCulloch 'Fees for Speculative Actions' 1994 SLT (News) 401.

the risk undertaken by the lawyer it is permissible for him to raise his fee by up to 100 per cent[1].

Many advocates hold full-time appointments as judges, sheriffs, academic lawyers etc. They take little or no part in the running of the Faculty.

The Faculty is headed by its Dean, who is its elected leader and also makes rulings on professional conduct and has disciplinary powers and duties. He is assisted by an advisory Dean's Council. The other elected officers are the Vice-Dean, Clerk of Faculty, Keeper of the Library and Treasurer. They are elected at an annual meeting held in January.

## Solicitors

The Law Society of Scotland comprises all solicitors qualified in Scotland. They are to be found throughout Scotland and a small number in England and elsewhere. In 2003 the roll of members numbered 11,076 of whom 8,926 held practising certificates. They elect by district constituencies a Council numbering, with co-opted and ex officio members, a total of over 50. Elected members serve for three years and may be re-elected[2]. From their number a President, who is the main spokesman of the Society, is elected each year. A Vice-President is also elected annually and usually becomes the next President. The statutory objects of the Law Society include the promotion of '(a) the interests of the solicitors' profession in Scotland and (b) the interests of the public in relation to that profession', two goals which may in practice be difficult to reconcile[3]. The Council conducts the business of the Society and, with the concurrence of the Lord President, the senior Scottish judge, can make regulations affecting its members, which have the force of law.

The Council puts much of its business through a plethora of committees and working parties which report to it. They are composed of Council members and others, the President and Vice-President being members of them all.

There are also other societies of solicitors, local and national. Membership is voluntary and members do not now have any public statutory privileges. They include the Scottish Law Agents Society, the Society of Writers to the Signet, the Society of

---

1 Law Reform (Miscellaneous Provisions) (Scotland) Act 1990, s 36.
2 Constitution of the Law Society of Scotland. Parliament House Book F359.
3 Solicitors (Scotland) Act 1980, s 1(2).

Solicitors in the Supreme Courts and local societies such as the Glasgow Bar Association and the Society of Advocates in Aberdeen.

Certain solicitors also have the additional qualification of being entitled to practise in the supreme courts and as such are colloquially called solicitor-advocates[1].

## LEGAL EXPERTISE

The body of specialised knowledge which advocates and solicitors profess to have is the law of Scotland, that is all the law from whatever source that prevails in Scotland. That includes both the substantive law and the procedural law. They should not advise on the law of any other country, even England, unless they are qualified in it.

### Advocates

Advocates tend to be ready to accept instructions on any branch of the law of Scotland. But some are known to be specialists in criminal proceedings only, and are unlikely to be instructed in other cases. With very limited exceptions[2] they may receive instructions only from a solicitor, never directly from an individual client. They thus have no contractual relationship with the client, as the solicitor does. They have a professional loyalty to the client, but subject to the rules of professional practice, which include obligations to the court[3]. This has several consequences. They are not supposed to pick and choose among clients but should accept instructions when given, if free to do so and offered a reasonable fee, giving priority to the party who applies first. This is called 'the cab-rank rule' and it militates against specialisation at the Bar. Sometimes, of course, they are double-booked, for instance when a trial takes longer than expected. Then they will have to drop out of one commitment, often at very short notice, and the instructing solicitor will have to find a replacement. Advocates may not be sued for professional negligence when in court, although it is assumed on House of Lords authority in English cases that they may be in

---

1 See p 349 below.
2 E g from the chief executive of a local authority or from a lawyer outside Scotland where no litigation in Scotland is contemplated or in progress.
3 *Anderson v HM Advocate* 1996 JC 29 at 35.

respect of forms of professional fault outside the court. And remarkably, according to a leading 19th-century judge, an advocate's 'legal right is to conduct the cause without any regard to the wishes of his client and what he does *bona fide* according to his own judgment will bind his client'[1] (that is, in court).

As well as their public appearances in courts of all levels, advocates are frequently consulted on questions of doubt which have arisen in the course of legal practice; for example, on the legality of a proposed course of action or the meaning of a will or, most commonly, on the prospects of success in raising or defending an action. This is known as taking the opinion of counsel. The consultation is initiated by a written document, drafted by a solicitor, called a memorial, in which the facts are stated and copies of any documents are produced, possible legal authorities cited and then a number of questions posed. The advocate will answer these one by one, supporting his response by legal authority and argument. Advocates may also be consulted on the drafting and revision of documents intended to have legal effect, such as important contracts. Advocates frequently also take part in arbitrations, which are hearings of disputes by an arbiter in private, according to procedure agreed by the parties and at a time and place to suit them. They may also be instructed to represent interested parties at public inquiries on planning applications.

*Solicitors*[2]

Solicitors are sometimes described as the general practitioners of the law, but this is misleading. Certainly, anyone can consult any solicitor on any point of law, but they have techniques for sliding away from difficult and unremunerative problems. Indeed, they are warned in their Code of Conduct not to undertake work for which they lack the necessary knowledge and experience[3]. Their work is overwhelmingly concentrated in procedures which can be routinised in a standard set of steps, many capable of being carried out by unqualified staff (sometimes called para-legals). The law utilised can be treated as given and simply ensures the legal effectiveness of the transaction, provided the required steps have been

---

1 *Batchelor v Pattison and Mackersy* (1876) 3 R 914 at 918 by Lord President Inglis, cited with approval in *Brodt v King* 1991 SLT 272 and *Anderson v HM Advocate* 1996 SLT 150.
2 On solicitors generally, see *The Laws of Scotland: Stair Memorial Encyclopaedia* vol 13, 'Legal Profession'.
3 Code of Conduct, to be found in *The Parliament House Book* section F.

correctly followed. When exceptionally a novel point of law does arise, it is likely to be referred to an advocate or in some subjects a specialised solicitor, such as a professor of conveyancing, to be researched. Thus, the work of solicitors can be concentrated in the more profitable areas of practice. By the use of advertising, which is now permitted within broad limits, the volume of desirable work such as the buying and selling of houses can be increased.

Advocates likewise are sometimes described as the consultants of the law and it is true that solicitors do consult them on difficult problems of law. But they are seldom consulted as specialists[1]. Their opinion is sought because they have the time to research a problem thoroughly and give a detached and reasoned answer to it, often with advice as to the course of action to take.

Nearly all solicitors engage in the buying and selling of property, both residential and commercial, and in drawing up the documents of offer and acceptance, called missives, the deed of transfer called the disposition, and the security, if any, over the property which enables the transaction to be financed. These and certain less frequent property transactions are called conveyancing. Nearly all also deal with the distribution of the estates of deceased people, which sometimes leads to the setting up and administration of a trust, under which assets are held for the benefit of someone or some public purpose. Many will form companies for clients, in which they may have a personal stake. This often leads to advising on all aspects of the law as it affects companies. Many are now licensed under the Financial Services Act 1986 to advise on financial investments, with their tax implications. Some firms avoid court work, some do it when their established clients require it, and a minority engage in it in a substantial way. Most civil cases relate to divorce and related family matters and actions for the recovery of debts. Criminal cases encompass all kinds from the most trivial to the gravest.

Since November 1996 all solicitors have been required by the Law Society to take steps to keep their professional expertise up to date, under the name of Continuing Professional Development. They must devote 20 hours each year to this end. At least 15 hours must be in group study. This usually takes the form of attendance at courses on new laws, which are organised by local faculties of solicitors, universities, training companies and some of the largest firms. Skills such as office management, accountancy, and client

---

1 A recent publication of the Faculty of Advocates, circulated to solicitors, provides a statement of the special knowledge claimed by each practising advocate. This may encourage the growth of specialisation.

relations are also acceptable as being relevant to the solicitor's practice and 5 of the hours must be on management topics. Up to 5 of the 20 hours may be spent on private study, including the preparation of and reading of articles. Solicitors are obliged to keep record cards of their studies. The Law Society calls in a random selection of them for scrutiny[1].

Solicitors who have acquired expertise by specialising in a particular branch of law may apply to have this recognised by the Law Society by being known as Accredited Specialists. So far 16 areas of specialisation have been approved. They include agricultural law, child law, employment law, medical negligence law and pension law. Holders of these qualifications are available to advise their fellow solicitors in their area of expertise.

Most solicitors also qualify as notaries public, for which no extra training or qualification is necessary. This enables them to perform such functions as receiving under oath written statements called affidavits which form the basis of the evidence in undefended divorces; receiving sworn statements from executors as to the items of property left by deceased persons; and drawing up and signing wills and other documents for blind people. Because of the international credibility of notaries they may also be asked by foreigners in Scotland to deal with documents under foreign legal systems[2].

The usual way in which persistent disputes with a legal basis are settled is by the judgment of a court or, less commonly, in private by an impartial arbiter[3]. However, since 1994 solicitors have been offering mediation services which help people in dispute to reach their own agreement. The Law Society sponsors a list of trained and accredited solicitor-mediators called ACCORD. There is also a list of mediators called CALM who specialise in family disputes, such as the care of children on the breakdown of a marriage. There are 20 authorised insolvency practitioners

*Solicitor-advocates*

Until 1993 solicitors could not appear in the High Court of Justiciary, the Court of Session and other superior courts, though they were usually much involved in the preparation of cases in these courts and would sit in court, while their client was represented by an advocate. But now solicitors can seek what are called

---

1 See *The Parliament House Book* section F, 272.
2 See Brand 'The Modern Notary in Scotland' 1997 JLSS 50.
3 See p 86.

'extended rights' enabling them to appear and speak in the superior courts. Solicitors who have not less than five years' continuous experience of court work may apply to practise in the superior civil or criminal courts or both. They must undergo an induction course, observe cases in the appropriate court(s), attend (subject to certain exemptions) a training course in the work of the courts, and pass examinations on subjects related to practice in the superior courts[1]. It is now permissible for a solicitor-advocate to be appointed an Advocate Depute. In 2003 there were 77 solicitor-advocates qualified to practise in the criminal courts, 58 in the civil courts and 2 in both. Like advocates, they are allowed to act according to their own discretion and judgment in the conduct of a client's case[2].

In the services that they profess to supply and do supply, advocates and solicitors define the law which matters to them. Predominantly it is the preservation and increase of substantial material assets, whether owned by individuals or corporations. That is what the clients set great store by and what they are willing to pay to defend and add to. In so far as most students of law in Scotland wish to enter the Scottish legal profession, the law courses which they elect to follow have to give prominence to those parts of the law which lawyers find remunerative.

## ADMISSION TO THE LEGAL PROFESSION

Admission to the offices of advocate and solicitor is controlled by the Faculty of Advocates (nominally on a remit from the Court of Session) and under statute by the Law Society of Scotland, respectively. Both bodies require three stages of training, which are similar, but not identical. The first is the stage of knowledge of the law. For the Law Society this is in the law of Scotland, conveyancing, evidence, taxation and European Union law. The Faculty's requirements are more extensive, in that the subjects of the law of Scotland are fully specified, and in addition to the Law Society's requirements international private law, constitutional law, jurisprudence and the Roman law of property and obligations are demanded. The great majority of entrants to both branches provide evidence of their knowledge by the possession of a degree

---

1 See Admission as a Solicitor with Extended Rights (Scotland) Rules 1992. On the process of admission, see 1993 JLSS 234.
2 *Anderson v HM Advocate* 1996 JC 29 at 35; 1996 SLT 155 at 158.

in law (LLB) from a Scottish university, with or without Honours, containing passes in the subjects specified. But both bodies also provide their own examinations in each required subject.

The second stage is study for and the acquisition of the Diploma in Legal Practice from a Scottish university. The course for the Diploma deals in a simulated way with the main forms of legal practice in Scotland. The course is uniform throughout the five participating universities, which share the same course materials. Much of the instruction is given on a part-time basis by practising solicitors. The Diploma courses are eight in number: conveyancing (in addition to that already studied in the LLB degree), accountancy, civil court practice, criminal court practice, professional responsibility, wills, trusts and executries, and finance, taxation and investment plus one of formation and management of companies or public administration. In exceptional circumstances exemption may be granted from the Diploma, where there is sufficient relevant professional experience. The course has lasted one academic year but has recently been reduced to the period from October to April.

The third stage is training in an approved legal office under a training contract. For an intending advocate it normally lasts 21 months; for an intending solicitor, two years. During that period the trainee attends a university for a further two weeks takes a Professional Competence Course provided by the Glasgow Graduate School of Law and the Writers to the Signet Society or in two cases a large firm of solicitors. Professional Competence is attested by appraisal throughout the traineeship and a log-book record of all work performed by the trainee. The intending advocate then has to spend a further nine months approximately in pupillage (known colloquially as 'devilling'), learning from and assisting an established advocate. During this period he or she has to pass a further examination in evidence, pleading, practice and professional conduct. Any payment in respect of pupillage is forbidden. The Law Society, however, stipulates minimum salaries for each of the years of the solicitor's traineeship. These are often exceeded by local and other public authorities. Intending advocates can expect similar salaries.

The would-be advocate or solicitor has also to name persons who will provide a reference as to his or her fitness to enter the legal profession. Any criminal convictions or bankruptcy must be declared and will be investigated.

Thus, the two professional bodies determine whom they admit to their number and so to a form of public office with certain unique privileges. For the last two decades the numbers admitted have far exceeded the numbers leaving the solicitors' profession.

The number of women admitted has for several years exceeded the number of men. The number of practising advocates has also grown steadily in recent years to about 435.

## STANDARDS OF PRACTICE AND BEHAVIOUR

It is difficult for the Law Society to supervise the activities of its members, once qualified and admitted. The work they may have the opportunity to do is very diverse, their numbers are large – over 11,000 in total, counting those with and without practising certificates – and they are scattered throughout Scotland and beyond. Advocates, on the other hand, being far fewer in number and concentrated in Edinburgh, and to a lesser extent Glasgow, around the courts, have a certain *esprit de corps* which enables standards of conduct to be absorbed informally by imitation or advice from colleagues, for example, as to clubs, sports and dress, though up to a certain point eccentricities and discreet deviant behaviour are tolerated.

The primary source of professional standards for the new advocate is the *Guide to the Professional Conduct of Advocates*, which was published in 1988, as a response to a recommendation by the Hughes Royal Commission in 1980. This slender publication of 26 pages also serves as an indication to the general public of behaviour to be expected of advocates. In 2003 it was under revision.

The conduct required of solicitors could be ascertained in two ways: certain aspects of legal practice, for example, keeping accounts and advertising or 'touting' for business, were regulated in Law Society regulations and rules; and behaviour which amounted to professional misconduct could be ascertained from the decisions of the Scottish Solicitors' Discipline Tribunal[1]. Following criticism from the Royal Commission on Legal Services in Scotland in 1980 in its Report at 18.4 and the adoption of a Code of Conduct by the Bar Councils of the European Community in 1988 (known in Scotland as the Cross-Border Code of Conduct), the Law Society of Scotland in 1989 issued a Code of Conduct for Scottish solicitors, which was revised in 2002, taking account of the Cross-Border Code of Conduct[2].

---

1 See p 361 below. See also JH Webster *Professional Ethics and Practice for Scottish Solicitors* (3rd edn, 1996). Ian Smith and John Barton *Procedures and Decisions* (1995).
2 For the Cross-Border Code of Conduct Rules, see *The Parliament House Book* section F, 274 and for the Code of Conduct for Scottish Solicitors, see section F, 1002.

The Code is 'a statement of the basic values and principles which form the foundation of the solicitor profession' and underlie the more specific rules, for example, on conflicts of interest between clients. It stipulates various obligations of the solicitor, which it acknowledges may conflict: to clients, to the courts, to the public and to the legal profession and its individual members. But the Code starts with an assertion of the independence of the solicitor in various senses. Thus, misleading arguments must not be put forward on behalf of a client because of the lawyer's duty to the court. He must give advice in the best interest of the client and not take action which he considers to be against that interest. He must not put forward advice which promotes his own interest. Many solicitors are literally dependent in being employed by the government, local authorities, banks, companies etc. Confidentiality towards clients is a fundamental duty, respected even by the courts. The concept of providing adequate professional services is extensively defined. Solicitors should not undertake work unless they can perform it adequately. That means they must have the requisite legal knowledge and skill, be able to complete the work within a reasonable period of time, and communicate effectively with the client and others. Having once undertaken work, they must not withdraw from it without good cause and, if the matter is before a court, normally with the agreement of the court.

There is also a Code of Conduct for Criminal Work, of 1996. It consists of short statements such as 'A solicitor should not accept instructions from more than one accused in the same matter', followed by longer explanatory guidance notes. The Scottish Legal Aid Board brought into operation in 1998 a Code of Practice affecting those solicitors who are registered to provide legal services remunerated by Criminal Legal Aid[1]. It stipulates in detail the manner in which these services are to be provided and the records which are to be kept[2].

Competition among solicitors has been encouraged by regulations on advertising and promotion of 1995. Formerly, any form of advertising was strictly curtailed. But since 1991 'a solicitor shall be entitled to promote his services in any way he thinks fit', with a few exceptions. He must not approach a person he knows or ought to know is the client of another solicitor. But that does not preclude the general circulation of promotional material, which may reach the clients of other solicitors. Advertising must be 'decent' and shall not claim superiority over another solicitor,

1 See p 365 below.
2 Crime and Punishment (Scotland) Act 1997, s 49.

compare fees with those of another solicitor, contain inaccurate or misleading statements, bring the profession into disrepute, identify any client without his consent, or be defamatory or illegal. The Council of the Society has power to order the withdrawal or cancellation of any offending material[1]. Breach of these rules can amount to professional misconduct[2].

Misuse of clients' funds has led to the tightening up of the rules relating to clients' accounts. All account books must be properly written up and a reconciliation of the firm's books with bank statements be made every month. 'Books and documents' are defined to include computerised records. For each accounting period, usually every six months, a certificate must be produced to the Law Society, signed by the cash-room partner and another, as to the state of the firm's accounts[3]. Inspectors of the Law Society have the power to inspect accounts on giving written notice[4]. A guide to the Solicitors' (Scotland) Accounts Rules was issued with effect from 1 February 2002.

Detailed Practice Guidelines are issued by the Professional Practice Committee of the Society on many and varied subjects, such as conflicts of interest, confidentiality and the use of fax and e-mail for transmitting documents. These Guidelines are collected in *The Parliament House Book* section F.

## NEW FORMS OF ORGANISATION

Most solicitors practise in partnerships, which means that each partner is fully liable for all the debts of the firm, a protection to some extent for clients. It is now possible for solicitors partnerships to be formed under the Limited Partnerships Act 2000. Some practise as individuals. Under Rules of 2001 (replacing ones of 1997) it is possible for solicitors to form an incorporated practice, if recognised by the Council of the Society. Incorporation may take various forms but could limit the firm's liability to pay its debts, though it is still obliged to contribute to the Master Policy against professional negligence (see pp 357–358 below) and its members to the Guarantee Fund (see p 357 below)[5]. It would also entail that

---

1 For the rules on advertising and promotion, see *The Parliament House Book* section F, 248.
2 Ibid F, 249.
3 *The Parliament House Book* section F, 1239.
4 *The Parliament House Book* section F, 1240.
5 *The Parliament House Book* section F, 1235.

the affairs of the practice be opened up to some degree of public scrutiny through the Registrar of Companies. So far only two incorporated practices have been formed and one of these has ceased to operate as such.

It has been a matter of acute controversy whether solicitors should be allowed to practise along with members of other professions such as accountants and surveyors in multi-disciplinary practices (abbreviated to MDPs). In a discussion paper in 1987 the government floated the idea, suggesting it would be advantageous to consumers to have one door to call at with their problems. The Law Society resisted the proposal strenuously in its response to the 1989 consultation paper *The Legal Profession in Scotland* on the grounds that it would erode the existing statutory protections to the public (see p 356 below), a position it still maintains. The Law Reform (Miscellaneous Provisions) (Scotland) Act 1990 by s 31(3) creates a curious compromise of the dispute in allowing the Law Society to regulate MDPs, but requiring that any regulation which would prohibit them should have the approval of the Secretary of State and the Director General of Fair Trading. The Law Society responded in 1991 by issuing regulations forbidding solicitors to form a legal relationship with a person or body who is not a solicitor with a view to their offering jointly professional services, but allowing the Council to waive the rule in unspecified circumstances[1].

The possibility of MDPs has also been thrust on a reluctant Faculty of Advocates, whose members have always practised as individuals and continue to do so. But the 1990 Act, by s 31, states that any rule prohibiting partnerships among advocates or of advocates and other persons is subject to the approval of the Lord President and the Secretary of State for Scotland, who must consult the Director General of Fair Trading.

At the level of the Commission of the European Union there is also pressure on the legal professions to allow MDPs. But the Council of Bars and Law Societies of Europe (CCBE) has resisted such moves as threatening the independence of lawyers and confidential dealings with their clients.

A further novel form of practice which is provided for in the 1990 Act is the multi-national practice. Under a European Community Directive of 1977 (77/249) lawyers from one member

---

1 *The Parliament House Book* section F, 330. The Secretary of State for Scotland approved the multi-practice Rules, but stipulated that a review should take place after five years to ascertain whether competition had thereby been distorted.

state can appear in the courts of any other member state, though practical difficulties mean that this right is rarely used. Provision is made for testing the competence of and admitting qualified applicants[1]. Ironically, lawyers from England and Northern Ireland could not thereby appear in Scottish courts (nor vice versa). Provision is now made by s 30 of the 1990 Act for regulations to be made for the admission of legal practitioners qualified in England and Wales or Northern Ireland to appear and conduct litigation in Scottish courts. In *Hoekstra v HM Advocate (No 3)* 2000 SCCR 676, a case concerning drug-smuggling at sea, three of the accused were represented by members of the Netherlands Bar. By s 32 of the same Act, Scottish solicitors may enter multi-national practices with foreign lawyers, defined so as to include those qualified in England or Northern Ireland. The Council of the Law Society is to maintain a register of such foreign lawyers.

## PROTECTION OF THE PUBLIC

Professions are to a large extent self-regulating bodies. As such they have traditionally set standards of conduct and policed their members' compliance with them. In recent years Parliament, dominated by governments committed to extending market principles and under pressure from the consumer movement, has taken more interest in how professional standards are maintained. There has been an increasing awareness that the knowledge and skills of professionals put them in a position of superiority over their clients and that the competitive pressures on lawyers in particular mean that there are temptations to take advantage of that relationship. Hence some protections for the public against any abuses by members of the Scottish legal profession have been adopted voluntarily and some have been imposed on it.

### Solicitors

The protections for the public against solicitors are: (a) the Guarantee Fund; (b) claims for damages for professional negligence, which may be met by compulsory insurance; (c) awards for inadequate professional services; and (d) refund of grossly excessive fees.

---

1 *The Parliament House Book* section F, 228.

## Guarantee Fund

Under the Solicitors (Scotland) Act 1980, s 43 the Law Society has to maintain a fund from which grants of compensation may be made to people who have suffered loss because of the dishonesty of solicitors (other than their partners or employees). The dishonesty may, but need not, have led to a criminal conviction. The scheme is a last resort, so any other remedies have to be pursued first. This Guarantee Fund is maintained by annual contributions from solicitors, plus levies to meet exceptionally large claims[1].

## Professional negligence insurance

Solicitors, in common with other professional people, are bound to exercise the standard of skill and care which can reasonably be expected of a competent practitioner in their profession. If they do not, they may be sued for consequential loss, certainly by a client, and possibly by affected third parties as well[2]. Delay in performing legal transactions is the commonest form of such negligence. For example, failing to raise an action for damages for personal injuries within three years, failing to make an application for unfair dismissal compensation within three months, failing to register security documents. As well as such negligence, deliberate fault, such as fraud, will give rise to a claim for compensation.

It might be difficult to find a solicitor willing to raise a court action against a fellow practitioner. However, since 1975 the Law Society has had a panel of solicitors, to one of whom a complainer who cannot obtain advice or representation on such a claim is referred. The services of such a person (sometimes called a 'troubleshooter') have to be paid for, either in the normal way for professional services or through legal aid.

Although a claim against a solicitor may eventually have to be decided in court, the great majority are settled by negotiation, under the threat of court action. Since November 1978 the Law Society has required all its members to be covered by a Master Policy of professional indemnity insurance, thus ensuring that legitimate claims will be met[3]. Proof that the premium has been paid must be exhibited each October when applications for renewal of the practising certificate are made. The number and size

---

1 *The Parliament House Book* section F, 280.
2 See *The Laws of Scotland: Stair Memorial Encyclopaedia* vol 13, para 1189.
3 For the Rules, see *The Parliament House Book* section F, 307.

of claims has soared and so inevitably there have been regular increases in the premiums. Premiums are calculated on a complex formula related to number of partners and staff. To encourage care, there is a low claims discount financed out of loadings on the premiums of those who have had above average claims. There is also an excess per partner, a sum which must be paid by the insured before the liability takes effect. The insurers are advised by a panel of solicitors on the more difficult claims, for it is by the standards of the average competent solicitor that liability is established.

*Inadequate professional services*

There may be many instances of an unacceptable quality of service by a solicitor which fall short of negligence or are too minor to pursue as such; for example, not replying to letters or telephone calls. In such cases arising from conduct after 3 June 1991 the Law Society, on receiving a complaint from a solicitor's client, has powers to order its member to reduce or waive the fees and outlays charged, to refund payments already made by the complainer, to rectify errors and omissions and to pay the complainer up to (now) £1,200 in compensation[1]. The Discipline Tribunal has similar powers in respect of cases prosecuted before it.

*Excessive fees*

Where fees charged by a solicitor are regarded by the Council of the Law Society as 'grossly excessive' it has power to order the excess, as established by the Auditor of the Court of Session, to be refunded and to suspend the solicitor from practice until this is done[2].

**Advocates**

By comparison with those against solicitors, the remedies of clients against advocates are less. In the case of *Batchelor v Pattison & Mackersy* (1876) 3 R 914, a celebrated judge of his day, Lord President Inglis, declared that because the advocate owed a duty to the court and must be independent of his client

1 Solicitors (Scotland) Act 1980, ss 42A–42C, 53A.
2 Solicitors (Scotland) Act 1980, s 39A.

'His legal right is to conduct the cause without any regard to the wishes of his client, so long as his mandate is unrecalled, and what he does *bona fide* according to his own judgment will bind his client, and will not expose him to any action for what he has done, even if the client's interests are thereby prejudiced'.

This pronouncement from over a century ago is fully subscribed to by all advocates today and is quoted with the surrounding passages in full in the *Guide to the Professional Conduct of Advocates* of 1988. It was also followed by Lord Justice-Clerk Ross in *Brodt v King* 1991 SLT 272. So however negligent an advocate may be in conducting a case in court, his client has no legal redress against him.

However, in the English case of *Rondel v Worsley* [1969] 1 AC 191 the House of Lords upheld the immunity of barristers (and, by inference, of advocates) for actions done in court, on grounds ironically called 'public policy', but left open the possibility that they might be liable for negligent advice. In a later English case, *Saif Ali v Sydney Mitchell & Co* [1980] AC 198, a driver sued his solicitors for loss incurred through the latter's delay in pursuing an action. The solicitors sought to claim indemnification from a barrister who, they said, caused the delay. The House of Lords held that the immunity extended only to what was done in court and pre-trial work closely connected with it. By a majority it held that this third-party claim was not close enough and so should not be struck out. It is probable that the same distinction would be made in Scotland and since 1976 advocates have collectively taken out insurance against actions against them for negligence out of court[1].

A further English case on this subject, on which the law in Scotland has arguably been developed, is *Arthur JS Hall & Co v Simons* [2002] 1 AC 615. In it, Lord Hope, a former Lord President, speaking *obiter*, opined that the 'core forensic immunity' (i e as to conduct in court) should remain in criminal cases in which the advocate might be harassed by a client who might well be 'devious, vindictive and unscrupulous'. However, in civil cases he regarded the core immunity as 'disproportionate', though it might be difficult to prove negligence. The same law, whatever it is,

---

1 On the likely scope of the immunity of advocates see *The Laws of Scotland: Stair Memorial Encyclopaedia* vol 13, para 1380, where the authors, then a judge and an advocate, attempt to extend the immunity affirmed in *Rondel's* case to settlements reached outside court, but immediately before or during a proof or jury trial.

that applies to Scots advocates also applies to solicitor-advocates, on the authority of the Scottish case of *Anderson v HM Advocate* 1996 JC 29 at 35. In the same case Lord Hope could only say of solicitors that they were agents of their clients but could not be asked to follow the clients' instructions beyond what is 'lawful and proper'.

## COMPLAINTS AND DISCIPLINE

Much of the cohesion of a profession derives from its ability to control the behaviour of its members, even to the extent of punishment. In this way the conduct of the offender is stigmatised and the correct norms of behaviour, which might be uncertain or taken for granted, are affirmed and reinforced.

### Advocates

Until 1988 the disciplining of advocates was a matter for the discretion of the Dean alone. However, when most professions and occupations, including solicitors, had disciplinary procedures with ultimate recourse to the courts in some circumstances, it seemed anomalous that advocates should enjoy no such protection. Rules were published in that year and re-issued with amendments in 2002. They regulate the disciplining of advocates and reduce the role of the Dean, though he remains the key figure.

Anyone may make a complaint about the conduct of an advocate, in writing to the Dean of the Faculty. It will not be entertained more than six months after the date of the conduct complained about, unless there are exceptional circumstances. The complaint will be copied to the advocate complained about. He is asked to respond within 14 days. Further correspondence may ensue to clarify whether the material facts are in dispute or not. The Dean may also act without a complaint. The *Guide to the Professional Conduct of Advocates* gives information as to the conduct to be expected of advocates.

If the facts are not in dispute the complaint is sent to a Complaints Committee, composed of the Dean or Vice-Dean, a senior advocate and a lay person. If the complaint is upheld, the Committee can impose a penalty, including a financial one, or it may remit the matter to the Discipline Tribunal of four practising advocates and at least two lay persons, whose powers of punishment are greater.

But if the facts are in dispute the Complaints Committee can remit the matter to an Investigating Committee who, after investigation, will submit a written report. Alternatively the complaint can be remitted directly to the Discipline Tribunal to determine the facts and impose a penalty if appropriate. The standard of proof required is beyond reasonable doubt. Penalties which the Discipline Tribunal can impose include a fine not exceeding £15,000, suspension from practice for up to five years, and expulsion from the Faculty.

## Solicitors

The machinery for disciplining solicitors is laid down in statute, with a right of appeal to the Court of Session. The first stage is that of complaint. The Law Society maintains a Client Relations Office which accepted 1,606 complaints in 2002. About one in five of these are referred to one of five Client Relations Committees which meet monthly. The rest are disposed of by some kind of administrative action, for example, where the complaint is of delay, by the delay being explained or the work resumed and/or by a cut in fees. The Society urges firms of solicitors to designate a complaints partner who will try to achieve a conciliated settlement.

The Client Relations Committees each have ten members: five solicitors and five lay members. They deal with the more serious or disputed complaints. They can censure the solicitor complained of or, if they find professional misconduct, reprimand the offender, make an order as for inadequate professional services[1], or recommend a prosecution before the Scottish Solicitors' Discipline Tribunal.

This body[2] is composed of ten to fourteen solicitors and four lay persons. A quorum is four, of whom one must be a lay person. In most cases the Council of the Law Society acts as a prosecutor and appoints a solicitor to present the case against its member, who can be legally represented. But if a solicitor has been convicted of an offence involving dishonesty or sentenced to imprisonment for not less than two years, then the Tribunal can decide what action to take on that information alone. The Tribunal also acts as an appellate body against disciplinary decisions of the Council of the Law Society.

The Tribunal has the power to strike off, suspend from practice, censure and fine up to £10,000 a solicitor, or revoke the

---

1 See p 358 above.
2 Solicitors (Scotland) Act 1980, ss 50–54 and Sch 4, Pt I. For Rules of 2002 see Parliament House Book F272.

recognition of an incorporated practice. Its decisions must be published, unless to do so would harm the interests of persons other than the solicitor, partners and their families[1].

## The Ombudsman

Overseeing all these complaints and disciplinary procedures is the Scottish Legal Services Ombudsman. Formerly, as the Lay Observer, he investigated allegations about the Law Society's handling of complaints. Since 1 July 1991, with a new title, he has had a wider role[2]. His remit covers complaints to the Faculty of Advocates and the now defunct Scottish Conveyancing and Executry Services Board, as well as the Law Society. The Ombudsman cannot overrule the decisions of the professional body. He can only make recommendations to it. He may recommend a particular form of redress or further procedure in relation to an individual complaint, and he may make broader recommendations about the manner of dealing with such complaints or complaints in general. Under the Scottish Legal Services Ombudsman Etc Act 1997, s 2 he can recommend that the profession complained of should pay compensation of up to £1,200 to the complainer for loss, inconvenience and distress. He also has power to refer cases directly to the Scottish Solicitors' Discipline Tribunal. In 2002–03 the Ombudsman received 206 complaints about the handling of complaints, all but 15 concerning the Law Society[3]; and prepared 210 Opinions. The Justice One Committee in it's report on the handling of complaints by the legal profession urged that the Ombudsman's powers should be strengthened.

## PRIVILEGES

Advocates have long enjoyed the monopoly of representing clients in the Court of Session, High Court of Justiciary, and equivalent courts. In addition they have the same rights as English barristers to appear before the House of Lords and Judicial Committee of the Privy Council. They now have to share representation in the Scottish superior courts with suitably qualified Scottish solicitors

---

1 Solicitors (Scotland) Act 1980, ss 50–54.
2 Law Reform (Miscellaneous Provisions) (Scotland) Act 1990, s 34.
3 Scottish Legal Services Ombudsman, Annual Report. His address is 17 Waterloo Place, Edinburgh.

and members of any other bodies who seek and obtain approval[1]. Members of Bars of European Community member states may also appear in these courts, in conjunction with advocates and now qualified solicitors[2]. Members of the Bars of England and Wales and of Northern Ireland may also apply to practise before the superior courts[3]. Advocates have the right to appear in any court and tribunal within Scotland.

Solicitors may appear in any sheriff or district court and tribunal in Scotland. Since 1993 certain of them have been granted the right of audience in the Court of Session, or the High Court or both[4]. For at least five years continuously before the application they must have had experience in advocacy or as a solicitor instructing advocates. They must undergo an induction course in the rules and practice of the court to which they seek admission and undertake 'sitting-in' for a certain number of days in that court. Finally, they must sit and pass an examination in civil and/or criminal procedures. Training courses are also provided by the Law Society and must be attended by any applicant with less than ten years' experience as an instructing solicitor in the Court of Session or advocacy in solemn criminal procedure[5].

Solicitors have enjoyed a legal monopoly of the preparation of deeds for reward, which led to the practical monopoly of conveyancing. Provision was made for the sharing of that monopoly with qualified conveyancers approved by the Scottish Conveyancing and Executry Practitioners Board[6]. Solicitors have also had a monopoly in the preparation for a fee of the papers needed to apply to a court for the confirmation of executors. This was to be shared with approved executry practitioners[7]. The Board is being abolished and it's powers transferred to the new society.

## ALTERNATIVE WAYS OF DELIVERING LEGAL SERVICES

The legal profession is the most conspicuous provider of legal services. However, being motivated primarily by profitability,

1 Law Reform (Miscellaneous Provisions) (Scotland) Act 1990, ss 25, 26.
2 European Communities (Services by Lawyers) Order 1978, SI 1978/1910.
3 Law Reform (Miscellaneous Provisions) (Scotland) Act 1990, s 30.
4 Law Reform (Miscellaneous Provisions) (Scotland) Act 1990, s 24.
5 Admission as a Solicitor with Extended Rights (Scotland) Rules 1992.
6 Law Reform (Miscellaneous Provisions) (Scotland) Act 1990, s 17; see p 300 below.
7 Law Reform (Miscellaneous Provisions) (Scotland) Act 1990, ss 18 and 19. But see p 376 *infra*.

without which its members would not remain in business, it understandably concentrates on those services in which payment of fees is virtually assured, such as home ownership, financial services, and the distribution of the assets of the dead. In recent years competition from estate agents, banks and accountants has led the legal profession to defend its stake in these areas vigorously. But there are many other needs for law. Those who are charged with crimes, or whose marriages break down, or who are dismissed from their jobs, are unwillingly caught up in the law. There are many other rarer events which lead people either to need to use the law or to find it being used against them. Yet the cost of legal services is such that most of these people will find them well beyond their means. Should they be enabled to get access to the law and, if so, how?

If people do not know of the laws that might benefit them, or lack the means to utilise them, they are at a profound disadvantage compared with those who do have such knowledge and ability. Moreover, the purposes of the state in providing through legislation certain benefits are thwarted. In the period of the foundation of the welfare state, following the Second World War, an attempt was made to correct these defects. The principle was first established that people who had limited financial means and a genuine case should be enabled to raise and defend proceedings in court. They might well not have to do so, for their bargaining position would be greatly strengthened because the state would pay in whole or part for whatever services of lawyers were necessary. This principle was given effect to in the Legal Aid and Solicitors (Scotland) Act 1949. It is now repealed but the principle is still embodied in its replacement, the Legal Aid (Scotland) Act 1986.

## The legal aid schemes

The first form that legal aid took was in civil proceedings, for which it was made available from 1950. In its present form it enables people who pass means tests regarding their income and capital to be represented by solicitors or advocates in the House of Lords, Court of Session, sheriff courts, Scottish Land Court, Lands Valuation Appeal Court, Lands Tribunal for Scotland, Restrictive Practices Court and the Employment Appeal Tribunal[1].

1 An Act of the Scots Parliament of 1424 allowed courts to appoint an advocate in civil cases to 'onie pure creature, for fault of cunning, or expenses, that cannot nor may not follow his cause' (see APS II, 8). In 1535 two advocates for the poor were appointed and Fridays were set aside by the new Court of Session for the hearing of the cases of the poor (*Acta Dominorum Concilii* III, 434, 438).

In 1964 legal aid for criminal proceedings in the High Court and sheriff courts was introduced and extended in 1975 to district courts. In summary cases there is a financial condition that the accused must be unable to defend himself without undue hardship to himself or his dependants and have no other means, such as insurance, to cover court expenses. No financial contribution is required. In solemn cases there is no financial test other than undue hardship. In addition, everyone being brought before a court from custody is entitled to initial free advice and representation from a duty solicitor.

In 1972 a scheme of advice and assistance was introduced. This is a comprehensive service offering through solicitors (and, where appropriate, advocates) (a) advice on any matter to which the law of Scotland applies and (b) the assertion of rights under it by any means short of going to court; for example, by correspondence, telephone calls and interviews. There are financial tests of income and capital, applied by the solicitor, who also collects any contribution. Expenditure of up to £80 (or in exceptional circumstances £150) can be incurred by the solicitor without any approval from the legal aid authorities.

The relative simplicity of the advice and assistance scheme and its administrative economy led to its being being extended to cover certain forms of representation under the name of ABWOR (assistance by way of representation). So far ABWOR has been applied to certain summary criminal proceedings, such as changes of plea to guilty and proofs in mitigation of sentence, to applications and appeals to the sheriff by patients under the Mental Health (Scotland) Act 1984, to disciplinary proceedings before a prison governor, to applications for removal of a driving disqualification, and to unopposed petitions for the appointment of an executor, those appearing from custody following breach of interdict and to life prisoners wishing to challenge their tariffs.

There are special provisions for legal aid for children, who are assessed without regard to their parents' resources.

## Administration of legal aid

Legal aid was administered from 1950 by committees of the Law Society of Scotland. The Hughes Royal Commission criticised this arrangement as 'wrong in principle' and by the Legal Aid (Scotland) Act of 1986 the Scottish Legal Aid Board was set up. It is classed officially as a 'non-departmental public body', sponsored by the Scottish Executive. It disburses on behalf of the Scottish

Ministers to solicitors and advocates payments in respect of fees and outlays incurred in giving legal aid to people found eligible under the various schemes. The Board consisted in 2003 of a chairwoman, Jean Couper, and eleven members, of whom two are solicitors, two advocates and one a sheriff[1]. It operates from one office at 44 Drumsheugh Gardens, in the centre of Edinburgh.

*Eligibility*

The Board, through its staff, is responsible for most of the decisions that have to be taken on whether legal aid is to be granted or not. In a limited number of cases, judges still decide.

**Civil legal aid.** In civil legal aid the legal tests are (1) whether as pursuer or defender the applicant has a probable cause for litigating, that is, an arguable case in law backed up by sufficient evidence, and (2) whether it is reasonable in the circumstances that legal aid should be made available. Solicitors submit a sketch of the client's case in law and statements taken from potential witnesses. In straightforward cases staff of the Board take the decision, but it has also a panel of solicitors and advocates, to whom, as reporters difficult cases can be referred. The opponent is given a chance to object to any proposed award of legal aid. Civil legal aid is not awarded if an organisation such as a trade union, insurance company or motoring organisation is available to pay. In actions of defamation or verbal injury it cannot be awarded.

There is also a financial test which is applied by the Board. Annual income and capital from all sources are separately assessed. Deductions are made in respect of dependants, housing costs, debts, National Insurance, tax etc. The applicant's home and its furnishings, clothing and tools are disregarded in assessing capital. If the applicant's income and capital, thus assessed, are below a certain level (in 2003, £2,851 for annual income, £6,100 for capital), then he is eligible without making a contribution. People who receive income support are automatically eligible. Those whose available income exceeds a certain level are ineligible (£9,307 for annual income, but less in an action of reparation for personal injuries). Those whose available capital exceeds £10,170

---

1 On the Board's operations see its annual reports. For a comprehensive collection of legal aid legislation, see *The Parliament House Book* Division G. For the fullest commentary on the legislation, see Charles N Stoddart *Law and Practice of Legal Aid in Scotland* (4th edn, 1994 and supplement).

may be refused civil legal aid. Those who fall in between these lower and upper financial limits are eligible, subject to having to make a fixed contribution, regardless of the length or complexity of the case. It may be paid by instalments from income, usually over ten months. In these calculations the income and capital of husband and wife (and of couples living together as such) is aggregated, unless they have opposed interests – as in divorce – or are separated.

To avoid financial hardship arising out of the award of civil legal aid, courts can modify the award of expenses in two ways. Normally the successful party is awarded the expenses of the action against the unsuccessful one. If an unassisted party wins, then the award of expenses against an assisted person is not to exceed a sum which in the opinion of the court it is reasonable for him to pay, having regard to the means of the parties and their conduct in the dispute (Legal Aid (Scotland) Act 1986, s 18).

That might leave the successful unassisted party in a position of hardship. So the court may, secondly, award him all or part of his expenses out of the Legal Aid Fund, provided severe hardship would otherwise result and it is just and equitable to do so (1986 Act, s 19).

**Criminal legal aid.** In applications for criminal legal aid in summary prosecutions the legal test is that it is in the interests of justice that legal aid should be granted. Until 1986 no specification of this vague test was given and, as the award was granted by different sheriffs and justices, widespread differences occurred. Now the 1986 Act lists examples where legal aid should be provided, such as that a substantial question of law may arise or that the accused has difficulty in understanding the proceedings (s 24(3)). The financial test of undue hardship to the accused or his dependants is interpreted by the Board in a broad way, without the stringency of civil legal aid (s 24).

In solemn procedure it is assumed that the matter is grave enough to justify the award of legal aid, provided the test of undue hardship is met. It is the court that takes that decision. Again, where a summary court is considering whether to impose a first sentence of imprisonment, it decides whether to award criminal legal aid on the hardship test (s 23). Applications for aid in criminal appeals are decided by the Board, which has to apply the hardship test and check that there are substantial grounds for making the appeal and that it is reasonable to do so (s 25).

Solicitors providing criminal legal aid have from 1 October 1998 had to be registered as such and agree to abide by a Code of

Practice laying down their responsibilities towards the Board and clients in a manner consistent with the Law Society's Code of Conduct for Criminal Work, of 1996.

From the same date the Board began, on an experimental basis, to provide criminal legal aid in summary proceedings in the Edinburgh sheriff and district courts by means of salaried solicitors. All persons wishing such assistance and born in the months of January and February must apply for it to the Public Defence Solicitors' Office. The experiment is to continue till at least 2008 and there is provision for it to be extended to two other areas.

The fees of solicitors for work done under criminal legal aid have since April 1999 been fixed in accordance with the category of work done, on submission of detailed accounts.

**Advice and assistance.** Advice and Assistance (and its off-shoot ABWOR) is relatively simple and cheap to administer. The only test of eligibility is a financial one and it is applied by the solicitor giving the service (or an employee on his behalf). As with civil legal aid, there is a range of persons whose assets entitle them to aid without contribution. From 7 April 2003 disposable income for eligibility (after deductions for dependants) must be £81 per week or less and disposable capital no more than £1,330. The upper qualifying income limit is £192 per week. Where weekly disposable income is over £81 and no more than £192, a contribution is payable on a sliding scale. Those who receive income support, family credit or income-based jobseeker's allowance are automatically eligible. The scheme is a comprehensive one, covering advice, written or oral, on all aspects of the law of Scotland and assistance in making use of it, for example by letters and telephone calls.

**Costs of legal aid.** Legal aid is not subject to cash limits (though its administration is). The demand in any one year could not be predicted with accuracy. The soaring costs of legal aid (in 2001–02 £135.9m offset by £8.5m in contributions and recoveries) have been a subject of concern to the Executive and UK Treasury. Great emphasis has been laid on efficiency at all stages of the award of legal aid, including the meeting of targets, and on value for money[1]. However, the use of contracts and franchises with particular firms, as used in England and Wales, has not been adopted.

---

1 On statutory legal aid see further *The Laws of Scotland: Stair Memorial Encyclopaedia* vol 13, para 1001ff.

*Deficiencies of legal aid*

Such is the official provision of legal aid, as distinct from voluntary efforts, which we have still to mention. What are its defects? There are problems with the legal aid schemes, with the lawyers who provide them and with the people who use them.

Unlike social security benefits, the entitlement conditions leading to the benefits of civil legal aid and advice and assistance are not linked to the cost of living. So, as all governments try to contain public expenditure where they can, legal aid entitlements tend not to be sufficiently revised.

Where the objective of an action is to recover compensation, then the sum recovered has to be paid into the Legal Aid Fund, pending decisions as to the expenses incurred by each side in the action. Normally the unsuccessful party has to pay the expenses of the successful party, but in matrimonial cases this is not always so. There can be disputes where each party succeeds to some extent. Settling the question may require another appearance before the court. Which expenditure is included is a matter for assessment by the Auditor of Court. There may also be decisions by the court under the Legal Aid (Scotland) Act 1986, ss 18 and 19[1].

Under what is often called the clawback, the Board takes from the sum paid to it all the outstanding expenses incurred by the Legal Aid Fund (s 17(2B)) (with certain exceptions in family and social security law). The successful litigant gets what is left. That can be little or literally nothing. For example, the sum may be reduced by contributory negligence, or the action may be settled out of court (sometimes without the knowledge of the pursuer) for a sum much less than the notional value of the claim or the sum sued for, because there would be difficulty in proving it. Of course, if the court expenses are all recovered from the unsuccessful side, then the Board may have been fully reimbursed. But the losing party may be unable to pay, or there may still be outstanding costs incurred in preparation for the action which are not covered by the court's award of expenses.

If the dispute is over property, whether heritable (such as land and buildings) or moveable, then, whether the assisted person has successfully made a claim to it or preserved it, the property becomes available to the Board to take unmet expenses out of its value. It has powers to sell moveable property and to require the owner to sell or grant a security over heritable property. This can

1 *The Parliament House Book* section G 47. See p 367 *supra*.

be particularly hard in a divorce case, where the wife has successfully asserted or defended her rights in the matrimonial home, and
there is no award of expenses or the husband is unable to pay
them. Then, except for the first £2,500 of its value, the home is
subject to the Board's claims in respect of the aid it gave. From this
power over property most social security and family law payments
are exempt[1].

The same clawback principle applies to advice and assistance,
but here there will be no payment of expenses by the other side,
unless it has been agreed in an out-of-court settlement and paid.
But the solicitor can apply to the Board, asking that the clawback
be waived on the grounds of hardship. The majority of these applications are granted.

There is a second type of clawback which is not linked to legal
aid, but as it affects those who receive most social security benefits,
it does act as a second factor reducing any apparent victory in the
courts. Where a person on benefit receives compensation for
personal injuries or illness over £2,500, by court decree or through
negotiation, then the person paying the compensation must first
deduct the amount of benefits paid, arising out of the occurence,
up to the date when final payment is made or for five years,
whichever comes first, and pay that sum to the Secretary of State
for Social Security. That recoupment takes precedence over any
reimbursement of the Legal Aid Fund[2].

To the successful legally aided litigant, it may look as if everyone
– the government, the solicitors, the advocates – is paid, except him.

However, for most people, involvement with the civil courts is a
rare and unwelcome experience. They are more likely to wish to
use one of the busier tribunals. Yet, for them, no legal aid for representation is available. The only exceptions are the Employment
Appeal Tribunal and the Lands Tribunal for Scotland, both of
which are presided over by judges and almost the same as courts,
apart from the participation of lay members along with the judge.
For proceedings in these tribunals, civil legal aid is available. If one
is financially qualified, it is possible to ask for advice under the
Advice and Assistance scheme on how to present one's own case.
But relatively little use is made of this possibility. In 1997–98 there
were 9,207 cases on state benefits of all kinds out of a total of
321,452.

The government's attitude is that tribunals are supposed to be
informal. The intervention of lawyers would tend to make them

---

1  Parliament House Book G 605.
2  Social Security Administration Act 1992, Pt IV.

more formal. But, of course, lawyers are not actually debarred from attending. And in the Employment (formerly Industrial) Tribunals, where two private parties, the employee and the employer, are in dispute, much as in a civil court, the employers are usually represented by a solicitor or advocate and the employee will have to speak for himself. The involvement of lawyers and a legally qualified full-time chairman has led to the procedure of Employment Tribunals becoming quite formal and complex. Hundreds of appeals have been taken, usually by employers, to the courts and thus the brief statutory provisions are surrounded by case law. This creates a legal minefield for the applicant making his one and only appearance before an Employment Tribunal, and puts him at a serious disadvantage.

Another weakness of the legal aid provisions is that they accommodate individuals, not groups. It is one person who must show an interest and be financially assessed. But nowadays many cases arise which affect groups of people, for example, tenants in a block of damp flats or victims of harmful medication. Even by pooling their resources, they may be unable to afford to prepare a case against a powerful and well-informed adversary. The best they can hope for is to put forward one of their number who does qualify for legal aid, seek a decision on his case and hope that, if favourable, it will be applied to the others as a test case[1].

Then there are obstacles on the part of lawyers. The range of possible inquiries under advice and assistance can extend over the whole of the law operating in Scotland. But lawyers tend to know best the parts that they make a steady living from: mainly conveyancing, wills, trusts and succession, contracts and delict, divorce and other family disputes. Although they should be able to discover the answer to any legal question or problem, given time, the remuneration that they get from the Scottish Legal Aid Board, in the opinion of many of them, simply does not adequately cover the cost. Solicitors expect to earn at least £80 an hour, to cover

---

1 See, for example, *McColl v Strathclyde Regional Council* 1983 SLT 616, where a Glasgow pensioner, with legal aid, sought to interdict the council from fluoridation of the public water supply. Lord Jauncey commented 'it would be naive to assume that the petitioner alone has an interest in the outcome of this action'. His decision that the council lacked powers to fluoridise water held up the practice throughout Scotland for several years. See also *McInally v John Wyeth and Brother Ltd* 1992 SLT 344 where, in an action arising out of damage allegedly suffered by the user of a tranquilliser, the success of one pursuer in obtaining production of documents benefited other claimants co-ordinated by a tranquilliser addiction solicitors group.

their constant overheads, such as paying staff, rent of premises and equipment, etc and their own pay. Those with commercial clients would charge far more. But the legal aid scales often fall far short. For instance, under advice and assistance a solicitor can be paid £10.55 for 15 minutes for a meeting with the client and £2.40 for a short letter or framing a formal document[1]. Moreover, authorised outlays such as the cost of police and hospital reports or advertisements have to be paid by the lawyer in the first place, in the expectation that they will eventually be recovered from the Board. The accounts have to be submitted in such minute detail and based on record-keeping of the length of each meeting, letter or phone call that many solicitors just refuse to have anything to do with advice and assistance, or in minor cases of pure advice they will opt for a standard fee of £25, regardless of the work involved, for that does not require the preparation of detailed accounts.

From the point of view of the person with a problem, there are barriers which are not so readily measurable, but are nevertheless real. Firstly, the person with a problem may not recognise that it has or might have a legal solution. For many people, the law means trouble and trouble equates with the police. Others with a wider view may not think of the law as having anything to do with social security. Even on learning, through advice and assistance, that a problem might be solved by raising a small claim action, a person may be put off by the idea of standing up in court (there being no civil legal aid for such cases) or put off by the risk of losing and having to meet the other side's expenses. These are restricted to £75, but that limitation does not apply if there is an appeal to the sheriff principal.

For people living in rural areas there may be no accessible solicitor or the only one may be acting for the opponent. Residents of peripheral city housing schemes for whom travel to a city centre is a costly matter may simply put up with a grievance that might have a legal resolution or they will pursue it through a councillor. But no doubt if recourse to a solicitor is unavoidable, they will make the effort and go to where one can be found. Recognising the difficulties, some firms have opened branch offices in housing schemes, but as the business is likely to be all legally aided, they have difficulty in making such offices pay.

Finally, there are matters of image. Among some sections of the population lawyers have the reputation of being aloof and grasping, and so best avoided, a reputation they have sought to dispel by advertising campaigns.

1 Parliament House Book G 592.

*Dial-a-law*

An attempt has been made to make the services of solicitors more accessible by the Law Society's Dial-a-law service. This is a list of over 40 recorded messages on common legal problems and how solicitors can help. It can be accessed 24 hours a day through the Society's website: http://www.lawscot.org.uk by clicking on Dial-a-law. In its first year Dial-a-law (then a much more accessible telephone service) received about 10,000 calls and referrals were made to 1,200 firms of solicitors.

## Other sources of aid

However, there are other means by which people can obtain help with the law besides the legal profession and also ways to ease access to professional legal services.

*Citizens Advice Bureaux*

The Citizens Advice Bureaux network (CABx) is prominently involved in both these developments. Founded in 1939 on the outbreak of the Second World War, it now has 70 offices and 100 other service points covering most of Scotland, including the islands. They are organised by full-time managers, but rely for their advisers almost entirely on over 2,500 trained, unpaid volunteers. No charge is made for help and the bureaux rely for their funding mainly on local authorities. The government sustains financially a supportive central organisation, Citizens Advice Scotland (or CAS), based in Edinburgh, which provides training and a continuously updated information system and ensures that standards are maintained in the local bureaux.

The CABx in Scotland dealt in 2001/02 with a total of 405,314 problems, a drop on previous years because of cuts in local authority funding requiring a reduction in opening hours. CAS does not gather separate figures for inquiries on law, but most of its categories are based on legal rights and obligations. For example, there were 56,762 inquiries on employment matters, 38,364 on housing and 121,682 on social security benefits, much the largest number.

In all these areas advice is given and negotiations are conducted on the basis of a basic knowledge of the relevant law. This is supplied initially in training courses for volunteers and kept up to date by CAS. To deal with the more difficult questions a full-time legal adviser can be contacted at CAS by telephone or fax. Where a problem seems to need the services of a solicitor, for example, in marriage breakdown, the inquirer can be put in touch with one. Many firms provide, on a rota basis, services at CABx legal clinics in the evenings, often utilising the advice and assistance scheme.

As well as legal advice the Citizens Advice movement is increasingly becoming involved in representing clients at certain tribunals, among them Employment Tribunals, Social Security Appeal Tribunals and Disability Appeal Tribunals. In 2001–02, 1,227 clients had their cases presented to tribunals by trained volunteers.

The figure of 405,314 inquiries compares with 331,890 intimations of the giving of Advice and Assistance given by lawyers in 2001–02. One may reasonably conclude, therefore, that the CABx are the largest providers of basic legal services in Scotland and the first port of call for a majority of people in need of them, albeit that a minority will have to be referred to solicitors.

*Money advice centres*

Overlapping with the Citizens Advice Bureaux are the specialised Money Advice Services, agencies which were set up in the 1980s in response to the increasing number of debt problems which followed the easier availability of credit through credit cards, store budget accounts, home mortgages etc. Some are adjuncts of Citizens Advice Bureaux, some are run by local authority consumer protection and trading standards departments and some are independent bodies started by local initiatives in deprived areas, some of them funded by Social Inclusion Partnerships. They specialise in negotiating payment arrangements on behalf of people faced with multiple debts and thus have to act within the constraints of the law on debt enforcement and bankruptcy.

*Law centres*

Law centres are non-profit-making charitable bodies, staffed by legally qualified staff and support staff. They exist to make up the lack of traditional legal services in deprived areas and concentrate on the branches of the law that could most benefit the residents of such areas, such as social security, housing, consumer protection and immigration. As well as advising individuals and groups, they give training to other users of the law, such as tenants' associations and disabled groups, and they raise awareness of the law and legal issues among residents generally. Some strive to change the law to the benefit of disadvantaged people by taking up test cases or campaigning for reforms in statutory law and law enforcement.

In England and Wales there are about 60 law centres, most of them funded by local authorities or the Lord Chancellor's Department. In Scotland they were later to develop and were denied central government funding. However, some were established with Urban Programme funding for limited periods. From April 1999 this has been replaced by the Social Inclusion Partnership, which is not confined to urban areas and not subject to time limits.

The longest-established law centre in Scotland is at Castlemilk, on the southern outskirts of Glasgow. It receives funding from the City of Glasgow Council. It holds conferences and produces publications, thus spreading knowledge of its more successful ventures, such as obtaining awards from the Criminal Injuries Compensation Agency for abused children and from landlords for illness attributable to dampness in defective houses.

For more than a decade Castlemilk was Scotland's only territorial law centre on the English model. However, in 1992 a similar law centre was set up in the Glasgow housing scheme of Drumchapel. Others followed in Glasgow East End, Dumbarton, Govan and Paisley. The Dundee North Law Centre was sponsored by the Dundee Legal Advice Association, which began in 1974. The Centre replaced it in 2002.

A law centre based on the needs of a particular class of people, though still within a defined area, was set up in 1992 – the Ethnic Minorities Law Centre in the centre of Glasgow. It was created on the initiative of the Glasgow Community Relations Council and specialises in immigration, nationality, racial discrimination and housing matters. It is staffed by a solicitor and an advice and development officer and is funded by Glasgow Council. Shelter provides an advice service on housing law.

Another agency organised around the needs of a particular interest-group is the Scottish Child Law Centre, based in Edinburgh. It was founded in 1988 to promote knowledge of and use of Scots law for the benefit of children and young people up to the age of 18. It offers them a Freephone telephone advice service (number 0800 328 8970) and also takes inquiries from social workers, teachers and others whose work is among children (number 0131 667 6333). It has a website at www.sclc.org.uk. It has played a prominent part in promoting reform of the law on children, especially as contained in the Children (Scotland) Act

1995, on which it has published an explanatory book. It is maintained by the Scottish Executive and local authorities.

Still another specialised venture in non-profit-making legal services is the Legal Services Agency, a limited company based in Glasgow, which undertakes case work, court and tribunal representation in cases likely to yield some clarification of the law. It also specialises in holding seminars and conferences in subjects of concern to disadvantaged groups. Prominent among these are the mentally ill. It runs a Mental Health Legal Representation Project which tackles not only mental health problems, but also those of dementia and brain injury.

*Insurance companies*

Certain insurance companies offer legal advice by telephone. The Automobile Association provides members with free legal advice and representation in relation to motoring matters.

*Trade unions*

Some of the major trade unions provide legal services for their members, either through their own staff or by standing arrangements with certain firms of solicitors. For example, the General Municipal Boilermakers and Allied Trade Union has arrangements with firms of solicitors to provide a free interview for members with any legal problem, whether or not related to employment, and, if there is a case to be pursued, how it can be financed, which in some cases might be through the union.

**Qualified conveyancers and executry practitioners**

To break the monopoly of solicitors in their most profitable areas of work and stimulate competition, the Conservative government in its Law Reform (Miscellaneous Provisions)(Scotland) Act 1990 made provision for two new kinds of supplier of legal services – qualified conveyancers and executry practitioners. They were, respectively, to supply solely conveyancing services and executry services (ingathering and distributing the assets of deceased persons). A Scottish Conveyancing and Executry Services Board was set up by s 16 of the 1990 Act to keep registers of 'fit and proper persons' to fulfil these roles, set standards of education and training and exercise disciplinary functions akin to those of the

Law Society. Financial institutions, such as banks and building societies and insurance companies, were to be permitted to provide executry services, under regulations as to the qualifications and training of those who provided the services. But that provision was not brought into effect. These opportunities did not prove attractive and in 2003 the Executive announced the abolition of the Board.

# 8. Law reform

## WHY LAW REFORM?

To be effective a law must be capable of being discovered and understood, so that people can know what is required of them. But there is no point in a law having these attributes if it is incapable of meeting changing human needs and wants or is plainly out of date. So an efficient law system must make provision for its own development. There has to be a mechanism for making brand-new laws, repealing outdated laws, and amending laws that are no longer able to achieve their goals.

Most changes in the law are of a minor character, adding to what is there already. A section in an Act turns out to be ambiguous and courts are interpreting it in different ways. Or it has left a loop-hole of which people, perhaps tax-payers or motorists, are taking advantage. The Misuse of Drugs Act 1971 has a provision enabling new drugs to be added to the list of controlled drugs by a resolution of both Houses of the UK Parliament. The highest court may resolve the problem by upholding one of the conflicting interpretations applied in lower courts. Or a department of government may secure an amendment of an unsatisfactory section by Parliament.

Apart from such deliberate changes, whenever existing law is applied by a court to new circumstances and a reasoned judgment is delivered and published, the law has been developed, even if only to a trivial extent. We can call this normal legal development. The law never stands still. It is always on the move, as it keeps being applied to new situations.

However, a law system should be capable of striking off in new directions or making a fresh start to some outmoded form of regulation. This is law reform and it is usually confined to the enacted law that Parliament produces, though occasionally judges can engage in law reform in what turns out to have been a dramatic way. Thus, in *Stallard v HM Advocate* 1989 SLT 469, 1989 SCCR 248 the judges decided that a wife could no longer be said to surrender herself to her husband's sexual demands. They were equal partners and he could be charged with raping her, as with any other form of assault. Law reform is usually prompted by some assumptions as to what is right or good or necessary and thus to reflect a presumed social need. But sometimes, as in laws against racial and sexual discrimination, the law has an educative role and sets new standards that are in advance of social behaviour.

## PRESSURES FOR LAW REFORM

### Technological change

What are these cues that signal a need for law reform? Perhaps the most tangible is when some new technology or technique becomes available that has a potential for harm as well as good. The most obvious example is the advent and expansion of motor traffic, which revolutionised the transport of goods and people, but at the cost of killing and maiming many road users. A vast array of laws and regulations has been devised to try to contain these unwanted consequences. The introduction of a 30mph speed limit in built-up areas in 1934 was followed by a dramatic drop in road deaths. The advent of the breathalyser in the Road Safety Act 1967, now followed, under the Road Traffic Act 1988, ss 6 to 8, by a test of the alcoholic content of breath, blood or urine, avoided the difficulties of proving unfitness to drive through drink or drugs.

Sometimes the law's reaction is of a less coercive and punitive kind than road traffic law. Medical science has advanced rapidly in recent years in two ethically problematical areas: the transplanting of human organs and the use of embryos in assisting pregnancy and medical experiments. The general public has shown some concern at these developments and the medical profession itself looked for a clear statement of what is ethically permissible. On the first issue the law has responded through the Human Tissues Act 1961, which allows the removal of organs from corpses with the consent of the deceased or without objection from relatives, and the Human Organ Transplants Act 1989, which forbids commercial dealings in human organs. The second matter is dealt with by the Human Fertilisation and Embryology Act 1990 which controls the use of human embryos, sperm and eggs and sets up a licensing authority.

Yet sometimes the new development appears out of the blue without human volition. The HIV virus, which is believed to cause the life-threatening condition of AIDS, has raised questions as to whether there is a role for law in charting its advance and impeding its transmission and whether tests for HIV should be performed, and if so, with or without consent. So far legislation is limited to the AIDS (Control) Act 1987, which requires health authorities to make reports on HIV and AIDS to the Secretary of State to facilitate the collection of statistics on their spread.

## Political pressure

Often the demand for law reform is put forward as part of the programme of a political party. Parties in a multi-party society such as ours exist to promote their vision of a better society (or, as some of them would say, to advance the interests of a class within it). So whatever they propose in and out of government is likely to meet with resistance from the other parties. But together they help through public debate to clarify the options for change. The reform, when it comes, will nearly always take the form of new law. Thus, throughout the 1980s industrial relations and the powers of trade unions were a highly contentious political topic. The prior law was transformed by six employment and trade union Acts between 1980 and 1990. Most were consolidated in the Employment Rights Act 1996 amended, in accordance with the policies of the Labour Government, in the Employment Act 2002.

A further form of pressure for law reform is created when a law system is expanded and the bounds of the territory in which it operates are redrawn. This has been one major consequence among many of the United Kingdom's membership of the European Community. As a member state the United Kingdom obliged itself to give effect to directives by the Commission. The implementation of the Single European Act by the end of 1992 with the object of equalising trading conditions throughout the Community impinges on innumerable areas of domestic law by setting uniform standards, such as on water quality and pollution.

## Political and moral values

Behind many of these demands for change there lie tacit or explicit changes in values or conflict among rival value systems. Thus, the policies of the Labour Party, for example, in education and health, tended to exhibit a preference for equality and community action which translated into the public provision of services, a tendency which has become less distinct under the Blair administration. Those of the Conservative Party show a preference for individual choice and thus encourage a variety of services privately supplied.

Sometimes, as on the suppression of dealings in dangerous drugs by the criminal law, the parties share a common stance. But some calls for law reform show straight clashes of values held by citizens, unmediated by political institutions. Thus, attempts to change the law on abortion, to make it either easier or more restrictive, reflect differing beliefs on the value of human life and the point from which it merits protection. The lowering to 16 of the age at which consensual male homosexual acts are permitted has cut across party political boundaries.

## THE INSTRUMENTS OF LAW REFORM

How is this requirement that the law be kept up to date achieved? As shown above, the normal means is through legislation. But before examining how enacted law is used to revise the law, we should first examine what scope other sources of law play in this task.

### Custom

Custom is so diffuse and unco-ordinated that one would not expect it to be of use in the purposive enterprise which law reform requires. But on rare occasions concerted and sustained action may have the effect of changing the law. Thus, before the passing of the Abortion Act 1967, abortion was an offence at common law only. But most gynaecologists in Scotland did perform abortions in hospitals to save the life or avert serious risk to the health of pregnant women; and in so far as they did not incur prosecution, it could be said that a custom had emerged among leading gynaecologists and the Crown Office, tacitly amending the criminal law on abortion so as to exclude those performed by medical practitioners for therapeutic reasons. Under the guidance of a Scottish Office circular the medical profession until the Age of Legal Capacity (Scotland) Act 1991 had a firm practice of requiring the written consent of parents and guardians to treatment of children up to the age of 16, which ignored the common law of minority in Scots law[1].

---

1  See Scottish Law Commission, Report no 110, para 27.

## Institutional writers

Institutional writers purported to declare and expound the law, including customary law, whether unwritten or evidenced in the decisions of courts. They did not therefore claim to be making law, though in gathering it, organising it and drawing inferences from it, they certainly developed it. But it would be misleading to describe this activity as an exercise in law reform.

## Judges

Judges do from time to time have opportunities to reform the law in a deliberate way. Whether they seize the opportunity depends in part on their temperament and in part on the scope that existing law affords them. It is mainly judges in the appellate courts who have the chance to reform the law. If the parties are able to pay for the full pleadings and exhaustive debate that civil appeals are given, it is likely that more is at stake than the outcome of the one case. An insurance company may want a ruling to settle some point concerning the assessment of damages. A local authority may want the legality of a financial practice followed by several others determined. (See e g *Morgan Guaranty Trust Co v Lothian Regional Council* 1995 SLT 299.) Judges will give a ruling arising out of the closest scrutiny of the facts of a genuine dispute. They are not considering the question, as Parliament does, in abstract terms. But if the matter is one in which the government of the day takes an interest, there is a risk that it will introduce a Bill to undo the change in the law, or even exceptionally to nullify the court's decision[1].

The response of the judiciary to the opportunity to reform the law can be expressed in some generalisations. Broadly speaking, Scottish judges in civil appeals are less willing to declare that they are changing the law than some English judges. This may be because they know there is the possibility of a further appeal to the House of Lords. Certainly some Scottish judges when sitting in the House of Lords have been at least as innovative as their English colleagues. Lord Kilbrandon, Lord Fraser and Lord Reid (though he was never a judge in Scotland) are examples. On the other hand, the criminal law of Scotland, which is not subject to appeal to the

---

1 This occurred when the decision of the House of Lords in favour of the company in *Burmah Oil Co Ltd v Lord Advocate* 1964 SC(HL) 117 was overturned in the War Damage Act 1965. See Stott *Lord Advocate's Diary* p 145.

Lords and most of which is the creation of judges, not statute, is regularly developed by judges, though often without their declaring that they are doing so. Thus, in a few unpretentious cases the law of theft was expanded to embrace situations where there was only a temporary removal of another's property with no intention to appropriate it[1], or merely unlawful retention of it[2]. The conduct in question was stigmatised as 'nefarious' and that was enough to make it criminal by extension of the law of theft.

*Signals to Parliament*

The responses of judges to an invitation explicitly to develop the law may be arranged on a scale from timidity to boldness. Firstly, a judge may note a gap in the law or an unjust consequence of the law, but declare that it is for Parliament to remedy it. Thus, the Adoption Act 1930 required that a minor child consent to his or her own adoption. In *B and B* 1965 SC 44 the child was mentally retarded and unable to give consent. Although the adoption would be to the child's benefit, Lord Clyde declined to approve it as to do so would in effect be to amend an Act of Parliament. But the case did draw attention to the need for reform and by the Law Reform (Miscellaneous Provisions) (Scotland) Act 1966, s 4 the child's consent can be dispensed with (now Age of Legal Capacity (Scotland) Act 1991, s 2(3)). Since the creation of the Scottish Law Commission judges have been able to point to it as able to give more thorough consideration to the need for law reform than can judges adjudicating in a single dispute[3].

*Overruling*

Secondly, judges may overrule an unsatisfactory past decision. Thus, in *Dick v Burgh of Falkirk* 1976 SC(HL) 1 the question was whether a widow, as well as taking over as executor her late husband's action of reparation for injuries sustained at work, could also seek an award for herself for solatium and loss of support. The Court of Session judges felt constrained to follow a decision of the

---

1 *Milne v Tudhope* 1981 JC 53.
2 *Kidston v Annan* 1984 SLT 279, 1984 SCCR 20. And see *Black v Carmichael* 1992 SLT 897, 1992 SCCR 709, where the wheel-clamping of a vehicle without removing it was held to be theft.
3 See Lord Reid in *McKendrick v Sinclair* 1972 SC(HL) 25; Lord Kissen in *Dick v Burgh of Falkirk* 1976 SC(HL) 1 at 7.

House of Lords in *Darling v Gray & Sons* (1892) 19 R(HL) 31 'despite the injustices which may follow from it' (per Lord Wheatley). But in the House of Lords the judges readily overruled the decision of their predecessors in *Darling* as 'wrongly decided', Lord Kilbrandon pointing out that 'your Lordships are here to do justice between the appellant and the respondents and should not leave it to Parliament to act on the recommendations of the Scottish Law Commission in Report 31 on the subject'. It was perhaps also significant that it was the Law Lords who created the injustice and it was therefore appropriate that they should remedy it at the first opportunity.

### Reformulating case law

Thirdly, judges of the highest courts may reformulate case law in a new and broader manner and thus open up the way to a new line of cases. The best known and most dramatic example of this practice is the celebrated snail-in-the-gingerbeer-bottle case of *Donoghue v Stevenson* 1932 SC(HL) 31. In the case of *Mullen v Barr* 1929 SC 461 the Inner House of the Court of Session had held that the law did not require bottlers to maintain an infallible system to exclude mice from ginger beer bottles. But in *Donoghue* Lord Atkin in the House of Lords not only held that the manufacturer of a product not open to intermediate inspection owes a duty of care to the consumer of it; he also stated a general principle of negligence, to the effect that 'you must take reasonable care to avoid acts or omissions which you can reasonably foresee would be likely to injure your neighbour' (at 44). Though the majority in the Lords was only 3 to 2, *Donoghue v Stevenson* has been as significant a reform of consumer protection law in the United Kingdom and many Commonwealth countries as any statute, and has also been the springboard for the development of liability for several other forms of negligence.

In another House of Lords 'reformulating' case, *RHM Bakeries v Strathclyde Regional Council* 1985 SC(HL) 17, Lord Fraser showed himself to be anxious to dispel any suggestion that a person who creates a structure on land, such as a dam, is strictly liable for any consequential damage. Single-handed (the other Lords concurring), he re-interpreted an earlier case, *Kerr v Earl of Orkney* (1857) 20 D 298, described the suggestion that the English strict liability case of *Rylands v Fletcher* (1868) LR 3 HL 330 was part of Scots law as 'a heresy which ought to be extirpated', distinguished the House of Lords decision of *Caledonian Railway Co v*

*Greenock Corporation* 1917 SC(HL) 56 as involving not a dam but a diverted stream, and thus reversed the decision of the Inner House.

### Prospective change

Fourthly, judges can go beyond the factual bounds of the case before them and address those who they foresee may face similar but not identical questions in the future. To them they give an indication of the court's thinking on such prospective questions. This can be justified as making a lengthy and expensive recourse to the courts unnecessary. But it has the drawback that the judges deprive themselves of hearing the arguments of counsel on the issue. Lord Denning was an enthusiastic exponent of this practice. In *Jefford v Gee* [1970] 2 QB 130 the Court of Appeal had to interpret a new Act on the award of damages in personal injuries. But Lord Denning as Master of the Rolls said

'Parliament has quite understandably left it to the courts to decide the principles on which they should act. Up and down the country people want to know the answer. Trade unions, insurers, accountants, solicitors, barristers, all want to know . . . . Such is the confusion that we feel it our duty to set out the guide-lines.'

Such a practice comes close to judicial legislation and was almost unknown in Scotland. But in *Smith v M* 1982 SLT 421 Lord Wheatley, who as Lord Justice-Clerk considered nearly all Scottish bail appeals, set out guidelines for all lower judges in saying that where 'the accused was in a position of trust to behave as a good citizen and not to break the law he should be refused bail unless there were cogent reasons for deciding otherwise'. But that the police were making further inquiries was not a sufficient reason for refusing bail. This guidance was not, however, well received by defence lawyers and social workers. In a case which carries the authority of a bench of seven judges, *Morrison v HM Advocate* 1991 SLT 57, 1990 SCCR 235, where the admissibility of a statement by an accused which was both incriminating and exculpating was in issue, Lord Justice-Clerk Ross, giving the opinion of the court, said 'The following is a statement of the law which applies to all such statements', that is, statements made by an accused after the offence and prior to trial, if accurately recorded and fairly obtained. However this clarification of the law in advance in the broadest of terms was not wholly successful. In *McCutcheon v HM Advocate* 2002 SLT 7 a court of nine judges was formed which disapproved of *Morrison* in part as being capable of creating injustice. And in the civil case of *West v Secretary of State for Scotland* 1992 SC 385 at 392 Lord President Hope, noting that guidance should be given as to the scope of judicial review, said he would 'set out what we consider to be the principles which may be used to define the limits of the supervisory jurisdiction of this court'.

## Procedural legislation

In the last of these practices judges come close to legislating. Through their power to control the procedure of the courts, they can widen remedies and thus give new access to the law. Through Acts of Sederunt in civil matters and Acts of Adjournal in criminal matters judges do engage in a specialised form of legislation and from their creation until 1756 the Court of Session and High Court produced a mass of law, much of it changing the substantive law[1]. Nowadays such Acts usually merely spell out the consequences for Scottish court procedure of some innovation in the law elsewhere. For example, the power of a court of a member state of the European Community to seek a ruling on a point of Community law from the Court of Justice (under article 177 of the Treaty of Rome) led to the Court of Session amending its Rules of Court by Act of Sederunt. But occasionally the court will be bolder. Thus, the lack of effective remedies against unlawful administrative action had been the subject of criticism in Scotland for many years without response. Lord Fraser (obiter in the House of Lords) in the case of *Brown v Hamilton District Council* 1983 SC(HL) 1, a case on the homeless persons law, observed 'It is for consideration whether there might not be advantages in developing special procedures in Scotland for dealing with questions in the public law area'. Lord President Emslie leapt into action and set up a working party under Lord Dunpark which quickly produced a simple scheme for judicial review of administrative decisions, that came into effect as Rule of Court 260B in 1985. A similar rapid reform was the provision of simplified commercial procedure in 1994 by amendment of the Rules of Court, following the recommendations of a Committee under Lord Coulsfield.

---

1 See *An Introduction to Scottish Legal History* (Stair Society, vol 20, 1958) pp 27, 53.

## The UK and Scottish Parliaments

### The UK Parliament

On the surface the most suitable vehicles for changing the law are the legislatures. The individual members that constitute the UK Parliament and the government which controls much of its activity are in touch with most aspects of public life and receptive to complaints of things that are wrong and which the law might remedy. Through select committees MPs who are not in the government can inform themselves on the current state of affairs in most government departments. The law that emerges from Parliament is general in its terms and seeks to determine some form of human conduct for the future. The manner in which it is expressed can be thoroughly considered through the legislative process. Its links with adjacent law can be checked. Finally, the ideology which holds that Parliament expresses the will of the majority of the people who have elected it, gives to measures of law reform approved by it a legitimacy lacking in changes made to law by other means, such as the judgments of judges.

However, most of these points are subject to some qualification. Governments are in fact usually elected by a minority of the electorate and obtain power through their ability to command a majority in the House of Commons. The exigencies of the parliamentary timetable and in particular the crude device of the guillotine by which parts of a Bill may receive no scrutiny at all mean that statutes can turn out to be unworkable in some respect. Sometimes too much activity at the committee or report stages can mean that late amendments are inserted without the draftsmen having a chance to consider fully their impact on other parts of the Bill. The conventions of legislative drafting make the resultant law often incomprehensible to the people who are supposed to comply with it. Nevertheless, the parliamentary process does provide a semblance of popular participation through representatives and an opportunity for careful forethought. It is thus better than any alternative method of law reform. And as we shall see shortly, in some areas of the law Parliament is assisted by the careful preparatory work of the Law Commissions.

Most parliamentary time is controlled by the government and in so far as it is used for drafting legislation is taken up with the enactment of the government's own programme as announced in the annual Queen's Speech. Much of that will take the form of new areas of legal coverage. But some kinds of government activity are constantly being monitored by the department concerned and new legislative proposals are frequently brought forward in the hope of improving the existing law and keeping it in line with the government's objectives. Thus, between 1980 and 1989 ten social security Acts were passed (including ones on contributions), an average of one a year. In the same period there were seven Acts on aspects of road traffic.

*Law reform Acts*

One kind of statute promoted by the government declares itself to be a law reform measure. This is the law reform Act. The low priority given to Scottish legislation led to many matters of Scots law being changed by this device. An example of this genre, which aroused much criticism from the legal profession and other quarters, is the Law Reform (Miscellaneous Provisions) (Scotland) Act 1990, which has 75 sections and 9 Schedules. It includes what amount to whole statutes on charities, on arbitration, and on legal services, including the restructuring of the legal profession, substantial amendments to the law on liquor licensing, provisions on the giving of blood samples in civil proceedings, on the giving of evidence by children and many other lesser matters. Given the heterogeneous character of such Bills, it is difficult to ensure that the standing committee which will scrutinise it in detail is staffed with members who will have an interest in or knowledge of its coverage or to avoid excluding members who are strongly concerned about one of its ingredients.

*The Scottish Parliament*

The limited opportunities for the examination of legislation affecting Scotland in the Westminster Parliament and the problems Scots people and organisations had in lobbying MPs and attending proceedings there were among the reasons why a devolved form of government for Scotland was created in the Scotland Act, 1998. By contrast, the Consultative Steering Group on the Scottish Parliament in its Report entitled *Shaping Scotland's Parliament* laid down as a key principle that 'the Scottish Parliament should be accessible, open, responsive and develop procedures which make possible a participative approach to the development, consideration and scrutiny of policy and legislation'. To promote these objectives it recommends that a structure of specialist Committees of MSPs should be set up. They should be able to influence the formulation of policy emanating from the Executive even before a

Bill is drafted. In this role they should be accessible to interested organisations and individuals. If authorised to do so under s 23(8) of the Scotland Act 1998 a Committee might require 'any person' to attend its proceedings to give evidence and to produce relevant documents. The Steering Group recommends that these specialised committees should also have the power to initiate legislation. Under the Scotland Act, 1998, Sch 3, para 6, the Parliament has created 16 committees.

The Scotland Act 1998 envisages modification of existing Scots private law or Scots criminal law which bears upon reserved matters as described in s 29(4). A simplified procedure can be created under s 36(3) for Bills which merely restate the law and ones which repeal spent laws and for private bills.

The procedures of the Scottish Parliament have on the whole fulfilled these objectives. It is possible for any individual or organisation to petition the Procedures Committee with some grievance which may result in a new or amended law. All Bills promoted by the Executive are examined in detail by one or more relevant committees who under the Scotland Act 1988, s 23 have the power to summon witnesses including, with certain qualifications, ministers and civil servants and to call for documents to be produced. The resultant output of legislation produced during the Parliament's first four years ranges from the Dog Fouling (Scotland) Act 2003, introduced by Mr Keith Harding, to two large Executive Acts on mental health and others making extensive changes to land law to the extent of the abolition of the feudal system, as one Act claims. In one of the earliest Bills the then Justice and Home Affairs Committee took evidence from various women's organisations and individuals who pointed to the need to have interdicts under the Matrimonial Homes (Family Protection) (Scotland) Act 1981 where abuse was claimed to be supported by a power of police arrest. This resulted in the Protection from Abuse (Scotland) Act 2001. The Law Society used its experience of operating the main Act of 1980, the Solicitors (Scotland) Act, to enable any power given to its Council to be exercised with some exceptions by a sub-committee or individual in the Council of the Law Society of Scotland Act 2003.

## Commissions and committees

Governments were formerly often prompted to introduce legislation by the reports of Royal Commissions and departmental committees, composed of people from various walks of life, which they set up to inquire into some particular problem. Major inquiries included the Crowther Committee on Consumer Credit, which led to the massive Consumer Credit Act of 1974, and the Clayson Committee on Scottish Licensing Law on whose report the Licensing (Scotland) Act of 1976 is based. Under the administrations of Margaret Thatcher this method of law reform fell out of favour as being too slow and liable to produce proposals unacceptable to the government. The major reform of social security in the Social Security Act 1986 was based on the work of small review teams chaired by ministers. Where, exceptionally, external bodies are created to recommend changes in public policy they are now given a clear indication of the direction of the reform expected of them and set a time limit within which to report[1]. The Scottish Executive has made little use of ad hoc committees, perhaps because of the accessibility of the Committees of the Parliament. Thus the Justice I Committee in 2001 began an investigation of the regulation of the legal profession, including under that term judges, sheriff officers and prosecutors. It soon decided that this was a burdensome task and confined itself to the treatment of complaints against solicitors, advocates and conveyancing and executry practitioners. The typical mode of paving the way for law reform practised by the Executive has been the issue of consultation papers, to which any interested party can respond.

*Private members' Bills*

At Westminster individual MPs who have limited access to the legislative process through the annual ballot for the chance to introduce a Bill can bring about law reform. Usually it takes the form of a limited amendment to existing law, which has been shown to be defective[2]. Large-scale innovations requiring new administrative structures and increasing public expenditure are unlikely to be supported by the government. But the Housing (Homeless Persons) Act 1977 is an example of an important social reform introduced by a Liberal MP, Stephen Ross, although in its early years it suffered from a lack of government funding and local government support[3]. Sometimes major matters on which the government does not wish to take up a position are left to the

---

1 Eg the Sheehy Inquiry into Police Responsibilities and Rewards (1993) (Cm 2280); the Maclean Committee on Serious Violent and Sexual Offenders (1999). A Royal Commission on reform of the House of Lords was set up in December 1998 to report by 31 December 1999.
2 Eg the Badgers Act 1991.
3 See now Homelessness etc. (Scotland) Act 2003.

initiative of individual MPs. Thus, the Abortion Act 1967 was steered through the Commons by Sir David Steel MP.

The Scottish Parliament also makes provision for members' legislation; of which the Dog Fouling (Scotland) Act 2003 (see p 389 above) is an example of general application. Legislation may also be introduced for the benefit of particular organisations within the devolved matters. Thus St Andrews University wished to be able to award degrees for research in medicine, despite losing the power to award any degrees in medicine in the Universities (Scotland) Act 1966. The local MSP, Mr. Iain Smith, introduced a Bill which became the University of St Andrews (Postgraduate Medical Degrees) Act 2002.

## THE LAW COMMISSIONS

In preparing comprehensive schemes of law reform on subjects which are neither of concern to political parties, nor likely to attract the interest of individual MPs, the United Kingdom and Scottish Parliaments have the benefit of the Scottish Law Commission. There is also a Law Commission for England and Wales. A wide area of law exists, covering, for example, contract, delict, succession and property, which is the everyday concern of members of the legal professions, but impinges only rarely on the lives of ordinary people. As such it is often called 'lawyers' law', misleadingly so, for of course it would not exist without the problems of the general public and its rules can dramatically affect their lives. If for instance a person is rendered paraplegic in the course of an operation, legal definitions of what constitutes medical negligence and how it can be proved will have a vital impact on his future standard of living. But such questions are not the everyday concern of the general public. The Law Commissions provide a process by which what the law ought to be on these matters can be exhaustively considered.

The genesis of the Law Commissions is to be found in a book entitled *Law Reform Now*, written by a barrister, Gerald Gardiner, and an academic lawyer, Andrew Martin, in 1964. In it they argued that the Lord Chancellor's Office (for England and Wales) should have attached to it a unit composed of five highly qualified lawyers, independent of government and civil service, to be called Law Commissioners. Their main task would be 'to review, bring up to date and keep up to date what may be called the "general law"'. In the same year Gerald Gardiner gained the opportunity to turn his vision into reality, for he was appointed Lord Chancellor in the

Labour government which took office in October 1964. The Law
Commissions Act 1965 was one of its first pieces of legislation.

Because of the wide differences between English and Scots law
in the areas to be the concern of the Commissioners it was decided
that there should be a separate Law Commission for Scotland. But
the two Commissions should act in consultation. Scotland had had
since 1954 a Law Reform Committee, but it was a part-time body
with no permanent secretariat. It had no power to take an overview
of the law but could act only on references from the Lord
Advocate. Like its English counterpart its output was small. Its
main achievement was the important Occupiers Liability
(Scotland) Act 1960, which followed its first report.

In 1965 the Scottish Law Commission was created, with, as its
first Chairman, a judge, Lord Kilbrandon, best remembered for
leading the committee whose report on children and young
persons led to the setting up of children's panels. The numbers of
the two Commissions are the same, at five. But the Scottish
Commission has usually included two part-time members.
Academic lawyers, seconded from the universities or combining
work for the Commission with their university duties, have been
prominent in the work of the Commission. There has also usually
been one advocate and one solicitor.

**Powers of the Commissions**

The powers of the two Commissions are laid down in s 3 of the
Law Commissions Act 1965. They have a general duty:

'to take and keep under review all the law with which they are respectively
concerned with a view to its systematic development and reform,
including in particular, the codification of such law, the elimination of
anomalies, the repeal of obsolete and unnecessary enactments, the reduction of the number of separate enactments and generally the simplification
and modernisation of the law'.

In fulfilment of that duty, they have the positive function of
submitting programmes of law reform to the Lord Advocate and
Secretary of State. Otherwise their functions are of a reactive
nature. When requested by these ministers they are to examine
specified branches of the law and make proposals for reform by
draft Bills or otherwise, and to prepare schemes for the consolidation and revision of statute law. They are also to respond to
requests for advice and information from government departments
on law reform. They are to receive proposals for law reform from

anyone. To facilitate their work they may seek information on the law systems of other countries.

## The Scottish Law Commission

The Scottish Law Commission consists in 2003 of five commissioners appointed by the Lord Advocate. The part-time Chairman is Lord Eassie, a judge seconded from the Court of Session. There are two full-time Commissioners, Professor Gerard Maher and Professor Joseph Thomson, and two part-time Commissioners, Mr Patrick Hodge QC and Professor Kenneth Reid. Thus within its small number the Commission has representation from the judiciary, the legal profession, and academic lawyers. There are no members who do not have some professional involvement with law. Section 2(2) of the Law Commissions Act 1965 so limits the appointments. However, the Commission has been scrupulous in seeking responses to its proposals from all interested bodies and persons and on some subjects commissioning social research. The Commission has a core staff of six full-time lawyers, drawn from the Government Legal Service for Scotland, and another six legal assistants and access to draftsmen, though this has not always proved sufficient.

### Its method of working

Each law reform project is assigned by the Commission to a Commissioner (occasionally more than one), who leads a team drawn from the Commission's staff. Their first task is to ascertain exhaustively the existing state of the law and uncover its deficiencies. Some, but not necessarily all, of these may have led to the reference to the Commission. Occasionally this research on the relevant law is entrusted to outside experts. Thus, Sheriff ID Macphail, later a member of the Commission, produced an extensive research paper on the law of evidence, which was revised and published as a book on the subject. Social surveys are sometimes commissioned on the way the existing law is used and perceived by users. The most extensive use of this technique was in preparation for consultative memoranda on debt recovery and diligence. Eight studies were conducted by or for the Central Research Unit of the then Scottish Office. Since then there have been surveys on public attitudes to succession law, on the financial arrangements made on divorce, as shown in a sample of 1,104 divorce actions, on the legal powers of young people and on attitudes to corporal punishment.

Commissioners meet fortnightly to debate and approve the work in progress and individual teams meet more frequently to advance their projects.

Once the Commissioners have formed provisional views on the options for change, they issue a discussion paper (formerly called a memorandum) to all organisations and persons likely to be knowledgeable and interested in the subject. Summaries are issued to legal periodicals and the press. More popular pamphlets aimed at the general public have occasionally been issued. Examples are the law regarding young people and that on inheritance. Any member of the public is entitled to a copy of a discussion paper on application to the Commission. Responses, often in the form of answers to specific questions, are invited by a certain date. Sometimes, on very specialised topics, for example the recognition of foreign nullity decrees, consultation is by means of consultation papers issued to a few selected experts.

When the Commissioners have considered the replies and come to a final view on the nature of the reforms, the team produce a draft report for consideration by the Commission, often mentioning the views of respondents. If a Commissioner disagrees with the final recommendations he is entitled to dissent and add a note of dissent to the report, but this has not so far been necessary in a report pertaining to Scotland only. Where legislation is recommended, the report will be accompanied by a draft Bill. Thus, the Commission has addressed itself not only to what reforms are desirable, but also to how they can be achieved. Finally, the government, as the recipient of the report, may choose to issue its own consultative document on how it should respond to the report.

This is the most visible part of the Commission's work and arguably the most important. But it also engages in some painstaking and less dramatic tasks. In its interpretation of its remit in the Law Commissions Act 1965, s 3 (see above) it examines old Acts to see which are ripe for repeal in a Statute Law Repeals Act. There have been 16 of these emanating from the two Commissions and enacted by the UK Parliament. The consolidation of laws covering a certain subject but still needed is another form of 'tidying up' in which the Commission engages. The process allows for obsolete words to be replaced by contemporary ones to make the enactment more comprehensible. For example, the law on criminal procedure in Scotland was consolidated in the Criminal Procedure (Scotland) Act 1995. But one cannot be certain that all the law relating to the topic in the title of the Act is there. The Court of Session Act 1988 consolidates only certain enactments relating to the Court of Session and repeals only some. Moreover, the Criminal Procedure Act has already been amended many times. In 2003 the work on both statute revision and consolidation was being held up by a shortage of resources.

## Its achievements

In its early days the Commission issued ambitious Programmes of Reform for the approval of the Lord Advocate, as it might be required to do under the 1965 Act, s 3(1)(b), undertaking to reform areas of law as extensive as obligations and succession. Some foresaw in this power the possibilities of codification on the scale of European systems of law, such as the French and German. But difficulties of achieving agreement on such complex areas, where continental and English models were at odds, doubts about the desirability of such a comprehensive reform, with its implications of permanence, and the number of small-scale referrals to the Commission combined to make progress on Programmes very slow. A major report on the law of succession, testate and intestate, was issued in 1990, as part fulfilment of the Second Programme of 1968 and has still to be implemented in legislation. A series of innovative Acts has brought a comprehensive restatement of family law in a single consolidating Act closer to achievement, as promised in the Second Programme. Diligence (debt enforcement), also in the Second Programme, was in part codified in the Debtors (Scotland) Act 1987, now heavily amended in the Debt Arrangement and Attachment (Scotland) Act 2002.

In its 32nd Annual Report in 1997 the Commission announced a new mode of operation. Its Fifth Programme is a rolling one, gathering up whatever has not been completed from previous ones. The projects are arranged under most of the main branches of law. Timetables have been set for each. A short-term project should take just one year; a medium one, two or more years; a long-term one is not time-limited. The 37th Report highlights what progress has been made with each project in these three categories under the Sixth Programme of Law Reform of 2000.

Another factor which can determine the allocation of the resources of the Commission is the collaboration in which it is bound to engage with the other Law Commission. Certain topics are referred by the Lord Chancellor and the Lord Advocate jointly to the two Commissions and result in joint reports; for example, on commercial law topics, such as partnership and the sale of goods, and on questions of private international law. Legislative change may go forward in a single Bill or parallel Bills. Then there are draft English measures which may impinge upon the law of Scotland and which have to be considered within the English Commission's timetable. Requests for informal advice from government departments, often at short notice, add to the Commission's workload and can alter its timetable.

The recommendations and draft Bills of the Law Commissions remain no more than aspirations until they are turned into law by Parliament. Except for consolidation (under the Consolidation of Enactments (Procedure) Act 1949), Bills have to go through the normal legislative process with the possibility of amendment. They have to compete for space in the government's legislative programme, but usually lack any political glamour. But sometimes a sympathetic MP, often a lawyer, who has been fortunate in the private members' ballot, or a member of the House of Lords, will take up a ready-made Commission Bill. For example, the Age of Legal Capacity (Scotland) Bill was introduced in the Commons by Sir Nicholas Fairbairn MP and piloted through the Lords by Lord Macauley QC in 1991. The Scottish Parliament may be expected to be a forum in which there will be more understanding of the objectives of the Scottish Law Commission's proposals and the means of accomplishing them. No special procedure is laid down in the Scotland Act for enacting its Bills, except, under s 36(3), those that restate the law or repeal obsolete laws. The abolition of the feudal system of land tenure, as proposed by the Commission in its Report No 168[1], is one recommendation of the Commission which received a strong ground-swell of support from most interested bodies and most political parties. It was given effect in the Abolition of Feudal Tenure etc (Scotland) Act 2000, s 1 and consequential legislation.

Once a report has been enacted it may be referred to in court to help to clear up an ambiguity in the statute or to discover what mischief it was designed to remedy.

The Scottish Law Commission has firmly established itself as the paramount means of keeping Scots law in line with changing social needs. With the coming of a Parliament wholly dedicated to Scottish affairs, the rate and speed of implementation of its reports may, it is to be hoped, improve.

---

1 See Rennie 'Abolition of the Feudal System' 1999 SLT (News) 85.

# Appendix 1

## A NOTE ON THE NATURE OF RULES[1]

### Two models of rules

Law is generally thought of as comprising rules. Rules can, however, be usefully divided into more than one type.

*Rules in fixed verbal form and rules not in fixed verbal form*

Some rules are written, usually in formal, even stilted, language. They are usually written to encapsulate as exactly as may be the intentions of those drafting them, and they attempt to cover all likely eventualities. Often they are broken down into sections, subsections, and the like, and these may be indicated by arabic or roman numerals, or letters, and indented. These are draftsman's devices to express the rule logically and unequivocally. Rules of golf clubs and other societies are generally of this nature, as are the rules within a university on who may be awarded an LLB degree. They are what we usually expect rules to look like. They have been referred to as 'rules in fixed verbal form'.

Some rules are not of this nature, however, and we are familiar with the idea of unwritten rules. One of the commonest ways of making a rule is by saying 'don't do that!' (or 'do it this way!', or 'watch me!'). Rules within families and workplaces are commonly of this kind. Here there is no written form of the rule, indeed quite possibly no attempt to articulate at all closely what the rule is. Nevertheless, a rule may be inferred, by observing the prohibition (or requirement) made and the behaviour which precipitated it, against a general knowledge of the relationship between the parties involved. It may be that no clear inference is possible from a single instance, and impartial observers might differ as to what inference

---

1 See W Twining and D Miers *How To Do Things with Rules* (3rd edn, 1991). The debt owed to them in what follows will be obvious to those who read that book.

is correct. Clarification might be sought by asking for a 'fixed verbal form' of it; in other words, for this unwritten rule to be written down. However, this may not be possible or reasonable in practice. In this case, only further examples are likely to specify more closely what the rule is. These have been called 'rules not in fixed verbal form'.

### The significance of the two types of rule

Both types of rule exist within the legal system. Legislation is generally speaking in fixed verbal form. It is laid down in advance, with reasonably precise instructions to cover foreseeable cases. Common law is not in fixed verbal form. It is inferred from a series of decisions by judges on more or less similar facts, and a clear view may emerge only after quite a number of decisions. These two types of rule require different handling.

With those in fixed verbal form, there is a text which has a single authoritative version. A person applying it cannot alter this text, but only apply what it requires. This may be straightforward, but where it is not, the interpretation applied must be one the text can reasonably bear. It follows that it is all-important to have an accurate version of the text, and that any text departing from the original is not authentic, and cannot be relied upon.

With those not in fixed verbal form, there is no authoritative text in the same sense, although there are decisions, expressed in words. It is important to have an accurate report of what the judge said, but the rule lies not in his precise words. It must be inferred from those words, for he is not constructing a rule in fixed verbal form. The inference can only be made in the light of the dispute which gave rise to the judgment, against the background of the already known rules of the system. Indeed, a clear view of the rule may often emerge only when a series of decisions has been made[1]. In any case, such rules are never in final form, for they can always develop through further precedents, and there can be reasonable argument as to the precise applicaton of the inferred rule to a new set of facts. Each case can indeed be seen as a 'rule-fragment'.

Dealing with rules in fixed verbal form is akin to dealing with a

---

1 Jeremy Bentham, a great legal philosopher of two centuries ago, observed (in relation to English law), that common law, working through precedent, operates in the same way as you train a dog. You do not draft precise rules for it in advance. You wait till it does something you regard as wrong, and then punish it. Bentham's mummified body can be viewed in University College, London.

fixed standard like Greenwich Mean Time. There is a correct version which is to be applied, and all other calculations of time of day are accurate only in so far as they accurately reflect it. Dealing with rules not in fixed verbal form is more like building a dry-stone dyke. Rules of thumb, born of long experience, must be applied to the materials to hand, which are less than ideal, in order to produce a structure which will stand up to the weather and keep the sheep in.

## The structure of rules

Rules, whether in fixed verbal form or not, can be said to have a certain structure. They are one class of 'if . . . then' statements. In other words, they appear, or can always be redrafted to appear, as statements which say 'if a certain thing or things happen, then there will be a certain result'. In the case of legal rules the result is a legal result, for example a permission or a penalty[1].

### Protasis and apodosis

The 'if' part of the statement is sometimes called the *protasis*, and is descriptive. That is, it describes those facts or conditions which have to be fulfilled if the result is to occur. The 'then' part can be called the *apodosis* and, in a legal rule, it is prescriptive. That is, it prescribes the legal result of the fulfilment of the facts or conditions in the *protasis*.

This structure may be obvious, for rules in fixed verbal form, particularly offences, are sometimes actually drafted in something close to this mould. For instance, s 3(1) of the Prevention of Terrorism (Temporary Provisions) Act 1989 read:

'Any person who in a public place –
  (a) wears any item of dress; or
  (b) wears, carries or displays any article,
in such a way or in such circumstances as to arouse reasonable apprehension that he is a member or supporter of a proscribed organisation is guilty of an offence and liable on summary conviction to imprisonment for a term not exceeding six months or a fine not exceeding level 5 on the standard scale or both.'

---

1 Not all 'if . . . then' statements are rules, let alone legal rules. 'If you hit a person without legal excuse, then you commit an offence' is a simplified legal rule. 'If you hit him, then you will be sorry' is a prediction.

Commonly, however, the structure is less than obvious[1], particularly so with rules not in fixed verbal form. Thus the rule laid down in *Donoghue v Stevenson* 1932 SC(HL) 32 could be rendered as something like: If you act in such a way as to make it reasonably foreseeable that you will injure someone, if that person ought reasonably to be in your contemplation, and if such a person is in fact injured as a result of your act, then you are liable to compensate that person for the injury suffered[2].

It is often useful to analyse rules in terms of this structure in order to understand them. Firstly, it may be useful in specifying what the facts in the *protasis* actually are[3]. Secondly, it may be useful in specifying the relationship between the various facts[4]. The relationship between the facts in a *protasis* is either cumulative (all must be true) or alternative (either must be true). Thirdly, it draws attention to, and requires specification of, the *apodosis*[5].

This form of analysis can usefully be done by constructing algorithms, although these are rarely found in legislation[6].

---

1 'No entry', 'Keep out' and 'Trespassers will be prosecuted' can all be redrafted into something like 'If a person enters, then he will be punished'.
2 But see pp 294–296.
3 The prevention of terrorism offence includes 'wears . . . any article' as well as 'wears any item of dress', so badges are included as well as uniforms.
4 Thus 'wears' or 'carries' or 'displays' are alternatives, so any one of them suffices. On the other hand, the requirement that it be 'in such a way or in such circumstances as to arouse reasonable apprehension . . .' of certain things is cumulative, and must be fulfilled in all cases, or no offence is committed. The important words (expressed or implicit) are 'and' and 'or'.
5 The penalty is imprisonment, or a fine, or both, subject to certain maxima.
6 One example found in quasi-legislation is Chart I in Annex 2 (NHS Charges to Overseas Visitors: Manual for Hospital Staff) to Scottish Home and Health Department Circular 1982 (GEN) 29 (NHS Treatment of Overseas Visitors: Summary) (reference NFE/4/2) dated 15 December 1982 to health board secretaries. These attempted to explain the effect of the National Health Service (Charges to Overseas Visitors) (No 2) (Scotland) Regulations 1982, SI 1982/898.

# Appendix 2

**SCOTTISH COURTS (SIMPLIFIED)**

**Civil courts**

European Court of Justice

House of Lords

Court of Session Inner House (1st and 2nd Divisions)

Court of Session Outer House

Sheriff Principal

Sheriff

Restrictive Practices Court

Land Court

Appeal

Optional

Obligatory
} reference of a question of validity or interpretation of Community law to the ECJ for a preliminary ruling

("devolution issue" pathways are ignored)

## Criminal courts

*Solemn procedure (with jury)*

————— Appeal

→ → Optional ⎫ reference of a question of validity or interpretation of
–➤–➤ Obligatory ⎭ Community law to the ECJ for a preliminary ruling
("devolution issue" pathways are ignored)

*Summary procedure (without jury)*

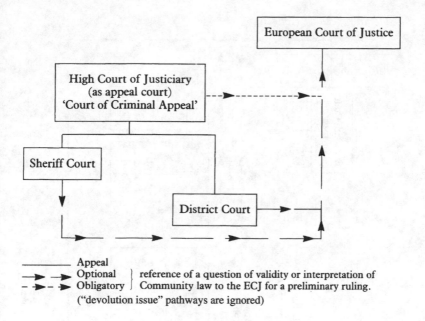

_____ Appeal

➤ ➤ Optional ⎫ reference of a question of validity or interpretation of
– ➤– ➤ Obligatory ⎭ Community law to the ECJ for a preliminary ruling.

("devolution issue" pathways are ignored)

# ENGLISH AND WELSH COURTS (SIMPLIFIED)

## Civil courts

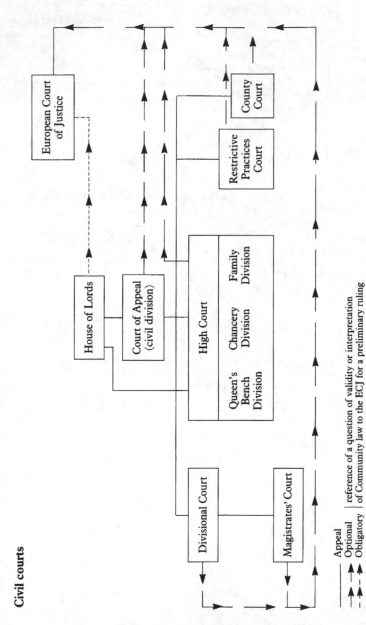

Appeal ——— 
Optional ——▲ reference of a question of validity or interpretation
Obligatory --▲ of Community law to the ECJ for a preliminary ruling

## Criminal courts

*Indictable procedure (with jury)*

_____ Appeal
◄— ◄— Optional ⎤ reference of a question of validity or interpretation of
◄ –◄ – Obligatory ⎦ Community law to the ECJ for a preliminary ruling
. . . . . . . . Committal for trial i e preliminary sieving process

*Summary procedure (without jury)*

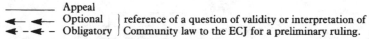

Appeal

Optional } reference of a question of validity or interpretation of
Obligatory } Community law to the ECJ for a preliminary ruling.

## SOME UNITED KINGDOM TRIBUNALS

References to the European Court of Justice omitted and otherwise slightly simplified.

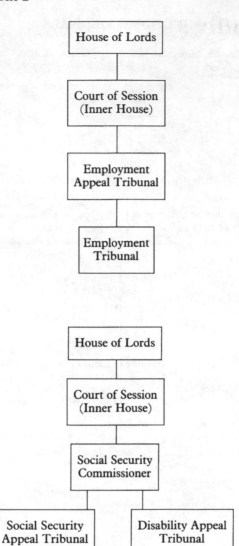

# Appendix 3

## 'EUROPE'

| COUNCIL OF EUROPE | EUROPEAN UNION (including 'three pillars' of: <br> – **European Community** <br> – **Common Foreign and Security Policy** <br> – **Police and Judicial Co-operation on Criminal Matters** – formerly Justice and Home Affairs) |
|---|---|
| **44 members (2003)** (founded 1948, UK founder member) | **15 Member States (2003)** (10 seeking accession in 2004) (founded 1950s, UK joined in 1972) |
| **Strasbourg** | **Brussels** <br> European Commission <br> Council of the Union <br> European Parliament (committees) <br> **Strasbourg** <br> European Parliament (plenary sessions) <br> **Luxembourg** <br> European Parliament (secretariat) <br> European Court of Justice and Court of First Instance (and 'judicial panels') |
| (**European Commission on Human Rights** – merged with European Court of Human Rights in 1998) | **European Commission** |
| **Committee of Ministers** | **Council of the Union** (*alias* 'Council of the European Union' and formerly 'Council of Ministers') <br> **European Council** |
| **Parliamentary Assembly** | **European Parliament** |
| **European Court of Human Rights** | **European Court of Justice** and **Court of First Instance (and 'judicial panels')** |

| | |
|---|---|
| **Nearly 200 treaties** between various members including principally:<br><br>– **European Convention on Human Rights and Fundamental Freedoms** ('ECHR')<br><br>– but also a variety of matters from social security to cybercrime, via patents, extradition, travel by young persons on collective passports, exchange of blood grouping reagents, liability of hotelkeepers for property of guests, protection of the archaeological heritage, protection of pet animals, cinematographic co-production, etc. | **Various treaties,** including:<br><br>– **Treaty Establishing the European Community** ('TEC', alias EC Treaty, and formerly EEC Treaty, aka, Treaty of Rome')<br>– **Treaty on European Union** ('TEU', alias, Maastricht Treaty')<br>– **Treaty of Amsterdam** ('ToA')<br>– **Treaty of Nice** ('ToN')<br><br><br>Also 'secondary legislation' (main means of legislating):<br>– **Regulations**<br>  (thousands every year)<br>– **Directives**<br>  (hundreds every year)<br>– **Decisions**<br>  (hundreds every year)<br><br>**TEC + secondary legislation = 'Community law'** (alias 'EC law' or possibly 'European Union law') |
| **No 'direct effect'** of human rights or other law (i e no direct incorporation into UK law), but:<br><br><br>– **most of rights under ECHR transferred into UK law by Human Rights Act 1998** and contents of various other treaties similarly taken into account in UK legislation<br><br>– **right of individual petition** to European Court of Human Rights, which may produce a favourable decision (including compensation), which the state is obliged by the ECHR to effect, but which is unenforceable in domestic law. | **'Direct effect'** (i e direct incorporation into UK law) of some Community law, i e:<br>  – **parts of Treaties**<br>  – **all Regulations**<br>  – **Directives under some circumstances**<br>  – **Decisions**<br><br>Community law **without 'direct effect'** transferred into UK law by:<br>– **statutory instruments under European Community Act 1972, s 2,** or<br>– **Act of Parliament.** |

# Index